To Dad
and the
Scottish Tradition
in canada
Love Linda

The Scottish Tradition
in Canada

RETURN TO.
KEITH HUNTER
ORANGEVILLE
519-941-5514

GENERATIONS

A History of Canada's Peoples

The Scottish Tradition in Canada

edited by
W. Stanford Reid

Published by McClelland and Stewart in association with
the Multiculturalism Program, Department
of the Secretary of State of Canada and the
Publishing Centre, Supply and Services Canada.

The Canadian Publishers
McClelland and Stewart
25 Hollinger Road
Toronto, Ontario

Printed and bound in Canada
by John Deyell Company

To David M. Stewart
President of the Macdonald–Stewart Foundation

Contents

Editor's Introduction vi

Introduction ix

ONE The Scottish Background *W. Stanford Reid* 1

TWO "The Auld Alliance" in New France *Henry B. M. Best* 15

THREE The Scot in the Fur Trade *Elaine Allan Mitchell* 27

FOUR Patterns of Settlement in the East *K. J. Duncan* 49

FIVE Scottish Settlement of the West *Alan R. Turner* 76

SIX The Highland Catholic Tradition in Canada *R. MacLean* 93

SEVEN The Scottish Protestant Tradition *W. Stanford Reid* 118

EIGHT The Scottish Military Tradition *George F.G. Stanley* 137

NINE The Scot as Farmer and Artisan *J. A. McIntyre* 161

TEN The Scot as Businessman *David S. MacMillan* 179

ELEVEN The Lowland Tradition in Canadian Literature *Elizabeth Waterston* 203

TWELVE The Gaelic Tradition in Canadian Culture *George S. Emmerson* 232

THIRTEEN The Scottish Tradition in Higher Education *D. C. Masters* 248

FOURTEEN The Scot as Politician *A. Margaret MacLaren Evans* 273

FIFTEEN The Scot and Canadian Identity *W. Stanford Reid* 302

APPENDIX Scottish Place-Names in Canada *Watson Kirkconnell* 311

INDEX 322

Editor's Introduction

Canadians, like many other people, have recently been changing their attitude towards the ethnic dimension in society. Instead of thinking of the many distinctive heritages and identities to be found among them as constituting a problem, though one that time would solve, they have begun to recognize the ethnic diversity of their country as a rich resource. They have begun to take pride in the fact that people have come and are coming here from all parts of the world, bringing with them varied outlooks, knowledge, skills and traditions, to the great benefit of all.

It is for this reason that Book IV of the *Report of the Royal Commission on Bilingualism and Biculturalism* dealt with the cultural contributions of the ethnic groups other than the British, the French and the Native Peoples to Canada, and that the federal government in its response to Book IV announced that the Citizenship Branch of the Department of the Secretary of State would commission "histories specifically directed to the background, contributions and problems of various cultural groups in Canada." This series presents the histories that have resulted from that mandate. Although commissioned by the Government, they are not intended as definitive or official, but rather as the efforts of scholars to bring together much of what is known about the ethnic groups studied, to indicate what remains to be learned, and thus to stimulate further research concerning the ethnic dimension in Canadian society. The histories are to be objective, analytical, and readable, and directed towards the general reading public, as well as students at the senior high school and the college and university levels, and teachers in the elementary schools.

Most Canadians belong to an ethnic group, since to do so is simply to have "a sense of identity rooted in a common origin . . . whether this common origin is real or imaginary."[1] The Native Peoples, the British and French (referred to as charter groups because they were the first Europeans to take possession of the land), the groups such as the Germans and Dutch who have been established in Canada for over a hundred years and those who began to arrive only yesterday all have traditions and values that they cherish and that now are part of the cultural riches that Canadians share. The groups vary widely in numbers, geographical location and distribution and degree of social and economic power. The stories of their struggles, failures and triumphs will be told in this series.

As the Royal Commission on Bilingualism and Biculturalism pointed out, this sense of ethnic origin or identity "is much keener in certain individuals than in others."[2] In contemporary Canadian society, with the increasing number of intermarriages across ethnic lines, and hence the growing diversity of peoples ancestors, many are coming to identify themselves as simple Canadian, without reference to their ancestral origins. In focusing on the ethnic dimension of Canadian society, past and present, the series does not assume that everyone should be categorized into one particular group, or that ethnicity is always the most important dimension of people's lives. It is, however, one dimension that needs examination if we are to understand fully the contours and nature of Canadian society and identity.

Professional Canadian historians have in the past emphasized political and economic history, and since the country's economic and political institutions have been controlled largely by people of British and French origin, the role of those of other origins in the development of Canada has been neglected. Also, Canadian historians in the past have been almost exclusively of British and French origin, and have lacked the interest and the linguistic skills necessary to explore the history of other ethnic groups. Indeed, there has rarely ever been an examination of the part played by specifically British – or, better, specifically English, Irish, Scottish and Welsh – traditions and values in Canadian development, because of the lack of recognition of pluralism in the society. The part played by French traditions and values, and particular varieties of French traditions and values, has for a number of reasons been more carefully scrutinized.

This series is an indication of growing interest in Canadian social history, which includes immigration and ethnic history. This may particularly be a reflection of an increasing number of scholars whose origins and ethnic identities are other than British or French. Because such trends are recent, many of the authors of the histories in this series have not had a large body of published writing to work from. It is true that some histories have already been written of particular groups other than the British and French; but these have often been characterized by filio pietism, a narrow perspective and a dearth of scholarly analysis.

Despite the scarcity of secondary sources, the authors have been asked to be as comprehensive as possible, and to give balanced coverage to a number of themes: historical background, settlement patterns, ethnic identity and assimilation, ethnic associations, population trends, religion, values, occupations and social class, the family, the ethnic press, language patterns, political behaviour, education, inter-ethnic relations, the arts and recreation. They have also been asked to give a sense of the way the group differs in various parts of the country. Finally, they have been asked to give, as much as possible, an insider's view of what the immigrant and ethnic experiences were like at different periods of time, but yet at the same time to be as objective as possible, and not simply to present the group as it sees itself, or as it would like to be seen.

The authors have thus been faced with a herculean task. To the extent that they have succeeded, they provide us with new glimpses into many aspects of Canadian society of the past and the present. To the extent that they have fallen short of their goal, they challenge other historians, sociologists and social anthropologists to continue the work begun here.

Jean Burnet
Howard Palmer

[1]   *Report of the Royal Commission on Bilingualism and Biculturalism.*
[2]   Ibid. Paragraph 8.

Introduction

The statement that the Scots have had a longer and more constant connection with Canada than any other European ethnic group, may come as a surprise to many people, but this would seem to be the truth. It is reported that among Thorfinn Karlsevni's crew in 1010 were two Scots whom he sent to explore Vineland (presumably Newfoundland or Nova Scotia) when he reached its shores. Coming down to more modern times, one of the first cartographers to draw a map of the mouth of the St. Lawrence River was Jean Rotz who published his atlas in 1542. Although a native of Dieppe, he was the son of David Ross, a Scot, who like many others had migrated to France. It is also likely that some of the crews of Cartier's ships were Scots for many Scottish seamen lived in the Brittany and Norman ports. It is reasonable, therefore, to hold that Scottish interest in Canada antedates that of the French, Portuguese and English, and has been more consistent and constant than that of the Scandinavians. To show what this interest has meant to Canada is the purpose of this book.

Scottish influence, however, did not really become strong until the eighteenth century, first with the establishment of Nova Scotia and then after the Cession of New France in 1763, with the advent of the Scottish administrator and merchant to the newly acquited territory. Yet because of their early arrival in the country and the subsequent constant immigration, Scots have spread in all directions across the land. The result is that more than most ethnic groups, the history of Canada is to a certain extent the history of the Scots in Canada. They have not remained in one area, as have the large majority of the French Canadians, nor have they tended to settle in concentrated groups either in towns and cities or in the countryside as have many other racial units. Instead they appear in every location and in every possible aspect of Canadian life.

While this is a matter of pride among Scots, it has not made the task of the historian who would record the Scottish contribution to Canadian development and identity easy. He has no particular geographical area nor typical organization to which he can point as the Scots' primary vehicle of expression, for they have been involved in practically all social activities from the Presbyterian and Roman Catholic churches to the Royal Bank of Canada and the Canadian Labour Congress. Some historians in attempting to describe the part played by the Scots in Canadian history have tended to talk in terms of individuals, classifying them in various professions or types of work. This, however, has usually resulted in a list of names of important people without much relationship to the whole pattern of Canadian development. In the present work we have sought to present another approach which may give a better picture of the Scottish contribution to Canada's growth and maturing as a nation.

The plan has been to present a series of chapters on various topics which bring out the Scottish place in Canadian history, rather than a list of names or a description of organizations. For this work some thirteen different authors have been persuaded to write. While the majority are professional or amateur historians; sociologists, literary critics and others are included in the roll. This means that although the approaches of the different chapters are by no means always uniform, the amount of unanimity in point of view and conclusion is obvious. All who have written, however, have had one major complaint: they have not had enough space to develop their themes as thoroughly as they wished. They have discovered that Scots have been even more active than they had originally anticipated when they commenced the research on their assignments.

The chapters have all been written independently of each other, and the editor has refrained from attempting to force any uniformity on them, as he believes that an author should be allowed to say what he has to say as long as his work is relevant to the subject and easily understood by those who read. The result is diversity within unity. It will be noticed, however, that in a number of cases the chapters are really preliminary studies of the topic under discussion. Little research has been done in some fields, such as the Scottish part in the development of Canadian labour movements, with the consequence that wide generalizations still await the intensive study upon which such conclusions can be based. It is interesting to note that as a result of having written a chapter for this book a number of the authors are now proceeding to produce monographs on the same subject.

Although the chapters have all been written independently by each author, they form a definite pattern. The editor has commenced the work by presenting a short history of Scotland in order to explain the background from which the Scots have come, highlighting those aspects of Scotland's story which seem to have influenced the migrant to Canada. Then follows a chapter on the Scots in New France and Acadia, succeeded by various chapters seeking to show Scottish influence in different aspects of Canadian life and development since 1763. It will be noticed, however, that most of the authors have concentrated on the years prior to 1900. The period since the beginning of the present century has seen such a change in Canada's story that it has become even more difficult to keep the Scots in focus as they have inter-married with and adapted to the new ethnic groups entering the country. Nevertheless, according to the latest census figures (1971) Scots or Canadians of Scottish origin still form the third largest ethnic group in Canada, making up 10.43% of the population. For this reason the editor in the final chapter has sought to point out that Scots and Scottish Canadians over the past seventy years have still played an important part in almost every aspect of Canadian life.

One criticism which may be made is that in some cases the different essays overlap each other as they both refer at times to the same sources and to the same material. This is of course true, but really unavoidable owing to the fact that they all deal with the same major topic: the Scot in Canada. At the same time, however, it must also be recognized that each essay approaches the topic from a different angle, so even if there is repetition of material occasionally, the use made of it is different.

Another criticism may perhaps be that there is no chapter devoted to the Scots in the professions such as medicine and law. Again this is true, but there are definite reasons for the omission. Already in the works of William Wilfrid Campbell, George Bryce, W.J. Rattray and others so much space has been devoted to this topic, that those who may be interested should turn to their works. Furthermore, as one goes over the roll of Scottish doctors, lawyers and judges in Canada he is simply inundated by the numbers involved in these professions to the extent that it is difficult to single out individuals for special mention. But probably most important of all, it is often impossible to separate the work and achievements of Scots from others in the same profession since these professions leave little room for manifesting any "Scottish traditon." Where doctors, lawyers, scientists and the like have played an important part in some other sphere of activity they have been mentioned, but it is very difficult to speak of a Scottish tradition in the treatment of the sick or in the development of English Common Law.

The editor would express his thanks to the various authors who have written chapters and who took his criticisms and urgings with such good grace. He would also like to say that he is appreciative of the support given to this work by the Department of the Secretary of State and particularly to Miss Jennifer MacQueen, a Canadian of Scottish origin, the original director of the ethnic history project, to her successors and to the two editors of the series, Prof. Jean Burnet of York University and Dr. Howard Palmer, University of Lethbridge.

One parting word is perhaps in order. The editor hopes that the following chapters do not sound too much as though the Scots are boasting. The authors have all sought to maintain an objective approach in order to tell the plain truth. They have had the same attitude as the Aberdonian servant girl in London, who when her mistress reproached her for not telling her that she came from Aberdeen, replied: "When I left hame, me mither's last words were, 'Lassie dinna blaw.'"

W. Stanford Reid
Guelph, 1976

ONE

The Scottish Background

W. Stanford Reid

1

Scots have played an important part in the development of Canada, as the subsequent chapters in this book will show, but in order to understand why this has been the case we must look beyond Canada to Scotland itself. The traits of character, the ways of thinking, the prejudices and the biases with which the Scottish immigrants came to this country and which they passed on to their descendants even to the third and fourth generations, found their origins in the homeland which they had left. It is therefore necessary that we should commence our survey of the Scottish tradition in Canada by looking at the Scottish background in order to gain some comprehension of the place which the Scot has made for himself in Canada.

Two basic forces which have made the Scot what he is are Scotland's geography and Scotland's history. The physical character of the land itself has wielded a powerful influence on Scottish development; along with that has gone the influence of its geographic position in the world. At the same time, history which includes the human development in this environment has played an even more important role in shaping the Scottish character. We must, therefore, take both these factors into account when we attempt to understand the Scot and his contributions to the New World.

Scotland, like Caesar's Gaul, is divided into three geographical areas: the far north, including Caithness, Sutherland and the Orkneys, which are flat, windblown and not very fertile; the middle portion, containing the Highlands lying north of the Firth of Forth-Firth of Clyde line, which are mountainous, rugged and on the west coast come down to the sea's edge with cliffs sometimes over two hundred feet high, with long coastal indentations or sea-lochs, deep valleys and poor soil; the southern area or Lowlands with a broad belt of fertile land running between Edinburgh and Glasgow, and the more southerly portion having low hills or uplands and relatively good soil. The Lowland area has always been the wealthiest part of the country, and since the eighteenth century and the beginning of the Industrial Revolution it has tended to dominate Scotland, drawing off much of the population from the northern areas to its factories and work-shops. It has also had a further advantage in that it has the best ports on both the east (Aberdeen, Dundee, Perth, Leith) and west (Ayr, Ardrossan, Glasgow) coasts, and is closer to England than the other regions, which means that its opportunities for commerce are considerably greater.

Although Scotland did not begin to develop as a nation-state until Kenneth MacAlpine, King of Dalriada in Argyllshire, succeeded to the throne of Pictland in 843, it had a long history before that date. Successive invasions and settlements of Stone Age, Bronze Age and Celtic peoples had populated the country. In the fifth century Celtic Scots from Ireland had landed in modern Argyllshire to found the Kingdom of Dalriada and probably about the same time the Picts, made up of a mixture of Celts and Bronze Age peoples, had established their kingdom in the central and eastern Highlands. Consequently, when King Kenneth I succeeded to the Pictish throne he began a process of unification which took place at first north of the Forth and Clyde line, but which eventually included the Britons of the Kingdom of Strathclyde in the southwest and the Angles who had pushed north from Northumbria to found Edinburgh (Edwin's Burgh) and settle the south centre and east.

Many factors helped to bring about the coalescence of these diverse elements into one nation. One of the most important was the Christian Church. Although at first Celtic Christianity from Ireland, which dated back to the third century, had begun the conversion of the various peoples, it was eventually ousted by Roman Christianity which, with its urbanized approach and highly structured organization, was able to set up a unified church which tended to bring the various parts of the country together. Another important factor was the advent of the Anglo-Normans after the Norman Conquest of England, for they brought with them the ideas of feudalism, centralization of government and nationalism, which came to dominate the Lowlands although they did not affect so strongly the clan-oriented society of the Highlands.

One other force which brought about the unification of Scotland was pressure from outside. From the eighth to the twelfth centuries the north of Scotland constantly suffered under attacks from Scandinavians who settled in the Orkneys, the Hebrides, and Caithness and Sutherland. This experience had forced the other parts of the country to draw closer to each other to resist the invaders. More significant in this process, however, was the Scottish resistance to the attempts of the English kings to make Scotland a vassal state. William the Conqueror had forced King Malcolm I (Canmore) to do some form of homage; Henry II had made William the Lion his prisoner and forced him to become his vassal, although Richard I sold him back his independence; and Edward, rightly known as "the hammer of the Scots," made the most determined effort to bring the Scots

2

to heel. At first Edward almost succeeded, but as a result of English oppression, the church, the nobility and the burghs joined together in resistance, the principal leadership being given at first by one of the lairds,
William Wallace of Elderslie, and then by Robert deBrus, Earl of Carrick,
who became King Robert I. Edward I was succeeded by his son Edward II,
who through ineptitude and problems at home was forced after the Battle
of Bannockburn (1314) to give up any hope of conquering Scotland. As a
result of this ordeal by fire Scotland had become a nation.

Yet the country still suffered from an internal division between the
Highlands and the Lowlands which was to endure down to the eighteenth
century. For one thing, there was a language difference. The Highlander
spoke Gaelic or "Old Celtic" which differed even from the language of
the Celts of southwest Wales and Ireland, and was completely different
from the Anglo-Norman language spoken in the central and eastern Lowlands. Added to this was the difference of social organization. In the
Highlands the land was regarded as the property of the clan as a whole
through the chief. Each crofter had his own "in-field" or plot and might
also cultivate an "out-field," but his principal interest was the pasturing of
his cattle, which grazed upon the common land. The Lowlander, on the
other hand, tended to follow the English practice of relatively intensive
arable cultivation of strips of land scattered throughout the lord of the
manor's fields. While in the Lowlands the tendency by the beginning of
the modern period was towards the consolidation of land into individual
farms, in the Highlands the farming methods changed little until the
eighteenth century. The linguistic and socio-economic patterns also had
their political effects. In the north the chief of the clan was the ruler, often
a kind of petty monarch who was supposed to take good care of his clansmen, who in turn were obliged to follow him in war, usually carrying a
broadsword or Lochaber axe. In the Lowlands the country was organized
along feudal lines with the vassals of the king serving both as his civil
service and the heavy cavalry of which his feudal army consisted. Added
to this force on occasion during the War of Indpendence and later, he
called out the peasants as a whole, who formed the "schiltrons" of
pikemen which defeated the English cavalry at Bannockburn and other
battles. The Scottish monarch's power in the north varied very much
according to his own ability, power and capacity to win the support of
powerful clans such as the Gordons in the northeast and the Campbells in
the west. The one constant unifying element in the country seems to have
been the church with its monasteries, its bishoprics, its parishes and its
services in a common Latin.

Yet while the Scots had maintained their independence and autonomy
against English encroachments in the early part of the fourteenth century,
they were not suffered to live in peace. During the War of Independence
they had become allied to France, who constantly sought to use them as a
cat's paw to cause England trouble during the Hundred Years War which
began in 1337. The English for their part repeatedly attempted to add

3

Scotland to the empire which they hoped to establish by the conquest of France. In the fifteenth century these difficulties were further compounded by the fact that from 1406 until the union of the crowns of England and Scotland in 1603, every Scottish monarch came to the throne as a minor. This gave full scope to aristocratic intrigue and conflict, resulting at times even in civil war. Yet despite, or perhaps because of their difficulties, the Scots during this period became increasingly conscious of their identity as a nation. To this was added a radical change in the church in the sixteenth century which gave further strength to the Scottish sense of uniqueness.

The Protestant Reformation began in 1517 when Martin Luther in Wittenberg, Saxony, made his protest against ecclesiastical corruption. This movement spread to other areas of Europe, particularly Switzerland, where Ulrich Zwingli and Henry Bullinger in Zurich, and somewhat later Jean Calvin in Geneva, led in the development of the reform movement. In Scotland the condition of the church, which had reached a low ebb, and the social and economic changes which were taking place prepared the way for the advent of the new religious thought and ideas. The church itself was in considerable disarray theologically, morally and socially, with the result that many of the rising bourgeoisie seem to have been becoming disillusioned and rather cynical. One has only to read the acts of the last two or three synods of the church before 1560 to gain an impression of its condition. At the same time, Scottish merchants, sailors, soldiers and scholars were bringing in the new ideas from Germany, France and Switzerland. These were taken up first of all in the port towns of Aberdeen, Perth, Dundee and Leith but soon spread into the hinterland to gain the support of the lairds or landed gentry and some of the nobles. By 1555 the Protestant movement had gained a considerable amount of support, although it was still without any effective organization.

The man who pulled the whole movement together was John Knox who, from 1549 to 1553, had been a refugee in England because of his beliefs and, on the Roman Catholic Mary Tudor's accession to the English throne, had found it necessary to move to Geneva where he became the pastor of the English refugee congregation. In 1555 he returned to Scotland for some nine months to encourage and help organize those pressing for ecclesiastical reform. Then in 1559, after Elizabeth, who favoured Protestantism, succeeded her sister Mary as Queen of England and his English congregation consequently departed to their homes, Knox went back to Scotland. There he quickly became the spiritual leader of the reform movement. Largely through his influence, in 1560 the Scottish Estates or parliament abolished papal authority and the recital of the Mass, while at the same time establishing a Protestant church which Knox believed to be "the best reformed church in the world," his sentiments being echoed by many of those who sat in the church's General Assembly. Thus by the time of Knox's death in 1572 the groundwork had been laid for a distinctively Scottish Protestant religious outlook.

Central to the doctrine of the Reformation was the basic Christian paradox of the depravity of man and the overflowing abundance of the grace of God in Jesus Christ, the Redeemer. Knox and his supporters were uncompromising Calvinists who believed that man's whole life is to be lived to the glory of God. This, however, could be done only by the way in which the Christian knew God's will for him through the guidance of the Holy Spirit speaking in Holy Writ. Consequently, the church had the tremendous responsibility of expounding faithfully the Word of God in the Old and New Testaments, of administering the sacraments and of "uprightly" enforcing Christian discipline. This in turn meant that the church must be autonomous, free from the control of the nobility, the government and even the universities. Nevertheless, the ministers of the church had the duty of admonishing the rulers concerning their obligations since they too were also citizens of the Kingdom of Christ, and of guiding the schools and universities that they might train the youth to take their proper places in both church and commonwealth. These ideas, set forth in the "Scots Confession" of 1560 and in the first *Book of Discipline*, became the foundation of Scottish Protestantism producing what one author has called "a nation of agressive thinkers and enquirers into the truth."[1]

Once the new church, with the support of the government, had established itself firmly in the country and the Reformation had been more or less generally accepted, a noticeable change took place. The Scots, who had never been particularly noted for religious devotion or even high moral conduct, seemed to experience something of a change of heart. A new and deep religious feeling seemed to develop among the people, including the Roman Catholic minority. Theology became a matter of consuming interest to many, and attendance at sermons almost a national pastime. Yet withal, we do not see the intense bitterness of conflict between Protestant and Catholic that appeared at the same time in other countries. The deposition of the young Queen Mary in 1567 probably forestalled a civil "war of religion" similar to that which plagued France for years. No Catholics were executed for their beliefs after the Reformation came into effect in 1560. Controversy was common, but systematic persecution was not. This may be partly because most of the Roman Catholic minority were either located in the Highlands or were to be found among the lower classes in the towns, but also because the Scot usually felt that argument was more effective than terror. Religion and religious controversy in this way came to provide another dimension to Scottish national identity.

Knox's work was carried on after his death in 1572 by those who had come under his influence: James Melville, Robert Pont, and Robert Bruce, but especially Andrew Melville who, influenced also by the thinking of Theodore Beza, Calvin's successor in Geneva, sought to set up a completely articulated presbyterian system of church government with an ascending hierarchy of church courts made up of elected members, from the session at the congregational level through presbyteries and synods to the national general assembly. Under the influence and drive of such men the Reformation spread across the country not only in the Lowlands but into the Highland glens and straths, with the result that by the end of the century the Reformed Church of Scotland was indeed truly national, wielding a broad and powerful influence upon the whole of Scottish life. From this point on Scottish character and life would be closely involved with a strong Calvinistic Protestantism. Even those opposed to it because of conflicting religious beliefs or simply because they did not like its practical effects would, nevertheless, have to take it into account.

Scotland throughout the latter part of the sixteenth century, however, was by no means a peaceful or prosperous country. Not only was she affected by the constant conflicts in Europe which damaged her trade, but she also suffered from the internal anarchy fostered by an unruly aristocracy. Nevertheless, some progress was made towards peace as James VI gradually took control of the government. Yet even he, though hailed as the "Scottish Solomon" and entertaining grandiose ideas of Divine Right, was not able to bring peace until he ascended the English throne in 1603 on the demise of Elizabeth.

The advent of James to the throne of England came as the result of the foresight of Henry VII who had married his daughter Margaret to James's great grandfather, James IV, who died fighting the English in 1513. Henry seems to have seen the ultimate outcome of this move as the union of the two countries; and although it took a century to bring about the preliminary step of the union of the crowns, it was on the way to achieving its purpose. The move, however, was by no means an unmixed blessing to Scotland. The Scottish court forsook Edinburgh for London, which resulted in Scottish interests being placed repeatedly in a secondary position to those of England. Furthermore James, who had been obliged to wage a continual campaign against his nobility and who had sought by every means to dominate the democratically governed Reformed Church, now had behind him the power which enabled him to control both, as he said, with a stroke of his pen from Whitehall.

It was the conflict with the Scottish church which finally led to an explosion which ushered in the Civil War between Charles I and the English Parliament. As a result of James's imposition of episcopacy on the Church of Scotland there had been growing discontent in its ranks. But when Charles I and Bishop Laud attempted in 1637 to impose an English form of liturgy on the congregation of St. Giles, Edinburgh, and Jenny Geddies tossed her stool at the dean's head for saying 'mass at her lugs,' not only did the other ladies follow Jenny's example, but the nation also rose in revolt. The result was the "First Bishop's War" which forced Charles to call his Parliament to pay off the Scottish forces encamped in the north of the country. From that time on one move led to another, until war broke out in England, to be followed by the formal alliance of the Scottish and English rebels in the Solemn League and Covenant of 1643. Yet, although the Scots proved to be valuable allies for the English parliamentary party, when they refused to accede to Charles's execution and gave their support to his son, the English parliamentary armies in 1651 moved into the country upon which they imposed an unequal union for close to a decade. This union, although it brought prosperity to some of the Scots, left a considerable legacy of antipathy to English rule, even among the church leaders who had so much in common with the Puritans.

Although many of the Puritan clergy had agreed with the Scots in their ideas of doctrine and church government, and as a result had drawn up the strongly Calvinistic Westminster Confession of Faith, the Larger and Shorter Catechisms, The Directory of Worship and the Form of Church Government, the English Parliament had rejected these documents while the Scottish Estates adopted them wholeheartedly. "The Westminster Standards" in this way became the hallmark of Scottish Presbyterianism which was opposed to both English Congregationalism and English Episcopacy. The rule of Cromwell's Independents, however, was relatively mild compared to that of the bishops who returned with the restoration of Charles II to the thrones of the two countries in 1660. Charles, whose principal interest was in ruling as an absolute monarch similar to his cousin Louis XIV in France, attempted to force even by musket, boot and thumbscrew the Scottish Presbyterians to accept an episcopal church order. The result was the rise of the Covenanters, who demanded the restoration of the National Covenant of 1638, but all that resulted was the "killing days" under "Bluidy Clavers" (Graham of Claverhouse). The outcome was the growth of an anti-Stuart, radical Protestant element in the country which was violently opposed to England and everything for which it seemed to stand.

Religion, however, was not the only cause for discontent with the unequal marriage to the English. Although Scotland had been given freedom to trade within the English Empire during the Cromwellian occupation, with the Restoration the English merchant lobby saw that this was brought to an end. Thenceforward, Scots might go as colonists to Virginia and similar places, a few Scottish articles of trade might be shipped to the colonies, but otherwise Scots were strictly foreigners. At the same time, Scotland had its own trade destroyed by being involved against its will in the English wars with the Dutch and the French, two of their best European customers. Gradually the Scots came to depend almost entirely upon trade with England, who was prepared to give no presents in return.

When the English rose in revolt against James II and placed William of Orange and his wife Mary, James's daughter, on the throne, the Scots went along with the move although with no great enthusiasm. One thing that did reconcile many to the new regime was the final establishment of presbyterianism and the abolition of episcopacy. William, however, soon wiped out the benefits of the favour obtained through this move by the massacre of the MacDonalds of Glencoe and his involvement in the failure of the Scottish attempt to establish a colony at Darien on the Isthmus of Panama. The feeling in most quarters was that they had returned to

'square one,' for the English, while insisting that the Scots were foreigners, did not recognize the rights of the Scots to independent action.

Although Scottish discontent did not come to a head during the reign of
William and Mary, probably due to a constant threat of the return of the
Roman Catholic Stuarts, it did during the reign of James II's second
daughter Anne. Scots were becoming so frustrated with the situation in
which they felt themselves always subordinated to English interests that
they believed that the only answer was total independence of England,
under a Scottish monarch. Although Roman Catholics, the Stuarts would
be the only possible candidates for this position, a point of view adopted
by even a good many Protestants. Anne's answer was complete union of
the two countries by an amalgamation of their parliaments. After much
argument and negotiation this was finally brought about in 1707. The
maintenance of the presbyterian character of the Church of Scotland as
established and the continuance of Scottish law were guaranteed, although both promises were soon forgotten by England once the union was
effected. At the same time, Scots were given complete freedom of trade
within the Empire, a privilege of which they took immediate advantage.

The eighteenth century was a century of very mixed feelings in Scotland. The mercantile community, particularly in Glasgow, came into sudden prominence, since by virtue of their geographic position they were
favourably placed to enter the North American markets, in which they
gained almost a monopoly of the tobacco trade. Thus, despite increased
taxes resulting from the union, certain sections of the country began to
prosper. Other elements in the population, on the other hand, were not so
happy. The 48 members of the House of Commons and the 16 elected
peers had little influence in Parliament, the MPs being usually under the
control of some "manager" such as Lord Dundas. Increasing discontent
within the Church of Scotland over the abrogation of the congregation's
right to choose its own minister (1712) led to two secessions, one under
Ralph and Ebenezer Erskine (1733) and the other under Thomas Gilles-
pie (1761). At the same time, for a mixture of reasons, religious, economic, political and social discontent came to expression in the Highlands
in the Rebellions of 1715 and 1745 in favor of complete independence
under a Stuart monarchy. Many Scots were by no means prepared to have
their country swallowed up by the English, either culturally, religiously or
politically.

Despite the resistance to change, however, both Highlands and Lowlands underwent many modifications as a result of the union with England. The Highlanders during this period experienced what was probably the most drastic alteration to their social structure and way of life. As a
result of the ruthless suppression of the rebellions, particularly of the '45,
the Highlands were "pacified." Every effort was made to destroy the clan
system by wiping out the authority of the chieftains, by banning the wearing of the kilt, by calling in all firearms and by building roads throughout
the whole area. These measures were followed by the enlisting of whole

regiments of clansmen to fight overseas in the Empire's wars, and by the beginning of the clearance of people from the Highland glens. These uprooted Highlanders either migrated to Lowland cities such as Glasgow or crossed the sea to America, bearing with them the traditions, sentiment, nostalgia and often anger of a displaced people.

While the pacification of the Highlands was enacted and enforced as the result of government legislation, "the clearances" took place because the chieftains, now deprived of their former authority and independence, sought to recoup themselves by becoming sheep graziers who could sell their wool to the growing textile industry in the south. Simultaneously the Lowlands, particularly in the region of Glasgow, which were developing industrially were quite prepared to take the influx of migrants who could find jobs in the burgeoning tobacco industry, in the cotton and linen factories, and in the building of ships or in the mining of coal. The English Industrial Revolution was radically altering the whole face of Scotland.

Yet the economic changes were by no means the only, nor perhaps the most important, changes affecting Scottish identity during the eighteenth century. One of the reasons for Scotland's development was its unique emphasis upon education ever since the establishment of the Reformed Church which had sought to set up a nationwide parish school system. G. M. Trevelyan believes that at the Union of 1707, the Scots were the best educated people in Europe. The eighteenth century saw a growth of education particularly at the post-secondary level. The universities under the leadership of men such as Dr. William Robertson, Principal of Edinburgh University, flourished as they never had before. Furthermore, the growing interest in science and technology owing to the expanding industrialization found the Scottish universities, much more than their English counterparts, prepared to develop the sciences. Chemistry and physics advanced under the direction of teachers and scientists such as Joseph Black of Edinburgh. What we now call economics was first set forth systematically by Adam Smith, Professor of Moral Philosophy at Glasgow; and technology expanded as the result of the work of inquisitive craftsmen such as James Watt, an instrument-maker, and the improver of the steam engine. The result was Scottish intellectual expansion and development which sometimes produced the scepticism of the philosopher David Hume and at others the piety and religious vigour of the preacher Robert Haldane, but laid a large part of the foundations for the development of English-speaking Canadian education in the nineteenth century.

With all these changes, Scottish identity became somewhat dimmed and the Scot tended to become increasingly anglicized. Political life under Lord Bute and Lord Dundas, who became First Viscount Melville, was centred in London, while English influence, economic, intellectual and religious, extended its hold on the Scottish outlook. Reaction came in the religious sphere with the founding of the Associate Presbytery (1733) and the Relief Presbytery (1761), but these were indirect manifestations since these bodies' primary interests were in maintaining the spiritual freedom of the church from the control of a frequently rationalistic or Anglican nobility and parliament. Added to this, the Associate Presbytery divided in 1747 over the issue of whether a Christian could take the oath of allegiance when he became a burgher of a Scottish burgh. The oath required the one taking it to promise his loyalty to the form of the Christian Church established in the land. Some believed that the oath could be taken by members of the Associate Presbytery, others said, "No." This was to have important repercussions in Canada as both the "Burgher" and "Anti-Burgher" synods were among the earliest churches to send missionaries to the British North American colonies. By 1820 these two bodies had reunited in Scotland to form the United Associate Secession Church and in 1847 they joined with the Relief Church to form the United Presbyterian Church which rejected any type of civil church establishment. Much more important to national identity, however, was the revival of Scottish self-consciousness under the influence of Robert Burns, Sir Walter Scott and John Galt who by their poetry and their novels reminded the Scot of his difference from the Englishman – indeed from all other men. It was the Romantic Revival in Scotland which brought about the effective resurgence of the feeling of Scottish identity and uniqueness.

This rebirth of Scottish consciousness came just in time, for the end of the eighteenth and the beginning of the nineteenth centuries saw Scotland experiencing a revolution unlike any she had known before. The Wars of Independence and the Protestant Reformation had both been important for the wide influence which they had exercised, but the increasing pace in the industrialization of the country was equally, if not more, far-reaching. To be sure, the Industrial Revolution was not a specifically Scottish phenomenon, seeing that its main centre was in England, but it did have important effects in Scotland that extended far beyond the walls of the factories and shops. It brought about radical changes which have left their impress not only upon Scotland, but also upon other countries such as the United States, Australia, New Zealand, South Africa and Canada.

The immediate impact was felt in the Lowlands. Scientific farming had become important shortly after the opening of the nineteenth century with the farmers of Lothian gaining the reputation of being some of the best agriculturalists in the world. But parallel with the agricultural development went the development of heavy industry based on Scottish mineral resources: ship-building, railway engine-building, general engineering. These were principally centred on Glasgow and the surrounding area. At the same time, light industry such as the production of cotton goods and other textiles became active in other parts of the country. J. and P. Coates, the sewing thread manufacturers, commenced operations in Kilmarnock. Swan and Co. in Kirkcaldy began with the production of jute bags, but soon turned to linoleum. Dundee, Aberdeen and other cities were likewise caught up in industrial development, while distilling, an ancient industry, expanded all over the country from the valley of the Spey in the east to Islay and Skye on the west. By the end of the nineteenth century new industry had begun to manufacture electrical equipment, chemicals and other products needed for an increasingly complex society.

The financing for all these developments was largely Scottish, for the Scots had already developed a banking system which gave monetary stability to the economy. Instead of following the English example of having one central government bank with individual banks set up all over the country, the Scots had relatively few banks, some going back to the early eighteenth century, but many bank branches. Thus the dangers of failure were minimal, while the possibility of bank investment in and financial support of industry was much greater. Although the government tried to make the Scots conform to the English pattern, it was defeated largely through the attacks by Sir Walter Scott on the idea in his *Letters of Malachi Malagrowther*. There were, of course, booms and busts throughout the century and although there were bank failures such as that of the City of Glasgow Bank in 1878, in general Scottish financial houses weathered the storms as well as if not better than their English or American counterparts. Usually such periods of depression led to outflows of immigrants to the colonies and United States.

Naturally, these economic changes brought about radical social changes. Class division became more marked and obvious as not infrequently "the rich got richer and the poor got poorer," to quote the song of the 1930s. Gradually also English capital began to flow northward to buy up Scottish industries and often to move them to England. But even when the industries were left in Scotland the profits were taken south, coming back in the form of money to purchase Scottish estates, which were used mainly for the deer or grouse hunting of the English capitalist and his aristocratic English and Anglo-Scottish friends. This in turn led to more clearances and the resulting migration of the ousted crofters either to the industrial Lowlands and England or overseas.

Along with these changes went an alteration of the whole ecclesiastical pattern. With its parish system in which one church served a fixed geographic area, the Church of Scotland was unable, and in some cases unwilling because of the cost involved, to take steps to meet the needs of the migrant workers moving into the industrial centres. Added to this, many of its leaders had so imbibed the eighteenth century rationalism that they had nothing to say to their working class parishioners who lived in poverty, squalor and degradation in the narrow dead-end side streets of Edinburgh, Glasgow and other industrial cities. As one critic put it, "they read cold moral essays to cold, but none too moral congregations." The reaction to this came through the work of men such as the Haldane brothers who brought about an evangelical revival within a segment of the established church. Their work was carried on by the Rev. Dr. Thomas Chalmers, a brilliant mathematician and economist, who sought to bring about the spiritual, moral and social reform of the whole country. His great problem, however, was that of obtaining churches for evangelical ministers since the power of appointment lay in the hands of the heritors, usually the local landlords, not in those of the congregations. After a ten-year struggle over the issue, the General Assembly backed by the civil courts refused to make any change and 451 ministers, followed by nearly one-third of the Established Church's membership, walked out in 1843 to found The Free Church of Scotland. This church, along with the United Presbyterians formed in 1847, did much to help solve the spiritual problems of the "lower classes" both in the Highlands and in the industrial areas of the country. At the end of the century the United Presbyterians and a majority of the Free Church merged to found the United Free Church, although the strongly Calvinistic wing of the Free Church refused to go into the union, continuing, principally in the Highlands, down to the present day.

Intellectually Scotland in the nineteenth century was influenced strongly by winds blowing from outside while at the same time keeping its own particular characteristic outlook. The impact of the Reformation continued strong in most areas of life showing its power in such movements as the ecclesiastical disruption of 1843, in the development of such bodies as the Free Presbyterian Church, and in strong sabbatarianism coupled with independence of thought and a liking for metaphysical and theological discussion. In the universities, however, with the rising influence of physical science, the acceptance of Darwinian evolution and similar trends, the Reformation doctrines were beginning to lose their hold, although the basic attitudes often remained. From Adam Smith and David Hume down to the end of the nineteenth century, Scotland produced its quota, if not more than its quota, of philosophers, scientists, doctors and others active in intellectual fields. At the same time the Scottish literary tradition was carried on by Thomas Carlyle, R. L. Stevenson, J. M. Barrie, "Ian MacLaren," Andrew Lang, George Brown and numerous others.

The changes in Scotland were not limited in their effects to Scotland alone however, for the nineteenth century was the century of imperialism, colonization and missionary activity, with people from the western world flowing out to the uttermost parts of the earth. And the Scots were in the vanguard of the movement. One one hand, there were soldiers such as "Chinese Gordon" who ended his days as a victim of the Mahdi in Khartoum, and David Livingstone, the missionary-geographer who fought the slave trade to his dying day. On the other, there were the nameless and almost countless immigrants who set sail from Glasgow and other west coast ports to seek their fortunes and to find free lands "down under" or in the New World of the Americas. Scots went everywhere, settling in the "outback" of Australia, on the veldt of Matabeleland in Africa, on the pampas of Argentina and in the wilds of the Yukon or the North West Territories in Canada. One Canadian newspaper in the 1920s even went so far as to say that when the first official flight was made to the moon, a Scot would be waiting to welcome it. While this was hardly possible, it is well to note that the first man to set foot on the moon bore the name of Armstrong, long associated with the clans on the Scottish borders!

Yet while separated from their "ain folk," the Scots have not changed radically. Their attitudes, prejudices and points of view have continued strong. Their nationalism, albeit no longer specifically Scottish, has been usually transferred to their new heath, as we can see for instance in the influential part they played in bringing about Canadian Confederation. Their aggressiveness in every field of activity into which they have entered has manifested itself repeatedly. In the areas settled by Highlanders the use of Gaelic has so continued that there are probably as many speakers of "the language" in Cape Breton today as there are in Scotland, and Scottish customs, particularly Highland dancing, have become so popular that one even finds Dutchmen and Germans happy to wear the kilt, although genuine Scots may sometimes object to such a profanation of their national garb. Usually the Scot also maintains a religious background which keeps coming to the fore, even when he likes to proclaim himself a freethinker or an agnostic. But above all one might say that he has not lost his clannishness. Robert Louis Stevenson was quite right when he said:

> The fact remains: in spite of the differences of blood and language the Lowlander feels himself the sentimental countryman of the Highlander. When they meet abroad, they fall upon each other's neck in spirit; even at home there is a kind of clannish intimacy in their talk.[2]

Because of this continuance of characteristics even through three and four generations, Scots are usually quite identifiable within even a cosmopolitan population. If one is asked to speak at a Scottish Masonic Lodge in Toronto, to a Highland Dance Society in Durham, North Carolina, to the St. Andrews Society in Montreal or to one of the dozen other Scottish organizations across Canada or the United States, one finds that there is a basic similarity and, consequently, understanding. The sense of humour, which is most important, and very different from English or American humour, is the same; the background traditions are similar and the reactions vary little. Even the differences between Protestant and Roman Catholic seem to have had their rough edges smoothed considerably by the removal from the old battle grounds to the new lands of conquest. They are all "brither Scots" together facing an uncomprehending and sometimes a sneering and often hostile, but obviously inferior world.

Yet the Scots have also been adaptable, making some of the best settlers history has known. Like the Jews they have been able to move into new situations, face new hazards and difficulties and by a power of adaptation overcome, while at the same time maintaining their identity. Various explanations have been offered for this capacity, but it would seem that the reason is the history of Scotland itself, the traditions which it has developed from the days of Wallace, Bruce, Knox, Burns, Scott to the present. It is this Scottish tradition which has played such an important part in the development of Canada and the Canadians.[3]

NOTES

1. W. Notestein, *The Scot in History* (London: Cape, 1947), p. 123.
2. R. L. Stevenson, "The Foreigner at Home," in *Memories and Portraits* (London: Collins, n.d.), p. 36.
3. For a more detailed account of the Scottish background the reader should turn to the *New Edinburgh History of Scotland* by W. C. Dickinson and G. Pryde, 2 vols. (Edinburgh: Nelson, 1961-2), or to the *Edinburgh History of Scotland* in four much larger volumes, edited by Gordon Donaldson (Edinburgh: Oliver & Boyd, 1971 ff.).

TWO

"The Auld Alliance" in New France

Henry B. M. Best

> Of the three groups who form what we now call Les Anglais, those who have been here longest and those who are the most remarkable are the Scottish Group. For us, French Canadians, this is also the most sympathetic and the most understanding of the three groups concerned.[1]

Statements such as this one made in 1898 are not surprising to those familiar with the relations between Frenchman and Scot throughout the history of Canada. There is considerable evidence that a special under-standing existed and may still exist between the French and the Presbyterian as well as the Catholic Scot, which did not develop between the French and others who joined them in Canada. André Siegfried wrote, "they [the Scots] manifested a real goodwill towards the French and these latter were the first to recognize it."[2] There are specific reasons for the harmony between them but it must also be realized that the Scot is not only unusually ubiquitous but also very adaptable to other cultures. It matters not in what part of the globe we search, the Scot is to be found, and very often he has been in the country of his adoption for many generations. Curiosity and a sense of adventure coupled with quarrels and crowding at home often led the Scot to become a mercenary or simply to seek his fortune in a new land while his ability to adapt and to succeed in a wide variety of circumstances contributed greatly.

Relations between France and Scotland appear to have started in the tenth century with negotiations between the Emperor Charlemagne and the Scots to devise some protection against the depredations of the Vikings. By the fifteenth century contact had increased to the extent that the destinies of France and Scotland were very much intertwined. Many Scots served in the Royal Body Guard of Louis XI, many were involved in business, and others studied at the Collège Écossais at the Université de

15

Paris or became members of religious communities in France. Intermarriage of royal families, alliances for political and military purposes, cultural contacts – all increased until the sixteenth century when they reached their greatest strength during the minority and reign of Mary, Queen of Scots. In 1600 Shakespeare wrote in *Henry V*, "Qui la France veut gagner, A l'Ecosse faut commencer!" giving an indication of Scotland's importance to France but also of its vulnerability.[3] The Auld Alliance, as the connection between France and Scotland came to be called, saw its last flowering in Europe with the events of the eighteenth century involving the attempts of James and Charles Edward, the Old and the Young Pretenders, to enlist the support of France in their attempts to recover the throne of the United Kingdom. Against this kind of background it is not surprising to find that the Auld Alliance had effects upon New France as well as old.

Contrary to the accepted view, the official policy in New France – that only French Catholics were allowed – was not rigorously applied. From the documents of the period it is evident that Austria, Belgium, China, England, Germany, Ireland, Italy, the Netherlands, Portugal, Scotland, Spain, and Switzerland were all represented, however minimally and unofficially, in the colony. The Scots were not only among those who had the closest and most cordial relations with the French but were also among the most numerous of the minority groups, if indeed that term is not too pretentious. There is no question, however, that the heady brew of Celtic twilight and the fumes from a Quebec sugar house were in evidence during the Ancien Regime, even though it did not achieve its full potency until the nineteenth century. One has only to read the very popular work of Philippe Aubert de Gaspé, *Les Anciens Canadiens*, to see what effects this brew could have.

Those Scots who came to New France under normal circumstances can be divided into two groups, neither of them very numerous. These were the settlers and the military. Possibly the first mention of a Scot in New France is in the writings of Champlain. When he returned to Canada from France in 1618 he found that the previous winter had been a very difficult one; however, only one individual of the small group then living in Quebec had died and he was a Scotch Huguenot who reportedly refused conversion on his deathbed.[4] Who was this solitary unfortunate? There is no indication to throw any further light on the subject.

Undoubtedly the best known of the reputed Scots in the early years of the history of New France is Abraham Martin dit l'Ecossais. The term "dit l'Ecossais" which was found in at least one document concerning Abraham Martin is a solid indication that he was indeed of Scottish ancestry.[5] The name Martin could also be English, German or French. Martin or Martine is one of the most international of names but there are other pieces of what could be called corroborative evidence of his ancestry. Martin's wife was Margeurite Langlois. The name Langlois was an adaptation of L'Anglais often given to those of English background. On the subject of the term "dit l'Ecossais," this is certainly the most obvious indication of Abraham Martin's background although it is only fair to say that it could also have been a false name, used by him when in military service, or as the member of an illegal organization. Another piece of evidence is the fact that when the Kirke brothers captured Quebec in 1629 and Captain David Kirke made his brother, Captain Louis Kirke, governor, Martin did not leave with Champlain and many of the colonists, but chose to remain under English rule. A case could be built to show that this proved certain sympathies with the Scots Kirkes, but the fact remains that other accounts assure us that a number of people chose to stay simply to avoid the horrors of an Atlantic passage. They thought that they might be better off remaining in Quebec with what little they had been able to accumulate by this time.

Was Abraham Martin a Scot or not? It is very difficult to say with complete certainty but the weight of evidence is clearly in favour of this conclusion. Certainly he was the first of the king's St. Lawrence pilots and the Plains of Abraham were named after him. For these reasons his name is known to us today. Martin, or Maître Abraham as one often finds him called, lived in Quebec until 1664, when he died at the age of 75. He had many descendants, same of whom should be mentioned. First of all, Anne Martin, probably born in France, married Jean Côté in 1635, and thus Abraham became the ancestor of the very, very numerous Côté families in Quebec today. Marguerite Martin married Etienne Racine in 1638 and, again, there are numerous descendants, including two bishops of the Catholic Church. Hélène Martin married Claude Etienne in 1640 and secondly, in 1647 she married a fascinating person, Médard Chouart, better known as Chouart des Grosseilliers, the explorer and pilot who led a very varied and colourful existence indeed. Marie Martin in 1648 married Jean Cloutier, and, again, there are very numerous descendants. Charles-Amador Martin, born in 1648, was the second Canadian to become a priest and he served successively at Beauport, Sainte-Famille, Château-Richer and Ste-Foi. He was a Canon of Quebec and composed the Mass of the office of the Holy Family, which is still sung. Thus he was probably the first Canadian composer.

The records of the Hôtel-Dieu of Quebec mention a young girl of Scottish ancestry who arrived in Canada in 1642, Marie Irwin.[6] The name was also written as Kirwin, Herovin and Hirouin. She is quoted in the annals of the Hôtel-Dieu as being the daughter of a noble Scotsman who took refuge in France with all his family in order to preserve his religion. Born in Scotland in 1626, Marie Irwin remained as a pensionnaire at the Hôtel-Dieu in Quebec from 1642 to 1647 when she returned to France. She entered a convent at Dieppe, where she became a nun, and returned to New France in 1657. Her name in religion was Mère Marie de la Conception. She died in October, 1687, in Quebec.[7]

Of the Scots who entered particularly into the military annals of New

France there are two names that stand out. They are Ramsay, or de Ramezay, and Douglas or Douglass, or Du Glas. There seems to be little question that Claude de Ramezay and his son, Jean-Baptiste-Nicholas-Roch, were of Scottish descent, but the actual connecting link poses some problems as yet. The first person who can be traced with some certainty is one Philibert de Ramezay, Sieur de Montigny et de Bélin. There are documents concerning him dating from 1532. His great-grandson, Claude de Ramezay, born in France June 15, 1659, came to Canada in 1685.[8] I shall not go further into the European connection except to say there seems to be little question that Claude was descended from a Scot. Most probably he was descended from Sir John Ramsay who spent some 15 years exiled in France, part of it as a member of a regiment raised by Sir John Hepburn. Claude de Ramezay, as mentioned, arrived in Canada in 1685 as an ensign with the troops of the marine. He was one of several "fils de famille" who accompanied the Marquis de Denonville on his arrival as governor of the colony. He rose swiftly to the rank of lieutenant and then captain. In 1690 he was made governor of Three Rivers and it was in that same year that he married Marie-Charlotte Denys de la Ronde at Quebec. In 1696 he was put in command of the colonial militia on the occasion of an expedition against the Indians. In 1699 he became commanding general of the troops of New France. He was called to Montreal in 1701 as Lieutenant-du-Roi and was made governor of the same city in 1704. He held this position until his death at Quebec in August 1724.

Claude de Ramezay received the highest military distinction available, the Cross of St. Louis and, during the absence of Governor Vaudreuil, he acted as Governor *par interim* of Canada. He was granted, over a period of years, three seigneuries. That of Sorel he received in 1672, but soon forfeited to the government when he did not carry out the attached duties. That of Monoir on the Richelieu was granted in 1708, and that of Ramezay on the Yamaska in 1710. Claude de Ramezay and Marie-Charlotte Denys de la Ronde had 16 children. Of these, Claude, born in 1691, was killed at the Battle of Rio de Janeiro in 1711. Louis, Sieur de Monoir, born in 1695 at Three Rivers, was massacred while commanding an expedition against the Cherokees in 1716. Charles-Hector, Sieur de la Gesse, born in 1695, became a captain of the colonial troops and was drowned in 1725 on the vessel *Chameau* crossing the Atlantic. Marie-Catherine, born in 1696, entered the Ursuline Convent in Quebec. Marie-Charlotte, born in 1697, entered the Hôpital-Général in Quebec as a nun and remained there until her death in 1767. Louise-Geneviève, born in 1699, married Major Louis-Henri Deschamps in 1721 and at his death in 1736 retired to the Hôpital-Général in Quebec. Of her children, one, Charles Deschamps, rose to the rank of captain in 1756 and received the order of Chevalier de St. Louis in 1758. Another, Louise-Charlotte, married, at Quebec in 1745, Roch de St. Ours of another well-known family. Françoise-Louise de Ramezay was born in Montreal in 1705. She never married but showed remarkable business acumen in attempting to improve the poor financial state of her family. She was one of the earliest successful businesswomen in Canada. Marie-Elizabeth de Ramezay, born in 1707, married Louis de la Corne, Sieur de Chapt and lieutenant in the troops of the Marine. He finally became a captain, Chevalier de St. Louis, and was Seigneur of Terrebonne when he died in 1762. His widow retired to the Community of the Grey Nuns in Montreal. One of their children will come into our narrative later – Marie-Charlotte de la Corne, who married one François-Prosper de Douglass. The only son to survive was Jean-Baptiste-Nicholas-Roch. He was born in 1706, became an ensign at the age of twelve, rising swiftly to captain, and was commandant of the area of Hudson Bay and of Acadia, a major at Quebec and finally Lieutenant-du-Roi, also at Quebec. It was while in this position that he surrendered the Citadel to a Scot by the name of Murray. He married Louise, the daughter of Réné Godefroy de Tonnancour, at Three Rivers in 1728. After the capitulation he and his wife returned to France. There are thus no de Ramezays left by name in Quebec but the family was obviously one of great importance during the French Regime.

We have already seen that Marie-Charlotte de la Corne, the daughter of Marie-Elizabeth de Ramezay and Louis de la Corne, married François-Prosper de Douglass. This was an interesting coincidence when two of the foremost families of Scottish origin in New France became allied. The marriage document of this occasion found in the Archives of the Superior Court in Montreal, provides a most interesting view of the period, apart from naming the parents of François-Prosper. The signatures of those present at the ceremony on April 12, 1757, form a roster of the important people of the time. Aside from the two principal persons, who signed simply "Douglass" and "Charlotte Lacorne," we have Marie-Elizabeth de Ramezay, the mother of the bride, who signed "de Ramezay Lacorne;" Pierre de Rigaud de Vaudreuil, the Governor of Montreal, who signed simply "Vaudreuil," and the Chevalier de Levis. There were several members of the D'Ailleboust family, including Charles-Joseph, who was Lieutenant-du-Roi of Montreal at this time. We also find the signatures of Montcalm, of Bourlamarque and of Montreuil.

Although the versions of the background of François-Prosper de Douglass are almost as numerous as the places in which they are mentioned, there seems to be little question that he was also of Scottish descent. The marriage record states that he was "fils majeur de défunt Messire Charles Comte de Douglas de Mégillac." The gentleman who interests us particularly arrived in New France as a lieutenant in the Regiment of Languedoc in 1743. He obtained a company in 1746, was wounded at the Battle of Carillon on July 8, 1758, and obtained the Cross of St. Louis in the same year. There are several references to an officer by the name of Douglas in the French forces at Quebec at the time of the capitulation, and there is some possibility that it may be another person, who is mentioned later. As far as they can be unravelled, however, these references are to François-Prosper de Douglass. The best known source is the memoirs of M. le Chevalier de Johnstone, himself a Scot. These memoirs are not notable for their great historical accuracy but there is no reason to believe that Johnstone did not know the other officers present at the siege of Quebec. In this sometimes very fanciful account there is mention of Captain Douglas as in charge of one of the posts at the top of the heights scaled by Wolfe's troops.[9] Evidence points to the station of Samos as the one that Douglass commanded.[10] In any case, François-Prosper de Douglass and his wife went to France after the capitulation, taking with them their two sons, Louis-Archembault de Douglass and Charles-Luc de Douglass.

It appears that there were two men by the name of Douglas among the officers of the regular militia or colonial troops who attained the rank of captain or lieutenant in the period 1670 to 1760. The list compiled by Benjamin Sulte only mentions one without specifying which, but there were undoubtedly two of this name.[11] The second person was Jean Douglas. He is referred to as the Chevalier de Bassignac and is variously mentioned as being a captain in the Régiment de Béarn and as a captain in the Régiment de Royal-Roussillon. He received the order of Chevalier de St. Louis, a slightly lower order than the Cross of St. Louis awarded to François-Prosper, but they both received their decorations on the same date, October 20, 1758. The Chevalier Jean Douglas de Bassignac is mentioned in the memoirs of Captain Pouchot of the Régiment de Béarn as being present, as was François-Prosper, at the Battle of Carillon.[12] According to the journal of Captain Pouchot, M. De Bassignac attached a handkerchief to the end of his gun, though for what purpose is not stated. The British thought that this was a sign that the French wished to surrender and immediately marched forward, expecting their adversaries to lay down their arms. According to the report, the French felled a number of British soldiers. Another story emanating from the Battle of Carillon is recorded as follows:

> Some highlanders, taken prisoner by the French and Canadians huddled together on the battlefield and, expecting to be cruelly treated looked on in mournful silence. Presently, a gigantic French officer walked up to them and whilst exchanging in a severe tone some remarks in French with some of his men suddenly addressed them in Gaelic. Surprise in the Highlanders soon turned to positive horror. Firmly believing that no Frenchman could ever speak Gaelic, they concluded that his Satanic Majesty in person was before them. It was a Jacobite serving in the French Army.[13]

It must be asserted that there is no proof of the authenticity of this tale nor of the identity of the Gaelic-speaking devil. There were, undoubtedly, a few Scots who, taking refuge in France following 1745, joined the French forces that came to the New World. Three of these are the Chevalier de Johnstone already mentioned, Chevalier de Montelambert and the Chevalier de Trion.[14] They took service at Louisbourg in 1749. It is uncertain whether the others ever actually went beyond Louisbourg and came to Quebec, but Johnstone took a ship for Quebec as he was not anxious to be captured by the British. He became aide-de-camp to de Lévis in 1759, stayed at Quebec with Montcalm and was there at the time of the capitulation. He was afraid of the treatment he would receive from the victorious army but General Murray showed leniency and Johnstone stayed for a few months at Quebec with a cousin who was a captain in the British artillery. He returned to France in 1760.

The value of the Scots as fighting men was certainly recognized throughout Europe and in New France as well. Louis-Antoine, Comte de Bougainville, who was one of Montcalm's better officers at the time of the seige of Quebec, wrote a memorandum in which he set down a number of necessary items for the defence of the colony. Among these he included the following:

> A troop of Scots, even of only sixty men, headed by a MacLean or a MacDonald, or some other of these Clan Chiefs, of whom the names are cherished and respected by all Highlanders. These last understand very well they are sent to America in great numbers by the British in order to depopulate their area and even in hopes of seeing some of them killed. Those that we have captured have told us a hundred times and over that if they saw in our army a troop of their own compatriots and a chief known by them a great number of them would come over to our flag and that the nucleus of sixty men would bring us a very considerable number indeed.[15]

There is undoubtedly considerable truth in these statements though it is entirely possible that the captured Scots were anxious to say anything that would please the French in the hope of better treatment and rations.

During the Old Regime, Scots were also found in the region of Acadia. Matters became very complicated at times because of the constant change of allegiance or change of ownership of this area and the people often did not know under which flag they were living. The first colonizing attempts took place in 1603 at St. Croix Island and later at Port Royal. In 1621 Sir William Alexander, knighted for his literary achievements by James VI and I, was granted Acadia, a huge domain stretching from the Atlantic to the St. Lawrence, and east from an extrapolation of the St. Croix River north. This territory he called New Scotland and he intended to found a large and prosperous colony of Scots. Alexander planned to grant parcels of land to individual gentlemen on whom would be conferred the title of Baronet of Nova Scotia and, in return, they would bring settlers to their lands, thus opening up the country. The Kirke family, already heard of in connection with the taking of Quebec in 1629, assisted Alexander in settling the colony. In 1628 two ships were sent out to Port Royal under the command of the son of William Alexander and, and according to the records, there were seventy colonists (described as more or less willing) who came to set up a colony near the ruins of the French port known as Port Royal or Charles Fort. The site is where one finds the present-day village of Granville, Nova Scotia. What happened over the next few years is rather vague, but in any case, with the Treaty of St. Germain-en-Laye in 1632, Canada and Acadia were returned to the French. There seems to be no question that the Scottish colony had had considerable difficulty; there was much sickness, and the Indians were not friendly. A number of colonists left in 1632, reportedly going back to Scotland, but a few stayed. One source gives the names of those families who stayed as the Paisleys, Collesons, Melansons, Peters and Kesseys.[16] The only name that appears in later records is Melanson, and it seems probable that the Melansons chose to remain under the French and, indeed, very quickly became French. There are other possible explanations for the arrival of the Melansons in Acadia, one being that they arrived in 1657 with Sir Thomas Temple, appointed Governor of Nova Scotia by Oliver Cromwell. Reportedly, Temple continued on to Boston leaving the Melansons, among others, at Port Royal.[17] But it would seem most likely that they came as part of the settlement of Sir William Alexander and then remained after 1632. La Mothe-Cadillac, in his *Mémoire sur l'Acadie*, states that he saw in 1685 at Port Royal two brothers who had become Catholics and had married French girls.[18] It would seem possible that these two brothers were the Melansons. In any case, we find in documents of this period two brothers, Pierre and Charles Melanson or Mellanson. The census of Port Royal for 1671 gives us Charles Melanson, labourer, aged 28, and his wife Marie du Gast, age 23, and four children. It also mentions Pierre with the following information: "tailleur, Pierre Melanson refused to give his age, the number of his stock, and information about his lands and his wife asked why anybody would be so stupid as to run around the country asking such questions."[19] This entry in the census is amusing, although not particularly helpful. The census of 1686 gives us a little more information of Pierre Melanson and his family, listing Pierre Melanson de la Verdure, 54 years old, and Marie Mius d'Entremont, 36 years of age, living at the Baie des Mines with their 9 children.[20]

Both Melanson families seemed to prosper and grow in number and they remained in Acadia after its cession to the British by the Treaty of Utrecht in 1713. A number of Melansons or Mellansons (also spelt a number of other ways such as Melensont, Mellson and so on in documents of the mid-eighteenth century) at that time signed statements promising to be faithful to their new king.[21] With the dispersion of the Acadians in 1755, the name Melanson seems to have spread to the four winds. It is among the names of the parishioners in the Church of Grand Pré;[22] the name is found in Pennsylvania and in many other parts of North America. Most of the Melansons seem to have returned later to Acadia or to have gone to Quebec. The name Melanson is still found in New Brunswick and Nova Scotia, usually spelled Melanson, but also Melançon, which is simply the French spelling of the same name.[23] The descendants of the

Melançon family are numerous and are spread throughout Acadia and Quebec. Claude Melançon, public relations officer with the CNR and writer of natural history books, is one; Msgr. Georges Melançon, the Bishop of Chicoutimi, was another, as is the Abbé Melançon, of the Bishopric of Joliette.

There is much pathos in the history of the Acadians, of which the Melançon family forms a part, as do the captives, particularly the many children, who were taken in the border raids on the frontier settlements. Whether France and England were at war or not, two things were carried on; one was trade, illicit or otherwise, and the other was a series of guerrilla raids to harass the enemy. With regard to trade, an official raid of 506 houses in Montreal in 1741 showed that 449 of the homes contained contraband goods.[24] The question of legitimate trade involving Scots is still to be properly investigated but one example of a financial transaction can be given. The archives of the colonies, "Extraits des Lettres du Canada" for October 22, 1705, contain the account of the case of one Samuel Belth or Beith, who arrived in Quebec from Boston on a mission concerning the exchange of prisoners.[25] One might think that he had another reason for taking on this mission when it is learned that he had loaned £3,000 to Claude de Ramezay in 1701 and was still awaiting payment. The same records show that Louis XIV had authorized the colonists to deal in matters of business "avec les Ecossais."

The record books of The Sovereign & Superior Councils yield a number of documents known as "Lettres de Naturalité" or naturalization papers which are useful in the search for non-French names in New France. These were given to people who were not citizens of New France, but who wished to have their status regularized and become citizens. A large number of those who received these letters were captives, taken either in the border raids or in other raids that took place on Hudson's Bay or in Newfoundland. Among the captives there were, of course, many children whose names were lost. Many of the Langlois families in Quebec today are descended from captives who were simply baptized Pierre, or Marie, or some other such Christian name followed by L'Anglais – English one – and this has become Langlois.

One captive whose name is of Scottish origin is Marie-Madeleine Warren. She is listed in the registers of Notre Dame de Montreal as having been baptized on May 9, 1693. She is referred to as Madame Kresek, born in New England, February, 1662, of the marriage of Jacques Warren, a Scottish Presbyterian, and of Marguerite, described simply as an Irish Catholic. She was captured June 28, 1689. On October 15, 1693, Marie-Madeleine Warren was married to one Philippe Robitaille in Montreal. When Marie Warren was captured she had with her her daughter from a previous marriage, Christine Otis. When Philippe married Madeleine Warren he adopted Christine.

A list of the English captives remaining in the hands of the French in

1695 gives Grysell Otis and Christen (sic) Otis among those held.[26] Without going into undue detail, it is interesting to note that Christine Otis married Louis Lebeau, a carpenter at Ville Marie, in 1707 and that she had several children by him. He died in 1713 and in the following year his widow was successfully wooed by a Captain Thomas Baker who came to New France as interpreter for Stoddart and Williams on their mission following the Treaty of Utrecht. This must indeed have been a very strange situation. Originally captured from New England at the age of three months, the young widow, with several children by her French husband, now returned to New England to remarry there. Apparently the state, the church and her mother all opposed Christine's departure from New France and attempted to prevent it. She was not allowed to take any money with her. She had intended to take at least one of her children and leave the others with her mother and step-father. In the end Governor Vaudreuil refused to allow her to take any children and Christine ceded all belongings to her mother and step-father, stipulating that she could take possession if she returned to Canada. Thus, Christine Otis Lebeau arrived in New England and married Thomas Baker. She was rebaptized as a Protestant before the marriage. There were several children by this marriage. Christine Baker and her husband made one trip back to New France in 1721 in the hopes of recovering her children, but they were unable to do so.[27]

Another captive of interest was John Reid (Reed), who was granted a letter of naturalization in June, 1713. Here he is referred to as Jean Reed.[28] Among others granted citizenship at the same time were several taken by D'Iberville in his attack on Fort St. John's, Newfoundland, in 1696. However, the fact that Reid appears in Montreal might lead one to think that it was more probable that he was captured in New England, but this is far from certain. The archives in the Palais de Justice in Montreal preserve the record of the marriage of Jean Ris in 1714 to Catherine Primeau in the parish of La Prairie. He is described there as Jean Ris, son of David Ris and of Elizabeth Madrianu, his father and mother both being declared to be of Verness [Inverness] in Scotland. The registers of the parish of Notre Dame, Montreal, in the year 1715, give the record of the baptism in the month of October of one Marie Caterine, two-day-old daughter of Jan Reidde, Ecossais, and of Caterine Primot his wife.[29] This, of course, shows the kind of change which can take place, even within the same document, in a name. There were six children of this marriage and from some of these are descended the many Reid families that we find in Quebec today, especially in the regions of Chateauguay, Beauharnois, St. Philomène, Montreal, La Prairie, Quebec and elsewhere. One must be careful, of course, not to mistake some of the Reids who arrived in the Montreal region after 1760 with those who arrived before. The spelling Reid appears to have practically disappeared for generations. It went through variations such as Ris, Ridde, and Riddey, but today the only spelling found of the descendants of John Reid is Reid, although none of the people concerned have any indication whatsoever that they are anything but of French descent.

There are several other names of interest which occur in examination of the records of naturalization; George Gray[30] and William Saderlan (Sutherland?) are two that are recorded as being natives of Scotland.[31] To be entirely thorough, one must, of course, look at the legal records of those who were malefactors, and even here we find question of Scots. One record shows the conviction on September 19, 1755, of Charles Kennedy and his accomplices of the crime of stealing several pieces of silverware from the home of one of the counsellors of Quebec. Kennedy and one other person were led to the gallows.[32] There is no record that he was a Scot, but the name might lead one to that conclusion.

Thus whether of high rank as were the de Ramezays or of humble origins as were most Scots who came to New France, Scots had already begun to play a part in Canadian history before the great influx began following the cession to Great Britain of Acadia in 1713 and of New France in 1763.

NOTES

1. Benjamin Sulte, "Les Ecossais au Canada," *La Revue des Deux Frances*, II (1898), 120.

2. André Siegfried, *Le Canada, les Deux Races* (Paris: Colin, 1906), p. 73.

3. William Shakespeare, *Henry V*, Act I, Scene 2.

4. Morris Bishop, *Champlain, The Life of Fortitude* (Toronto: McClelland and Stewart, 1963), p. 270.

5. Notre Dame de Québec, Régistre de Baptême, le 24 Octobre, 1621.

6. *Les Annales de l'Hôtel-Dieu de Québec* (Quebec: l'Hôtel-Dieu, 1939), p. 42.

7. Mgr. Cyprien Tanguay, *Dictionnaire Généalogique des Familles Canadiennes* (Montreal: Senécal, 1971), I, 307.

8. Victor Morin, *Les Ramezays et leur Château* (Société Archéologique et Numismatique de Montréal, 1955), p. 26.

9. James Johnstone de Johnstone, "Memoirs de M. le Chev. de Johnstone," *Literary and Historical Society of Quebec* (Montreal: Société d'Archéologie et de Numismatique, 1955), Series IX, Part II, p. 130.

10. Abbé H-R Casgrain, "Les Plaines d'Abraham," *Literary and Historical Society of Quebec Transactions, 1889-1900*, No. 23, p. 51.

11. Benjamin Sulte, "Canadian Militia Under the French Regime," *Mélanges Historiques* (Montreal: Ducharme, 1918), I, 143.

12. Pierre-Georges Roy, "Officers du Régiment de Béarn," *Bulletin des Recherches Historiques*, LI (1945), 425.

13. J. Murray Gibbon, *Scots in Canada* (Toronto: Musson, 1971), p. 78.

14. Johnstone, pp. 63-199.
15. Pierre-Georges Roy, ed., "Memoir pour le Ministre de la Marine sur 1. Les Pandres Alimentaires; 2. Les Canons Portifs; 3. Une Troupe d'Ecossais à envoyer au Canada, 17 janvier, 1759," par M. Bougainville. *Rapport de l'Archiviste de la Province de Québec, 1923-1924*, p. 40.
16. Emile Louvrière, *La Tragédie d'un Peuple* (Paris: Bossard, 1923), I, 64.
17. Bona Arseneault, *L'Acadie des Ancêtres* (Quebec: Laval, 1955), p. 40.
18. *Ibid.*, p. 42.
19. Placide Gaudet, *Généalogie des Familles Acadiennes*, Archives of Canada, Documents de la Session, No. 18, 1906, p. 62.
20. "Recensement de L'Acadie en 1686," in *Bulletin des Recherches Historiques*, XXXVIII (1932), No. 12, 725.
21. *Proceedings and Transactions of the Royal Society of Canada, 1886*, VI, Sect. I, p. 52.
22. Arsenault, p. 285.
23. It has been suggested by Professor W. Stanford Reid that Melanson is an anglicized form of MacMillan, which means "son of Millan." This is an interesting possibility, although the family tradition is that they were MacClellands.
24. Marcel Trudel, *Introduction to New France* (Toronto: Holt, 1968), p. 198.
25. Archives des Colonies, Paris, C11, A23, fol. 196, 198.
26. Emma Lewis Coelan, *New England Captives Carried to Canada, 1677-1760* (Portland, Me., Southworth, 1925), I, 75.
27. *Ibid.*, pp. 150-154.
28. Archives de la Prov. de Québec, *Régistre des Insinuations du Conseil Supérieur*, Vol. D, No. 4, fol. 9.
29. Tanguay, VI, 574.
30. *Ibid.*,74,124, pp. 378-9. See also Tanguay, IV, 356.
31. Tanguay, VII, 108.
32. Archives de la Prov. de Qué., *Régistre Criminel*, IV, fol. 150-1.

THREE

The Scot in
the Fur Trade

Elaine Allan Mitchell

It would be almost impossible to overemphasize the pre-eminent position which Scots of every stripe, Highlander, Lowlander and Islander, attained during the eighteenth and nineteenth centuries in the North American fur trade. The same political, economic and social pressures which forced them as a people to emigrate in such large numbers, brought them as a matter of course into this expanding trade. But it is clear that, in addition to the paramount need to earn a living, they possessed certain advantages of character or education, or both, which admirably fitted them for the service of the two principal and diverse interests in the northwest, the Canadians operating from Montreal and the English on Hudson's Bay. If the dashing Highlanders of the North West Company have captured the imagination of the general public, still they must yield pride of place to the less spectacular Orkneymen of the Hudson's Bay Company, who preceded them in that part of North America formerly known as Rupert's Land. In later years, too, the sons of both groups, the majority of them born of marriages with Indian women, were frequently to succeed their fathers and grandfathers, and themselves to play a substantial and worthy part in the continent-wide and virtually monopolistic corporation on whose foundations the modern Canadian nation has been built.

The fur trade dates back to the earliest days of the discovery of Canada. The Basque, Breton and other European fishermen who followed the explorers to the Gulf of St. Lawrence (and may even have preceded them) were the first to barter furs from the Indians with goods and trinkets, but the trade continued to be subsidiary to the fishing industry and of minor importance until the hatmakers of Europe discovered the superiority of beaver in the manufacture of their increasingly popular felt hats. The hooked ends of the under fur particularly suited it to the felting process and the most prized pelts came from the robes which the Indians wore to protect themselves from the cold. These skins, taken when prime during the winter, were subjected to a special treatment which caused the guard hairs to fall out, leaving the soft fur underneath, while constant wear for fifteen to eighteen months further improved the quality, making them well-greased, pliable and yellow in colour.[1]

The new French colony, which Champlain founded on the St. Lawrence River in 1608, soon came to rely on the fur trade as its principal source of revenue and the adventurous *coureurs de bois*, preferring the free life of the woods, with its relatively high rewards, to the harsh and unremunerative toil of Quebec farms, spread out in all directions by way of the Ottawa River and the Great Lakes in pursuit of beaver. The story of Radisson and Groseilliers and the founding of the Hudson's Bay Company is too well known to be repeated here, but the presence of English traders after 1668 on the bay which the French regarded as their own had immediate repercussions on the St. Lawrence. Not only did it give fresh impetus to the French movement inland, in order to intercept the furs going down to the Bay, but it led to numerous attempts, first by sea and then by land, to oust the English from their posts. These campaigns featured the daring exploits of de Troyes and Iberville and constitute one of the most exciting periods in the history of New France.

In 1713 the Treaty of Utrecht ended the struggle for the Bay by returning all the posts there to the English, and a glut of beaver in Europe gave temporary pause to the pace of French expansion in the interior. A few years later, however, it was again taken up by explorers like La Verendrye and his sons, who continued to press inland towards the Rocky Mountains and to establish posts in strategic places along their route.

Meanwhile the Hudson's Bay Company, emerging from a quarter of a century's precarious tenure of the Bay, was experiencing acute personnel problems. Its officers, as Professor Rich has pointed out in his history of the Company,[2] were typical products of the English artisan class at the beginning of the eighteenth century, mostly promoted servants not bred to command. They proved unable to control obstreperous subordinates largely drawn from the slums of towns (principally London and its environs) and much given to excessive brandy-drinking and promiscuous Indian women. Restricting their access to these vices, the governor and the London Committee recognized, was no permanent solution and they began to look round for more biddable labourers. They had already tried the Scottish mainland (two presumably Scottish servants, James Mudie and Thomas Bannatine, signed the protest against Henry Sergeant's surrender of Fort Albany to de Troyes in 1686[3]), but the distances involved and perhaps English distrust of the latent Jacobitism[4] of the Highlanders had led them to give over their interest in Scots. Prospects for recruitment in the Orkneys, however, now seemed promising. The Company's ships frequently made Stromness their last port of call before sailing for Hudson's Bay and the islanders' hardihood, docility and diligence, as well as their obvious poverty, were likely to make them good servants.

Even today, despite centuries of patriotic adherence to the rest of Scotland, Orcadians (their proper connotation, although the Hudson's Bay records invariably refer to them as Orkneymen) are inclined to regard themselves as a separate people. And in a manner of speaking they are, for the Norse invasions obliterated every trace of the Celtic peoples who formerly inhabited the island. Until 1468, when they came under the Scottish crown, they were part of the Kingdom of Norway, although their hereditary earls had belonged to Scottish families for over two hundred years and Scottish influence had also come in through many of their bishops. The change of rulers was not a happy one for the islanders. Their ancient landholding system gradually disappeared as Scots became the largest proprietors, with little interest in their tenants' welfare. By the middle of the seventeenth century agriculture was backward, fishing on a commercial scale unknown and education only for the few, while the ordinary crofter was generally both impoverished and miserable. "Considering the oppression they had had to suffer, and the penalties and humiliation they had endured," *The New Orkney Book* observes, "the wonder is that they had any spirit left in them."[5]

Stromness harbour provides a splendid anchorage for ships and in the eighteenth century captains bound for North America used it to avoid privateers and French cruisers in the English Channel. During the Napoleonic Wars fleets of merchantmen assembled there to be taken in convoy by the Royal Navy, while whalers and sealers on their way to Greenland found it a convenient rendezvous for completing their crews. For the Hudson's Bay ships, the route by Stromness afforded a direct passage to Hudson Strait, allowing their captains more time in port to replenish stores and enjoy themselves, but the advantages of securing servants there probably outweighed all other considerations.

The London Committee wanted sober, industrious, dependable, strong and healthy young men, and the Orkneymen filled the bill. Bred as crofters and fishermen, handy both ashore and at sea, accustomed to cold and hunger, loyal, obedient and hard-working, they became the backbone of the Company's overseas operations, as essential to its prosperity as the French-Canadian voyageurs to the Montreal traders. In turn, they benefited from service with the Company. Small as their wages were, they could spend little money in the wilderness and, being extremely parsimonious, they often accumulated enough in a few years to retire, buy a small croft and settle down, to the envy of their neighbours. At a later date, after the Red River Settlement was founded on the present site of the City of Winnipeg, many of them remained in the country with their Indian wives and children, frequently to enjoy a more prosperous way of life than if they had returned home.

Naturally the Orkneymen were not without defects of character, although these were apparently of little consequence until the Hudson's Bay Company came up against the Canadians in the interior during the second half of the eighteenth century. Those with ability rose to the most important positions in the country as traders and officers but, with some notable exceptions, they were generally less enterprising and aggressive than their Canadian opponents. The common servants, on the other hand,

29

showed less steadiness and reliability and, compared to their French counterparts, were overly cautious, deficient in energy and unwilling to stand
up for themselves or their employers. Often dour and stubborn, they also
lacked the French ability, or desire, to make themselves agreeable to the
Indians. As individuals, they were usually docile but in numbers they were
inclined to combine against authority and their clannish attachment to
one another sometimes made governing them difficult. Despite his recognition of their virtues and their suitability for the country, Samuel Hearne,
the Hudson's Bay officer who explored the Coppermine River, called them
"the slyest set of men under the sun."[6]

The Hudson's Bay Company seems to have recruited Orkneymen as
early as 1708. In January of that year, after consulting their captains, the
governor and committee wrote to a "Mr Grimsay at the Orkneys," instructing him to hire twelve or fourteen servants, lusty young men
between the ages of twenty and thirty of whom two were to be tailors.[7]
Isaac Cowie, a clerk in the Company's service from 1867-74 and himself a
Shetlander, asserts that although the London Committee sent special
agents four years later to engage another forty men, it was not until 1740
that the Hudson's Bay ships regularly called at Stromness.[8] He gives no
authority for his statement, however. Certainly the captains and outgoing
officers, working through local contacts, played an important part in recruitment for many years, until the Company finally employed an agent at
Stromness, paying him a commission on each recruit. The necessity for
doing so was probably the result of the much larger numbers being hired.
The New Orkney Book states that between 1700 and 1800, an average of
seventy were enlisted yearly for a considerable period and that by 1799, of
the Company's 530 men in North America, almost four out of five were
Orkneymen.[9]

A carpenter recruit of 1876, N.M.W.J. McKenzie, who rose to become
general manager of all the Company's eastern districts, has described the
annual arrival of the Hudson's Bay ships as one of the two memorable
events of the year in Stromness, the other being the Lammas market.[10]
During their stay, he relates, the captains and Company officers held high
carnival, with dinner parties on board and ashore and dancing every
night. At least one matrimonial match was made during those halcyon
days in 1848, when the agent's daughter, Anne Rose Clouston, became
engaged to Edward Pelly, a clerk in the service and a cousin of the governor, Sir John Pelly. She followed him to York Factory on Hudson's Bay in
1849, in the care of the new Church of England bishop, who married them
there. Anne Rose may have been the first girl to come from the Old Country to be married at York, for the officers usually married when on leave or
chose their wives in the country. Letitia Hargrave, wife of the chief factor
at York, remarked caustically in a letter to her family in Scotland that the
bride had "brought an immense quantity of finery 5 perfectly new bonnets besides that she wore on board, & scarves, handkerchiefs & shawls as
if she had been going to Calcutta, & napery, blankets & all from her

Father and Mother. They have not much money & I am sure will feel the effects of such disbursement for many a day."[11]

About 1810, when the need for more aggressive servants to oppose the North West Company became imperative, the Hudson's Bay Company engaged young men from other parts of Scotland as well, principally the Highlands, Lewis and Shetland, assembling them at Stromness for embarkation. The ships usually came direct from Gravesend on the Thames and remained for a couple of weeks. When N.M.W.J. McKenzie joined the Company in 1876, the candidates, variously classified as clerks, carpenters, boat builders, blacksmiths, coopers, tinsmiths, sloopers and labourers, had to be between the ages of eighteen and twenty-five and pass a rigid medical examination before being accepted. At other periods, however, and especially during the Napoleonic Wars, when young men were scarce everywhere, the Company could not afford to be so choosy and many were the complaints from the country of the quality of recruits being sent out. As more men became available in Rupert's Land and Canada during the latter half of the nineteenth century, recruitment of Orkneymen diminished but was not finally discontinued until 1891, when the Company's ships ceased to call at Stromness.

Among Orkneymen who rose to prominence in the Hudson's Bay Company prior to its coalition with the North West Company in 1821 were Alexander Kennedy, Joseph Isbister and William Sinclair (the latter said to be descended from the old earls of Orkney). Another Orkneyman, William Tomison, the Company's dominant figure on the Saskatchewan for twenty years, is also remembered for his courage in caring for the Indians during the terrible smallpox epidemic of 1781-2. About 1826 the Company's agent in Orkney was John Rae, father of the famous Arctic explorer, Dr. John Rae, of whom we shall be hearing more later. Edward Clouston, a lawyer, took on the post in 1836, retaining it for almost thirty years. Gentle and kindly, he was affectionately remembered by many of the young men who passed through his hands. His two sons, Robert and James Stewart Clouston, became clerks in the service, Robert rising to the rank of chief trader before his premature death and James to that of chief factor. Both married into the Company's hierarchy. Robert's wife was Jessy Ross, daughter of Chief Factor Donald Ross of Norway House, and James's, Margaret Miles, whose father, Chief Factor Robert Miles, was his chief at Moose Factory. Jessy Clouston died from tuberculosis after a year of marriage and is buried in Playgreen cemetery at Norway House. James's eldest son, Edward Seaborn Clouston, had a distinguished career in Canada. Entering the Bank of Montreal at the age of sixteen, he became successively general manager and vice-president. He was honoured with a baronetcy in 1908.

It was only after 1763 that other Scots, Highlanders in particular, but Lowlanders too, began to play an increasingly influential part in the Canadian fur trade. As in the Orkneys, the principal spur for emigration was poverty. But in the case of the Highlanders, the poverty was not only more immediate and acute but intensified by political and religious persecution and social decay. The erosion of the power of their chieftains and of the old system of land tenure, which culminated in the defeat of the clans at Culloden in 1745, left many young Highlanders with no prospects for the future and still others no choice but exile. North America received the larger share of this emigration. The West Indian islands offered vast sugar plantations and a thriving foreign trade, while in Canada, once the French had withdrawn from the northwest, the most rapidly expanding and profitable field for exploitation was the fur trade.

Beyond all these considerations, however, Scots, generally speaking, seem to have had a natural affinity for the trade. In the first place, partly no doubt as a result of early political and commercial ties with France, as well as a shared dislike (or envy) of the English, they got along well with the French in Canada, without whose help the Canadian trade could never have been revived so soon. It appears moreover that the Highlanders at least (perhaps because of the intricacies of their own Gaelic) possessed an innate linguistic ability, which enabled them to acquire quickly a fluency in French and in the Indian tongues of the districts to which they were posted. Isaac Cowie noticed this facility in 1867, remarking that the newly engaged Highlanders in his group were picking up both languages much more readily than their companions.[12]

Cowie observed, too, that the Highlanders were generally livelier and more active than the others, besides adapting themselves more rapidly to a new and alien environment. Their native climate, which could be harsh at times, probably fitted them better for a country with a decided winter, while their own hills were rugged enough to predispose them to a liking for the Rockies. With lands at home only partly suitable for cultivation and even when arable worked with difficulty, they were more inclined to accept the hardships of the northwest and to be less intimidated by its overpowering physical characteristics than men used to gentler and lusher landscapes.

Aggressive, enterprising, courageous, ambitious, determined and shrewd, the Scottish recruits were finally, because of their common school system, better educated on the whole than their English counterparts of the day. One must not, of course, rate them too highly. Other nationalities share these desirable traits and undoubtedly Scottish clannishness, as we shall see, played a major role in their eventually overwhelming predominance in the Montreal trade. But when every tendency to exaggerate is discounted, a sufficient core of truth remains to sustain our argument that the Scot fitted naturally into the fur trade world.

Like the Orkneymen, needless to say, the Highlanders exhibited the defects of their virtues. If they were lively and quick, their tempers were equally so; with generations of clan wars behind them, they were apt to be quarrelsome, while their daring frequently led them into untenable positions. Excessively proud and often conceited, they were as easily offended and, when their numbers gave them superiority, sometimes hard to handle. At their best, however, they made loyal, capable, brave and intelligent officers and servants.

Some of the Scots who came to Canada at the close of the Seven Years' War to pursue the fur trade were, like Simon McTavish, already engaged in the Albany trade and merely moved north to be closer to the centre of activity. Others, like Richard Dobie and his associate, William Grant of Three Rivers, came directly from the Old Country. They represented all classes and degrees. Dobie, a Lowlander from the neighbourhood of Edinburgh, had a sister married to a poor Gilmerton weaver and presumably came from the same milieu. Grant's father farmed a small Highland holding, Inverlochy, in Strathavon, upper Banffshire, but William's uncles, John and Francis Grant, owned large plantations in Jamaica and John was Chief Justice of the island from 1783-90. When he retired, John bought Kilgraston, a Perthshire estate, to which his brother succeeded in 1793. Other Grants in the fur trade were so numerous and their relationships so confusing that so far no one has been able to sort them out.

The sons of Scots settled in the English colonies before the Revolutionary War, and who later came to Canada as United Empire Loyalists, also figured largely in the Montreal trade. One of them was the famous Nor-'Wester, Simon Fraser, explorer of the tempestuous river which bears his name, who was born in Bennington, New York, in 1776. Still others were the sons and grandsons of men attached to the Highland regiments disbanded after the Seven Years' War and again after the American Revolution, the best known being the 78th, or Fraser Highlanders, who settled about Murray Bay, Quebec, and the Glengarry Highlanders, who made homes for themselves in what is now Glengarry County, Ontario.

From the height of their own royally-chartered and century-old company the Hudson's Bay men referred to the early Canadian traders as "pedlars." Although intended as a term of opprobrium, that, in essence, was what they were – daring, resourceful and adventurous individuals, risking their own or borrowed capital, to say nothing of their lives, in an attempt to make their fortunes. Some of the earliest of them exploited fields relatively close to Montreal, Richard Dobie, for example, turning his attention to Timiskaming in 1764. William Grant of Three Rivers traded at Michilimackinac and in the Illinois country, while the Montreal firms of Todd, McGill & Co. and Forsyth, Richardson & Co. not only had extensive interests southwest of the Great Lakes but also secured a hold on Nipigon. James McGill, Thomas and John Forsyth, and John Richardson were all Scottish-born. Isaac Todd's birthplace is not known and he retired in England, but he was an active member of St. Gabriel's Presbyterian Church in Montreal and presumably also a Scot.

The first trader on the Saskatchewan after 1763 appears to have been a Frenchman previously engaged in that trade, known as "Franceway" (François). He wintered there in 1765 or 1766, probably outfitted by Isaac Todd and James McGill. James Finlay, Sr., a Scot trading on his own account, followed him in 1768. Another Scottish trader, Thomas Corry, spent the winters of 1771-2 and 1772-3 on the Saskatchewan and a measure of the profits to be made in those early days may be judged from the fact that he accumulated sufficient capital in the two seasons to allow him to retire from the trade.[13] But although two Scots were thus apparently the first to follow a Frenchman to the northwest, French, Swiss, English, Irish and American traders were all soon to be found there.

Almost from the beginning, because of the high capital risk and the extended credit necessary for trading over such great distances, individual "pedlars" tended to combine forces. At first these unions were temporary, usually made for one year only and sometimes ending unhappily. Indeed it was hostilities among the various factions, climaxed by a murder in the interior, which led to the formation in 1783 of the first association of traders known as the North West Company. This amalgamation was primarily the work of Simon McTavish who, with the Frobisher brothers, Benjamin and Joseph, held six of the sixteen shares in the concern. The Frobishers were Yorkshiremen, the only two Englishmen among the original partners, while of the remaining seven, McTavish and three others were Scots, with one Irishman, one Frenchman and one American comprising the rest.

The infant North West Company was strongly opposed by another influential Montreal firm, Gregory, McLeod & Co., which had been left out of the new arrangement. One of its founders in 1773 had been James Finlay, Sr., who retired ten years later and was replaced by Normand McLeod, a Detroit trader born in Skye. Young Alexander Mackenzie entered its service about 1779, to be followed by his cousin, Roderick, in 1784. The increasing bitterness between the rivals in the northwest culminated during the winter of 1786-7 with the murder in Athabasca of John Ross, a partner of Gregory, McLeod & Co. Roderick Mackenzie and Simon McTavish's nephew, William McGillivray, brought the news down to the central depot at Grand Portage in the summer of 1787 and their respective principals, fearing that Ross's death would lead to reprisals, immediately decided to unite their interests under the name of the North West Company. Shortly afterwards the newly formed firm of McTavish, Frobisher & Co., whose partners, Simon McTavish and Joseph Frobisher, held the dominant interest in the North West Company, became its Montreal agents.

Meanwhile, in their turn, the English on Hudson's Bay had been pushing inland. Apparently the opposition of French traders in the interior had never been serious enough to force them to alter their original mode of conducting their trade and for some years after 1763 they had continued to maintain large, impressive and well-stocked factories on the seacoast and to wait for the Indians to bring down their furs. But it was not long before it became clear that, with active Canadian traders swarming inland and intercepting their customers, they must try a new approach. Accordingly, in 1774 they built Cumberland House on the Saskatchewan and quickly established other posts in the interior to enable them to meet the Indians on their own lands. It was now that the disadvantages of a long residence on the Bay, as well as the drawbacks of their Orkney servants, became glaringly evident and their situation was even more serious, of course, when the independent Canadian traders combined to form the North West Company.

To begin with, there was the vexing problem of transporting goods and servants inland. On the larger rivers, where boats could be used, the Orkneymen fared well enough, being accustomed to handling them from childhood. Indeed the development of the famed York boat, which was to be the Company's standby in the northwest until modern transportation reached the area, was directly due to Orkney knowledge and skill. Unfortunately, most of the rivers on the Laurentian Shield, which forms a vast collar about the Bay, were not only tortuous, but shallow during most of the summer and broken by falls. On them only canoes would answer.

The English suffered from grave disadvantages even in the matter of obtaining canoes. There was no suitable birch bark within a considerable distance of Hudson's Bay and they had therefore to depend largely on the inland Indians to supply them. But many of these Indians were strongly attached to the Canadian traders, or afraid of offending them, and when it suited their purpose, the Canadians did not scruple to pre-empt canoes which the English had ordered or, if necessary, take them from the Indians by force. Since the Orkney servants were unfamiliar with such unsteady craft, the Hudson's Bay Company had to rely for crews on its homeguard Indians (those about the Bay) and run the risk of having them "enticed" by the Canadians in the interior. Even if a few Orkneymen did become accustomed to handling canoes during the period of their contracts, they often left the country for good at their expiry, to be replaced by inexperienced hands. Moreover, hardy though they were and patient under hardships, the Orkneymen were slow in acquiring wilderness skills, many of them being intimidated by the prospect of living and travelling in the forests of the Shield. Worse still, they were neither as active nor as aggressive in the pursuit of furs as were the Canadian traders and their French and Scottish servants. All these handicaps took years to overcome and even up to the time of the union in 1821, as several Hudson's Bay officers frankly admitted, their own men rarely attained the standard of their opponents.

In these circumstances, the London Committee recommended hiring Canadians, who would not only be useful themselves but serve as examples and teachers for the Orkneymen. The officers in the interior did manage to entice a few from the opposition but this solution (again with some exceptions) proved unsatisfactory. Few Canadians would accept the salaries offered, and those who did frequently turned out to be not only untrustworthy but undisciplined, perhaps the most heinous of sins in a semi-militaristic organization like the Hudson's Bay Company. As N.M.W.J. McKenzie was later to remark of his chief factor at Fort Ellice, Archibald

MacDonald, "you might break all the ten commandments in one clatter, but to break any of the rules and regulations of the service, that was quite another thing."[14] On the whole, it would seem, deserters on both sides generally tended to be misfits or malcontents, unlikely to make good servants for either company.

During these same years changes were also taking place in the Canadian trade, and in the process the French in the country were losing out to the Scots. The partners of the various interested firms were bringing in needy, or deserving, relatives and friends as apprentice clerks and these newcomers were gradually replacing the French masters inland. It was not always, however, a case of nepotism or greed. Often the French servants or clerks, like Panneton, master of Fort Abitibi until 1776, were men of little or no education. Although they had grown up in the country and were at home with the Indians, they were probably not the organized and efficient managers which an increasingly complex and competitive trade was coming to need. Where the French were qualified, they appear to have held their own, but when they retired, as they were more and more often replaced by Scots, the general trend was unmistakable.

Even when there were no relatives or friends to consider, the North West Company apparently favoured Scottish clerks and servants. In October, 1798, McTavish, Frobisher & Co. requested Aneas Cameron of Fort Timiskaming, who was returning to Scotland on leave, to engage "four or five decent young men from the Age of 18 upwards, of good character & Sufficient Education as Apprentices or Clerks to the Concern, for 5. 6. or 7 years" on very favourable terms indeed. The agents also directed Cameron to write to a gentleman in the Orkneys, who was known to them, and to assist him in getting any servants he might be able to hire for them to Greenock. Should the gentleman fail to secure any, the agents added, Cameron himself should search out and engage an equal number of seamen from any other part of Scotland, as well as two or three good ship's carpenters, able to navigate the Company's small vessels on the Great Lakes and willing to double as seamen. To the latter he might offer from £50 to £100 a year, provided they had sufficient education to keep their cargo accounts.[15]

It is surprising to find the Nor'Westers looking to the Orkneys for servants, but we must remember that these were the days of the Napoleonic Wars, when labour was so scarce in Canada and Europe as to be at times virtually unobtainable. Whether they ever tried again is not disclosed, but certainly the practice of hiring Highlanders continued until eventually, in Dr. Wallace's words, their predominance in the Canadian trade made "the names of the North West Company partners sound like a roll-call of the clans at Culloden."[16] It also presumably helped to account for the "much-changed" Montreal, which the retired Alexander Henry the Elder, one of the early "pedlars" and himself of English descent, found so incongenial. "The country is over run with Scotchmen," he wrote disparagingly.[17]

Despite the distressing effects of the war in Europe, which rapidly inflated the cost of goods and salaries and at first depressed the price of furs, the years from 1787 to 1798 were probably the most prosperous and peaceful for the Nor'Westers. Fur prices gradually recovered and the Hudson's Bay Company, though a palpable threat, was not yet affecting their profits. Besides, any progress the English achieved in the interior was counterbalanced by their own expansion in Athabasca and by Alexander Mackenzie's journeys to the Arctic and Pacific Oceans, which opened up vast new possibilities for trade. Although the opposition of independent Montreal traders still troubled them, like the partnership of David and Peter Grant from 1793-5, it was short-lived. By 1795, when the Nor-'Westers signed a new agreement to come into force in 1799, Simon McTavish's ambition to unite all the Canadian trade under the aegis of his own firm seemed close to becoming a reality.

But it was not to be. The subsequent defection from the agreement of the two influential firms of Todd, McGill & Co., and Forsyth, Richardson & Co., opposition to the agents both within and outside the North West Company, and the jealous enmity towards McTavish of men like Daniel Sutherland and Angus Shaw, was to shatter the dream. At Grand Portage in the summer of 1799 Alexander Mackenzie, who had been a partner of McTavish, Frobisher & Co. since 1795, announced his intention of withdrawing from that concern at the same time that Forsyth, Richardson & Co. and several other interests were launching an opposition in force against the North West Company. The new association was known as the XY Company from the markings on its bales (the letters X and Y following W in the alphabet) and after 1800, when Mackenzie joined its ranks, as the New North West Company.

Some have ascribed the disastrous rivalry which followed to the uncompromising individualism and divisiveness of the Scots on both sides and there is reason in their arguments. The obdurate Highland pride of the principals, McTavish and Mackenzie, was intensified by the personal rift which had opened between them. The latest evidence indicates that Mackenzie, the younger and apparently the more intransigeant, his influence in the Company bolstered by his feats of exploration, may have been more to blame for the quarrel.[18] On the other hand, it is clear that he considered himself greatly injured by McTavish and his nephews, William and Duncan McGillivray, so much so, he wrote to Aneas Cameron in the spring of 1800, that he might for a time forget his former fur trade friends "& even forget that which we seldom Lose Sight of, my Interests."[19] Pride can go no further.

Only the currently high prices for furs, as Richard Dobie pointed out in a letter to Cameron, allowed the two factions to indulge in such foolishness. Dobie had heard that McTavish and the McGillivrays had sworn to sacrifice £200,000 to be revenged of all opposition, and his grandson-in-law, James Finlay, Jr., a North West wintering partner, had told him that although the Nor'Westers did not expect to get a sixpence of profit during the seven years of the new agreement, still they reconciled themselves "with totally Ruin to Opposers." "Mutuality woud anser better," Dobie concluded drily. But the Scots, after all, are not the only uncompromising controversialists and, given human nature in general and the lure of high profits, perhaps the battle between the Canadian fur interests for what they considered a fair share in the riches of the northwest would have been inevitable, whatever the racial derivation of the protagonists.

The opposition between the two Canadian companies continued until 1804, when McTavish's death cleared the way for a union between them. By then it must have been apparent to all that to continue as they were doing would mean ultimate ruin for both parties, and indeed it now seems likely that the financial losses which the Canadians suffered during these bitter years were a significant factor in their eventual defeat at the hands of the Hudson's Bay Company.[20] For the time being, however, with the reunited Montreal interests free to devote all their energies to overcoming their remaining rival, the situation of the English company was to become so critical that again, as a century before, years were to pass without any dividends being paid to its shareholders.

Nevertheless the Hudson's Bay Company, with its advantages of a shorter and cheaper supply route through Hudson's Bay and its capital reserve fund, survived the crisis by instituting a rigid system of retrenchment, by adopting some of the better features of the North West Company's organization, and by renewing its pressure against the Canadians in the interior. After 1813, moreover, as its fortunes began to improve, those of the Canadians took a downward turn with the twin misfortunes of war with the United States and the intrusion into the northwest of Lord Selkirk's Red River Settlement. The war seriously interfered with the Nor-'Westers' main transport route by way of the Great Lakes and hampered the trade in other ways, while the clash between the colony and the North West Company was in the end to ruin the Montreal trade.

It is in the tradition of tragic irony that the final defeat of the North West Company should have been precipitated by another Scot, Thomas Douglas, Earl of Selkirk. In 1812, with the support of the Hudson's Bay Committee, he founded a colony at the forks of the Red and Assiniboine Rivers for poor Scottish crofters displaced by the Highland clearances. It was in the heart of the Nor'Westers' pemmican country; this easily portable and highly nutritious food, compounded of dried and pounded buffalo meat mixed with grease and berries, was the mainstay of diet for all their brigades in the interior. When Selkirk's governor, Miles Macdonell, forbade the export of pemmican from the settlement, his action confirmed the Canadians' belief that the colony was part of a new and dangerous threat to their trade and they recklessly embarked on a course of intimidation which ended in 1816 in the notorious massacre of Seven Oaks.[21]

These years witnessed the crumbling of the North West Company under extreme pressure, its assets rapidly dwindling, a number of its wintering partners at odds with the Montreal agents and its trade in the northwest dislocated. Hoping to conclude a working arrangement with the
Hudson's Bay Committee, William and Simon McGillivray were in London in 1820, when two of the dissident wintering partners, John
McLoughlin and Angus Bethune, arrived to negotiate a settlement on
behalf of themselves and their supporters. The British government was
drawn into the affair because of the virtual state of war in the northwest,
and the result of the negotiations was a coalition of the two opposing fur
trade interests which was, in fact, a defeat for the North West Company.

Critics of the Nor'Westers have frequently imputed to the overweening
pride and arrogance of its Highlanders, and the excesses to which they led,
a large share in the retribution which overtook them. Washington Irving,
with his partiality for Astor and the Americans, condemned "the swelling
and braggart style" of these "Hyperborean Nabobs"[22] and could charge
with considerable truth that the wintering partners, many of them of good
Scotish families, with a score of retainers at their bidding, fancied themselves in the role of Highland chieftains. He equally decried the convivial
fraternity of the Beaver Club in Montreal, and the extravagant frolic and
feasting of the summer gatherings at Fort William which, he claimed,
communicated even to the lowliest of employees a dangerous sense of
solidarity and superiority.

Their most partisan admirers do not deny these Highlanders' faults but
the spell of their tremendous achievements remains undimmed, and even
Irving could not resist it. The very phrase he coined to describe them, "the
lords of the lakes and the forests," is likely to outlast the memory of their
failings. The Hudson's Bay Company's victory over the Nor'Westers was
the classic one of the tortoise over the hare, of the sober and canny over the
gambler and adventurer, of the staid and durable chartered company over
the loose partnership of individualists, with its inherent tendency towards
disruption. Nevertheless the day would come when the English company,
in its turn, would have to give way to pressures set in train by these same
Nor'Westers who, in building Canada's first great industry based on the
exploits of the French before them, laid secure foundations for the modern
Canadian nation.[23] In that sense, at least, although it would probably have
been cold comfort at the time, their defeat was not as final as it appeared to
be in 1821.

The union of the two companies changed many things in the northwest,
but the predominance of Scots in the fur trade was not one of them.
George (later Sir George) Simpson, the Hudson's Bay chief in Athabasca
during 1820-1, soon rose to be overseas governor of all the Company's
territories, and his rule spanned the years of its greatest power and prosperity, lasting until his death in 1860. Although more gifted than most,
Simpson was typical of those energetic, shrewd and ambitious Scots with a
genius for organization, economy and hard work, who have built empires

and made names and fortunes for themselves all over the world. In contrast, his closest friend in the country, John George McTavish, a former Nor'Wester, whose advice helped him to salvage the best features of the Canadian company for the united concern, represented the high-spirited and intelligent but easy-going and extravagant Highlander, whose day in the northwest was almost over. For in the Rupert's Land of Simpson's day, men of his own type were increasingly to prevail, if only because his decisive and far-reaching control of affairs left little room for individualists.

In the early years of his governorship, Simpson was concerned with the problem of redundant servants left over from the years of competition. Dissatisfied with many of the Canadian halfbreeds, both former Nor-'Westers and those who had been recruited in Montreal for the Hudson's Bay Company, he favoured Orkney servants and "European" clerks, particularly for those districts bordering on the settled areas of Canada. The Canadians in the service, he argued, prided themselves on their knowledge of the country and their friendship with the Indians and were fully aware of their value to any opposition. This situation tended to make difficulties for the Company, not only in terms of employment and wages but also in the very real danger that they might leave the service and set up in the trade on their own or with others. If they were moved inland, or to the Bayside districts, and were replaced with "Europeans," all these drawbacks could be overcome. But Simpson had in fact an even more compelling reason for preferring "European" servants and clerks. The fewer the Canadians in the service, he was convinced, the less other Canadians would know about the Company's business.

Most of his officers on the frontier (largely former Nor'Westers) disagreed with him, objecting that Orkneymen were fit neither for voyaging nor for going after Indians, but Simpson was not to be deterred. Although conceding that they were seldom of much use during their first season, he continued to advocate them on the ground that they were steady and well-conducted. His preference for Orkneymen, however, did not preclude Highlanders and here he and his officers, many of them Highlanders themselves, found common ground. "Do not lose sight of our Sturdy Glenlivat men," he adjured Chief Factor Angus Cameron of Timiskaming in November, 1839, when that gentleman was home on leave, "and let three or Four of them be such as may look forward to the rank of Postmasters in due time. Stout strong active intelligent men who will not be above putting their hands to anything." Yet a decade later, outraged by the behaviour of two highly recommended men, Simpson had harsh words even for Highlanders. As a class, he declared indignantly, they had become "so uppish, self-sufficient, & selfish that I must say my countrymen do not now stand quite so high in my estimation as formerly."

For apprentice clerks, Simpson preferred young Scots with a reasonable degree of education, a view obviously shared by Chief Factor Alexander Christie, a Scot who had joined the Hudson's Bay Company in 1809.

"Without any partiality to my Countrymen," Christie wrote to Cameron in 1826, "really in my humble opinion they will ever be found the most proper persons for this Country. I mean respectable Farmers sons who have received a plain education, and who's morals have not been neglected, having no prospects but what may be derived from perseverance and industry, – give me such for Indian traders in preference to any Dandy from behind a counter, or from the desk of a Counting house."

Following the earlier custom of both companies, Simpson and the London Committee were always ready to engage the sons of officers and servants in good standing, either active or retired, and as the quality of Orkneymen willing to emigrate fell off during the nineteenth century, they came to depend more and more on this pool of labour. The original Orkneymen had intermarried with the Crees, particularly the Swampies who lived about the Bay, a steady, reliable people of considerable character. The Orkney strain blended well with the Cree and the daughters of the first marriages, in turn, became wives of the newcomers to the country.[24] After the Red River Settlement was founded, many of these men chose to retire there with their families. In some instances, the succession in the service went from father, to son, to grandson, a circumstance which further strengthened the *esprit de corps* of a company remarkable for that quality. Alexander Christie, twice Governor of Assiniboia, who eventually took his "country" wife to settle in Edinburgh, was one of those whose sons and grandsons followed him into the service and achieved distinction there.

Another kind of Scottish succession was exemplified in the rich Timiskaming district where "a dynasty of Camerons"[25] followed one another over a period of almost a hundred years. The Camerons came from upper Banffshire (Strathavon and Glenlivet), and the first of them, Aeneas Cameron (a cousin of William Grant of Three Rivers and like him a nephew of Chief Justice John Grant of Jamaica), went to Fort Abitibi in 1788 as a clerk for Dobie & Grant, the Montreal firm which then owned the Timiskaming posts. After some years there and at Grand Lac he assumed command of Fort Timiskaming in 1793, two years before the North West Company bought the posts. He became a partner in the North West Company in 1798 and remained at Fort Timiskaming until 1804. By that time his nephew, Angus Cameron, was serving at Matawagamingue, one of Fort Timiskaming's subsidiary posts, having come out to Canada in the spring of 1801. On his uncle's retirement Angus became master of Matawagamingue (Mattagarni) and in 1816 a partner in the North West Company and head of the Timiskaming district. With the exception of seven years from 1827-34, which he spent at Lake of Two Mountains, Angus Cameron remained in charge of the Timiskaming district until he retired in 1843, having become a chief factor in 1837. He brought out two others of his family who eventually succeeded to the command of the district, his nephew James Cameron, who began his career in Timiskaming in 1836 and was in charge of the fort from 1847 until his untimely death in 1851, and a cousin, Charles Stuart, who served in the district from 1840-72, during the last four years of which he, too, commanded Fort Timiskaming. It is indeed a remarkable record.

George Bryce, an early historian of the Hudson's Bay Company, asserts that from 1821 to 1870, the year in which the Company's territories became part of the new Dominion of Canada, 171 out of a total of 263 commissioned officers, or 63%, were Scottish in origin, a situation which he credited entirely to Simpson's recruitment policy. Whether his figures are reliable or not, it seems safe to say that the Company's personnel during most of the nineteenth century were predominantly of Scottish blood and that even in the twentieth Scottish candidates enjoyed a preference. A case in point is that of Mr. Robert Laurence of Sault Ste. Marie, Ontario. Born in Lerwick, Shetland, he applied from Chicago in 1906 in his early teens for a clerkship in the fur trade and was taken on immediately, sight unseen, subsequently serving for several years at the post of Matawagamingue in northern Ontario, before leaving the service to pursue a different career.[26]

Selecting the names of a few representative Scots from among all those who contributed so much to the fur trade is a truly bewildering task. We can do little more here than to mention some of the most outstanding, adding the caution that these men built on the achievements of lesser men, both their own countrymen and others, most of whom never rose to positions of importance in the country and are now largely forgotten.

The explorers necessarily come first, for without them there would have been no transcontinental trade. The earliest of course were French, although the Hudson's Bay Company also sent emissaries inland at an early date – Henry Kelsey in 1690, Anthony Henday in 1754-5 and Samuel Hearne in 1771-2. But the exploration "explosion" only really began after 1763, with the aggressive Montreal traders pushing into the northwest, and the predominantly Scottish character of the later North West Company insured Scots an important role in opening up the country. We should always remember, however, that without the friendship of the Indians the whole process of exploring the continent would have been much more arduous and dangerous than it actually was.

The man who made the most powerful impact on his contemporaries and more than any other, perhaps, has stirred the imagination of later generations of Canadians was the Nor'Wester Alexander Mackenzie, born near Stornoway on the Island of Lewis. In 1789 he reached the Arctic Ocean by the river named after him and four years later was the first white man to cross overland to the Pacific in the northern part of the continent. But the fact that he published his famous *Voyages* in London in 1801, and a year later received a knighthood, doubtless contributed much to his reputation in his own day. His book has reappeared in numerous editions since then, one of the most recent being Dr. Kaye Lamb's definitive volume of his journals and letters for the Hakluyt Society, published in 1970. In contrast, Simon Fraser, the Nor'Wester who in 1808 conquered the turbulent Fraser River by incredible feats of daring and endurance, was largely neglected in his lifetime and had to wait for general recognition until 1960, when Dr. Lamb edited his letters and journals.[27] The name of Fraser's redoubtable companion, John Stuart (born in Strathspey), is commemorated in Stuart Lake, northern British Columbia, but he seems more often to be remembered, even by historians, as the uncle of Lord Strathcona.

At the time of the union of 1821 British exploration was principally concerned with the renewed search for a northwest passage. The Hudson's Bay Company, besides assisting the official expeditions at considerable cost to itself, undertook to complete the survey of the Arctic coastline. To this project two Scottish officers made the most significant contributions, Thomas Simpson, Master of Arts of King's College, Aberdeen, and a first cousin of Governor Simpson, and Dr. John Rae, an Orkney surgeon with an Edinburgh degree.

Simpson shared the command of the 1837-40 expeditions with an older officer, Peter Warren Dease, who seems to have been content to let him take the lead, a role for which he was eminently suited. By the time of his tragic death in 1840 most of the unknown portion of the coastline had been surveyed and the governor assigned the task of finishing it to Rae, who was already famous in the service as a marksman and for his feats of endurance in travelling about the country.

Rae's explorations covered the years 1846-53, during which he not only completed the survey of the coast but also discovered the first clues to the fate of Sir John Franklin and his men. His methods of travel anticipated the modern age of Arctic exploration in adopting the clothing and living habits of the Indians and Esquimaux but, in reality, he was only exploiting to the full practices which, in modified form, had long been in use in the fur trade. He was the first since Hearne, however, to depend on the food the land provided. The ten men he chose to accompany him on his first expedition represented a cross-section of the Company's personnel – four Orkneymen, one Shetlander, one Hebridean, two French Canadians, a boy from York Factory and an Indian deer hunter. Like Mackenzie, Rae was knighted for his services to exploration and his memorial in Stromness Cathedral is a particularly moving and appropriate one, the life-sized figure of a man asleep in a buffalo sleeping bag, with his moccasins on, and a gun and open book at his side.

During these years there were still vast unexplored areas of what is now Canada, especially in modern Yukon Territory and the northern parts of Labrador and Quebec. Four Scottish officers shared largely in opening up the Yukon. In 1834 John McLeod penetrated to the headwaters of the Stikine River by the hazardous Liard River route. John Bell established Fort McPherson on the Peel River and explored the Porcupine to its confluence with the Yukon. Alexander Hunter Murray built Fort Yukon there in 1847, the Company's most remote post and actually in Russian territory. Finally, Robert Campbell explored most of the Liard country between 1838 and 1852 and discovered the Pelly River (the upper portion of the Yukon), which the Company would have named for him, had he not modestly refused the honour.

The exploration of much of northern Labrador was the work of two other Scottish officers, Nicol Finlayson, brother of Duncan Finlayson, Sir George Simpson's brother-in-law, and John McLean. In 1831, from Moose Factory, Finlayson established Fort Chimo on Ungava Bay, travelling partly by way of the seacoast and partly overland. Six years later the governor assigned the Fort Chimo post to McLean, instructing him to open up communications with Esquimaux Bay (now Hamilton Inlet) on the Atlantic coast. McLean made a spectacular journey there and back in 1838 and the following year again travelled inland, being the first white man to see the Grand Falls of Labrador (later Hamilton and now Church-ill Falls), half as high again as Niagara. At odds with the governor, McLean left the Company in 1845 after twenty-five years in the service, and the book he wrote about his experiences is still a fascinating account, if somewhat marred by his bitterness against his former employers.[28]

After the explorers came the administrators, whose genius transformed the fur trade into Canada's first transcontinental industry. We have already assessed the contributions of two outstanding Scots to fur trade affairs during the eighteenth and nineteenth centuries. Indeed the names of Simon McTavish and Sir George Simpson are virtually synonymous today in the popular mind with their respective companies. In vision and enterprise they were very much alike, but while one of Simpson's greatest assets was his ability to get along with all sorts of men, McTavish's basically understanding and generous nature was embittered by the quarrel with Mackenzie and his supporters, which darkened the last years of his life and earned him the reputation of the haughty "Marquis" of the Montreal trade. Simpson's nickname, "the little Emperor," on the other hand, fitted him perfectly and although he was not, perhaps, as sympathetic a character as McTavish, he probably excelled him in optimism and energy, and in the close attention to detail which turned the disaster of the pre-union period into the triumph of the united company.

When Simon McTavish died in 1804, his nephew, William McGilli-vray, succeeded him as head of the North West Company. McGillivray appears to have inherited both his uncle's attractive personal traits and his business ability but, faced with the effects of the disastrous years of conflict, 1799-1804, and the difficulties raised by the Red River Settlement, it is unlikely that even a much greater man could have forestalled the eventual absorption of the Canadian concern or the failure of the former North West Company agents in 1825.

Two other administrators of Scottish ancestry, Dr. John McLoughlin (born in Riviere-du-Loup and part Irish) and James Douglas (born in Demarara, British Guiana), made their names on the west coast. McLoughlin, as we have seen, was one of the spokesmen for the rebellious North West wintering partners in 1820, and after the union he was sent to the Columbia district. A very able, if passionate and arrogant man, he built an empire which extended as far north as Russian Alaska but which dissolved rapidly after 1840 with the advance of American settlement into Oregon. In the end he left the service and became an American citizen, revered by the settlers as "the Father of Oregon" or "The White-Headed Eagle."

Douglas replaced McLoughlin as the Company's chief on the west coast, his headquarters being Fort Victoria, which he himself had established in 1842 on Vancouver Island. The British government appointed him Governor of the colony of Vancouver Island in 1851 and he held this office in conjunction with his chief factorship in the Hudson's Bay Company but when, seven years later, he became the first Governor of the new colony of British Columbia, he left the service. He was knighted in 1863. Alexander Grant Dallas, another Scot, formerly of Jardine, Matheson & Co. and a newcomer to the Hudson's Bay Company, succeeded him at Fort Victoria. Dallas married Douglas's youngest daughter, Amelia, and followed Sir George Simpson as overseas governor from 1862-4. His successor in that office was Chief Factor William MacTavish, nephew of Simpson's old friend, John George McTavish, who had spent his life in the country and was to be the Company's last overseas governor. The difference in spelling of the surnames is because John George, second son of the then MacTavish chieftain, had changed his to accord with that of his patron, Simon McTavish.

Far and away the most successful of them all in terms of monetary reward and public acclaim was Donald Smith (born in Forres, Morayshire), who spent most of his fur trade years at the remote North West River post in Labrador. He was a canny investor and many of his fellow officers entrusted their funds to him. In 1869 he was appointed head of the Company's Montreal office and a few months later chief commissioner to deal with the rebellion at Red River. His real career, begun in his fifties, was remarkable. Member of Parliament, first in Manitoba and then at Ottawa, he also made a fortune in railways, later playing a prominent part in the financing of the Canadian Pacific and becoming in turn Governor of the Hudson's Bay Company in London, President of the Bank of Montreal and Canadian High Commissioner in England. In 1897, after having received several previous honours, he was raised to the peerage as Baron Strathcona and Mount Royal. His benefactions, both in Canada and Britain, were legion.

The fur trade also boasted a good many writers within its ranks, a number of them Scots. Fascinating journals of travel and exploration are preserved in the Hudson's Bay Archives and the Hudson's Bay Record Society has already published several, Rae's among them. Other fur trade letters and diaries have appeared in various forms, while still other authors have used their experiences either as a basis for reminiscence, like

Isaac Cowie and N.M.W.J. McKenzie, or for fiction, like Robert M. Ballantyne. A nephew of Sir Walter Scott's publisher and a clerk in the Company's service from 1841-7, Ballantyne was a prolific writer and his books of adventure are still popular with boys. The first of them, *Hudson's Bay: or Every-Day Life in the Wilds of North America*, published in 1848, is an account of his years in the country. Such was the romantic attraction of his stories that Cowie warned all boys against reading them, declaring that they had lured him, to his regret, into the service. Let them instead, he advised, "mark and digest" its realities as revealed by McLean.[29]

Alexander Ross, who settled in Red River in 1825, was probably the first of the fur trade historians. A clerk in Astor's Pacific Fur Company, he had taken part in the founding of Astoria, subsequently joining the Nor-'Westers, and his three books, *Adventures of the First Settlers on the Oregon or Columbia* (1849), *The Fur-Hunters of the Far West* (2 vols., 1855) and *The Red River Settlement* (1856) are still read by those interested in the subjects, the last two having been reprinted in the 1950s.[30] Another Red River historian was Joseph James Hargrave, son of Chief Factor James Hargrave and Letitia MacTavish, born at York Factory, educated at St. Andrew's and Edinburgh universities and secretary to his uncle, Governor William MacTavish. His book, *Red River*, was published in 1871. Alexander Hunter Murray contributed notes and drawings on the Loucheux Indians to Sir John Richardson's *Arctic Searching Expedition*,[31] while his own *Journal of the Yukon, 1847-8*, edited by L.J. Burpee, was published by the Canadian Archives in 1910. Chief Trader Bernard Ross wrote articles on natural history and gathered specimens for the Smithsonian Institution, while Chief Factor Roderick Macfarlane's *Notes on Mammals collected and observed in the Northern Mackenzie River district* form a valuable section of Charles Mair's *Through the Mackenzie Basin*.[32]

Reminiscences or diaries, written by Scots employed in the Hudson's Bay Company's service, continue to come out and to attract enthusiastic readers. J.W. Anderson's delightful *Fur Trader's Story* (1961)[33] deals mostly with the country around James Bay. *Behind the Palisades* (1963)[34] is the autobiography of George Simpson McTavish, great-grandson of Sir George's illegitimate daughter, Maria, who married Donald McTavish. *In Rupert's Land* (1970)[35] contains the memoirs of Walter Traill, whose mother was Catherine Parr Traill and his father a member of a well-known Orkney family, one of whose ancestors Scott immortalized as Magnus Troil in *The Pirate*. In *Campbell of the Yukon* (1970)[36] Clifford Wilson, a former editor of *The Beaver*, has brought together the reminiscences and other records of the valiant and persevering Robert Campbell, discoverer of the Pelly River.

Many of the fur traders' descendants have long privately cherished their ties with the trade but their interest in it, like that of other Canadians, has immeasurably increased in the last fifty years, during which the achievements of the North West and Hudson's Bay Companies have at last been accorded their rightful place in our early history. Now the rebuilding of some of the most famous posts, among them Grand Portage (in upper Michigan), Lower Fort Garry and Fort Edmonton, as well as the current reconstruction of Fort William, is not only helping to bring the fur trade to life for all Canadians but must surely arouse in those of Scottish origin an even greater pride in the part played by their forbearers, or fellow countrymen, in the development of our nation.

NOTES

Although this study is based primarily on secondary sources and on private papers in her possession, the author is much indebted to the Governor and Committee of the Hudson's Bay Company for permission to use their Archives over a period of years, during which, among other benefits, she came to appreciate the vital role played by Scots in the success of the Hudson's Bay Company.

1. Harold A. Innis, *The Fur Trade in Canada* (Toronto: University of Toronto Press, 1962), pp. 10-14.
2. E.E. Rich, *The History of the Hudson's Bay Company* (The Hudson's Bay Record Society, 1958-9), I, pp. 497-9.
3. W.A. Kenyon and J.R. Turnbull, *The Battle for James Bay* (Toronto: Macmillan, 1971), p. 111.
4. See Chapter I.
5. John Shearer, W. Groundwater, J.D. Mackay, *The New Orkney Book* (London: Thomas Nelson & Sons, 1966), pp. 15, 23. This collection of essays on Orkney and original poems updates *The Orkney Book*, published in Edinburgh in 1909, and prepared for use in the schools of Orkney by a group of young Orcadians resident in Edinburgh. *The Orkney Book* has long been out of print and the present volume was written in the hope that new readers would find pleasure in the story of Orkney.
6. Rich, II, pp. 128, 157, 168-9.
7. Rich, I, p. 499.
8. Isaac Cowie, *The Company of Adventurers* (Toronto: William Briggs, 1913), p. 62.
9. *The New Orkney Book*, p. 64.
10. N.M.W.J. McKenzie, *The Men of the Hudson's Bay Company, 1670 A.D. - 1920 A.D.* (Fort William, Ontario: Times-Journal Presses, 1921), pp. 7ff.
11. *The Letters of Letitia Hargrave*, Margaret Arnett MacLeod, ed. (Toronto: The Champlain Society, 1947), p. 247.
12. Cowie, p. 123.

13. *Documents Relating to the North West Company*, W. Stewart Wallace, ed. (Toronto: The Champlain Society, 1934), pp. 3, 434.
14. McKenzie, p. 40.
15. Private papers in the possession of the author.
16. Wallace, p. 35.
17. Alexander Henry, *Travels and Adventures in Canada and the Indian Territories Between the Years 1760 and 1776*, James Bain, ed., Introduction to the new edition by L.G. Thomas (Edmonton: M.G. Hurtig, 1969), p. xii.
18. E.A. Mitchell, "New Evidence on the Mackenzie-McTavish Break," *Canadian Historical Review*, XLI, 1, pp. 41-7.
19. Letter in possession of the author, printed in *The Journals and Letters of Sir Alexander Mackenzie*, W. Kaye Lamb, ed. (Cambridge: The Hakluyt Society, 1970), p. 499.
20. R. A. Pendergast, *The Economic Organization of the Montreal-Based Fur Traders*, Paper presented at the Second North American Fur Trade Conference, October, 1970.
21. Rich, II, pp. 317ff.
22. Washington Irving, *Astoria* (London: Richard Bentley, 1836), I, p. 17; III, p. 227.
23. Innis, p. 262.
24. See W.J. Healy, *Women of Red River* (Winnipeg: The Women's Canadian Club, Peguis Publishers, 1923), Centennial Edition, June, 1967, and Sylvia Van Kirk, "Women and the Fur Trade," *The Beaver*, (Winter, 1972), pp. 4-21.
25. W. Stewart Wallace, *The Pedlars from Quebec* (Toronto: Ryerson, 1954), p. 83.
26. We may add that Scots did not confine themselves to the Canadian fur trade but figured prominently in that of the United States as well, in the early St. Louis trade, in Astor's Pacific Fur Company, in the American Fur Company and among the ranks of the free traders.
27. *Simon Fraser, Letters and Journals 1806-1808*, W. Kaye Lamb, ed. (Toronto: Macmillan, 1960).
28. *John McLean's Notes of a Twenty-Five Years' Service in the Hudson's Bay Territory*, W. Stewart Wallace, ed. (Toronto: The Champlain Society, 1932).
29. Cowie, *op. cit.*, p. 473.
30. *The Fur Hunters of the Far West,* K. Spaulding, ed. (Norman: University of Oklahoma Press, 1956); *The Red River Settlement* (Minneapolis: Ross & Haines, Inc., 1957).
31. London: Longman, Brown, Green and Longmans, 1851, 2 vols.
32. Toronto: Briggs, 1908.
33. Toronto: Ryerson.
34. Published privately by his wife's sister, Evelyn Gurd.
35. Mae Atwood, ed., (Toronto: McClelland & Stewart).
36. Toronto: Macmillan.

FOUR

Patterns of Settlement
in the East

K. J. Duncan

Until early in the nineteenth century, Britain and the other European powers, in accordance with prevailing mercantilist theory, discouraged emigration on the grounds that it weakened the nation both militarily and economically through loss of manpower at home, and offered no compensating advantages abroad. Colonies, it was believed, should be exploited for the benefit of the mother country and their populations kept as small as possible consistent with that end. Nevertheless, it is evident that people did emigrate from Britain to Europe and the North American colonies in rather substantial numbers before the Seven Years' War.[1] A few might have ended up in Newfoundland or in the environs of Halifax and some Scots even found their way as settlers to the French colonies, but overwhelmingly they went to the older British colonies on the mainland, particularly the Carolinas.

In 1763, by the Treaty of Paris which ended the Seven Years' War, France surrendered to Britain substantially all of her Canadian territories. And in that same year, the first sizable grants of land of which there is record were made to soldiers of disbanded Scottish regiments who had fought in North America. Thus began a history of over two hundred years of Scottish settlement in Canada.[2] There were, during the period, several patterns of settlement: military settlement of disbanded regiments from the various wars, proprietary settlement of groups and individuals organized and often financed by people with charitable or profit motives or both, and free settlement by groups or individuals either on tracts held by various land companies or on property somehow acquired in the open market.[3] Military settlement and proprietary settlement always took immigrants directly to the land, but much of the free settlement was preceded by a period in which the immigrant acquired either the skills or money or both to achieve his goal. In the most general terms military and proprietary settlement can be thought of as underwriting, where necessary, a period of apprenticeship in frontier farming, which free settlers were obliged in some way to manage themselves.

49

Despite sometimes generous aid and encouragement, some proprietary settlements failed. It is not surprising then that free settlers who went directly to wild lands paid a high cost in suffering and privation and that while many ultimately triumphed, many failed and left. Even those who brought or earned funds to buy made farms often had lean years until they had adapted fully to local agricultural conditions.

Whatever the particular type of settlement, there were problems common to all which form a uniting thread. Among them were ignorance of agricultural techniques appropriate to the location, lack of skill in the essential techniques of axemanship and land clearance, the overwhelming presence of the bush and the sense of helplessness and isolation it fostered, poor communications with towns and a general lack of public services of any kind. In addition, there were problems peculiar to each type of settlement which will be touched upon below.

The various types of settlement did not follow each other in strict chronological sequence; rather they overlapped, particularly in the early part of the period, and there were points in time when two or three were in existence at once, sometimes in the same general area, sometimes in locations separated by hundreds or even thousands of miles.[4] However, the block settlement of disbanded regiments ended with the post-revolutionary period, and with the increased flow of immigration during the rest of the century, the other types of settlement were ultimately of far greater importance. As the nineteenth century wore on, proprietary settlement became less important as people became aware of the impossibility of building landed estates on the British pattern in the face of available cheap land and a chronic shortage of labour in frontier conditions.[5] In the end, land company settlement, small groups and individual settlement, which were frequently not all that different in their essentials, became the dominant patterns.

This chapter will examine the main types of settlement in which Scots played their parts and discuss the problems they faced and the adjustments they made to them.

THE MILITARY SETTLEMENTS

If wars solve old problems, they inevitably produce new ones. The end of the Seven Years' War presented several problems to the British government and the measures it took to solve them had profound and permanent effects in the New World. Among them three stood out: how to re-establish the large numbers of disbanded troops with the minimum disruption of civil society; how to occupy the newly conquered French territories at a minimum cost; and finally, how to increase garrison strength in North America as unobtrusively as possible given the political and economic discontent already evident in the English-speaking colonies to the south.

To all of these problems the establishment of settlements of disbanded soldiers in the newly won territories seemed the ideal solution.

The Highland regiments raised for service in the Seven Years' War presented the British government with the problem of what to do with discharged troops in aggravated form. The collapse of the clan system, which had been under way since the turn of the eighteenth century, had been accelerated by the defeat of some of the clans at Culloden in 1746.

The chief no longer found advantage in a large number of retainers who were costly to keep and whose presence no longer guaranteed military might. The old days of raiding were past and the Highlands, with Europe let in upon them, were no longer a world unto themselves. The response of many chiefs was to force out the hereditary tacksmen who held land in return for marching with their armed tenants, and either to lease their holdings to the highest bidder or to deal directly with the tenants themselves. The new lessees, to recover their costs, usually forced out the tenantry in order to graze the more profitable cattle. Thus there was widespread dispossession of both tacksmen and tenants which undoubtedly applied heavy pressure to emigrate.[6]

After 1760, the introduction of sheep herding accelerated the Highland clearances and produced a very complex pattern of population movements. Some areas rapidly lost population, others continued to grow. There was large scale movement to the western coasts where the thriving kelp industry offered employment. In short, the Highlands underwent rapid and profound social and economic change in the eighteenth century.[7]

It appears evident that the British government was reluctant to turn large numbers of disbanded soldiers, with doubtful prospects of successful re-establishment, back into this rapidly changing society and, at the same time, was anxious to reward faithful service. In an era when land represented wealth and security as nothing else could, free land in North America seemed the ideal solution.

The settlement of disbanded regiments in the New World was also attractive on other grounds. Established in the new territories, they would be self-supporting colonies of people with proven loyalty and the military skill necessary to deal with possible French-Canadian insurrection, or, settled in the older colonies, they would be available for service if the discontent already evident there should issue in open rebellion. Altogether, the settlement of disbanded veterans of the Seven Years' War in the New World appeared to be the solution to a whole complex of problems, both at home and in America. Small wonder Britain abandoned, in this instance, her fixed opposition to emigration.

As remarked earlier, the first settlement of Scottish immigrants in any part of what is now Canada was of disbanded soldiers. The Fraser Highlanders and the Black Watch had been raised in the Highlands and both had fought with distinction in North America in the Seven Years' War. At the war's end, men from these regiments settled in Quebec and

Nova Scotia with the largest concentrations at Murray Bay and Mount Murray. Captain John Nairne received three thousand acres and Lieutenant Malcolm Fraser received two thousand acres from General James Murray in the year 1762 in accordance with government regulations, while the non-commissioned officers and men who accompanied them each received two hundred and fifty acres respectively.[8]

Although the countryside around Murray Bay is very picturesque and rather reminiscent of Scotland, the soil is not of the best, and military considerations, the protection of Quebec on the seaward side, unquestionably played the major part in the location of the settlements. There was no outside communication by road but that was not as serious a matter as might be thought, since the river, except at freeze-up in the fall and break-up in the spring, provided excellent communications. Salmon and whales abounded in the St. Lawrence and formed the basis of a fishery which was soon begun by men who had fished in Scotland before answering the call to arms.

Little is known of the day-to-day trials of the settlement. In accordance with government policy the settlers were supplied with implements of husbandry, tools, provisions, arms, etc., a practice to be followed in all subsequent military settlements. There is no record of particular difficulty or hardship in establishing the settlements. The twin bonds of clan membership and military service must have ensured a high level of co-operation in the construction of houses and the other necessary tasks of settlement. Land was soon cleared and crops of oats and potatoes planted in among the stumps. Churches were begun and the inevitable grist and saw mills were constructed. However, the building of the settlement was slowed by the outbreak of the American Revolution in 1775.

Although it is generally conceded that the long term results were bad, the British policy of military settlement was in the short run vindicated by the events of that year. Lieutenant-Colonel Allan MacLean of the 104th Highland Regiment went through the military settlements in Quebec, largely in and about Murray Bay, and recruited the 1st Battalion, the Royal Highland Emigrant Regiment. This regiment served faithfully throughout the Revolutionary War until disbanded in 1784.

With the return of peace and a good part of its manpower, the area began to thrive. By 1832, Murray Bay had a population of over 3,000. Churches flourished, good roads linked farms and villages; grist and saw mills, blacksmith shops and breweries gave evidence of a well-established and prosperous community.[9]

The second period of military settlement began with the end of the American Revolution. Highland regiments had been raised for that conflict both in North America and in Scotland, and with the end of hostilities Britain faced essentially the same problems she had had in 1763. The major difference now was that she, Britain, had to plan the defence of the very territories she had wrested from the French but a few years earlier.

Once again the decision was made to give grants of land to disbanded regiments, a decision which at once rewarded faithful service, helped hold down population in the Highlands and established loyal settlers with military skills in an area where it was hoped they could counter any attack. Of all the Scottish military settlements, those of Glengarry, in what is now eastern Ontario, are the best known and perhaps the most successful.

At the outbreak of the Revolution, Sir John Johnson and his cousin Guy Johnson, who held lands in New York, had recruited among the newly arrived Scots in the Mohawk Valley. Macdonells, Chisholms, Grants, Camerons, McIntyres and Fergusons flocked to their banners leaving behind their barely completed houses and steadings at the call to arms. Two battalions were finally raised and both served throughout the conflict.

At the end of the Revolution in 1783, men of the 1st Battalion, nearly 1500 strong, were granted lands in Lancaster, Charlottenburg, Cornwall, Osnabruck and Williamsburg townships on the St. Lawrence and men of the 2nd Battalion received grants to the west of them, upriver from Cataraqui. Some men of the 1st Battalion Royal Highland Emigrants also took land in the area. The Highlanders, along with Hessian veterans and a variety of civilian loyalists, spent the winter in camp at Sorel. With the spring break-up, they were conducted up the St. Lawrence by barge to the areas of settlement accompanied by wives, children and all the appurtenances of settlement. The British government did not stint.

> The settlers were provided by Government with everything that their situation rendered necessary . . . food and clothes for three years . . . , seed to sow on their new clearances . . . . Each received an axe, a hoe and a spade; a plough and one cow were allotted to two families, a whip and a cross-cut saw to every fourth family . . . . Pork was then as now the staple article of animal food.[10]

Work proceeded very rapidly in clearing the land and erecting huts of logs with wattle and daub fireplaces and chimneys. This was, of course, to be expected. Most of the men were familiar with axe and saw and many had pioneered before or were the sons of pioneers with experience in the Mohawk Valley or the Murray Bay area. In a very short time they were established with their wives and children in their new homes.

This is not to imply that there was no difficulty or suffering. In the best of conditions, felling huge trees, scrubbing brush, whipsawing logs, building shanties, and breaking the soil are arduous tasks. Supplies sometimes ran short. The cold in winter and the black flies and mosquitoes in the spring and summer were great trials. MacGregor perhaps exaggerates a little when he writes, "The Highlanders at Glengarry . . . had extraordinary difficulties to overcome and suffered great privations."[11] Nonetheless, the trials of the first two years were considerable. Some of the less robust left but the great mass stayed on and within two or three years had made the wilderness bloom.

The success of this venture is attributable to several factors – free land which allowed the settlers to apply such capital as they had to other purposes; provision of food, clothing and implements to see the settlers through the first cropless year; the prior experience of the settlers in frontier clearing and agricultural techniques; the social and moral solidarity of the groups based on clan, family and military ties; and the good transportation facilities provided by the St. Lawrence River.

There could be no better indication of the success and satisfaction of the settlers in Glengarry than their action in sending to Scotland for friends and relatives to join them. At their urging, over 500 people from Glengarry, the men mostly discharged veterans of the Glengarry Fencibles, arrived in 1785 under the leadership of the Rev. Alexander Macdonell. In 1791, MacDonell conducted a second group to the Glengarry area and yet another group of Scottish Glengarrians arrived in 1803. Once again the men were mostly veterans of the Fencibles and at the instruction of Lord Hobart, Secretary of State for the Colonies, each was granted the usual 200 acres of crown land because of "the merit and service of the Regiment" as well as "their connections now residing in the District of Glengarry of whose industry and general good conduct very favourable representations have been received here."[12]

In 1793, a group of MacLeods left Scotland and took up land about Kirkhill and in 1799 another large group settled at Lochiel. These new arrivals typically had relatives and friends in the area and were able to draw upon their help and experience while becoming themselves established. The whole Highland settlement in the eastern extremity of modern Ontario had, and long continued to have, all the characteristics of a closed community. Many years later, Sir Francis Bond Head, in his book *The Emigrant*, remarked upon this: "As the inhabitants of the township of Glengarry speak nothing but Gaelic, there is scarcely a stranger among them." Speaking specifically of the MacDonells (sic) he observed "their religion, language, habits and honour have continued there ever since, unaltered, unadulterated and unsullied."[13]

It is a fundamental fact of migration that an immigrant community once established becomes a destination for new immigrants from the common area of origin. Glengarry quickly came to have that role for many Highlanders in the first half of the nineteenth century. Although there was no further large scale movement of disbanded troops, small groups and individuals who continued to arrive from Glengarry, Scotland, were certain of a welcome and practical assistance from those upon whom they had claims of kinship.

There can be no doubt that the Glengarry settlement was economically and socially successful. In the opinion of near contemporaries, at least, it also vindicated British policy so far as its potential military role was concerned, providing troops for the War of 1812 and the suppression of the rebellion in Lower Canada. Bond Head remarked of the latter service that the settlers had by no means lost their Highland characteristics for "while they went down as infantry, they came back as cavalry."[14]

Other military settlements also took place after the American Revolution both in Canada and in the Maritime colonies. Men of the 1st Battalion Royal Highland Emigrants who were disbanded in 1784 were granted lands in Chatham Township in what is now Quebec in 1788. By 1793, all available land there had been taken under the usual conditions of settlement but, for reasons that are not clear, the settlement did not initially succeed. Almost all of the enlisted men sold out to their officers, particularly to Colonel Robertson, who accumulated much land in addition to his own grant. It seems probable that those who left simply realized what money they could and returned to the Murray Bay area where they had been recruited. Ultimately this settlement did flourish. Robertson actively sought settlers and by 1804 had fifty families well-established on the land.

There was also extensive settlement of disbanded troops in Nova Scotia and New Brunswick. After much debate with British authorities about the size and location of their grants – their officers seemed particularly voracious – most of the men of the 2nd Battalion of The Royal Highland Emigrants settled on the north side of Pictou Harbour, while the 82nd (Hamilton's) Regiment took their grants on the south side. Although many of the men of the 2nd Battalion of The Royal Highland Emigrants were recruited as they stepped from the ship at the outbreak of the Revolution and had not, therefore, had time to learn frontier agricultural techniques before enlisting, there is no evidence that they experienced abnormal difficulty. Aided, no doubt, by their proximity to the established settlement at Pictou, as well as generous government assistance in the form of supplies, implements and clothing, the veterans quickly built houses and cleared their lands. Their Highland background, good physical condition, disciplined habits and sober outlook must also have stood them in good stead. They and their neighbors of the 82nd Regiment are described by MacDonald as "a sober, industrious lot who cleared immense tracts of land."[15]

The veterans of these regiments added considerably to the population and helped to confirm the Scottish cast of society in the eastern third of Nova Scotia begun by John Pagan and reinforced by the famous "Hectorians" whose settlement at Pictou will be described below. Many disbanded soldiers were also settled in what is now New Brunswick. There was excellent unoccupied land on the St. John River from its mouth up to where Woodstock now stands and it was upon this land that the military settlements took place. Officers and men took up their lands regiment by regiment, almost as if falling into line of battle. This extensive settlement gave a conservative and loyalist character to the province, conspicious even today. A number of Scots were among the settlers and as one reported, they, in common with the others, "suffered very great hardships for the first few years after settling . . . . There were some idlers and faint hearted people . . . among us who left the settlement but all those who have remained have prospered."[16]

Looked at from the point of view of the settlers themselves, the military settlements following the Seven Years' War and the Revolutionary War can only be regarded as successful. There were early hardships and significant numbers failed, but the great majority became established, independent freeholders, with a wealth in land and possessions and a stature in the community that few of them could ever have achieved in the land of their birth. Highland Scots, as seen, were deeply involved in this type of settlement and although they might echo the words of a veteran of the 42nd Regiment who settled in New Brunswick, "never will we forget the tales, the songs, the music we heard in the Highlands,"[17] yet like him, they were content in their new homes.

The last military settlements established in Canada were those in the Bathurst district of Upper Canada following the War of 1812. The pattern was somewhat different in that civilian settlers from Britain, as well as disbanded soldiers from the late war, were induced to settle in this agriculturally inferior and geographically remote district by offers of free land, rations and equipment. This was the first instance of government assistance to civilian immigrants and the abandonment of the mercantilist position on emigration.

The War of 1812 had demonstrated to Britain how tenuous was her hold on Upper Canada and the territory to the west. It was widely believed that only the loyalty of the inhabitants of the central and eastern parts of the colony, particularly the Scots between Kingston and Brockville, had prevented the Americans from occupying everything west of Montreal.

With only the width of the St. Lawrence as protection against attack, the need for an interior line of communication from Montreal to the upper colony was evident. The Rideau Lakes system promised to fill the need. The settlements at Perth (1816), Richmond (1818) and Lanark (1821) were in direct pursuit of a policy of establishing loyal citizens with military potential to serve this strategic end. Drummondville in Quebec was established for much the same reasons.

The histories of the Perth and Lanark settlements are well known and may be summarized here. The Perth settlers were recruited by John Campbell in Scotland. Most appear to have been Highlanders. They left Glasgow in July and August and in September, 1815 reached Quebec whence they proceeded up country at once, only to discover that the surveys had not been completed and their allotments were not ready. Understandably there was much dissatisfaction among them. Several, upon learning more about the proposed area of settlement, petitioned to be allowed to locate elsewhere, naming "early frost," "lack of water communication," and "poor land" as their reasons, but no attention was paid them.[18] The Scots spent the winter at Brockville and in the following spring and summer were conducted to their new lands on the newly named River Tay where the depot of Perth had been established.

Although the settlers had considerable aid, there was also considerable hardship, most of it consequent upon their lack of skill with the axe and unfamiliarity with frontiering techniques. The first days of settlement could hardly have been worse. Constant bickering between different departments of government involved in transport and surveying, and a joint civil-military administration, often halted all action. Most settlers had long since run out of money and there was almost no food. No one seemed willing to help the settlers locate their lots, or advise them in the unfamiliar techniques of land clearance, house construction and frontier agriculture. Dishonest officials diverted supplies and as a final blow the first crop sown among the ragged stumps was an almost total failure. It is hardly surprising that many left to join friends and kinsmen in the United States and it is likely that many more would have done so had they had the wherewithal to make the journey. However, many remained upon the promise of continued rations, and the long term advantages of the area began slowly to become apparent. The soil was good and the location, although it had first seemed remote, proved in the end to be most convenient.

When Robert Gourlay carried out his survey of the settlement in July, 1817, only thirteen months after its commencement, some forty-two settlers interviewed all expressed themselves as "well satisfied"[19] with their condition. In 1828, it was referred to as a place of "happiness and contentment" and by 1850 it was unquestionaly one of the most prosperous, orderly and contented settlements in British America.

The subsequent settlements in New Lanark, drawing upon the experience gained at Perth, were much better organized. A recurrence of severe distress among Scottish weavers led Lord Bathurst to encourage emigration to Canada once again with the active assistance of emigration societies in Paisley, Hamilton and Lanark. Private philanthropy, painfully accumulated savings and government assistance combined to transport some 1200 settlers to Canada where they were expeditiously located on their lots some miles northwest of Perth in Lanark and Dalhousie townships. The settlers received the by now usual 100 acres, seed and implements, as well as a government loan of £100 to be repaid within ten years.

Although the initial organization and settlement was handled much more efficiently than at the Perth settlement, the New Lanark settlement was, in the long run, less successful. Most of the land was swampy and heavily treed or composed of rocky ridges with deceptive pockets of fertile soil between. The settlers knew nothing of agriculture in any form and moreover were many miles from market and without roads or transport to get there. Growth was painfully slow and no real prosperity ever arrived. The original settlers undoubtedly bettered themselves somewhat and certainly they provided their children with hope for the future. It is regrettable, however, that the time, money and energy expended by all concerned in the enterprises were not directed to the populating of areas with a better agricultural potential. The long term experience of the area has proved to be much rural poverty and large scale depopulation as the indifferent soil lost what initial fertility it had.

PROPRIETARY SETTLEMENT

Proprietary settlement began early in what is now Canada and continued sporadically throughout the nineteenth century, sometimes successfully and sometimes disastrously. In its essentials, proprietary settlement involved the acquisition of land by an individual and the active recruitment of immigrants to settle upon it according to terms agreed upon between themselves and the proprietor, subject of course to the ordinary protections of law and such conditions as the government had laid down.

The motives of the proprietors were various. Some acted from motives of pure philanthropy. Others clearly hoped to establish great landed estates upon which they expected to establish a social structure not unlike the clan system already dying in Scotland, while others sought only financial gain. The first setttlements that might properly be called proprietary took place on Prince Edward Island (Isle St. Jean) in the years 1768-72. The whole island had been allotted to some sixty-seven proprietors (most of them Scots), subject to a number of conditions. The principal conditions were the settlement of Protestants from Europe and the old colonies to the south, and payment for the whole of their properties at the end of ten years, at an average rate of about four shillings per hundred acres. Few lived up to their commitments. Some sold out at once and no more than five ever lived upon their estates. The remaining proprietors found they could not compete with the older colonies for Protestant European settlers and not unnaturally turned to Scotland and recruited among largely Catholic Highlanders.

Of the early proprietors, Captain John MacDonald, Chief of Glenaladale and late of the 84th Regiment, was most energetic. Having seen the island, he sold his Scottish holdings and purchased two townships with the express purpose of settling Highland Catholics upon them. Between the years 1770-1773 he brought in some 300 families from Uist and Moydart to locate at Tracadie and to this area headed many more in succeeding years.

Chief Baron Montgomery and Peter Stewart also arranged the dispatch of over 200 families between them, but settlement of the island went slowly and unevenly. In 1779 only 16 of the 67 townships had any settlers at all. Some of the settlers suffered great initial difficulties. In 1772 many arrived late in the season and without provisions, and some were reported to have starved to death in Prince Town. In 1774 a plague of locusts which destroyed their crops so discouraged settlers from Dumfries that they abandoned their lands and resettled at Pictou in Nova Scotia. MacGregor reports, " . . . the early settlers were . . . subjected for one or two years to all but perishing by famine."[20] The "absence of steady industrious habits" as well as "ignorance in clearing and managing land" commented on by MacDonald, also created problems.[21] Settlement continued very slowly for the next thirty years. The proprietors appeared more interested in speculative gain than in peopling their lands and busied themselves with political intrigues that gave the winners leverage in land sale manipulation. The advent of the American Revolution, providing military employment as an alternative to emigration and adding, of course, to the perils of travel, also had a dampening effect. It was not until the dawn of the nineteenth century that settlement in Prince Edward Island began again to thrive.

In 1803, in Prince Edward Island, Thomas Douglas, Earl of Selkirk, established the first of the Canadian settlements that place him among the best known of all the proprietors. Selkirk, perhaps the most benevolent and philanthropic man ever involved in Scottish emigration, devoted himself to the welfare of his countrymen and expended both his fortune and his life in the effort.

Selkirk had originally planned to found a settlement in Upper Canada, but under pressure from the British government which preferred maritime settlement, he abandoned his original intention and instead bought land in Prince Edward Island. In 1803, Selkirk himself led out some 800 people from Skye, Ross, Uist and Argyll. His plans were well worked out. Land was sold very cheaply or on credit to those without money, supplies were provided and, above all, instruction and leadership were provided to meet both the agricultural and social needs of the settlers.

> To obviate the terrors which the woods were calculated to inspire, the settlement was not dispersed as those of the Americans usually are, but concentrated within a moderate space. The lots were laid out in such a manner that there were generally four or five families . . . who built their houses in a little knot together. Each of them was inhabited by persons nearly related who sometimes carried on their work in common . . . . [22]

All went well. A year later Selkirk reported,

> I found the settlers engaged in securing the harvest . . . they had a small proportion of grain of various kinds but potatoes were the principal crop . . . several boats had been built . . and . . . a supply of fish obtained.[23]

More immigrants were brought from Stornoway, Lochiel, Kintyre and Perthshire in 1804 and in 1807-8. Selkirk, by this time, had matters so well in hand that later arrivals were usually able to settle on land that had at least a few acres cleared for them, a critical matter for people without the axeman's skills.

There were, as always, difficulties. Grasshoppers devastated one crop and a plague of mice destroyed another but by 1810 the Selkirk settlement was the most progressive and prosperous on the island. Emigrants from Scotland continued to join relatives in succeeding years and there can be no doubt that Selkirk's initial colonizing effort was an almost unqualified success.

Selkirk's second venture in colonization, this time in Upper Canada, was an almost unqualified disaster. Encouraged by the results of his work in Prince Edward Island, he again applied for land and after some difficulty with the colonial administration, he received a grant in Dover Township near Lake St. Clair. In 1804, some twenty families from Scotland arrived at the new settlement of Baldoon.

Selkirk had employed Alexander McDonell of Glengarry to superintend the new colony and from the start all went wrong. McDonell's part in it is clouded by conflicting testimony. Some viewed him as a tyrant, others, more sympathetic, saw him as a man facing an impossible task in trying to establish a parcel of drunken and idle rogues. The truth likely lies between. In addition to clashes of personality, there were other problems. The land, though fertile enough, was swampy and ill-drained. It proved nearly unworkable using the standard frontier agricultural methods. In any event the settlers arrived too late to plant a crop, food was scarce through the winter and there was much illness and nearly fifty deaths. The first crop in 1805 was parched by a summer drought and destroyed by an autumn flood. Finally, despairing of success, McDonell removed most of the remaining settlers to Sandwich.

Selkirk was sadly disappointed. However, he accepted the failure and lent the survivors sufficient money both for immediate needs and to buy cleared farms elsewhere. He now realized that his lands in Dover and Chatham were not well suited to settlement and he did not renew his attempts there. By 1820 most of this property has been sold to help meet the enormous debts he incurred in his next venture.

Undeterred by failure in Baldoon, Selkirk next turned his attention to the Red River Valley in the vast western territories of the Hudson's Bay Company. The story is well known. He set out to gain control of the Company and by 1810 he had done so. In 1811 he acquired from it 116,000 square miles of land which he meant to settle with immigrant Scots. From the outset, the Montreal-based North West Company, which had long traded in the area, did everything possible to hinder progress. The Hudson's Bay Company and the North West Company had long been rivals in the fur trade and had just broken off bitter and prolonged negotiations aimed at an equitable division of the vast western territory. It is not surprising then that the North West Company was alarmed at the prospect of a settlement dominated by the Hudson's Bay Company's largest shareholder, occupying the territory south of Lake Winnipeg through which ran the rivers vital to the North West Company's communications sytem and where Métis produced the pemmican necessary to provision the traders in winter. Despite the strong possibility of armed conflict, Selkirk pressed on. He employed Miles McDonell to take a reconnaissance party west to prepare for the main group to come. It arrived in the spring of 1812 and chose a site below the forks of the Red River.

The first group of settlers left Stornoway in June of 1811 and was followed by others from Kildonan and elsewhere in 1812 and 1814. The vast distances and primitive transport caused great initial difficulties. The parties of 1812 and 1813 were both forced to spend the winter on the shores of Hudson's Bay "living on oatmeal and ptarmigan" and suffering much hardship from cold and illness before going on to the colony. However, once arrived, the settlers found lightly timbered fertile land and settlement itself went well. But they were not left long in peace.

Food was scarce in the colony and the governor, fearing starvation among the people expected to arrive in 1814, prohibited the export of pemmican. Shortly after, he seized the supply which had been prepared for the winter rations of the North West Company's trading parties. To the North West Company's directors these constituted acts of open hostility, clearly intended to ruin their trade, and they now determined to eliminate the colony at any cost. Under the leadership of Duncan Cameron and Alexander MacDonell who enlisted the local Métis, the North West Company in essence made war on the Hudson's Bay Company and the settlers. In 1815, the settlers were attacked and dispersed and their houses and steadings burned. Many of the dispossessed made their way with the help of friendly Saultaux Indians to Upper Canada where eventually they were located with some government aid in various parts of the colony, notably in the Talbot Settlement. Some merely withdrew to the shores of Lake Winnipeg and when joined by a new group of Highlanders returned to re-establish the settlement.

The North West Company failed in attempts to incite the Cree and Assiniboine Indians to attack the colony but pursuaded the Métis to do so by representing the settlers as a threat to the Métis way of life. In June of 1816 a group of Métis attacked at Seven Oaks and killed Governor Semple and twenty-one of his followers. Selkirk, already on his way with an armed party of French and Scottish veterans of the late War of 1812, arrived within a few days, arrested the ringleaders and founded a new settlement, Kildonan. With characteristic generosity, he forgave all previous debt because of the hardships the settlers had endured and gave them new lots free.

These events on the Red River were followed by legal battles in the Upper Canadian courts. The case went against Selkirk and he was fined heavily. What Selkirk believed to be manifest injustice was a heavy blow to him. He left Canada in poor health in 1818 and died in 1820 while on holiday at Pau. It seems ironic that the rivalry of two great companies both dominated by Scots and with large numbers of Scots in their employ should have inhibited Scottish settlement on the Red River.[24]

Immigration declined markedly without Selkirk's active interest and promotion. The Hudson's Bay Company and the North West Company amalgamated in 1821 and thereafter many of the company servants took up land in the area and eventually outnumbered Selkirk's settlers. Thus, in the end, and despite great difficulties, Selkirk's belief that a permanent colony could be established on the Red River was vindicated.

Thomas Talbot, on the other hand, founder and director of the Talbot

Settlement, was beyond question the most successful colonizer in the history of Canada. An Irishman of good family and connections, while in service as a young man under John Graves Simcoe he saw the Lake Erie country, which he resolved to devote his life to settling. Not without difficulty he arranged, in 1803, an initial grant of 5000 acres in Dunwich Township. Over the next thirty-odd years, the settlement grew to total twenty-eight townships on the shores of Lake Erie. Talbot's general plan was to form tight-knit settlements of people loyal to British institutions as a defence against United States influence and possible attack. He directed his efforts to recruiting Britons in the United States and throughout the British Isles, in the process inducing many Scots, both Highland and Lowland, to settle in Upper Canada.

His method of settlement was efficient and practical. He had learned from Simcoe the importance of good roads and the free grant of 50 acres was conditional, not only upon building a substantial house and sowing ten acres within three years, but also upon satisfactorily completing half of the road the lot abutted. If this was all done to Talbot's satisfaction, and he usually conducted a personal inspection, the settler was then able to buy additional land at 12/- per acre. If, in Talbot's view, the settler had failed, he was simply and literally "rubbed out." His name was removed with an eraser from where it had been pencilled in on the master lot plan and he was forced to vacate forthwith.

Although at first all went slowly many Scots, both Highland and Lowland, took land in the Talbot Settlement. The first sizable body appears to have been composed of Highlanders from Caledonia, in New York State, who took up land in Aldboro. Later Mr. Buchanan, the British consul in New York, sent others to the Talbot Settlement. About 140 refugees from Selkirk's Red River colony were also granted land. The glowing accounts of the settlement arriving in Scotland in the period 1818-21 persuaded many people from Argyllshire and Perthshire to emigrate thence. It was not long, however, before the Highlanders were involved in a bitter dispute with Talbot.

Briefly, he settled them upon fifty-acre plots on a tract reserved for but not yet granted to him and promised them additional Crown land which he proved in the end unable to give. The Highlanders for their part came to believe Talbot was defrauding them of land to which they had a right and applied to the Legislative Council for remedy. The Council reluctantly confirmed Talbot's grant to "regularize" the situation and, at his suggestion, reduced the fees payable by the settlers for additional grants. The Highlanders were not satisfied and in an insulting memorial to the Council demanded their "rights." A stiff reply informed them they had no rights to further land and that only an apology for the unfounded charges would induce the Council to confirm the grants already promised. Not until 1824 did the Scots submit, after over five years of conflict.

There can be little doubt this experience soured Talbot's attitude to Highlanders. He cautioned Peter Robinson against them as "they make the worst settlers for new Roads."[25] While he continued to accept Highland settlers, his dislike of them was clear and where possible he gave preference to English, Irish and Lowland Scots, many of whom settled about St. Thomas and in Lobo, London, and Williams townships.

By 1835 most of Talbot's lands had been settled. Although he was eccentric, domineering and arbitrary, there can be no doubt he had, according to his own lights, the interest of the country and his settlers foremost in his mind, going to enormous lengths to help those he thought deserving. He was by all odds the most successful of the proprietors and was instrumental in setting the feet of a great many Scots upon the road to independence and prosperity.

Two other early proprietors should also be mentioned, Donald Cameron and Archibald McNab of McNab, although neither in fact brought many settlers to Upper Canada. Cameron was in some ways a tragic figure although he was the author of much of his own misfortune. He spent a considerable sum of his own money assisting some 600 Scots and then applied for a grant of land upon which to settle them. He was at first refused but shortly after the Executive Council granted him lands in the townships of Thorah and Eldon for the settlement "of a few Scottish settlers" within one year. This time limit was his undoing. He was unable to collect his settlers before the deadline and applied, over the years, for extension after extension. An unsigned complaint led to an investigation which concluded that Cameron had heavily padded his lists of settlers and otherwise falsified his records – quite a usual practice at the time. Cameron denied the charges but did not escape arrest and jailing at York. His settlers rallied to his defence with petitions on his behalf and years of contention followed. Several investigations were carried out apparently complicated by the political struggles between the Executive Council and the Legislative Assembly. In 1849 Cameron's last hope failed when the Colonial Office refused to consider the matter. Cameron was generous in the extreme, diligent in the service of his settlers and highly regarded by them, none of which can be said of the notorious Archibald McNab.[26]

McNab's machinations are in the main so well known and in detail so complex that they can only be summarized here. McNab was a man of immense energy, charm and determination. He arrived from Scotland "bankrupt and a fugitive from justice" but was well-received by Lord Dalhousie, which gave him access to the highest levels of government and society. He sought and without difficulty procured a township (to be called McNab) on the Ottawa River. In some way he secured with the grant a most unusual condition, that the Scots settlers he recruited would receive no deed until he certified they had met his required terms of settlement. In the light of subsequent events, it seems evident he meant, by the simple expedient of never certifying they had done so, to keep them in permanent dependency and *de facto* create for himself a vast estate worked by what amounted to a tenantry. The settlers, recruited by Dr. Hamilton of Arnprior in Scotland, arrived some twenty-eight families strong in 1824. Each family was committed to yield McNab one bushel of wheat per cleared acre forever after, having three rent-free years at the outset, and to repay a debt which averaged about £85 per family.

McNab began at once to behave with all the arrogance of a feudal lord. He demanded and received from the settlers, who were totally ignorant of their rights and completely trusting of their clan chief, mortgages to their lands. He refused to give the provisions Hamilton had promised would await them, claimed all the standing timber on the settlers' lots, even convinced them they could not depart the township without his leave. As discontent arose, he used his interest with government, his power as justice of the peace, and his traditional authority to punish savagely all who opposed him. When Hamilton, hearing of his behaviour, refused to recruit more settlers, McNab himself met immigrant Highlanders disembarking at Montreal and persuaded them to settle on his lands.

Very quickly his settlers came to hate and fear him and a fifteen-year struggle commenced which finally broke his arbitrary power. Arrests, lawsuits and finally two government investigations punctuated by the Rebellion of 1837 in which his settlers refused to serve under McNab as Colonel, finally came to an end in 1841. An order-in-council granted the settlers full title to their lands upon payment of a fair valuation. All of McNab's powers were removed from him and he was given a final cash settlement of £2500. Abandoned by his friends, hated by those he had tried to defraud and suffering withal from a lively sense of injustice, McNab retired to a small estate in the Orkneys where he died in 1860.[27]

A less well-known but much more successful proprietor than either Cameron or McNab was William Dickson. He emigrated to Upper Canada from Dumfries and practiced law at Niagara. In 1816 he bought outright the Township of Dundee and proceeded to bring out Scottish settlers. He gave them sound instruction, easy credit for supplies and good terms of purchase. Within twenty years his township had a population of over 6,000, almost all Scots, well supplied with schools, churches and mills, and by common consent highly prosperous. Dickson also wrote a well-publicized series of letters on emigration and was responsible for encouraging many other Scots, besides his own settlers, to seek their fortunes in Canada.[28]

Proprietary settlement had a number of distinguishing characteristics. Among them was the direct personal interest of the proprietor, be it philanthropic or otherwise, in procuring the land, recruiting the settlers and so far as possible personally supervising the settlement itself. Settlers were conducted directly to their lots, provided with tools, provisions and seed, sometimes at little or no cost, given some instruction in clearing and farming methods and in some instances at least helped and encouraged through the first lean years. They were very often group settlements too, in which people could rely on assistance from friends and relatives settled around them. In all of this, of course, the proprietary settlements much resembled the military settlements which they just overlapped in time.

When the proprietor was energetic and able, the settlers well-chosen and the land good, proprietary settlement proved to be a useful and economical way to reduce Scotland's population and increase that of the colonies. Without that combination of talents and conditions, it created hardship and disappointment for the emigrant and heartbreak, frustration and bitterness for the proprietor. By 1850 it had largely disappeared and free settlement because of its character had become the dominant pattern.

FREE SETTLEMENT

Although both military and proprietary patterns of settlement were of great importance in Scottish emigration to Canada, free settlement still accounted for the largest part. At its simplest, it involved a decision to leave Scotland for the colonies, arranging a passage and upon arrival, if the place of settlement was not already decided, choosing a destination either urban or rural and going there. In practice it took many different forms. Much emigration, although technically free, was forced either by unemployment after the Napoleonic Wars, by the Highland clearances, or by repeated failures of the potato crop, for the potato in Scotland had long since become a stale of diet among the poor.

Interest in emigration as a remedy for Scottish ills was widespread. Every city and town appeared to have an "Emigration Society" active in raising passage money. The hand weavers, who had suffered much from mechanization, were very active in both forming and using them.[29] Many landlords paid all or part of the passage money for thousands of their tenants, among them such people as Colonel Gordon, Lady Sutherland, the Duke of Argyll, Ramsay of Kildalton, the Duke of Hamilton and much later, Lady Gordon Cathcart who founded Benbecula in Saskatchewan in the 1880s in almost proprietary fashion and peopled it with Scots from her Hebridean estates.[30]

Nor were destinations haphazardly chosen. There was a large volume of correspondence between the colonies and Scotland. Would-be emigrants usually had friends or relatives to join. Thus, areas once settled by Scots were constantly reinforced by new immigration and people continued to go to the Maritimes and to Ontario until all good land (and much bad) was occupied. Immigrant guides, published collections of letters, travellers' accounts and land company agents offered an embarrassment of advice, so that many people set out with a good idea of where they were going and what they would do when they got there. Indeed, it became common practice to send a member of the family or representatives of a group to spy out the land and decide upon the best location in advance of the main body.

People who were not involved in proprietary settlement but wished to farm, as most Scots appeared to do, had several choices open to them. They could buy a farm at some stage of development at a price that varied with the amount cleared, buildings erected, closeness to services, and access to market. They could buy wild land held by speculators, of whom there were many. They could homestead Crown land for payment of the standard fees or they could buy from land companies, some of which had lands in various stages of preparation ranging from a few cleared acres with a house and barn close to essential services, to wild land remote from any. After 1825, land companies progressively came to dominate settlement in the eastern half of what is now Canada. Although in the end few ever returned much profit to their shareholders, they had an enormous impact on the development of Canadian society.[31]

The settlements of Pictou in 1765, so overwhelmingly important in the subsequent heavy Scottish immigration into the whole of eastern Nova Scotia, began as a colonization company, i.e., a land company venture. After the capture of Louisbourg in 1758, John Pagan, a native of Greenock living in Philadelphia, bought three shares in the Philadelphia company which held land in the Pictou area. Thither, he conducted a few Scots and Ulster Irish from the older colony and began through his agent John Ross to seek emigrants in Scotland. His efforts led to the departure of some 189 people from Loch Broom in the ship *Hector* which arrived in Pictou in July of 1773.

The Hectorians suffered much hardship. They had no tools, seed or supplies, most were illiterate, had no skill whatever with the axe and possessed only rudimentary agricultural knowledge. Many had hoped to fish but that hope was frustrated since all of the shorelands so necessary to fishing were already granted and they were compelled to settle inland. The first few years and particularly the first winter brought dreadful hardship but slowly the Scots learned the necessary techniques, cleared their lands and finally prospered. In succeeding years they were joined by many others from Inverness, Perth, Ross and Sutherland as well as the discharged veterans mentioned earlier. By 1830 all the available land was gone and the population of the settlement was over 21,000.[32] Most of the early settlers were Presbyterian but they were later joined by Catholic immigrants, many of whom worked their way into Cape Breton Island when it was thrown open to settlement after 1784. The nearness of Nova Scotia to Scotland itself, the rugged terrain and the sea both so reminiscent of home and, of course, the presence of other Scots, all made Nova Scotia immensely attractive to Scottish immigrants who arrived in large numbers for generations thereafter. Parts of eastern Nova Scotia, particularly Cape Breton Island, became as Gaelic in speech and outlook as the Highlands themselves and to some degree remain so.[33]

Settlement was again attempted in Canada in the nineteenth century. Many companies were proposed, some formed but hardly any prospered. The Canada Company, promoted and first directed by John Galt and with another well-known Scot, William "Tiger" Dunlop as a senior officer, was most important in Scottish settlement. The Company acquired the vast Huron Tract of some 1,100,000 acres and another 1,384,413 acres of

Crown Reserves scattered across nearly every township in Upper Canada in return for £348,680, less some remissions for public improvements.

The Company was chartered in 1826 and began a vigorous campaign to recruit settlers. Agents were established in the principal cities of Britain, two in Scotland at Edinburgh and Glasgow. Agents were also established at the principal Canadian ports of entry and at New York. Galt and Dunlop were both well-known in Scotland and many prominent men recommended the Company to intending emigrants and, although many English and Irish emigrants took Company lands, there always seemed to be some particular affinity between the Company and Scotsmen, many of whom were diverted to Canada from intended destinations in the United States.

Numerous Scots settled along the Maitland Road which Dr. Dunlop had slashed through the bush to the site of the new Town of Goderich, and around the area of Seaforth in what is now Huron County. The Scots tended, understandably, to settle in groups which grew by increments of new settlers and the names of many towns in Company-settled territories reveal their Scottish link. Leigh, Rothsay, Holyrood, Rannoch, and West Montrose, among others, come easily to mind. Many Scots were also settled on Company lands in other parts of Upper Canada where all contributed to the markedly Scottish cast of society in central and southwestern Ontario evident even today.

Galt, after many disagreements with his directors, was removed from his post in 1829 to the great regret of most of his settlers and those who had worked with him in Upper Canada. His offence was that of having more care for human beings than for profits. His importance in the history of settlement could hardly be exaggerated, however, for he set in motion and in part oversaw the transformation of a wilderness into a rich agricultural territory with a sturdy, industrious and independent population.[34] Although one may find fault with a policy which in fact turned over to a private company what ought to have been accepted as a public responsibility, there is no reason to suppose any government of the time could have planned or worked to better purpose than Galt did in promoting settlement in Upper Canada.[35]

Among other land companies involved in Scottish settlement were the British American Land Company and The New Brunswick and Nova Scotia Land Company. The former, which was opposed by local and particularly French-Canadian interests, was finally given a charter in 1834. The Company, pointing out economic stagnation in Britain and the consequent availability of a good quality of immigrants and playing on official fears of American infiltration into the Eastern Townships on the one hand and French-Canadian infiltration on the other, was finally able to convince Lord Aylmer, the lieutenant-governor, that this militarily sensitive area should be settled by the loyal Britons the Company would undertake to provide. The prospect of receiving some 120,000 over a period of ten years, at a time when the Legislative Assembly was refusing to vote the Civil List, must also have been a consideration.[36]

The Eastern Townships were by no means empty of settlers, many of them American, and about a third of the Company land was already surveyed and reasonably well served by mills, stores, churches, etc. The remainder was unsurveyed wilderness. The Company was given 847,661 uninhabited acres in the counties of Shefford, Stanstead and Sherbrooke. Agents recruited actively in Britain and the United States with special appeals addressed to Highland Scots who in the end formed the bulk of the settlers. The campaign was, in its initial phases, a little too successful. Poor immigrants were promised work in road-building, etc., to help pay for their lots. They began to arrive when plans for development were incomplete and many had no money, no work and no food. However, accommodations and compromises were worked out, jobs did begin to appear and later arrivals found the situation much improved.

In 1844, after much bickering with officials, the Company was deprived of much of its best land by the Government of Lower Canada which then proceeded to sell some lots on easy terms and to give free title to many others. This generous policy attracted many more immigrants, many of them Scots, but made the operations of the Company doubly difficult.

In 1844 Alexander Galt, John Galt's son, took over as commissioner. While he vigorously recruited settlers, he also became heavily involved in financing the St. Lawrence and Atlantic Railroad which he thought would materially benefit the area. By the 1850s a change in the character of settlement was evident.[37] British settlers were passing through to Canada West while more and more French Canadians were moving to Company lands as a result of population pressure in other areas.[38] Although the Eastern Townships were once home to many Scots and their children, the area today is almost totally French Canadian.

The New Brunswick Company, among whose organizers was the well-known Samuel Cunard, received a grant of 550,000 acres in 1833, in York County, N.B., in return for a note for £56,250. Agents recruited heavily, almost exclusively in Scotland and the north of England. Their lavish promises of cleared land and log houses awaiting on hundred-acre hold-ings with easy fifty-year leases attracted Highlanders and Lowlanders alike. Cowan reports the Gaelic-speaking agents even promised free trans-port. As often happened, promises exceed delivery, development costs far exceeded revenues and the immigrants, particularly those from Skye, were most discontented. They arrived on the Nashwaak River to find no lands cleared nor houses built. Many who were fishermen and wished to remain so objected to clearing land or working in the lumbering industry, and left. The Company struggled along for many years, sometimes in direct com-petition with the provincial government, which for its part granted long and easy leases on Crown lands to poor settlers. It was never profitable for its backers, and although it did settle Scots, their numbers were not great.[39]

As was pointed out above, military and proprietary settlement involved the movement of people directly to the land from their points of origin, and encouragement and assistance, sometimes lavish, in the process of settlement itself. Free settlement was quite different from this. Although many settlers, particularly those with money, went direct to the land, many did not, either from preference or necessity.

Perhaps the most widespread misapprehension about the pattern of free settlement is the fixed belief that the immigrant boarded ship at Glasgow or Liverpool, debarked at Montreal, made his way up country, went immediately to the farthest frontier, put up his shanty and began an individual assault on the forest primeval, ending up a couple of decades later a prosperous freeholder. It is true that many people tried to follow such a pattern and it is also true that many who tried succeeded, but the failure rate was high and as travellers' accounts and immigrants letters home accumulated, it became more and more recognized that pioneering was for specialists and fewer and fewer immigrants went directly to the woods. Two things were necessary for successful settlement on wild land – pioneering skills and money. There is an impression abroad that one could begin in the bush with nearly nothing. This was far from true. Aside from the cost of land if purchased in 1855-60, a man would need at least £100, which would amount to about $2000.00 at today's prices. A pair of oxen, a yoke, a logging chain, a harrow, a year's supply of food and the hire of some assistance in clearing and building easily ate up such a sum. If a man were an expert axeman, he might dispense with some hired help and thereby save a little, but few immigrants were familiar with the axe.

Of all the pioneering skills, that of the axeman was paramount. A good axeman could clear land, make a house and steadings, build furniture and make many of his other tools with the axe alone. The experienced wife could make soap, spin, knit and weave, recognize useful wild herbs and fruits, and do a myriad of things necessary to the isolated life of the agricultural frontier. Above all, the pioneer family must become used to the drudgery and isolation of life in the wilderness. There was even a specialized frontier agriculture – corn, beans and pumpkins grown together, with the beans twining round the corn and the pumpkin vine spreading over the hillock in a perfect symbiotic relationship. Pioneering, in fact, became a specialized way of life for some people who acquired the land, cleared a few acres, put up a log house and outbuildings, fenced the clearing, took a few crops from among the burned stumps and then moved on to do it all over again. These people were almost all Canadian or American-born. They were, so to speak, the cutting edge of the agricultural frontier. When in the late 1850s good land became scarce in Canada West (Ontario), they simply moved out to the U.S. agricultural frontier or to Manitoba. It was not their intention to create a property for succeeding generations but, to quote from Jones' valuable study, *A History of Agriculture in Ontario*, "their livelihood came not from the sale of . . . produce but from the increase of their farms consequent upon being cleared."[40] In short, the professional pioneer made a new farm and just when it was coming to a state when a British farmer might begin to consider it fit for use, he would begin to think it time to sell, in order to move on to where he could once again put his specialist skills to use. So clear was this pattern that it was commonly remarked of Upper Canada that within a few years in any area, the original settlers were nearly entirely replaced by British immigrants. Lynch in 1855-56 wrote of a man who "cleared up a new farm almost entirely with his own hands every five or six years, until he came to the ploughing when he became dissatisfied and sold out."[41] Even so, there were always those among the immigrants prepared to take the risk of true pioneering. Those with money could maximize their holdings by purchasing uncleared or, as it was called, "wild" land, and paying expert axemen to clear it but, in the main, immigrants seemed to prefer to buy a made farm, close to settlements and their amenities, where they could use their superior agricultural knowledge.

Since a great many immigrants arrived without sufficient funds even to take up Crown land, how did they go about getting farms, the grand aim and intention of almost all of them? There appear to have been two general patterns, either to work at a trade or some non-agricultural pursuit or to work as an agricultural labourer. Persons who adopted the first procedure usually bought cleared farms, which of course cost more, and this might mean a lapse of some years while savings were accumulated. Persons who "hired out" to established farmers quickly learned the techniques of Canadian agriculture and, most important of all, how to use the North American axe with its distinctive curved handle as well as native Canadians could. It was most often such persons as these who, when the time came to purchase, bought uncleared land on the back lots and really did pioneer in the frontier fashion in the '50s and '60s. Yet another common practice was to take a farm on a sharing arrangement. This was ordinarily done with partially cleared farms, the contract calling for the owner to supply stock, implements and seed, and to receive half the produce of the farm while the tenant worked the land and continued to clear it. There were other more complex arrangements developed after the 1860s. However, the aim was always to own land. Renting, leasing and sharing arrangements were always thought to be temporary measures to be abandoned as soon as the accumulation of savings made purchase possible.

The time lapse between arrival and farm ownership was of course quite variable. A Lieutenant Cook reported a man near Cornwall who, as he said, earned enough as a labourer in two years to buy a farm in part because "he was not encumbered by a wife." A Wellington County farmer who first settled in Simcoe "worked in Toronto as a carpenter for one year, most of the time making coffins for people who died of cholera ... then settling in ... Simcoe County purchasing a farm for $400.00."[42] For a man starting from nothing in Upper Canada, it took about eight years on an average to save enough to buy in the period 1840-1860. It appears that as the century wore on the length of time increased somewhat.

A study of early agricultural settlers in Wellington County reveals some had been lawyers, weavers, smiths, ministers, coopers, millwrights, etc. In all, forty different occupations were represented. Even more interesting, most persons with trades and professions seemed to have continued them even when farming. John Harland's prize essay, "A Report of The State of Agriculture in Wellington County 1852," reports "Persons who are styled farmers here are a very different class of men to those who follow the same occupation in the British Isles . . . . Numbers have settled here who were brought up to the plough, but the *great majority* of those who now live by cultivating the soil, were educated to some variety of trade . . . . They have an idea of commerce and decline selling to an old customer if a new one will offer a high figure."[43] Sad to say, he quotes no numbers and cites no sources, but his assertions have not been disputed. The observation is interesting in that it implies the new style of farmer using business techniques was very much market-orientated in contrast with a more traditional subsistence farmer of the period before 1840.

To summarize, the pattern of free settlement on the agricultural frontier went like this: (1) First clearing and making of farms by a specialist group of pioneers with the appropriate skills. Intermingled with this group were numbers of immigrants. These were of two sorts, those who had the money to pay for clearing and thus maximize land holdings, and those who in ignorance or hardihood went to the frontier and learned pioneering skills as best they could. For the latter, the failure rate was high and the suffering considerable. (2) The pioneering group was followed by immigrants, many of them Scots who, if they had cash, bought a "made" farm by preference. Those who recognized their ignorance sometimes deliberately hired out to learn Canadian techniques in agriculture before taking up their own holdings. (3) Finally, people without money worked either as farm labourers, or in villages and towns, in order to accumulate the necessary cash through savings.

A hundred years ago land represented the ultimate security. Most men, even professional men and tradesmen, sought and bought land as soon as they were able. Thus, the phenomenon we think so modern – the man who farms and also works at another job – proves not to be new at all. A study of the emergence after 1870 of the specialist farmer who did not do anything but farm, remains to be done. Tradesmen and mechanics who saved and bought farms seem to have done just as well at farming as those with agricultural backgrounds. This could imply several things: first, some prior knowledge of agriculture gained in Scotland; second, the use of hired labour for the day-to-day work of the farm, which was a fairly common pattern; third, and least likely, there was not much to farming. The real difference between these groups was the tendency of the town worker or tradesmen to buy a made farm in preference to wild land, while

71

those Scots who had worked on farms for others were much more likely to take wild land and clear and build themselves.

A study made by the author of the course of Scottish settlement in Wellington County revealed that at most one Scot in five bought wild land on arriving in the county and cleared it himself and that he might have worked in agriculture in Scotland beforehand. About four Scots in five who ultimately owned farms in Wellington County in the period before 1905 either bought farms which had been cleared by others or bought wild land which they then had cleared by local axemen. Some of the wealthier immigrants were able to afford to have a house and outbuildings constructed although this did not happen with great frequency.

The same study showed that Scots settlement did not diverge markedly from what appears to have been the general pattern of immigrant settlement on an open agricultural frontier. They were, however, somewhat less likely to buy land immediately upon arrival than were other immigrants, which may run counter to the belief that most Scottish immigrants were relatively well off *vis-a-vis* English and Irish immigrants. They avoided where possible the pitfalls of true pioneering, preferring to buy made farms, but if they did go on wild land they were at least as successful as others.[44]

In discussing patterns of settlements, very little has been said of the individual pioneer experience, the techniques required to farm successfully in Canada, the influence of the landscape, etc. There is a wealth of information but these areas are studies in themselves. This chapter has dealt with eighteenth and nineteenth century rural settlement, mainly in Eastern Canada. The subject is of great interest and importance and deserves a far more detailed presentation than has been possible here. The contribution of Scots to rural society in Western Canada is considered in another chapter. The whole subject of the migration of industrial and commercial workers from Scotland to Canada is now beginning to receive the attention it deserves.

To sum up, Scots have played an extremely important part in the settlement of Canada. In the earliest days of British settlement, the Scottish role was clearly the most important. Although with time Scots were outnumbered by English and Irish immigrants, they always came and continue to come today. Their contribution to Canadian society as evidenced in other chapters has been out of all proportion even to their substantial numbers.

NOTES

1. See Stanley C. Johnson, *Emigration from the United Kingdom to North America* (London: George Routledge and Sons Ltd., 1913), p. 1.

2. The settlements on the Annapolis Basin made in 1629 under the sponsorship of Sir William Alexander were abandoned when Nova Scotia was returned to France by Charles I.
3. Of the many proprietors, Selkirk, Talbot, McNab and Lady Gordon are, for very different reasons, best known.
4. The settlement at Perth in 1816 and Selkirk's settlement on the Red River in 1811-15 are cases in point.
5. The most interesting attempt to transplant the Old World to the New was that of Archibald McNab. Cf. the short account below and the detailed study by M.J. Fraser, "Feudalism in Upper Canada," *Ontario History Society, Papers and Records*, 12 (1914).
6. It is impossible to do more than guess at the numbers leaving Scotland annually in this period. Cf. contemporary issues of *Scots Magazine* for references to emigration from Scotland.
7. For a good short description of social and economic change in the Highlands see Gordon Donaldson, *The Scots Overseas* (London: Robert Hale, 1966), Chapters 3 and 4.
8. Norman MacDonald, *Canada, 1763-1841 Immigration and Settlement: The Administration of The Imperial Land Settlements* (Toronto: Longmans, Green and Co., 1939), p. 43.
9. *Ibid.*, p. 44.
10. J.S. MacDonell, *History of Glengarry County*, cited in J. Murray Gibbon, *Scots in Canada* (Toronto: Musson, 1911), p. 66.
11. J. MacGregor, *Emigration to British America* (London: Longman, Rees, Orme, Brown and Green, 1829), p. 46.
12. Lord Hobart to Lieutenant-General Hunter, reprinted in *A Short Account of the Emigration from the Highlands of Scotland to North America: and the Establishment of the Catholic Diocese of Upper Canada* (Kingston: Whig Office, 1839), p. 19.
13. Sir Francis Bond Head, Bart., *The Emigrant* (London: John Murray, 1846), p. 116.
14. *Ibid.*, p. 118.
15. MacDonald, p. 50.
16. *Ibid.*, p. 49.
17. *Ibid.*, p. 50.
18. Andrew Haydon, *Pioneer Sketches in the district of Bathurst* (Toronto: The Ryerson Press, 1925), I, p. 37.
19. Robert Gourlay, *Statistical Account of Upper Canada* (London: Limpkin and Marshall, 1822) I, p. 525.
20. MacGregor, p. 48.
21. MacDonald, p. 103.
22. Thomas Douglas, Earl of Selkirk, *Observations on the present state of the Highlands of Scotland with a view of the causes and probable consequences* (Edinburgh: A. Constable, 1806), p. 206.
23. Quoted in J.M. McGibbon, *Scots in Canada*.

24. For more detailed accounts cf., among others, George Bryce, *MacKenzie, Selkirk, Simpson* (Toronto: Morang and Co. Ltd., 1905) p. 115 *et seq.* in the Series "The Makers of Canada," Duncan Scott and Pelham Edgar, eds., and the excellent monograph by John Gray, *Lord Selkirk of The Red River* (Toronto: The MacMillan Company of Canada, 1963).

25. Quoted in F.C. Hamil, *Lake Erie Baron* (Toronto: MacMillan of Canada, 1955), p. 146.

26. Cf. MacDonald, pp. 181-186. It is appropriate here to pay tribute to the enormously useful and detailed work of Professor MacDonald to be found in the volume cited and in *Canada, Immigration and Colonization: 1841-1903* (Toronto: MacMillan of Canada, 1966.) Both have been used extensively in preparation of this chapter.

27. This account draws upon Marjorie J.F. Fraser, "Feudalism in Upper Canada," *Ontario Historical Society Papers and Records*, 12 (1914), pp. 142-152, Roland Wild, *McNab, The Last Laird* (London: Methuen, 1938) and MacDonald, p. 186 *et seq.*

28. J. Young, *Reminiscences of the Early History of Galt, and The Settlement of Dumfries* (Toronto: Hunter, Rose, 1880).

29. Johnson, p. 55.

30. Helen Cowan, *British Emigration To British North America*, (Toronto: University of Toronto Press, 1967), p. 209 ff.

31. W.T. Easterbrook and Hugh Aitken, *Canadian Economic History* (Toronto: The MacMillan Company of Canada, 1967), p. 277.

32. George Patterson, *A History of The County of Pictou Nova Scotia* (Montreal: Dawson Brothers, 1877), Chapters 4 and 5.

33. G. Campbell, *A History of Nova Scotia* (Toronto: The Ryerson Press, 1948), p. 182.

34. C.f. Easterbrook, p. 132 *et seq.*, and for a detailed and fascinating account of life in Huron Tract, Robina and Kathleen Lizars, *In The Days of The Canada Company* (Toronto: W. Briggs, 1896).

35. Oscar Skelton, *Life and Times of Sir Alexander Tilloch Galt* (Toronto: Oxford University Press, 1920), Chapter 1.

36. *Ibid.*, Chapter 2.

37. *Ibid.*, Chapter 4.

38. *Ibid.*, p. 43.

39. W. MacNutt, *New Brunswick, A History: 1784:1867* (Toronto: MacMillan of Canada, 1963), p. 305.

40. R. Jones, *History of Agriculture in Ontario* (Toronto: University of Toronto Press, 1946), p. 52.

41. J. Lynch, "Report of the Agricultural Condition And Prospects of the County of Bruce," *Journal And Transactions of The Board of Agriculture of Upper Canada*, Vol. 1 (1856), p. 615.

42. Historical Atlas of Wellington County (Toronto: Historical Atlas Publishing Co., 1905), p. 55. This Atlas is almost unique in Ontario in containing several hundred thumb-nail family histories of great interest to scholars.

43. J. Harland, "Report On The State of Agriculture In The County of Wellington," *Journal And Transactions of The Board of Agriculture of Upper Canada*, Vol. I (1856), p. 216.
44. K. Duncan, "Aspects of Scottish Settlement In Wellington County," *Scottish Colloquium Proceedings* (Guelph: University of Guelph, 1970), 3, 15-20.

FIVE

Scottish Settlement of the West

Alan R. Turner

The Scottish tradition in Western Canada originates with the predominance of Scots in the enterprises which first penetrated the area now comprising the Provinces of Manitoba, Saskatchewan, Alberta and British Columbia, who exploited its fur resources, explored and mapped its waterways, and established forts and trading posts, some of which formed the nucleus of permanent settlements. The fur trade era, a period of British sovereignty exercised through the Hudson's Bay Company by virtue of its charter and trading licence, persisted for two centuries, until the 1850s on the Pacific coast and until 1870 on the prairies. During that period persons of mixed Scottish and Indian parentage emerged as an important element among the indigenous peoples; the first agricultural settlement had been undertaken by Scottish people at Red River where the first local governing unit, dominated in its administration by Scots, was established; and a number of church missions and parishes were founded, achievements in which Scottish clergymen also played a part.

The Scottish presence was still evident in the colonial and provincial institutions which superseded the fur trade hegemony, and Scotsmen were influential in public programmes for settlement and development of the West, as well as in the direction and financing of private enterprises related thereto. Scottish people from the home land, Eastern Canada, and the United States contributed to the tide of settlers which reached flood proportions by the end of the nineteenth century, continued undiminished until World War I, and thereafter more slowly advanced into the forest fringe north of the prairies and into the interior of British Columbia. Few entirely Scottish settlements were founded in Western Canada after 1870 but there were both rural districts and urban centres in which Scots comprised a substantial element. Statistics confirm the number of Scots who peopled this new country and their augmentation over the years; their widespread presence and contribution to its development are reflected in the careers of numerous persons of regional or national stature. Peculiarly Scottish traditions tended to fade in the process of acculturation but some at least became widely dispersed among the population. In absolute numbers, in individual achievements in many fields of endeavour, and through significant involvement in public affairs, Scottish people had a marked effect on the settlement and development of Western Canada.

Although the Scot and the fur trade is the subject of a separate chapter in this book, it should be noted that this activity accounted for the establishment of numerous trading posts, among them Cumberland House, built by Orkneymen in 1774, the first inland post of the Hudson's Bay Company and the oldest permanent settlement in Saskatchewan. Scottish fur traders or their descendants were among the first settlers about some of these posts, as far-flung, for example, as Lower Fort Garry in Manitoba, Fort Pelly in Saskatchewan, Fort Edmonton in Alberta, and Fort Victoria in British Columbia. Many retiring Company servants and their families found a home in the Red River Settlement, one of the objectives for the colony founded by Thomas Douglas, Fifth Earl of Selkirk, in 1811.[1]

Lord Selkirk primarily intended that his colony should provide a home for Scottish immigrants, along the lines of the settlements he had previously sponsored in Prince Edward Island and Upper Canada. He expected, too, that the colony would increase and diversify provisions for the trading posts and brigades of the Hudson's Bay Company, at the same time confirming the Company's title to the soil in face of the challenge of the Montreal traders who also were predominantly Scots. Assiniboia, the considerable inland district of Manitoba granted in absolute proprietorship to Selkirk, received its first colonists in 1812, a small party of Scots led over the arduous route from Hudson's Bay by Governor Miles Macdonell. Opposition to the colony from the North West Company, whose trade route and operations were threatened by it, reached a climax in the violence of 1816 during which Cuthbert Grant, of mixed Scottish and Indian parentage and natural leader of the plainsmen and Métis, led an attack on it and dispersed the residents. In the aftermath Selkirk organized a force in Canada, reoccupied the settlement, and restored it on a surer foundation. By the end of 1817 the colony was relatively secure, but growth thereafter was slow as frosts, floods and grasshopper infestations hampered progress. In 1821 the population is said to have reached 419, of whom 221 were Scots.[2]

After the union of the fur trading companies in 1821 the Métis were no longer incited against the colony and came to see it as a place of settlement for themselves. Cuthbert Grant himself became "Warden of the Plains" on behalf of the Hudson's Bay Company and founded the settlement of Grantown at White Horse Plains, west of Winnipeg. As the years passed many Scottish halfbreeds became prominent in the life of the Red River Settlement – for example, Captain William Kennedy, who commanded two of the expeditions which searched for evidence of Sir John Franklin, and James McKay, trader, freighter, legislator, and negotiator of Indian treaties.[4]

By 1870 "the farmsteads of the halfbreeds and the Orkney and Kildonan Scottish settlers presented an almost unbroken line along the west bank"[5] of the Red River. Farther west, along the Assiniboine, the emerging settlement of Portage la Prairie included many Scots, among them John McLean, the first farmer, 1862,[6] and the colourful Thomas Spence who inaugurated and assumed the presidency of the abortive "Republic of Portage la Prairie" in 1867.[7] The District of Assiniboia, despite the growth of other ethnic groups, reflected in its council the dominance of the Scots – the Macdonells, Semples, Christies, Finlaysons and McTavishs occupied the position of governor of Assiniboia for forty-two of the fifty-eight years from 1812 to 1870![8] Justice was administered, from 1839 to 1870, by the Recorder of Rupert's Land. There were four recorders in this period; Adam Thom and John Black served a total of nineteen years, and Dr. John Bunn, who was Scottish on his maternal side, served four years.[9] Actually the pure Scottish element at Red River could not have exceeded 700 people, of whom 240 were born in Scotland, in a population of 12,000 when Manitoba became a province in 1870, but many of the 4,083 "English halfbreeds" enumerated at that time must in fact have been of Scottish and Indian parentage.[10]

At first served by Anglican clergy, the Scottish Presbyterians at Red River secured the services of a minister only in 1851 in the person of Rev. John Black who built the stone church at Kildonan. Scottish names abound, however, among the pioneer clergy of the West. The Reverend James Nisbet, who joined Black in 1862, travelled overland in 1866 to found a mission on the Saskatchewan River some miles below Fort Carlton. James Isbister, son of an Orkneyman, was already the first settler there.[11] Nisbet called his mission Prince Albert, whence grew the modern city of that name. The McDougalls of the Methodist Church founded Morleyville, now Morley, Alberta, within a few years.

Aside from such missions, along with the few settlers gathered about them and the fur trading posts, there were still only the native peoples in the old North West Territories when that area was acquired by Canada at the same time as the founding of Manitoba. However, the way for settlement had been paved by a long line of explorers and surveyors associated with the fur trade, including Alexander Mackenzie and Simon Fraser. In 1841 and 1854 James Sinclair, free-trader son of an Orkneyman, had pioneered overland routes from Red River across the Rockies in conducting parties of settlers to the Oregon country.[12] Increasing interest in the 1850s in the possibilities of the West for settlement had also resulted in the dispatch of exploring expeditions from Great Britain and the old Province of Canada. The British (Palliser) expedition included Dr. James Hector, Scottish geologist, who was responsible for much of its journal and for its descriptions of the geological formations and mineral potential from the Great Lakes to Vancouver Island.[13] A principal figure in the Canadian (Dawson-Hind) expeditions,[14] which explored the eastern prairies, was Simon J. Dawson, Scottish-born civil engineer, who subsequently, in

1868, opened communication between Canada and Red River by what became known as the Dawson Route.

In British Columbia colonial government had replaced Hudson's Bay Company rule for some twenty years before that province's entry into Confederation. The Scottish presence, manifest in the several trading posts almost without exception established by Scots, could be discerned in the governing structure first of Vancouver Island and then of the mainland in the commanding figure of Governor James Douglas. Of eight men who served on the Legislative Council of Vancouver Island between its inception in 1850 and 1859,[15] probably no less than six were Scots, including John Tod, the noted fur trader who after his retirement in 1852 became a gentleman farmer at Victoria. David Cameron was appointed judge of the new Supreme Court of Vancouver Island in 1853, and in 1858 Matthew Baillie Begbie (later Chief Justice) became judge in the new Crown Colony of British Columbia where he was renowned for maintaining law and order during the gold rush. By 1853 the Puget Sound Agricultural Company, a subsidiary of the Hudson's Bay Company, had been assigned four large tracts of land at Victoria for farming purposes, and Kenneth McKenzie, a native of Scotland, was appointed bailiff for the new Company. Arriving in 1853, McKenzie vigorously promoted the development of the farms, and established a saw mill, flour mill, bakery, kilns, slaughter house, smithy and other facilities.[16] In 1862 a group of settlers was dispatched from Victoria to Cowichan Bay where names such as Bell, Duncan, Flett, Kier, McKay, Montgomery and Morton among the newcomers of the first two years signify the presence of a considerable number of Scots.[17] At that same time a numerous party, known as the Overlanders or Argonauts of '62, journeyed from Ontario and Quebec via Forts Garry and Edmonton to the Cariboo gold fields of B.C. Many of them were Scottish and some of them were to become permanent and substantial citizens of the province[18] – for example, Edinburgh-born Richard H. Alexander, businessman and civic official of Vancouver; Robert Burns McMicking, who organized an electric light plant and managed a telephone company at Victoria; Archibald McNaughton, postmaster at Quesnel; George Baillie, rancher and hotel owner at Lytton; John Andrew Mara, merchant and miller of Kamloops. Undoubtedly there were Scots among the other thousands who rushed into the interior during that decade but many of the gold seekers failed to take up permanent residence. The total population of British Columbia had declined by 1870 when an enumeration showed only 8,576 "whites," of whom the number of Scots was not recorded.[19]

Upon the acquisition of Manitoba and the North West Territories in 1870 the Canadian government retained their lands and resources for the new Dominion and initiated within the decade policies for their settlement and development, including the extinction of Indian claims, maintenance of law and order, institution of a survey system, provision of transportation and communication, and procedures for disposition of lands.

Scots played a part in the administration and execution of these policies, instituted, it should be remembered, in the first instance by federal governments headed by two Scottish-born prime ministers, John A. Macdonald and Alexander Mackenzie. Lieutenant-Governor Alexander Morris of Manitoba and the North West Territories was the principal commissioner in negotiating five Indian treaties in the West; and for the three treaties which covered virtually all of what became the settled areas of Alberta and Saskatchewan, all of the commissioners were Scots.[20] Law and order was imposed on this frontier through the North West Mounted Police, whose early officers included James F. Macleod, appointed assistant commissioner, 1874, commissioner, 1876-80, the founder of Forts Macleod and Calgary, and Lieutenant-Colonel A.G. Irvine, appointed assistant commissioner, 1875, and commissioner, 1880-1886. Much of the administration of western affairs was assigned to the Department of the Interior wherein another Scot, A.M. Burgess, became deputy minister for a significant period, 1883-1897. This department directed the topographical and other surveys which were basic to the disposition and settlement of the western lands.

Scottish names abound among the surveyors[21] who carried out arduous duties in remote areas under often difficult circumstances. Surveys for the route of a Pacific railway were conducted by Sandford Fleming, and the selection of the eventual route for it across the southern plains was influenced by the findings of the botanist-surveyor, John Macoun, who reported much more favourably on their agricultural possibilities than had the Palliser and Dawson-Hind expeditions. The federal government also sent geologists into the West, none more distinguished than George M. Dawson, who was responsible for numerous pioneer geological reports, including those on the lignite tertiary formation of the Territories, and the first geological survey of the Yukon, where Dawson City was named for him. He became assistant director of the Geological Survey of Canada in 1883 and director in 1895.

The federal government, in addition to initiating a homestead policy to attract settlers, made grants of land to colonization and railway companies, and also sold blocks of lands to developers. Construction of the first transcontinental railway was subsidized through land grants, such that the Canadian Pacific Railway became a huge landowner and promoter of settlement. Most significant in the founding and financing of this enterprise were two Scots, George Stephen and his cousin, Donald A. Smith. The latter had become a principal shareholder, and at length Governor of the Hudson's Bay Company which through its agreement with the Dominion government retained not only tracts of land about its posts but one-twentieth of the lands in the fertile belt of Western Canada. The Company's ancient fur trade was increasingly overshadowed by its land sales; its posts became trading centres for new communities, leading eventually to its modern department stores. Throughout its history the Company continued to recruit Scots, and three hundred years after its inception in 1670 the Company, now headquartered in Canada, still has in its directorate a number of men of Scottish ancestry.[22] Other major land developers in the West included the Galts, Sir Alexander and his son Elliott, who acquired a large tract for irrigation near Lethbridge, and the Saskatchewan Valley Land Company, organized by D.H. McDonald of Fort Qu'Appelle, son of an HBC factor, together with Colonel A.D. Davidson and Senator A.D. McRae. This Company purchased and settled a large area of government and railway lands between the Qu'Appelle Valley and Saskatoon in the early years of the twentieth century.

That period saw the building of another transcontinental railway, the Canadian Northern, the enterprise of William Mackenzie and Donald Mann, which opened up further areas to settlement. Meanwhile capital from Scotland had also been directed into prairie settlement, as illustrated in the huge Bell Farm at Indian Head in the 1880s which was financed by Scottish loans,[23] and in the Scottish Canadian Land and Settlement Association which in 1884 secured 500,000 acres from the CPR in the Turtle Mountain and Souris districts of Manitoba.[24] Dundee investors in American cattle enterprises had organized the Matador Land and Cattle Company in 1882 which extended its operations into the Saskatchewan Landing area north of Swift Current in 1904.[25] All of these land and colonization companies, the railway companies, the Hudson's Bay Company, together with the federal government, through advertising, subsidization and direct sponsorship attracted the flow of settlers among whom were many Scots.

The first satisfactory source of statistics relating to the origins of the peoples of Western Canada after Confederation is the census of Canada for 1881. In that year there were 3,892 Scots in B.C., 16,506 in Manitoba and 1,217 in the North West Territories, a total of 21,615 Scots in a population of 137,234 in the area now comprising the four western provinces. The major increase in the decade ending in 1881 had occurred in Manitoba, where the largest concentrations of Scots were then in the Winnipeg (2,470), Springfield (724), St. Andrew's (1,184), Mountain (713), and Portage (722) census sub-districts. In the North West Territories only the Prince Albert district in 1881 had a concentration of Scots (651) approaching those centres, and in British Columbia 917 Scots were enumerated in Victoria City, with the next largest group being 580 at Nanaimo. It is clear that the increase in Manitoba had not come in any large measure from Scotland. Canadian government immigration agents in Scotland during that decade made such comments as "a great many people are looking towards Manitoba" but recorded that only a few families had gone there each year.[26] In 1881 only 2,868 Manitobans had been born in Scotland; hence some 14,000 Scots in that province had been born in Canada, many of whom had recently migrated from Eastern Canada.

The special census of the North West Territories in 1884-85 showed 6,788 "Scotch" and 762 "Scotch halfbreeds," a remarkable influx in five years into the area which would become the Provinces of Saskatchewan and Alberta, and where the total population had reached 48,362, of whom 20,170 were Indians.[27] The major concentrations of Scots were in the provisional district of Assiniboia (4,762) and, within it, in the Broadview (2,123) and Qu'Appelle-Regina (1,710) census sub-districts.

Regina, the territorial capital, then had a population of perhaps five or six hundred but an analysis of the 195 male residents listed in the first Regina *Director* (1885) suggests that at least forty of them, over 20%, were Scots.[28] They represented a wide range of occupations, and many were obviously of influence in the affairs of the town, since they included several barristers, a banker, the postmaster, the school teacher, the deputy sheriff, the clerk of the court, a druggist, a brewer, an auctioneer, a surgeon, a clergyman, a surveyor, a Dominion Lands agent, such tradesmen as a painter, a tinsmith, several carpenters, a butcher, a printer, and the proprietors of five general stores, a furniture store, a book store, a lumber yard, a livery stable, and two boarding houses. They found themselves living in a town which in its initial administration and street names had a markedly Scottish flavor, the latter conferred for the most part in honour of the principals of its joint developers, the Canadian Pacific Railway and the Canada North West Land Company. The railway and the land company, with their astute Scottish-Canadian directors and financial backing, were responsible for the establishment and development of forty-seven townsites between Brandon and the eastern boundary of British Columbia, including Regina, Moose Jaw, Swift Current, Medicine Hat, and Calgary.[29] These townsites were initially administered by a commission of four trustees, comprised of R.B. Angus and Donald A. Smith for the CPR and E.B. Osler and William B. Scarth for the land company. At Regina the townsite trustees, except for their control of unsold lots, had given way by 1884 to a municipal government, headed by barrister David L. Scott, the first mayor, 1884-85, whose successor was Daniel Mowat, 1886-87.[30]

Already on the plains about Regina, stretching northward to Lumsden in the Qu'Appelle Valley, Ontario-born Scottish, such as the Balfour, Martin, Sheriffs and Mutch families, had homesteaded.[31] Farther east, as previously noted, the essentially rural Broadview census sub-district included many Scottish farmers. There Lady Cathcart's philanthropic efforts had led to the settlement of nearly 300 Scottish crofters at St. Andrew's and Benbecula, near Moosomin and Wapella, in 1883 and 1884.[32] This was the forerunner of subsequent attempts, financed by the British government, to send impoverished crofters and cottars from the Western Isles to Manitoba and the North West Territories.[33] In 1888 thirty families, 183 persons in all, were enabled by Her Majesty's Board of Commissioners established for the purpose to settle at Killarney, Manitoba. This work was then assigned to the Imperial Colonization Board which, in

1889, assisted another forty-nine families, a total of 252 persons, to take up homesteads near Saltcoats, NWT (now Saskatchewan). The Killarney settlement was a success whereas that at Saltcoats collapsed by 1900, largely due to adverse climatic conditions. While this colony failed, the board's objective of relieving the distress its settlers had suffered in Scotland was attained as they found employment in neighbouring towns or moved to then more prosperous farming districts.

Elsewhere groups of Scots settled independently on the land. Family ties and favourable reports from friends who had emigrated tended to lead Scots, like members of other ethnic groups, to the same districts where they might sustain traditional folkways and assist each other in the struggles of pioneering. One such district lay south of Wolseley, Saskatchewan, where between 1885 and 1907 there was a steady influx of Lowland settlers from Ayrshire, Perthshire, Aberdeenshire, and the Lothians.[34] They spread over four townships, with the rural post office and Presbyterian Kirk of Moffat the focal point of the community. Not all of these settlers had previous experience in farming; they included carpenters, harness-makers, blacksmiths, drapers, butchers, bricklayers, and well-trained stonemasons. Using field stone, with locally fired limestone and sand for mortar, the latter were responsible for building the fine stone houses which still distinguish Moffat from most settlements on the prairies, where frame structures usually replaced the original sod houses and log cabins.

Although it is not apparent that there were many Scottish group settlements, whether formally organized as at Killarney and Saltcoats, or independent aggregations as at Moffat, there is no question that Scots both from the homeland and Eastern Canada were well represented in the great flood of immigration which developed at the beginning of the twentieth century. Annual statistics confirm the number of arrivals from Scotland. In the year ended June 30, 1904, for example, the Canadian government agent at Glasgow reported that 12,627 persons of Scottish nationality had left for Canada, of whom according to destinations registered at the ports of entry in Eastern Canada, 3,391 intended to go to Manitoba, 1,005 to the North West Territories, and 445 to B.C.[35] Included therein would be 911 Scots who filed entry for homesteads and 171 unmarried male labourers recruited for farm employment. Their disposition throughout the West is impossible to determine, although occasional references such as "135 Scotch" received at the immigration hall, Calgary, in that year sometimes indicate the general localities in which they settled. Comparative figures five years later, for the year ended March 31, 1909, showed 11,810 arrivals from Scotland, of whom 1,886 were destined for Manitoba, 1,776 for Saskatchewan and Alberta, and 1,495 for B.C.[36] It is impossible to determine how many persons of Scottish ancestry may have been among the thousands of settlers from Eastern Canada in this period. By the time of the census of 1911 Scots numbered 282,991 of the total population of 1,715,189 in the four western provinces. The passage of another thirty

TABLE 1: Total and Scottish Populations, Western Provinces

	1881		1901		1911		1941	
	Total Population	Scots	Total Population	Scots	Total Population	Scots	Total Population	Scots
Manitoba	62,260	16,506	255,211	51,365	455,614	82,861	729,744	109,619
Sask.	NWT 25,515	1,217	158,940	21,501	492,432	70,753	895,992	108,919
Alberta					374,663	54,884	796,169	112,540
B.C.	49,459	3,892	178,657	31,068	392,480	74,493	817,816	152,677
Totals	137,234	21,615	592,808	103,934	1,715,189	282,991	3,239,721	483,755

Source: *Census of Canada*

years may be said to have brought to a close the whole period of settlement. Certainly by 1941 the vast bulk of the agricultural lands had been occupied, the forest and mining frontiers at least initially tapped, and virtually all of the urban communities founded. Pioneer settlements had grown and developed, and there had been a natural increase over one or two generations in the population, as well as the immigration which resumed after World War I. While a marked rural-urban shift in population was still to come, the prolonged drought and depression of the 1930s had prompted the internal migration of farmers from the southern prairies and of some city dwellers as well. On their own or with inadequate government assistance these people, Scots among them, trekked into the northern parklands to take up the axe, grub-hoe, and breaking plough in a second pioneering venture in one generation.[37] Others left the prairies for British Columbia. While recognizing that these developments must be taken into account, the census figures of 1941 are instructive in confirming the steady growth of population of Scottish origin (see Table 1) and in identifying communities where Scots had settled in substantial numbers.

Nowhere do the Scots appear to have become a majority of the population, but there were communities in which they represented more than their average proportion of 14.9% for all of Western Canada in 1941. In Winnipeg, centre of the first Scottish colony, Scots were still fully 18% of the population, and they represented over 22% in Calgary. Examples of other places where Scots exceeded the average were (approximate percentage in brackets): St. James, rural (23%), Minnedosa (28%), and Russell (27%) in Manitoba; Avonlea (35%), Saltcoats (23%), Wapella (29%), Lumsden (28%) and Lashburn (28%) in Saskatchewan; Banff (23%) and Carstairs (27%) in Alberta; and New Westminster (21%) in British Columbia.

The widespread dispersal of the Scots and their contributions to western settlement and development can be seen in the careers of many outstanding persons, only a few of whom can be identified here. Although, as we have seen, some Scottish settlers had never farmed, many of this "race of gardeners," as they have been called, brought with them knowledge and experience which was of benefit to prairie agriculture.[38] A catalogue of them would include Angus MacKay,[39] who became first superintendent of the Indian Head experimental farm and promoted tree planting and the dry-farming technique of summerfallowing, and Frank L. Skinner, who in his nursery at Dropmore developed many varieties of fruits and flowers.[40] It would also include pioneer importers and breeders of livestock such as Archibald Wright of Winnipeg,[41] who imported the first Holstein cattle to Western Canada and who grew the first sweet clover there, Glen Campbell, who imported Highland cattle for his ranch at Riding Mountain,[42] James D. McGregor,[43] who specialized in Aberdeen Angus cattle at Brandon and also directed the irrigation projects of the Southern Alberta Land Company near Medicine Hat, William Rutherford and John Oman, who managed pioneer sheep ranches at Maple Creek and Swift Current, respectively,[44] Major James Walker, first manager of the Cochrane ranch at Calgary,[45] and the noted horseman, livestock judge and educator, William John Rutherford,[46] who was first Dean of Agriculture at the University of Saskatchewan. Scots were also among the early large scale "bonanza" farmers; for example, J.W. Sandison at Brandon[47] and William R. Bell at Indian Head,[48] both of whom went bankrupt, while Adam MacKenzie of the Arden and Carberry districts[49] and James Bruce of Lashburn[50] were successful, the latter aided by an inheritance which enabled him to donate a hospital and a church to his community.

Scots were also active in the organization of farmers' co-operatives, one of the most notable being A.J. McPhail,[51] first President of the Saskatchewan Co-operative Wheat Producers, Ltd., and of the central selling agency of the three prairie wheat pools. Earlier, the pioneer Grain Growers' Grain Company had been enabled to survive through sales to the Scottish Co-operative Wholesale Society of Glasgow;[52] prairie co-operatives, especially Interprovincial Co-operatives Ltd., of which another Scot, James McCaig, was first president, maintained an association with that organization.[53] Scots were prominent, too, among the private grain merchants, flour millers, and founders of elevator companies. William and John Ogilvie, of the Montreal firm, were the pioneer wheat buyers in Manitoba, and with other grain merchants such as D.H. McMillan, C.G. Galt, and K. MacKenzie formed the Winnipeg Grain and Produce Exchange in 1887.[54]

Scots were of course pioneers in other lines of business across the West. They were among the first merchants in many towns, representative of them being John A. McDougall in Edmonton,[55] James Clinkskill in both Battleford and Saskatoon,[56] R.D. McNaughton in Moosomin,[57] Wm. Douglas in Leduc,[58] W.F. Cameron in Vernon,[59] Tweed and Ewart, partners in the first store in Medicine Hat,[60] and Robert Gerrie, who opened the first furniture store west of the Great Lakes in Winnipeg in 1873.[61] The variety of businesses and industries founded by Scots is further illustrated in the careers of Wm. C. Garson, who established the Garson Quarries at Tyndall,[62] Duncan Macarthur, Winnipeg banker,[63] John McKechnie, founder of the Vulcan Iron Works, Winnipeg,[64] and such lumber millers and merchants as Douglas C. Cameron[65] of Rat Portage (Kenora) and Winnipeg and D.H. MacDowall[66] of Prince Albert. Colonel A.D. McRae, in association with Mackenzie and Mann, extended his interests beyond prairie lands and an important saw mill at New Westminster to found the Canadian Western Lumber Company, and entered the salmon canning industry in 1911.[67] H.R. MacMillan, founder of an exporting company at Vancouver, developed one of the largest lumber companies on the continent.[68] The Galts opened the coal mines at Lethbridge; Robert Dunsmuir also went into coal mining on Vancouver Island, becoming "the province's first capitalist," with interests in iron works, railway and steamship lines as well.[69] The Scottish enterprise in early transportation was duplicated in the air age in the success of G.W.G. McConachie who began his career as a northern bush pilot and founded an air transport firm, later absorbed by Canadian Pacific Airlines in which he rose to be president.[70]

The influence of Scots, noted in the administration of the old district of Assiniboia and in the colonial period of British Columbia, is also evident in the politics and government of the western provinces after Confederation. The first premiers of Alberta, Alex Rutherford, 1905-1910, and Saskatchewan, Walter Scott, 1905-1916, were Scottish. Both provinces have had ten premiers to 1975 since they were founded 68 years ago in 1905 and in both provinces five premiers have been Scots, occupying the position for a total of 21 years in Alberta and 50 years in Saskatchewan, the latter accounted for in part by the lengthy term of Thomas C. Douglas, 1944-1961. Manitoba since 1870 has had sixteen ministries to 1975, four of which covering a total of twenty-five years were headed by Scots, including John Norquay, 1878-1887, and to which could be added a fifth ministry, the nine-year term, 1958-1967, of Duff Roblin (Scottish only on his maternal side). In British Columbia at least eight Scots have served as premier, for a total of 41 years since 1871, including the twenty-year term of W.A.C. Bennett, 1952-1972. No attempt has been made to analyse the ethnicity of the membership of the ministries or legislatures of the four provinces, but it is of relevance that the first Saskatchewan ministry was comprised of Walter Scott, James Calder, J.H. Lamont, and W.R. Motherwell, certainly the first three of whom were Scottish, and Motherwell, born in Ontario, was probably of Irish-Scottish ancestry. In addition to the premiership, the Scots have been well-represented in the western legislatures in view of their electoral success in the federal arena.

Scottish representation in the House of Commons from Western Canada far exceeded their numerical proportion of the population. This is not to suggest that either federally or provincially there was a Scottish position or cause; the evidence confirms that many Scots took an active interest in public affairs and politics, the latter by no means confined to any one party. In office and in opposition they represented the traditional Liberal and Conservative parties as well as being active in the later Social Credit and CCF-NDP parties, and in the Progressive movement of the 1920s. No less than fourteen of thirty-nine Progressives elected to the House of Commons from Western Canada in 1921 were Scots, including such leading figures as T.A. Crerar and Robert Forke of Manitoba and Robert Gardiner of Alberta. Also elected, as a Labour member, was William Irvine of Alberta. A recent analysis of twenty-nine persons in the "middle leadership" of the Progressive Party in Saskatchewan showed that twelve of them were either born in Scotland or of Scottish descent.[71] Scots had earlier participated in nineteenth century farm protest movements, including the Northwest Farmers' Union, organized at Brandon in 1883, of which Dr. Alexander Fleming[72] was president, and the Patrons of Industry, of whom James M. Douglas of Tantallon was an exponent and successful candidate for Parliament in 1896.[73] They were

87

also leaders in the organization of grain growers' associations after the turn of the century. In the territorial association, founded 1902, W.R. Motherwell and John Millar were first president and secretary respectively. The secretary of the Manitoba Association, formed the following year, was Roderick McKenzie of Brandon, and the first board of directors included at least three more Scots.[74]

These illustrations of early concern about settlers' problems and of active participation in the organized farm movement and in politics generally demonstrate a strong public-spiritedness and social conscience among the Scots who settled in Western Canada. Combined with their business acumen and enterprise, and their contributions in other fields noted herein or examined elsewhere in this volume, it can be maintained that the Scots wielded an influence beyond their numerical strength in the population. They were probably less successful in preserving a Scottish way of life in the West. There were, as we have seen, few strictly Scottish settlements, and Scottish settlers, even where they comprised a sizable part of the community, tended to merge culturally with their neighbours. It does not appear that schools were taught in Gaelic or that the language persisted much beyond the first generation. Although some journals were once published in Winnipeg, no Scottish press flourished in Western Canada.[75] To be sure there were any number of Scottish editors of pioneer newspapers, such as P.G. Laurie of the *Saskatchewan Herald* (Battleford),[76] John Robson of the New Westminster *British Columbian* and Victoria *Colonist*,[77] and Richard Waugh of the *Nor'West Farmer* (Winnipeg).[78] Various Scottish societies were founded and, with annual observances of Robert Burns' birthday, persisted. Pipe bands, traditional dancing, and to some extent Highland games, also flourished in the West. The game of curling was imported, and often played on the river ice or outdoor rinks, as it was at Prince Albert and Battleford. Prior to 1890 four Scottish devotees from near the former place loaded their "rocks on a toboggan, drawn by a team of ponies, and walked alongside" all the way to Fort Qu'Appelle where they took the train to curl in the Winnipeg bonspeil![79] It is noteworthy that curling and Scottish dancing and music were adopted by the generality of the population, and, in a recent manifestation of that trend, the Province of Saskatchewan adopted an official tartan, duly registered with the Lyon King of Arms of Scotland, in 1961. George Bryce concluded his 1911 volume on the Scotsman in Western Canada with the assurance that here "the Scottish immigrant will find a favourable, remunerative, and socially suitable sphere of action for himself and his children."[80] In retrospect, despite some failures and periods of drought and depression, Scottish settlers found that to be their experience; moreover, they had helped significantly to make it true for themselves and for all newcomers.

NOTES

1. The literature on the Red River settlement is extensive; this summary is based on the relevant chapters in W.L. Morton, *Manitoba. A History*, rev. ed. (Toronto: University of Toronto Press, 1967).
2. G. Donaldson, *The Scots Overseas* (London: Robert Hale, 1966), p. 138.
3. M.A. McLeod, *Cuthbert Grant of Grantown* (Toronto: McClelland and Stewart, 1963).
4. A.R. Turner, "James McKay," *Dictionary of Canadian Biography* (Toronto: University of Toronto Press, 1970), pp. 473-474.
5. Morton, p. 151.
6. G. McEwan, *Fifty Mighty Men* (Saskatoon: Modern Press, 1958), Ch. XLVIII.
7. *Ibid.*, Ch. XLIV.
8. G. Bryce, *The Scotsman in Canada* (Toronto: Musson Book Co., n.d.), II 200-201.
9. R. Stubbs, *Four Recorders of Rupert's Land* (Winnipeg: Peguis Publishers, 1967).
10. Canada, *Sessional Papers*, 1871, No. 20, p. 92.
11. Sask. Archives, SHS File no. 29, "James Isbister."
12. D. Geneva Lent, *West of the Mountains* (Seattle: University of Washington Press, 1963), Chapters 6, 11-14.
13. A.R. Turner, "Palliser of the Triangle," *The Beaver*, Autumn, 1957.
14. L.H. Thomas, "The Hind and Dawson Expeditions," *The Beaver*, Winter, 1958.
15. Margaret Ormsby, *British Columbia: A History* (Toronto: Macmillan of Canada, 1958), pp. 122-123.
16. *Craigflower Manor*. A National and Provincial Historic Site (Victoria, B.C., n.d.).
17. E. Blanche Norcross, *The Warm Land* (Nanaimo: Evergreen Press, 1959).
18. M.S. Wade, *The Overlanders of '62* (Victoria: King's Printer, 1931), pp. 158-174.
19. Canada, *Sessional Papers*, 1872, No. 10, Appendix Z, p. 152.
20. For text of negotiations, signatories, etc., see A. Morris, *Treaties of Canada with the Indians of Manitoba and the North-West Territories* (Toronto, 1880).
21. Canada, *Sessional Papers*, 1892, No. 13, Pt. VI, List of Dominion Land Surveyors, 1872-1891.
22. E.g., G.T. Richardson, governor; A.J. MacIntosh, deputy governor; J.R. Murray, managing director, D.S. McGivern, managing director, retail stores (Source: *Financial Post Directory of Directors*, 1971).
23. E.C. Morgan, "The Bell Farm," *Saskatchewan History*, XIX, 57.
24. Norman Macdonald, *Canada. Immigration and Colonization, 1841-1903* (Toronto: Macmillan of Canada, 1966), p. 247.

25. W. Turrentine Jackson, *The Enterprising Scot* (Edinburgh: University Press, 1968), p. 299. For operations in Saskatchewan see Sask. Archives, Matador Land and Cattle Company records, 1905-1924.

26. Canada, *Sessional Papers*, 1875, No. 40, Appendix 40, p. 129.

27. Canada, *Census of the Three Provisional Districts of the North-West Territories*, 1884-5 (Ottawa, 1886).

28. *Regina Directory for 1885* (Regina: Leader Steam Print, n.d.).

29. J.B. Hedges, *Building the Canadian West* (New York: Macmillan Company, 1939), pp. 85-87.

30. Earl G. Drake, *Regina. The Queen City* (Toronto: McClelland and Stewart, 1955), p. 239.

31. Sask. Archives, S.H.S. files no. 2, 42, 44, 58.

32. James N. MacKinnon, *A Short History of the Pioneer Scotch Settlers of St. Andrew's, Sask.* (n.d., n.p.).

33. Kent Stuart, "Scottish Crofter Colony, Saltcoats, 1889-1904," *Saskatchewan History*, XXIV, 40-50.

34. Kay Parley, "Moffat, Assiniboia, North-West Territories," *Saskatchewan History* XX, 32-36.

35. Canada, *Sessional Papers*, 1905, No. 25, Pt. II.

36. *Ibid.*, 1910, No. 25, Pt. II.

37. Sask. Archives, Department of Municipal Affairs, L.I.D. Branch, Northern Settlers Re-establishment and Relief files (e.g. Angus and Hugh Black, Saskatoon to Loon Lake; George Gordon, Langham to Paddockwood; Walter Guthrie, Moose Jaw to Loon Lake, etc.)

38. Ian Finlay, *The Highlands* (London: B.T. Batsford Ltd., 1963), p. 79.

39. G. MacEwan, *The Sodbusters* (Toronto: Thos. Nelson and Sons, 1948), pp. 27-33.

40. *Ibid.*, pp. 232-236.

41. *Ibid.*, pp. 140-145.

42. MacEwan, *Fifty Mighty Men*, pp. 116-122.

43. MacEwan, *The Sodbusters*, pp. 66-72.

44. Sask. Archives, Clippings file: "76" Ranch.

45. Sheilagh S. Jameson, "The Era of the Big Ranches: The Romantic Period of Southern Alberta's History," unpublished ms., 1968, p. 7f. (Copy in Saskatchewan Archives)

46. MacEwan, *The Sodbusters*, pp. 53-59.

47. MacEwan, *Fifty Mighty Men*, pp. 308-314.

48. Morgan, *op. cit.*

49. MacEwan, *The Sodbusters*, pp. 20-26.

50. Sask. Archives, S.H.S. file no. 7, "James Bruce."

51. H.A. Innis, ed., *The Diary of A.J. McPhail* (Toronto: University of Toronto Press, 1940).

52. Hopkins Moorhouse, *Deep Furrows* (Toronto: George J. McLeod, 1918), pp. 103-107.

53. J.F. C. Wright, *Prairie Progress* (Saskatoon: Modern Press, 1956), pp. 16, 120.

54. H.G.L. Strange, *A Short History of Prairie Agriculture* (Winnipeg: Searle Grain Company, 1954), Ch. 10.
55. J.G. McGregor, *A History of Alberta* (Edmonton: Hurtig, 1972), P. 153.
56. James Clinkskill, "Experiences of Starting and Conducting a Store in Saskatchewan," *Saskatchewan History*, XVII, pp. 24-30.
57. J.N. MacKinnon, *Moosomin and Its Pioneers* (Moosomin: World-Spectator, n.d.), pp. 6-7.
59. *Vernon. Diamond Jubilee. 1892-1951* (Vernon: Vernon News Ltd., 1952), p. 5.
60. J.W. Morrow, *Early History of the Medicine Hat Country* (Medicine Hat: Val Marshall Printing, n.d.), p. 20.
61. *Pioneers and Early Citizens of Manitoba* (Winnipeg: Manitoba Library Assn., 1971), p. 83.
62. *Ibid.*, p. 83.
63. *Ibid.*, p. 128.
64. *Ibid.*, p. 142.
65. Bryce, p. 359.
66. G. Abrams, *Prince Albert: The First Century* (Saskatoon: Modern Press, 1966).
67. Ormsby, p. 357.
68. Article on MacMillan, *Encyclopedia Canadiana*.
69. Ormsby, p. 285.
70. J. McGregor, pp. 274-279.
71. L. Courville, "The Saskatchewan Progressives," unpublished M.A. thesis, University of Saskatchewan, Regina Campus, 1971, pp. 223-235.
72. *Pioneers and Early Citizens of Manitoba*, p. 78.
73. Gilbert Johnson, "James Moffat Douglas," *Saskatchewan History*, VII, pp. 47-51.
74. Moorhouse, p. 295.
75. Bryce, p. 422.
76. A.R. Turner, ed., "The Letters of P.G. Laurie," *Saskatchewan History*, XIV, pp. 41-63.
77. Ormsby, pp. 177.
78. *Pioneers and Early Citizens of Manitoba*, pp. 247-248.
79. *Saskatchewan Curling Association Golden Jubilee, 1904-1945* (Regina: 1954), p. 32.
80. Bryce, p. 430.

SIX

The Highland Catholic Tradition in Canada

R. MacLean

The largest groups of Scottish Catholics settled in the Glengarry district of eastern Ontario, Prince Edward Island and eastern Nova Scotia. Though there were other pockets of settlement in Ontario, Quebec, at the Red River, and other western communities, it was mainly in the above-named regions that their traditions developed. While it may be risky to write on a tradition it must also be borne in mind that history must include attitudes and impressions, the material from which traditions are made.

Canadians have usually referred to the Scottish presence in Canadian history without making any strong distinctions between Highlander/ Lowlander or Catholic/Protestant. The general effect of this lack of categorization has been beneficial, for it has largely ignored certain aspects of the Scottish historical past which might possibly have led to a re-opening of old wounds in the New World.[1] For most Scots in Canada it has been sufficient that they be known as Scots or as Canadians of Scottish origin. The common homeland bound them together, regardless of their former geographical or religious situation in Scotland. Yet for anyone who has made any attempt to understand the Scottish-Canadian character it is quite evident that there are definite differences among those of Scottish background and that such distinctions have in part determined their attitudes and roles in Canada. In effect, they have helped to mould views concerning man and his role in Canadian society. They should not therefore be lightly dismissed.

One of the most obvious differences in those with a Scottish background has been the factor of religion, particularly the views held by Presbyterians and by those of the Roman Catholic faith. Those within Presbyterianism have been numerous and have occasioned remarks on the propensity of Presbyterians to dispute fine theological points.[2] It may also be argued the tensions within this denomination[3] have been creative. Certainly there was, in the Presbyterian fold, an opportunity for the concerned individual to express his views. The organization allowed for a greater participation in church affairs through the realm of debate and discussion. Such was not the tradition in the more tightly-structured church of the Roman Catholics; the hierarchical pyramid distributed authority from the peak downward and assembly meetings were not a part of the system. They were, however, assured of security and therefore had little compulsion for debate and discussion. This basic difference in style and orientation, it is suggested, had a definite influence on the subsequent roles played by Presbyterians and Roman Catholics in Canada.[4] Often criticized as being motivated by the cult of success, the individual Presbyterian would be described by some as the typical Canadian. This is both unfair and inaccurate, for while Presbyterians have made an enormous contribution to Canada's historical development, other groups of different religious and ethnic backgrounds have counterbalanced this stereotyped Presbyterian projection. One such group has been the Roman Catholic Highlanders.[5] Like other Scots, they are found in every province and territory of Canada.

This characteristic of mobility has been noted of Scots for centuries and even during the so-called Middle Ages they could be found in many countries of Europe as traders, teachers, religious or soldiers. The urge to move was also common to those who came to the New World and the early records of our fur trading companies reveal the names of many Scots. The voyages of men such as David Thompson, Alexander MacKenzie and Simon Fraser also bear testimony to this fact. Generally, the Scots, including the Highland Catholics, did not tend to remain together in specific geographical areas for long periods of time; though some stayed and carried on their traditional life style, many others moved to compete elsewhere. Largely through the traditions preserved in the regions mentioned above it is possible to discern patterns rather different from those of other ethnic-religious groups. In the changes which occurred between the late eighteenth and mid-nineteenth centuries, we witness the emergence of a sub-culture that had become an integral part of the Canadian mosaic.

By the 1850s these Highland Catholics had well fashioned their own society in the New World and their traditions were solidly established. They were less Scottish and more Canadian or Nova Scotian, or Islanders. Completely at ease in this society, they had been active participants in all religious, economic, educational and political developments. Their life pattern was their own and in the rural areas it was to remain essentially unchanged until World War II. It is true that they were becoming Anglicized and that the Gaelic was losing its grip, but other cultural traits and traditions have survived to the present time. In studying their traditions it is fair to argue that, with the exception of later patterns of outmigration, these were formed by the 1850s.

The most westerly of what may be considered one of the Highland Catholic regions in Canada, Glengarry, is also the most easterly county of the Province of Ontario. Alexandria, named after the first Bishop, Alexander Macdonell (Alastair Mhor), located approximately midway between the St. Lawrence and Ottawa Rivers, is considered to be the centre of the county.[6] The Scottish defeat at Culloden and the subsequent economic changes were the remote causes of this Glengarry settlement, for many Scots emigrated to America in search of greater opportunities. Some joined British regiments and fought for the King during the American Revolution, only thirty years after Culloden.

When the hostilities finally terminated in 1783 it was evident that they could not remain in their former locations; British North America would be their new home and thousands trudged northward. The families of many of the soldiers had been departing during the last years of the war, to be reunited later with the husbands and fathers. In 1783 the King's Royal Regiment of New York and the Royal Highland Emigrant Regiment were disbanded; the men moved northward in search of a new life.[7] The Catholics among them asked to be allowed to settle in a body and the government tried to meet their request. As a result several strong Catholic colonies were planted in Glengarry and Stormont.[8] Other Catholic Loyalists, though not Scottish, were attracted to the region; also among the disbanded members of the Royal Highland Emigrants were many Presbyterians whose chaplain, Reverend John Bethune, acquired a 3000-acre grant near Williamstown where he built the first Presbyterian church in Upper Canada.[9]

The Presbyterians and Catholics in those areas shared many basic traditions; their loyalty to the Crown, their repugnance toward certain aspects of society to the south, and, for many, their common Scottish inheritance. The religious hatreds which had kept them apart in Scotland were largely ignored or sublimated; pioneer conditions and common political problems helped in forcing a greater tolerance.

The Catholic settlers received their first Gaelic-speaking priest in 1785:

> Sir:
> Having laid before the King a memorial of Mr. Roderick MacDonell, stating that at the solicitation of a considerable number of Scots Highlanders and other subjects of the Roman Catholic persuasion who, prior to the last war, were inhabitants of the back settlements of the Province of New York, and to whom, in consideration of their loyalty and services, lands have lately been assigned in the higher parts of Canada, he is desirous of joining them in order to serve them in the capacity of a clergyman, in the humble hope, that on the arrival at the settlement, he shall be allowed by Government an annual subsistence for the discharge of that duty.[10]

The priest was Reverend Roderick Macdonell of the family of Leek, the man who was to make possible the success later enjoyed by Bishop Alexander Macdonell. Though his territory extended south to the Mohawk Valley and westward to Illinois, he thoroughly enjoyed working with his Gaelic-speaking Scots in Glengarry and Stormont. With the assistance of kinsmen in the North West Company, most of whom were Catholic, he completed the first stone church, St. Andrew's, Stormont, in 1792.[11] Presbyterian Scots also made contributions to the building of the edifice; the frontier was doing what post-Reformation animosity had made impossible in Scotland.[12] Reverend Roderick Macdonell was joined by Reverend Alexander "Scotus" Macdonell[13] who led the entire parish of Knoydart in Glengarry, Scotland, to the New World.[14] Some passengers disembarked at Ile St. Jean but the great majority continued on to the Glengarry district. "Of those who came, not all were Catholic, but the Catholic settlers, as a rule, banded together and formed groups where, later on, missions were opened or parishes were formed – thus St. Andrew's, thus St. Raphael's, thus Alexandria, etc."[15] During the decade of the 1780s others arrived from Scotland and as the population west of the Ottawa River increased, largely through Loyalist migration, there began an agitation for a separate province for those of British extraction. Partly as a result of such agitation the Constitutional Act of 1791 was passed in the British Parliament; among its provisions was one creating two provinces, Upper Canada for those generally west of the Ottawa River, Lower Canada for the French Canadians to the east. On June 16, 1792, Lieutenant-Governor Simcoe issued a proclamation dividing the province into counties, the easternmost of which were styled Glengarry, Stormont and Dundas.[16]

The people of Glengarry remained isolated during the early decades of settlement and as a result the oral culture remained strong. "It was the old man's delight to take me on his knee, while he sat on the old log bridge, and tell me of times gone by, of strange adventures, of giant men, of haunted hills, of blessings and of curses."[17] As with their fellow Scots in Nova Scotia, the bard held an important cultural ranking:

> The bard is old but tall and of a dignified bearing. His long flowing white beard gives him almost a venerable look, his memory is unbelievably retentive; the unwritten songs and tales which entertained our grandfathers, and their grandfathers before them, he still remembers word for word . . . his marvellous memory has permitted him to retain almost everthing of interest in genealogy, history and folklore.[18]

As early as the 1790s the Glengarry Scots were making their presence felt in other avenues of Upper Canadian life.[19] The influence of the Catholic Highlanders was to find its fullest expression under Reverend Alexander Macdonell, an astute cleric who cultivated the lines of civil and ecclesiastical power very shrewdly in efforts to advance the welfare of his religious followers. Not only was he the first Roman Catholic bishop of Upper Canada but he also led the way in promoting the temporal advancement of his people. In education, and particularly in aligning the faithful with the British connection, the man showed strong qualities of leadership. "An ardent patriot and Conservative, he saw no inconsistency in defending Catholicism and British interests, at a time when Catholics were not admitted to full citizenship in the British Empire."[20] It has also been said that support of Tory rule was secondary to his desire to extend Catholicism; McGee is reputed to have called him "the greatest old Tory in Canada."[21] In addition to building schoolhouses and churches, he supervised the training of native clergy and more than 40 were trained during his tenure, with much of the expense borne by himself.

Appointed a bishop in 1819, he was also made a legislative councillor in 1831; he shrewdly used both positions to advance the interests of his people, for he realized that concessions to Catholics were made for political reasons. Constantly, and sometimes successfully, he sought government aid for Catholic schools and teachers.[22] In return he gave the government of the day strong support and was outspoken in his views on American republicanism and the radicalism of William Lyon MacKenzie.[23] By 1828, there were at least 36,435 Catholics in Upper Canada[24] and their growing numbers forced the government to listen to requests.[25] Macdonell cultivated good relations with the Protestant population and a healthy rapport existed between him and his non-Catholic friends:

> A tablet was set up to his memory in his church at St. Raphael's by the Highland Society of Upper Canada. It is not without significance that the motion for its erection was made in the Society by the Rev. Hugh Urquhart, Presbyterian and late Headmaster of the Grammar School at Cornwall. While Roman, the Bishop's work and approach had always been Catholic.[26]

Bishop Macdonell had no problem in being accepted as a Scot and in his way he made many friends among his Presbyterian countrymen. Along with William McGillivary of the North West Company, he was one of the founders of the Highland Society in Canada.[27] Religious differences that may have existed could often be sublimated under a common sense of ancestry and tradition. In 1852 there were 3,228 Macdonells or MacDonalds in Glengarry and thirty other clans numbered from 50 to 545 each.[28] It is hardly surprising that their Scottish ancestry should be a relative source of unity.

Though rather isolated at Glengarry, the Highlanders, Catholic and Protestant, soon made themselves known in every area of provincial life, even to becoming members of the "Establishment." Alexander (Sheriff) McDonell represented Glengarry in the House of Assembly;[29] his brother Angus represented York; another Angus McDonell (Sandaig, Glengarry) was also in the Assembly in 1804. All were Catholics and Alex (Sheriff) was elected as Speaker in the session which opened in 1805.[30] Two other brothers, John and Hugh Macdonell, were members of Simcoe's first Parliament in 1792-96.[31]

> Were not Glengarry's men, even within that generation, to take their places among the country's leading citizens? In law there was Angus Macdonell, member and first president of the Law Society of Ontario, 1792; in commerce, Alexander Macdonell, Greenfield, and Finnan

Macdonell, chief factors of the Hudson' Bay Company; in exploration, Simon Fraser, discoverer of the Fraser River, whose remains lie buried here at St. Andrew's; in politics, Colonel John Macdonell, M.P., first Speaker of the House of Assembly, 1792; in war, Colonel Macdonell, A.D.C. to General Sir Isaac Brock, the hero of Queenston Heights; in education and religion, the Honourable and Right Reverend Alexander Macdonell, first Bishop of Ontario; in diplomacy, Hugh Macdonell, consul-general in Algiers. But enough; these and the Colonel Chisholms, the Colonel Frasers, the Sandfield Macdonalds, and a host of others, have their names written on the pages of Canadian history for all to read.[32]

The society of Glengarry was rapidly maturing in the 1820s; the log cabins of the original settlers had almost completely disappeared and were replaced by frame, or occasionally brick, structures. Properties were being improved or enlarged; those not wishing to remain in agriculture were seeking opportunities elsewhere. By 1824 there were 7,084 people in Glengarry alone.[33] This had increased to 10,333 by 1831;[34] coach roads, though not always providing comfortable rides, were common, and informed discussion on public issues in Upper Canadian society was quite noticeable.

As one might expect from the foregoing the Macdonells were the most prominent of all the Glengarry settlers. "Of the members elected to the Assembly from Glengarry from 1791 to 1840, all were connected either by blood or marriage with the Macdonells who came to America on the *Pearl* in 1773, except Alexander McMartin and John Cameron."

Generally, it appears that the Highland Catholics accepted the existing political situation partly out of self-interest, partly from deference to those in authority. If any of them thought along radical lines there is little evidence to suggest that they so acted. Bishop Macdonell even cautioned those of his followers who supported the Reformers instead of Lieutenant-Governor Bond Head.[35] For such loyalty to established authority he was praised by the Orange Order although he also had his differences with members of that body.[36] The same loyalty was given to the government during William Lyon MacKenzie's efforts towards abrupt changes in the political system. Generally, he reflected the views of his people. They and their ancestors had supported British institutions and causes at Quebec in 1759, during the American Revolution and in the War of 1812. They were not about to change drastically for William Lyon MacKenzie.

The expansion of the settlement was steady, without dramatic changes. The decade between 1841 and 1851 represented the period of fastest growth, for the population rose from 12,546 to 17,596.[37] The highest population figure in the history of the district was reached in 1891 with 22,447. Thereafter there was a slight decline in each decade as out-migration continued to other parts of Ontario and the western provinces.[38] Throughout the nineteenth and early twentieth centuries the population was heavily Scottish and approximately 50% Catholic, the latter figure increasing throughout the twentieth century.[39]

The value of farm produce had increased by mid-century to the point where it was estimated at $4,006,952 in 1861, with the value of livestock at $660,548.[40] This expansionist trend continued through to the last decade of the century, but with increasing farm mechanization and a diminished demand for such skills as blacksmithing and carriage-making, the non-farm dweller dependent on such trades moved elsewhere. Out-migration had been a fact of life with the Glengarry Scots almost from the beginning. As in Nova Scotia, the attractions of family life were not irresistible to people with a marginal agricultural background. Moreover, the district had developed into a comfortable routine; like others in Canada West they had adapted to the Act of Union and responsible government, though not entirely without complaints. Through a combination of older cultural traits and adaptation to New World conditions, these Catholic Highlanders had fashioned their own society.

There are certain differences, as well as similarities, to be noted in the conditions of the Highland Catholics in Prince Edward Island, even in a brief treatment of their story. The first significant settlement began with the Glenaladale pioneers in 1772, though some Highlanders, "Scots by Montgomery," and others, had come earlier.[41] As in the Glengarry district the name of one priest stands out strongly in memory: this was Reverend Angus MacEachern, who arrived in 1790 and who remained to become the first Bishop of Charlottetown. During the pioneer period he, more than any other, provided leadership and spiritual guidance to the Highland Catholics of Prince Edward Island and eastern Nova Scotia. His tenure corresponds roughly to that of Bishop Macdonell in Glengarry;[42] their contributions were similar, for they firmly established both Catholicism and an ethnic influence in their respective areas.

Organized by Captain John Macdonald, the Laird of Glenaladale, a group of 210 Highlanders left Scotland aboard the ship *Alexander* on May 1, 1772, intending to improve their situation on the Island of St. John. Captain Macdonald's attention had been drawn to the island by letters received from its earliest Scottish settlers, a party of disbanded Fraser Highlanders who had settled there after the fall of Quebec.[43] Approximately 100 of the group came from Uist, while the others, among whom were many Macdonalds, came from the mainland of Scotland.[44] Their departure differed from the majority, for they left for religious[45] as well as economic reasons. Settling initially at an area where Captain Macdonald had originally purchased lands, they gave it the name of Scotch Fort. With them was the Reverend James Macdonald, a cousin of Captain John, who had chosen to accompany his countrymen; he spoke Gaelic, English, Italian and French, having learned the last two languages while studying in Rome. His ability in French was appreciated by the Acadian families already on the island and living around Malpeque.[46] Father Macdonald remained there as a missionary with the Acadians and Highlanders until his death in 1785. Also with the immigrants was Doctor Roderick Macdonald, another cousin of Captain John.

Since Captain John Macdonald owned the lands and was willing only to lease them, some of the settlers left Scotch Fort[47] within the first few years in an attempt to get land of their own in Cape Breton or elsewhere.[48] In this way, settlement was dispersed throughout the island with the original settlement, Scotch Fort, becoming a distributing depot. Those who came in the 1790s and early 1800s tended to move to other parts of the island, particularly the area now known as King's County. By the mid-nineteenth century the Scottish-born were heavily concentrated in western and southeastern Queen's County and widely scattered in King's and Prince as well.[49] Some of the early settlers were recruited for the British Army during the Revolutionary War and in conjunction with a body of Nova Scotia Highlanders, those recruited became the Second Battalion of the Royal Highland Emigrant Regiment.[50] Another well-known group of settlers who came together were those brought over by Lord Selkirk in 1803, settling at Orwell Bay.

The population expanded[51] relatively slowly during the final decades of the eighteenth century, but through natural increase and immigration it increased quite rapidly in the first three decades of the nineteenth.[52] People on the island had been exporting agricultural goods since the 1790s and their export figures rose dramatically by the 1820s, with significant amounts of oats and potatoes. During the same period the occupied and improved acreage increased considerably, as did the number of livestock.[53] Generally, such expansion continued in most categories until the early 1880s;[54] it was about this time also that the highest population of the nineteenth and the first half of the twentieth centuries was recorded.[55] Like their Highland brethren in Nova Scotia, these Islanders were not particularly noted for being, as a group, good farmers. Many combined fishing or lumbering with their agricultural endeavours, often to the detriment of the last-named operation. The routine and drudgery of nineteenth century farming operations appeared to have little appeal when contrasted with the greater freedom to be found in other occupations. Undoubtedly, this was a factor in the high rate of out-migration later in the century; the family farms could accommodate only a fairly fixed population and many people had little desire to remain in the occupation anyway.

As in Glengarry and eastern Nova Scotia, it was the clergy who provided the initial leadership in education. During 1831, in an effort to supply native clergy, Bishop MacEachern used his house as a college. Having been made Bishop of Charlottetown in 1829, hereby gaining greater independence from the Bishop of Quebec,[56] he was anxious to meet in his way one of his most pressing needs. This venture also marked the beginning of what may be termed higher education in Prince Edward Island. This first institution, Saint Andrew's, was later replaced by St. Dunstan's, founded by Reverend Bernard Macdonald, the first native

Islander to be ordained to the priesthood, and the successor of Bishop MacEachern in 1835.[57] It was Bishop Macdonald, and Bishop Peter MacIntyre who succeeded him, who bore the responsibility of gaining an educational system suitable to the Catholic population. Scores of priests, many of them descendants of Highland Catholics, received their early training in the above-named institutions and went on to service in other parts of Canada and the United States.[58] By mid-century the Catholics were receiving the guidance of some of their native clergy and though they were drawn into local religious feuds of the period they were apparently not singled out for criticism as Highland Catholics. Here, as elsewhere, their approach was moderate. However, in issues involving the entire Catholic population, such as separate schools, they generally supported their fellow non-Scottish Catholics. At Confederation, when the school issue was involved, they followed the lead of their bishop and gave it their support through the Assembly.

The evidence of a Catholic tradition is stronger in Nova Scotia than in the other regions. Catholics were present in greater numbers and they occupied larger regions; as in Glengarry and Prince Edward Island, they remained relatively isolated for a long period of time and this enabled them to retain their traditions with some degree of strength.

Economic hardship in Scotland provided the basic motivation for emigration, though some of the early settlers had, like those in Glengarry, a background of military service in British regiments during the American Revolution. One scholar attributes this support of the monarchy to the tenant relationship: "The loyalty of the Highlander in America to the Crown was a logical extension of his unquestioning obedience to his immediate landlord."[59] It is possible that the close association between the tacksmen and the crofters led to an assumption of obedience which was, upon the disintegration of the clan system, transferred to others in authority. There were several heavy waves in the tides of Scottish immigration, the first large permanent settlement arriving at Pictou aboard the *Hector* in 1773.[60] The pre-Revolutionary emigration[61] was affected by the events of 1775-1783 in the American colonies, but much the same set of causes was important during the period 1783-1803, which marks another phase. The year 1803 saw the first serious government effort to regulate the emigrant trade to North America.[62] Generally, those who left during this period were not "the wretched helpless exodus that was to come in the next century." They were of varying trades and occupations, and some of them travelled unassisted.[63] During the period 1803-1815 there were more who left Scotland through lack of alternatives than in the preceding decades of the eighteenth centry. As the "clearances" intensified, more Scots found themselves forced to emigrate. Following the smashing of Napoleon's delusions at Waterloo, many Highlanders returned home to find glens filled with the bleating of sheep but empty of human voices. Evictions, over-population and widespread economic distress in Britain after 1815 brought on the final and heaviest phase of Scottish emigration to Nova Scotia. This was the last, and most distressing, major influx of population. Thousands of Scots, both Protestant and Roman Catholic, managed, without government assistance, to survive the "coffin ships," disease and poverty, and to establish themselves in a new land. The immigration of this period shaped the character of Cape Breton.

> The great influx of Scottish immigrants (said by some authorities to have exceeded 25,000 souls), gave quite a new complexion to the population of Cape Breton.... The island is now decidedly "Scotch," with every probability of its continuing so to the end of time.[64]

Population moved from Pictou eastward and thus Cape Breton was the last to be settled. While much of the island was still in the pioneer phase, Pictou was leading in the struggle for educational and political reforms. Heavily Presbyterian, and situated closer to Truro and Halifax, Pictou was the first Scottish community to be influenced by the stronger Anglo-Saxon customs. As a result, Pictou County changed more quickly, and its cultural traditions, particularly the use of Gaelic, were transformed or weakened. The language lasted longer in Antigonish, and maintained a strong foothold in Cape Breton well into the twentieth century.[65] By mid-nineteenth century the character of the eastern part of the province was definitely Scottish and Nova Scotian in flavour.

As an ethnic group the Highland Catholics in Nova Scotia had characteristics peculiar to themselves and these remained largely unchanged in the new environment for well over a century. Their attitudes on education, their loyalty to the state, to institutions, to individuals, their conception of the role of religion, the maintenance of a folk culture and a strong attachment to their native soil — all these lived on with them and were reinforced in eastern Nova Scotia. Nor did they forget the old: "In pride of origin Nova Scotia Scots are equalled, if that is possible, only by the Norsemen overseas."[66] In time they came to be recognized on their own merits and weaknesses, through a composition of ethnic and regional traits, as Nova Scotians of Scottish descent. A Nova Scotia society was maturing by the end of the second decade of the nineteenth century. "Nova Scotians as such were emerging, rubbing the sleep out of their eyes and facing their own problems, in various ways, but with discernment and energy. They were conscious that they were Nova Scotians."[67] "Between 1789 and 1826, when the *Acadian Recorder* began its all-too-brief career, a new generation had grown up, proud of their province and the things that were theirs by right of birth."[68]

The year 1791 marked the arrival of the first large number of Highland Catholics in Nova Scotia. They came largely from the Western Isles and landed in Pictou in September of that year, practically destitute. Forced out by economic conditions in Scotland, their initial period in the province did not constitute much of an improvement:

But the emigrants landed at Pictou in September practically penniless and though that small community, itself containing only seven hundred individuals, made an effort to support the newcomers, eventually it was necessary to appeal for aid to the colonial government.[69]

They were treated as well as conditions would warrant by the people of Pictou, few of whom had any surplus of food to dispense. Upon the urging of Bishop Angus MacEachern of Prince Edward Island, many of them moved eastward.[70] Reverend James McGregor, an Anti-Burgher cleric and the only minister in the Pictou district, exhorted his people to treat the newcomers with kindness, but he was disturbed by some of their values and his comments illustrate certain differences in attitudes between the Catholics and the Presbyterians:

> Much of their time was spent in naughty diversions, jestings which are not convenient nor decent, in telling extravagant stories of miracles done by priests, and absurd tales about ghosts, witches, fairies, etc. The minds of the Protestant Highlanders, being partly tinctured with these superstitions before the arrival of the Roman Catholics, were less prepared to resist their influence than the minds of more reasonable and sceptical Christians. They had been pretty much weaned from the remains which the first settlers brought from Scotland, but we have not got wholly over these bad lessons.[71]

Apparently, denominational differences were not yet strong enough to erase the Highland predilection for ghost stories and other elements of their folk culture.[72]

The first Scottish settlers in Antigonish County came in 1784[73] as a result of British imperial policy, and land grants were awarded on both sides of Antigonish harbour, as well as at the eastern end of the present town boundaries. Included in this group, which also had a military background, were a number of English and Irish settlers. The first Highland settler in the area was Angus MacDonald, who acquired 500 acres of land at Arisaig. He had earlier taken up a grant at Merigomish, but fear of the Indians caused him to return there. The honour of being the first permanent settler on the gulf shore goes to John Ban Gillies, who was followed by McAra and former members of the 82nd Highland Regiment.[74] The last-named settled along the shore and established permanent settlements to which they gave such names as Knoydart, Moidart and Arisaig.[75] Some had moved eastward from Pictou to settle with their fellow Catholics. By 1820 there was a string of small scattered settlements, populated by Scots from the western Highlands and the Isles, all along the Gulf Shore from Merigomish to Ballantyne's Cove on the eastern side of Cape George. Many came from Barra and they worked at both farming and fishing in their new homes. The vast majority were Catholics who had first landed at Pictou before moving eastward. Subsequent patterns of settlement naturally turned toward the inland parts of the district where initially they settled along the rivers and rich intervales. By 1817, and certainly by 1820, settlement patterns were following those already laid out.[76] Like their pioneer countrymen elsewhere in British North America, they faced the formidable task of clearing the forests and establishing homes and though they had very little experience in cutting trees, they seemed to do so with a vengeance in the new environment.

Dorchester Village (Antigonish) developed as the principal trading town of the county because of its central location. It was

> one of the prettiest villages in the eastern section of Nova Scotia
> .... It has but one principal street ... and contains about 45 dwelling houses, exclusive of other buildings. The Court House is built on a hill of moderate ascent, and commands a pleasing view of the whole village .... The Roman Catholic chapel ... is by much the largest and most respectable looking building in the County ... not at all disproportioned to the extent of the congregation .... There is also in the centre of this village a small Presbyterian meeting-house.[77]

By 1827 the total population of Nova Scotia was estimated at 142,548, with 123,848 on the mainland and 18,700 in Cape Breton, giving an increase of 41,795 on the mainland since 1817. Sydney (Antigonish-Guysborough) had increased from 6,991 to 12,760 during the decade.[78] There were also marked increases in cultivated acreage, in the production of potatoes, hay, wheat and other grains, and in livestock.[79]

Contemporary accounts show certain similarities to other regions populated by Highlanders:

> Gaelic is the language of this part of the country – I Mean, it is that tongue which you hear in every cottage, and that which strikes the ear on passing through the street of each little village.
> Scotch, both from the High and Lowlands, are here [Sherbrooke][80] found without intermixture: the former make but indifferent farmers: accustomed to a hard and penurious mode of life, they are too easily satisfied with the bare existence that even indolence can procure in this country .... In the course of another generation, a very different order of things will prevail, for the sons of these Highlanders, more accustomed to think for and depend upon themselves, and instructed by an occasional excursion to other districts, appear to be a more promising race and to inherit but little of the apathy generally exhibited by their fathers.[81]

This apparent lack of ambition among Highlanders was referred to on other occasions but always in the context of agriculture, in which they had no tradition. Upon leaving the farm to compete in other activities they acquitted themselves at least as well as others. There was less criticism of this nature in reference to the Highland farmers of Pictou County, thus suggesting that the hybrid of Highland Presbyterians and Lowlanders were more ambitious. Writing in the late 1820s Haliburton commented:

> The Highlanders are not so advantageous a class of settlers as their Lowland neighbours. Their wants are comparatively few, and their ambition is chiefly limited to the acquirement of the mere necessaries of life. If in some instances they extend their clearings they derive not so much advantage from them as others. Their previous habits have fitted them better for the management of stock than the cultivation of the soil, and they are consequently more attached to it . . . . The Lowlanders, on the contrary, to the frugality and interest of the Highlanders, add a spirit of persevering diligence, a constant desire of improvement, and a superior system of agriculture which renders them a valuable acquisition to the Province.[82]

While there is justification for such an assessment it must be kept in mind that the habits of the Highlanders were rooted in centuries of tradition. Nor were they to be generally disturbed by appeals to efficiency and progress; this is particularly true of the Catholic Highlander, who was taught that his reward would come eventually. Soon after settlement they were providing for their necessities and for the majority this was sufficient. Never having known prosperity, they did not miss it; thus, they were good pioneers.

There are obvious and understandable differences to be noted between Pictou, with its Presbyterian majority, and Antigonish, with its predominant Catholic population. But the Scottish fact also promoted tolerance in each area.

> At the hospitable board of R.N. Henry, Esq., the then postmaster of Antigonish, I met four men, each differing in training, professional character, but each in his own time sufficiently remarkable to make his society very attractive. These were Dr. Fraser, who became Catholic Bishop of the Diocese, Dr. MacDonald, then in full enjoyment of a large country practice, the Rev. Thomas Trotter, Presbyterian pastor of the village congregation, and our old friend, Sandy MacDougall. They were all Scotchmen or of Scotch descent, were fast friends and cronies. Each would stand up for his own Church or his own snuff box, but they would all stand up for Scotland and fight to prove a thistle more fragrant than a rose. I would have given a trifle to have seen and heard our four old friends once more chaffing each other in Latin, English, Greek and Gaelic. With these four men I remained on terms of intimacy and friendship while they lived. Nothing impressed me so much as to hear questions of philosophy, of practical or abstract science or of European politics, discussed in the County of Sydney with the keenest of logic and fullness of information scarcely met with in the capital.[83]

The above words of Joseph Howe are revealing particularly with regard to the Catholic Bishop Fraser and the Presbyterian cleric, Reverend Thomas Trotter. This toleration of each other's views was not unusual and has also been noted with the Catholic Highlanders and Presbyterians in Prince Edward Island and Glengarry.

With regard to education, the Scottish Catholics followed the lead of their Presbyterian brethren. Pictou Academy received its charter in 1816 through the leadership of Reverend Thomas McCulloch who became the first Principal of Dalhousie University in 1838. St. Andrew's Grammar School was founded in 1838 by Reverend C.F. MacKinnon, the same man who established St. Francis Xavier University for his Scottish constituents in 1853.

During the peak immigration years of the 1820s, patterns of settlement were established and there were very few who would willingly have exchanged their place for a return to Scotland. Largely Gaelic-speaking, Roman Catholic and Presbyterian, they were laying the basis for a social pattern that lasted until World War II. Their fondness for entertainment changed little in the ocean crossing: "I had to try to abolish dancing and drunkenness, which things the people had been accustomed to. Dancing is rarer now and there is less drunkenness."[84] Religion would remain a very important part of their social pattern; it was a factor that grew stronger with the Highland Catholics during the nineteenth century. Whether or not the relative isolation sustained this view is worthy of consideration. Certainly, it permitted those of Highland descent to retain their language and customs long after both were weakening on the mainland.

Victoria County, which received its name in 1851, had a majority of Scottish Presbyterians, although the first permanent Scottish settlers there were Catholics from the Isle of Barra who came via Pictou shortly after 1800.[85] Those from certain districts and of similar religious persuasion tended to settle together and it became possible to distinguish many origins by accent. Because of this pattern of settlement it was somewhat easier for contemporaries to make comparisons:

> The Highland Scotch, unless intermixed with other settlers, are not only careless, in many particulars, of cleanliness within their houses, but are also regardless of neatness and convenience in their agricultural implements and arrangements. All this arises from the force of habit, and the long prevalence of the make-shift system; for whenever a Scotch Highlander is planted among a more promiscuous population, no one is more anxious than he to rival the more respectable establishment of his neighbour.
> The Scotch settlers from the Lowland countries, although they generally know much better, yet remain, from a determination first to accumulate property, for some years regardless of comfort or convenience in their dwellings; but they at last build respectable houses, and enjoy the fruits of their industry.[86]

The same author adds:

> Few people, however, find themselves sooner at ease than the

> Highland Scotch . . . . They acquire what they consider an indepen-
> dence in a few years . . . . I have observed, that wherever the
> Highlanders form distinct settlements, their habits, their system of
> husbandry, disregard for comfort in their houses, their ancient hos-
> pitable customs, and their language, undergo no sensible change.
> They frequently pass their winter evenings reciting traditional poems
> in Gaelic, which have been transmitted to them by their forefathers
> . . . . At their weddings, and often at their dances, and even at their
> militia musters, the piper is considered indispensable.[87]

Thus, if the work ethic and progress are to be the historical standards, the
Catholic Highlander, at least in agriculture, must be considered a failure.
But if one is to judge by the fulfilment of aspirations and the retention of
values, they were highly successful. Since their ambitions were few, it is
hardly fair to berate them for a lack of ambition. And when the barriers of
isolation were broken they showed themselves equal to any intellectual
challenge, despite a barren background. Satisfied with little, many preferred not to extend themselves, but as the nineteenth century moved onward
they moved with it, though retaining many of their peculiar ethnic, cultural and regional characteristics.

By 1843 the heaviest Scottish immigration was ending in Nova Scotia,
and a few people were leaving the province for other parts of Canada,
Newfoundland and the United States. The economy was expanding steadily.[88] Farming was easily the major occupation and in many coastal areas
it was combined with fishing. Agricultural societies had been formed but
they were carried on by a few dedicated individuals with most of the
Highlanders giving only intermittent support.[89] The number of schools
and students was increasing but government support and direction was
clearly insufficient.[90] In eastern Nova Scotia, as in Glengarry and Prince
Edward Island, the Catholic Highlanders had established traditions recognized, by mid-century, as being different from those of their fellow
countrymen.

The evidence indicates that religion was the most important single factor influencing the lives of these people, for it permeated their homes as
well as their churches. Most of their early clergy were educated at the Scots
College in Paris or the Royal Scots College in Valladolid, Spain. It was not
until the 1820s and 1830s that the Catholic Highlanders began to have
native sons as priests. These clergy, often the best educated men in the
district, played a role similar to that of the *curé* in rural Quebec. They were
consulted on a great variety of matters touching the daily lives of the
people and they took the lead in such important areas as education. Thus,
they commanded respect and their views were rarely ignored. Usually
Gaelic-speaking and deeply concerned for their people, they won and
retained their staunch support. Once that support was given, it was rarely
changed and the highest ambition of many Catholic families was to have a

son study for the priesthood. The status attached to this has been especially noticeable in Cape Breton, where an unusually high number of priests have had their origin. In addition to his role in the community the priest obviously had the great powers of his ministry, the Mass, the pulpit and the confessional, all grounded in the deep faith of the people.[91] And at the last moment of mortal existence it was the priest who directed the steps of the dying to Heaven. The actions of these men, admirable as they were, also reflected their personalities which were quite often remote and severe. Their views on temperance were closely allied to those of the strictest Presbyterian cleric, and the priests executed their charge with vigour.

A pastoral visit to a household was an occasion of special note; here, the visitor would be nervously entertained by the head of the household and a sense of relief was often felt upon his departure. Since leisure activities were frowned on by some pastors, they tried to discourage fiddling and dancing, which were often associated with drinking and fighting. Despite their position of prestige, the priests were never very successful in these matters for they were trying to change an intrinsic cultural tradition. The approach of some clerics in matters of temperance and entertainment was extremely rigid.

The church structure was usually the most eye-catching building in the community and would appear to set the tone for the daily routine of families, which was interspersed with religious devotions. There would be morning and evening prayer, mealtime blessings, and the family rosary during the weeks of Lent and Advent. On the walls of the house would hang a number of religious pictures, a crucifix, and occasionally a piece of palm. In some homes the use of holy water for protection during times of danger, such as thunder storms, was common. Lending a physical presence and support to the church structure was the "glebe," the dwelling of the priest, usually presided over by a devout and discreet Catholic housekeeper. The "glebe" reinforced the religious atmosphere and kept people mindful of where they were.

The most important events of the community were given "from the altar," usually announced by the pastor before the sermon. Few ever dared to confront the priest, for public support would not be forthcoming and the folklore contains stories of misfortune concerning those who contradicted this part of the social mores.

There were similarities and differences between the priest and the minister, with the most obvious being the fact of one being a celibate and the other usually a married man. The greatest difference was in leadership, which the minister came to share through his body of elders. The wardens of the Catholic parish went along with the will of the priest who was accountable only to his bishop. He was considerably more secure in his position and the Catholic communities acted accordingly. Another important area of difference was in language; the Catholic Highlanders and their clergy retained the Gaelic much longer. This delayed Anglicization and enabled a longer retention of cultural traditions, but it was also a handicap to economic and social mobility for some people. Generally, Catholic Highlanders were devout in their religious practices and gave strong loyalty to their church and clergy.

In education, the Scots have made noteworthy contributions to Canada and here the Highland Catholics appear to have followed the lead established by their Presbyterian brethren. It was the Catholic Bishops, Macdonell, MacEachern and MacKinnon, who supplied leadership in Glengarry, Prince Edward Island and eastern Nova Scotia.[92] They were succeeded by clergy who followed in their tradition. The institutions established sent hundreds of clergy, teachers, lawyers and other professional people to all parts of Canada and there is not a Canadian province which has not benefitted from them. This, really, has been the essence of their contribution to the Canadian mosaic. With the Catholic Highlanders, education was necessary to provide priests and teachers, as well as upward mobility in an English-speaking society. The emphasis on the classical system and the education of the "whole man" underlay what they believed. St. Francis Xavier University in Nova Scotia became the best known institution of the Catholic Highlanders and its administration and faculty still retain a number whose first language was Gaelic.

With regard to the economic sphere, the most distinctive feature of the Catholic Highlanders, which is obvious from the foregoing comments on agriculture, is that they have never fully adopted the "work ethic." In areas where they had to compete with other groups they performed very well but, when left to themselves, they worked only as hard as necessary and left themselves time to enjoy their music, their ceilidhs, and their conversation. Hence, they have often been charged with laziness, at least in eastern Nova Scotia. And while there is some truth in this charge, their scale of values must be kept in mind. The time to enjoy a good conversation with a friend or neighbour, the time to attend a "wake" or wedding, the time for fishing or hunting, were all of high priority in their daily lives. In this respect they were "people-oriented" and therefore anticipated the revolt against the dominance of technological control in our times.

Politically, two factors stand out in their tradition, one following from the other. The most important is that of loyalty; once given to a party or an individual, only an event of catastrophic proportions could shake it. Such loyalty in turn led to conservatism in voting behaviour which has not always worked to their benefit, for the politician could usually count on their support regardless of his record. "I think the Highland people are more traditional. I mean they are more apt to vote the way their parents would."[93] "When the family was for one party they didn't want to be turncoats, so they all voted for the one party."[94] At least some of the Scot's adaptability to any new environment arose from his willingness to give his loyalty to his superiors, in every phase of endeavour. It is far more noticeable among Catholic Highlanders, however, than among their Presbyterian countrymen.[95] With these people politics may be described as a secular religion, for it has enabled them to have a consistent interest and has also provided an opportunity for identification and emotional release. When fellow Highlanders, and particularly Catholic Highlanders, were involved in an election contest, the interest and identification were especially strong:

> A land of hospitality,
> A land of song and story.
> A land where everyone you see
> Is either Grit or Tory.[96]

Men such as John Sandfield Macdonald of Glengarry and Angus L. Macdonald of Nova Scotia were held in esteem not only for their political views but also because they were Catholic Highlanders and could command support on that basis. The concept of loyalty is most important in any attempt to understand their political behaviour.

Culturally, the evidence indicates that the Catholic Highlanders retained their customs and language longer than their Protestant countrymen. One reason for this is that the Presbyterians turned much more quickly to the use of English in their religious service and Bible reading. However, there has been a steady diminution in the number of those speaking Gaelic in all districts. Out-migration, the pressures of an English-speaking society, and the lack of efforts made to retain the language on the part of the people themselves, are the contributing factors in this decline. Presently, those speaking Gaelic are found largely in a few rural areas and they are predominantly over fifty years of age.[97]

The customs and traditions, especially in music, have lived on with the Catholic Highlanders; in addition to well-known Highland gatherings such as Maxville and Antigonish, there are others held in Cape Breton and eastern Ontario. Outdoor Scottish concerts featuring Scottish violin selections and Gaelic singing have become highly popular within the last decade in these areas also. Former residents flock home by the thousands from other parts of Canada and the Eastern United States during July and August in order to attend such gatherings. The pipe bands, the violin music and the step-dancing are major attractions for these "pariah" people and tourists. Although efforts are being made to revive the Gaelic, it is probably too late. Other cultural activities such as story-telling and certain Scottish sports attractions enjoy but limited participation. The art of story-telling was dealt its final blow through television and the cliché-ridden conversation of people everywhere reflects their lack of imagination.[98]

In the retention of certain cultural traditions the Highland Catholics have shown their strong desire to remain their own people. Though they have all but lost their language, they have not lost their appreciation of other aspects of their culture, and they especially resent being classified as Anglo-Saxons, a term often applied to them by government employees and others for the sake of convenience. There has been a long association between the Scottish Catholics of the three major areas. Scottish Catholic students from the Glengarry district have often attended St. Francis Xavier University; the Highland gatherings in Glengarry have been attended and competed in by athletes and pipers from Antigonish, all of whom claim that they feel "so much at home" in Glengarry. Scottish Catholic relations between Prince Edward Island and the Diocese of Antigonish have, beginning with Bishop Angus MacEachern, been long and close.

The central theme of their contribution to Canada has been the fact that they have quietly resisted homogenization. Their loyalty has been strong and quickly given, but they want to be recognized for who they are. Their view of Canada is shaped by their origin and by the region in which they live; the constant interplay between the federal and local levels of government and the thousands who have migrated to all parts of Canada have kept the views of these people nationally attuned. Through the federal system and the prism of party loyalties their attention has been drawn to the centre of power; the love of their cultural traditions and the freedom to enjoy them has kept these alive at the regional level. These are the freedoms all Canadians must enjoy.

NOTES

1. For some religious differences in Scotland, see C. MacKenzie, *Catholicism and Scotland* (London: Routledge and Sons, 1936). p. 28; W. Notestein, *The Scot in History* (New Haven: Yale University Press, 1947); J.H. Burton, *The History of Scotland*, 2nd ed. (Edinburgh: Blackwood 1873), VII.

2. W. Gregg, *Short History of the Presbyterian Church in the Dominion of Canada* (Toronto: Robinson, 1892); A. MacLean, *The Story of the Kirk in Nova Scotia* (Pictou: Pictou Advocate, 1911).

3. All of those calling themselves Presbyterians.

4. At this point it should be stressed that the linkage between Scots and religion has greater meaning and accuracy when applied to the post-Reformation period, to Presbyterianism, and largely to the Lowland region and parts of the Highlands. It was the Presbyterianism propagated by John Knox that did so much to create the disciplined Scot who contributed so greatly to the corporate life of Britain and Canada. See J. Porter, *The Vertical Mosaic* (Toronto: University of Toronto Press, 1965), p. 290.

5. For the remainder of the paper the term Catholic Highlander will be used.

6. J.A. Macdonell, *Sketches Illustrating the Early History of Glengarry in Canada* (Montreal: Foster, Brown, 1893), p. 60.

7. Approximately 1462 Highlanders moved in 1784 to settle the townships of Lancaster, Charlottenberg, Cornwall, Osnabruck and Williamsburg.

This had been the corps of Sir John Johnston in the Mohawk Valley.

8. Bull, p. 75.
9. *Ibid.*, p. 76.
10. Lord Sidney, Secretary of State, to Lieutenant-Governor Hamilton of Canada, 24 June, 1785, PAC, Series Q, 24-2, p. 29. Quoted in Msgr. E.J. Macdonald, PA, VIG, "The Diocese of Alexandria – Past and Present," Unpublished manuscript, p. 1.
11. According to the late Msgr. E.J. Macdonald, the parish of St. Andrew's was the oldest English-speaking Catholic settlement in Ontario. The stone church was partly paid for by a contribution of £222 from Highlanders of the North West Company. Another church of the district, St. Raphael's, was gutted by fire in 1970. The former mother church for Upper Canada, it was reputed to have been built in 1821. See Macdonald manuscript, pp. 43-45.
12. Bull, p. 78. Built without tower or steeple in 1792, the church was 78' by 39', with a height of 15' and walls 3' thick. Replaced by a larger structure in 1860, it was later used as a church hall.
13. Commonly known as "Scotus" in order to distinguish him from the "Warrior Bishop," Reverend Alexander Macdonell (1762-1840).
14. 604 people.
15. Macdonald manuscript, p. 3.
16. Macdonell, p. 75.
17. Macdonald, *supra.*
18. *Ibid.*, p. 42
19. Angus Macdonell, first president of the Law Society of Ontario, 1792; Alexander Macdonell, Greenfield, and Finnan Macdonell, Chief Factors of the Hudson's Bay Company; Colonel John Macdonell, MP, first Speaker of the House of Assembly, 1792. See Chapter IV by K.J. Duncan for settlement patterns in the east.
20. F.A. Walker, *Catholic Education and Politics in Upper Canada* (Toronto: Nelson, 1955), p. 18.
21. *Ibid.*
22. Ibid., pp. 18-34.
23. J.A. Macdonell, *Alexander Macdonell* (Alexandria, 1890). See pp. 79-83 for a list of Macdonells who supported the government during the uprising of 1837.
24. Rev. H.J. Somers, *The Life and Times of the Hon. and Rt. Rev. Alexander Macdonell, D.D., First Bishop of Upper Canada, 1762-1840* (Washington: Catholic University of America, 1931), p. 96.
25. *Ibid.*, pp. 214-221.
26. C.S. Sissons, *Church and State in Canadian Education* (Toronto: Ryerson, 1959), p. 10.
27. Macdonell, *Early History* . . . , p. 185.
28. E.C. Guillet, *Early Life in Upper Canada* (Toronto: University of Toronto, 1963), p. 45.

29. 1800-1812, 1813-1816, 1820-1834. See Brother Alfred, *Catholic Pioneers in Upper Canada* (Toronto: MacMillan, 1947), pp. 20-21.
30. *Ibid.*, pp. 22-23. The relationship between Scottish Catholics and Presbyterians was sometimes better than that which existed between Scottish and Irish or French Catholics. This was as true in Nova Scotia as in eastern Ontario.
31. Guillet, p. 39.
32. E.J. Macdonald, p. 6.
33. With 3,101 in Dundas and 4,714 in Stormont, *Census of Canada*, 1870-71, IV, 83.
34. *Ibid.*, p. 104.
35. Bull, pp. 109-110. John Sandfield Macdonald, first Premier of Ontario, Member for Glengarry and later Cornwall, lukewarm Catholic and moderate Reformer, became the best known political figure in the history of the district.
36. *Ibid.*, pp. 110-111.
37. Of the 17,596 people in Glengarry in 1851, 8,870 were Catholics. *Census of Canada*, 1870-71, Vol. IV, 104, 131, 180. Of a population of 18,732 in 1941, the number of Catholics had risen to 13,388, many of them French Canadians who moved into the district. Between 1861 and 1871 the population actually declined from 21, 187 to 20,524. *Census of Canada*, 1870-71, I, 24-26.
38. The lowest population was recorded in 1951, with a figure of 17,702. *Census of Canada*, 1951, I, 6-41, Table 6.
39. The patterns were similar in eastern Nova Scotia, though a decade earlier in each case, the peak being reached in the early 1880's, the decline most marked in the early 1940's. *Census of Canada*, 1860-61, 272-277.
40. Expansion is easily noted in the following table, although there is a decline in the number of horses used.

	Potatoes	Turnips	Horses	Wool	Sheep
1860–61	180,302 bu.	5,079 bu.	8,445	56,154 lb.	11,728
1881	287,254 bu.	6,722 bu.	6,447	81,871 lb.	22,800

41. A.H. Clark, *Three Centuries and the Island* (Toronto: University of Toronto, 1959), pp. 54-56.
42. Bishop Macdonell, 1804-1840; Bishop MacEachern, 1790-1835.
43. A. MacLeod, "The Glenaladale Pioneers," *Dalhousie Review* XI, (1931-32), 316.
44. J.C. MacMillan, *The Early History of the Catholic Church on Prince Edward Island* (Quebec: L'Evènement, 1905), p. 43.

45. *Ibid.*, pp. 41-42.
46. *Ibid.*, pp. 44-45.
47. The Tracadie district.
48. *The Arrival of the First Scottish Catholic Emigrants in Prince Edward Island, and After*, Memorial Volume, 1722-1922 (Summerside: Journal Publishing Co., 1922).
49. Clark, p. 88.
50. MacLeod, pp. 319-320. In 1778 the name of the Regiment was changed to the 84th.
51. With 4372 in 1798, of whom 1814 were Highland Scots. See Clark, pp. 60-61.
52. Clark, pp. 66-69. The Highland Catholic settlement became concentrated to the north and east of the major Scottish settlement areas, Tracadie Harbour, and Orwell Bay. *Ibid.*, p. 207.
53. *Ibid.*, pp. 69.76.
54. *Ibid.*, 1853: 30,000 cattle; 50,000 sheep; 20,000 pigs; 6,000 horses; 1881: *Census of Canada*, 1881, IV, 86-87: 25,182 horses; 166,496 sheep; 40,-181 pigs.
55. *Census of Canada*, 1881, IV, 2. The census gives the population of 1881 as 108,891. Of this number, 48,933 were of Scottish origin; 47,115 were listed as Catholics; 33,835 were Presbyterians (pp. 6-11). The population in 1871 had been 94,021 (p. 116).
56. *The Arrival of the First Scottish Catholic Emigrants . . .*, pp. 66-67.
57. A son of Angus Macdonald, one of the original immigrants.
58. J. Donahoe, ed., *Prince Edward Island Priests* (Minneapolis: Webb, 1945). Though incomplete, the book does give an indication of the religious attitudes of Prince Edward Island Catholics. Two of the best-known natives of the Island were Reverend James Morrison and Reverend Alexander Macdonald, the respective Bishops of Antigonish and Victoria.
59. I.C.C. Graham, *Colonists from Scotland: Emigration to North America, 1707-1783* (Cornell: University Press, 1956), p. 150.
60. The first Scottish settlements in Nova Scotia were established in 1629, one at Baleine Cove in Cape Breton, the other at Port Royal on the mainland. The Baleine Cove settlement lasted but a few weeks, while that at Port Royal survived until 1632, when the Treaty of St. Germain-en-Laye restored Acadia to the French. See C.B. Fergusson, *The Boundaries of Nova Scotia and its Counties*, Bulletin No. 22, 1-6, Public Archives of Nova Scotia (PANS).
61. M.I. Adam, "The Highland Emigration of 1770," *Scottish Historical Review*, XVI. There is some disagreement with certain views put forward by the author. See: Ian Grimble, "Emigration in the Time of Rob Doun, 1714, 1778," *Scottish Studies*, VII (1963), 129-153.
62. H.I. Cowan, *British Emigration to British North America* (Toronto: University of Toronto Press, 1967), p. 48.

63. Graham (p. 189) estimates that fewer than 25,000 Highlanders emigrated to British colonies between 1763 and 1775. Another source states that ten vessels of Highlanders went to the American colonies in 1773, "and yet these persons . . . were in general, extremely averse to an entire and abrupt rejection of British authority." See R.C. MacDonald, *Sketches of Highlanders* . . . (Saint John: H. Chubb and Co., 1843), p. 60.

64. It could be argued that this is a mixed blessing. For the quotation see R. Brown, *A History of the Island of Cape Breton* (London: S.L. Low, Son and Marston, 1869), p. 425. An estimate of the number of Scots in Nova Scotia in 1803 would approximate 9,000-10,000. Scottish settlement there slowed in the period 1803-1815, but it did not cease completely. Despite the slowness of migration to Cape Breton between 1802 and 1817, the population had reached 6,000 by 1815. See *Council Books*, Cape Breton, 1785-1820, Vols. 318-323, PANS. By 1838 the population of the island had risen to about 38,000. During the period 1815-1838 the population of Pictou increased from 8,737 to 21,449, while that of Sydney (Antigonish-Guysboro) went from 7,090 to 16,359. See J.S. Martell, "Immigration to and Emigration from Nova Scotia, 1815-1838," Publication No. 6, PANS, 1942), 10. In the final phase of immigration to Nova Scotia, 1838-1851, 16,000 people moved into the province; of these, 14,000 were of British extraction. See Mrs. R.G. Flewelling, "Immigration to and Emigration from Nova Scotia, 1839-1851," *Collections of the Nova Scotia Historical Society* (Halifax: 1949), pp. 75-105.

65. The extinction of Gaelic is a very strong possibility. By 1961 only 0.05% of Nova Scotians and 6.4% of those in Inverness County, the most Scottish area, claimed Gaelic as the mother tongue.

66. A.H. Clark, "Origins and Religions in Nova Scotia," *The Geographical Review* 50 (1960), 340. Many of Scottish descent still seem to believe that the "greatest lot on earth is to be born a Scotsman."

67. D.C. Harvey, "The Intellectual Awakening of Nova Scotia," *Dalhousie Review*, XIII, 21.

68. A. MacMechan, "The Nova-Scotia-ness of Nova Scotia," *The Canadian Magazine*, XXV (1905), p. 566.

69. Cowan, pp. 20-21.

70. Included in this group were the parents of Colin Francis MacKinnon, who was to establish St. Francis Xavier University in 1853. Pictou remained a major point of entry through the entire period of immigration.

71. G. Patterson, *Memoir of Rev. James McGregor*, D.D. (Philadelphia: Martien, 1859), pp. 257-258.

72. Patterson also made certain comments on the Highlanders: "Accustomed to extreme poverty, they readily endure hardship, but it is said that they are apt to be content with a condition but little beyond what they previous enjoyed, and do not show the same eagerness for progress that others do. This had, to some extent, been the case where they have settled by themselves, but where they have mixed with others, there is so

much of the spirit of emulation in them, that they will soon compete with their neighbours in almost everything." *A History of Pictou County*, p. 174. In a reference to the Lowlanders, Patterson states: "They were distinguished by steady industry and rigid economy, and they generally not only made a living but saved money." *Ibid.*, p. 275.

73. J.W. MacDonald, M.D., Manuscript History of Antigonish County, (1876), 2-3. Also C.J. MacGillivray in "Timothy Hierlihy and his Times," a paper read before the Nova Scotia Historical Society at Province House, Halifax, November 3, 1935. More space will be devoted to Antigonish County, for it had a higher proportion of Catholic Highlanders in its population than had any similar district in the country.

74. A.A. Johnston, *A History of the Catholic Church in Eastern Nova Scotia* (Toronto: Longman's; 1960), I, 133.

75. Among the Highlanders were John Smith, Dugald Dan MacDonald, Malcolm, Martin and Donald MacDonald. Martin MacDonald, a relative of John Sandfield MacDonald of Glengarry, is also credited with being the first settler on the Gulf Shore, having settled at Knoydart in 1784. See G.S. MacDonald, "West Highland Emigrants in Eastern Nova Scotia," *Collections of the Nova Scotia Historical Society* (Halifax, 1959). Another source, Patterson, states that MacDonald arrived there in 1778. *A History of Pictou County* (Montreal: Dawson, 1977), p. 160.

76. The population of certain districts in 1817 is given as follows: Gulf Shore-Malignant Cove, 399; Ohio-West River, 103; St. Mary's 262, Manchester Road, 113; Settlement of Cape George, 279; Morristown, 118; Little River and Tracadie, 391; Harbour Busher [sic]204; Pomquet, 163; Antigonish, 835; Addington Grant, 56; *Census of Canada*, (1817), 445, Document 6, PANS.

77. T.C. Haliburton, *An Historical and Statistical Account of Nova Scotia* (Halifax: J. Howe, 1829) II, 79-80.

78. B. Murdock, *A History of Nova Scotia or Acadie*, 3 Vols., (Halifax: J. Barnes, 1865-67), II, 591. In 1827 there were 18,659 Anglicans, 37,225 Church of Scotland Presbyterians, 20,410 Catholics, 9,408 Methodists, 19,790 Baptists and 8,365 others. Sydney County had 7,180 Catholics, 1,473 Church of Scotland, 4,107 Church of England. See W. Moorsom, *Letters from Nova Scotia Comprising Sketches of a Young Country* (London: Colborn and Bentley, 1830), p. 353.

	Horses	Sheep	Horned Cattle	Swine
1808	214	5,485	4,474	2,101
1827	848	24,349	15,706	7,705

79. Sydney County.
Statement of Stock in the Province of Nova Scotia, G.D. 45/3/456. General Register Office, Edinburgh.

80. 40 miles from Antigonish, now in Guysborough County.
81. Moorsam, pp. 331-332, 344.
82. Haliburton, p. 279.
83. Quoted in Johnston, pp. 465-66. Sandy MacDougall was Alexander MacDougall, a young barrister who later became Attorney-General of Nova Scotia. MacDonald was a Dr. Alexander MacDonald who came to Antigonish from Scotland some time between 1805 and 1810. R.N. Henry was the father of W.A. Henry (1816-1888), one of the Fathers of Confederation.
84. Reverend Joseph Moll, May 1821. Quoted in Johnston, pp. 420.
85. G. Patterson, "History of Victoria County," unpublished manuscript, 1885, pp. 6-8.
86. J. M'Gregor, *British America* (Edinburgh: Blackwood, 1832) I, 183.
87. *Ibid.*, pp. 184-186.
88. Exports of farm products, fish, lumber and coal in Cape Breton rose from £45, 170.2.6. in 1830 to £100,403.9.10 in 1838.
89. See *Agriculture: Local Societies, 1841-1860*, Sydney and Cape Breton, Vols. 20, 22, PANS.
90. See *School Papers, Inverness County, 1833-1883*, PANS.
92. The history of many Catholic communities in Saskatchewan and Alberta also indicates that religious leadership was supplied by priests of Scottish descent from Nova Scotia and Prince Edward Island.
93. Interview, Scottish Presbyterian farmer, Pictou County.
94. Interview, Catholic Highlander farmer, Antigonish County.
95. An analysis of voting behavior among the Scots of eastern Nova Scotia from Confederation to 1960 confirms this view. See D. Campbell and R.A. MacLean, *Beyond the Atlantic Roar: A Study of the Nova Scotia Scots* (Toronto: McClelland and Stewart, 1974) pp. 236-280.
96. From a Cape Breton folk-song.
97. The 1961 census listed only 3,702 people in Nova Scotia who could claim Gaelic as their mother tongue.
98. In interviews carried out with 100 people of Scottish descent the most impressive factor noted was their flexibility and beauty of expression in English. All of those interviewed had Gaelic as their first language and had grown to adulthood in an oral culture. Their love and appreciation of words was both refreshing and admirable.

SEVEN

The Scottish
Protestant Tradition

W. Stanford Reid

THE SCOTTISH BACKGROUND

In order to understand the Scottish Protestant tradition's influence in
Canadian development, it is necessary to turn back to Scotland itself. The
Reformation of the sixteenth century is the crucial factor in Protestant
beginnings. In fact some historians have maintained that it is the most
important event in Scottish history, for it set the Scots apart as different
from all other peoples. Although tied closely to the French and Genevan
Protestant movements it was yet different and helped to produce a people
who have differed from all other nationalities, even the English, a fact
recognized in the sixteenth century itself by men such as John Knox and
stressed more recently by Robert Louis Stevenson, Wallace Notestein and
others.[1] While a general outline of the Scottish ecclesiastical background
has been given in the introductory chapter of this book, it would perhaps
be well, before looking at the Scottish Protestant tradition in Canada, to
remind ourselves of some of the main characteristics of that tradition.

One important point that must be kept in mind, to appreciate Scottish
religious developments, is that the Scottish Reformation was not imposed
from above as it was in England, but grew up from the grass roots in spite
of much opposition at the higher levels of society. John Knox came of a
small farming family and was trained as a notary, which brought him into
contact with the middling element in society, the burgesses of the towns
and the lairds. He gave the leadership and guidance that shaped the Protestant forces into an effective reforming body which in spite of much
opposition from Crown and Church made the Reformation a fact in 1560.
Believing strongly that God had called him to "blaw his maister's trum-
pet" for reform, and that if necessary to accomplish this end force must be
used by the nobles, or failing them, by the people, he gave a rationale to
religious "rebellion" which brought the Protestant cause to victory.[2]

Probably the most fundamental element in the tradition from the days
of Knox onwards has been its Calvinism. In more recent days, some have

118

attempted to prove that the Scottish church was not Calvinistic or at least not as Calvinistic as the Dutch and French Reformed Churches. Yet as one examines the Scots Confession of 1560 and the Westminster Standards – The Confession of Faith, the Larger and Shorter Catechisms, the Common Order of Worship and the Form of Government which replaced the earlier doctrinal statement in 1649 – he can hardly doubt that the Church of Scotland was committed to a well-reasoned, strongly Calvinistic position. Furthermore, even though later groups broke away from the Established Church, their Calvinism still remained. Within the Church of Scotland itself, although the eighteenth century rationalist climate of opinion for a time gained the day, Calvinistic movements eventually developed in opposition to the prevailing ideas, sometimes, it is true, leading to the formation of new Presbyterian denominations as in the case of the Free Kirk (1843), but also stimulating a revival of Calvinism within the parent body.[3] Even today the same struggle is going on and a recent attempt to abolish the Westminster documents as the basis of the established church's doctrine and government has been defeated in the General Assembly.[4] Furthermore, although today the Scottish Episcopal Church has been strongly influenced by the Anglo-Catholic movement of the nineteenth century, in its origin it also held to the Reformed theological position.[5] This Calvinism as well as the struggles to modify and to maintain it has had much the same history in the Scottish Protestant tradition in Canada.

Coupled with its Calvinism has gone a stress upon the presbyterian form of government. Although some of the Scottish Protestants known as the non-jurors refused to accept William and Mary as king and queen in 1692 and formed a separate episcopal church, presbyterianism has been characteristic of Scottish Protestantism since the 1570s. With its concept of the government of the church by an hierarchy of courts, each appointing representatives to the court above it, it established a twofold concept of church organization. One was that all those who participated in the direction of the church should be elected to their offices, and the other that church government of clearly defined form and with recognized authority for administration and discipline was divinely ordained. In fact some even went so far as to assert the "divine right of presbytery" over against the "divine right of monarchy and of episcopacy." The presbyterian view of church government had also implications which went far beyond the actual ecclesiastical organization. It involved the view that there was no earthly head of the church, that position being solely the prerogative of the risen Lord.

This brought the Scottish church into direct conflict with such would-be absolute rulers as James VI who was not far wrong when he asserted: "Presbytery agreeth with [absolute] monarchy as well as God doth with the Devil. No bishop no king." When absolute kings attempted to dominate the church as did both Charles I and Charles II, the Presbyterians were prepared to resist in the name of "The Crown Rights of Jesus

Christ."[6] Furthermore, there was the constant insistence that while the state had the obligation to support and defend the true Reformed religion, Christ ruled his church by his Word and Spirit speaking through the faithful people in the church. This concept produced a number of divisions as resistance to government interference and aristocratic patronage arose, ultimately leading some Scottish Presbyterians to deny the validity of the whole principle of establishment and to insist on voluntarism. This opposition to government control of the church was and still is part of the Scottish tradition in Canada, as was revealed in the continuing Presbyterians' denial of the validity of the Church Union Act of 1924.[7]

The stress upon the "Kingship of Christ" was not limited to matters primarily ecclesiastical. There was a constant stress upon the idea that since Christ was Lord over all of life his will and law must be obeyed in every sphere of activity. This applied to both corporate and individual activities. Andrew Melville's calling James VI of Scotland "one of God's sillie subjects" in his Kingdom was a constant theme in much later Scottish Protestant thinking. For this reason the Scottish churches have always believed that it is their responsibility to speak to contemporary society concerning the divine requirements for a society which should manifest the Lordship of Christ. Similarly, the churches have also sought to train the individual from his or her youth to recognize the solemn responsibility of each Christian to manifest God's will in the activities of everyday life. The Christian's chief end is "to glorify God and enjoy him forever," in all he does.[8]

Although not all Scottish Protestants were trained up in the Calvinistic-Presbyterian tradition, this point of view seems to have entered the very bloodstream of Scottish culture. As both Robert Louis Stevenson and more recently Professor Wallace Notestein have pointed out, the Scottish Calvinistic-Presbyterian outlook on life has formed one of the basic drives in the Scottish character. It has meant an emphasis upon personal responsibility which manifests itself in what has often been labeled "the Protestant work ethic." This has meant, however, not only a sense of divine calling to work, but a God-given responsibility to show initiative, foresight and risk-taking. Yet, contrary to many people's thinking, it has not resulted merely in a desire to accumulate worldly goods. A concept of "stewardship" has gone along with it. The individual is responsible to use his gifts, talents and the wealth which they may bring for the benefit of others. The outcome of such an outlook on life has often been the formation of an individual who is hard-working, frugal sometimes to penuriousness, but also capable of acts of considerable generosity when the occasion requires. And all of this bred a race of people who were inclined to be independent, sometimes irascible, argumentative and often very sure of their own correctness of vision and action. Thus the Protestant Scot, although by no means always a 'lovable' character, has very often been a person possessing the necessary drive and self-assurance to make a good colonist.

120

These are but a few of the characteristics of the Scottish Protestant tradition which were brought to Canada by the influx of British immigrants since 1763. At the same time, we must also recognize that, as in Scotland, the tradition has been very much diluted over the past century. In Scotland the rise of scepticism, materialism and the acceptance of a Higher Critical approach to the Bible have all had their effect upon the church, with the result that the Scottish Protestant churches of nearly every hue have experienced a decline in membership, in giving and in influence. This has been partially responsible for various church union movements, as for instance the union of the majority of the Free Kirk of Scotland and the United Presbyterians as the United Free Church in 1900, the reunion of the UFC with the Church of Scotland in 1929, and the subsequent discussions of the union of the Church of Scotland with the Episcopal Church of Scotland and the Church of England in the 1950s and '60s.[9] There have always been, however, minorities who have refused to accept any watering-down either of doctrine or of the presbyterial form of church government, and have continued to maintain their original stance. The same trends have shown themselves in Canada, for although the Presbyterian Church in Canada has been completely independent of the Scottish churches since 1875, Scottish influences in the church have been very strong through the coming of ministers from Scotland, the publication of books and periodicals which have received a wide acceptance in Scottish Canadian Protestant circles, the study by Presbyterian theological students in Scotland, and the general, perhaps indefinable, sense of attachment and filial relationship to the Scottish Presbyterian churches.[10] Depending upon one's point of view, this influence has been good or bad, but that it has had a major impact no one can deny.

SCOTTISH CHURCHES AND CHURCHMEN IN CANADA

The Protestant Scots who came to what is now Canada in the early part of the eighteenth century usually settled in Nova Scotia, Prince Edward Island and New Brunswick. They were, however, neither numerous nor wealthy enough to call a minister until the middle of the century. Eventually they obtained the services of the Rev. James Lyon, a graduate of Princeton Seminary, and also of Rev. James Murdoch, an Irish missionary Scottish-trained, and sent out by the Irish Associate Synod. The first permanent presbytery was established by the Associate (Burgher) Synod at Truro in 1786, to be followed in 1795 by the Presbytery of Pictou in connection with the General Associate or Anti-burgher Church. Of those involved in the formation of these Presbyterian churches two men stand out most prominently. One was the Rev. James McGregor who arrived in 1785 and devoted some forty sacrificial years to ministering to the needs of Scottish settlers throughout the area now known as the Atlantic provinces (with the exception of Newfoundland.) The other was the Rev. Thomas McCulloch who in 1803 settled in Pictou where, despite the

121

opposition of members of the Church of England, he established both an academy and a theological college which prepared the sons of the immigrants for service in church and commonwealth. He later became the first Principal of Dalhousie University.[11]

Since many of the Scots who came to the "eastern provinces" were members of the Church of Scotland, with the settlement of the disbanded Scottish regiments and United Empire Loyalists after the American Revolution, increasing demands were made for ministers of the Established Church. Its response was, however, rather slow, much slower than that of the secession churches, but by 1787 ministers from the Kirk were beginning to consider the possibility of coming to British North America. Consequently when in 1817 the two secession presbyteries decided to unite and form a Synod of Nova Scotia, there were three Church of Scotland ministers who joined, bringing the number of Scots in the Synod to seventeen. As two English independent ministers also came into the union, the Synod began operations with nineteen ministers on its constituent roll.[12]

In the meantime Scots had been moving into the recently acquired territories along the St. Lawrence River which fell to British arms in 1760-1763. Among those who took part in the conquest were the Fraser Highlanders, many of whom were Presbyterians. As they were soon afterwards disbanded it may well have been that it was their chaplain, the Rev. George Henry, a minister of the Church of Scotland, who about 1765 took charge of the small Presbyterian congregation in Quebec City. In 1795 Henry was succeeded by another Scot, Rev. Alexander Sparks, under whose aegis the present St. Andrews Church was erected in 1810.[13] By this time there seem to have been about 150 members in the church, most of them Scots holding important government or commercial positions within the community.

While Quebec was the administrative centre of the region, Montreal soon became the commercial capital, for that was the jumping-off point for the fur traders who were pushing out to the West. Since many of these were Scots it is not surprising that a Church of Scotland congregation was organized there also soon after the American Revolution. The first minister was the Rev. John Bethune, who had served with the loyalist forces in North Carolina and later as chaplain of the 84th Regiment. So far, however, no one has been able to trace a record of his ordination. He was, nevertheless, always regarded as a *bona fide* minister of the Church of Scotland in whose name he established St. Gabriel Street Church, to which most of the Scots in Montreal belonged. Later he moved to Williamstown, Upper Canada, where he received a large grant of land, but continued to carry on his activities as a minister among the Scottish settlers of that area until his death.[14]

Before the end of the century troubles had begun to arise over the question of the right of non-Anglican churches within the Province of Canada to be recognized as bodies with a legal civil status. Efforts were made to deny to all Protestant communions but the Church of England the authority to perform civil acts such as marriages, on the ground that the Church of England was the established church of the country. To this the representatives of the Church of Scotland took very strong exception, claiming that they were part of an established church in Britain by the Union of 1707, and since the conquest had taken place after that date, they had an equal right to civil status and financial assistance in the form of subsidies and participation in the Clergy Reserves set aside for the support of clergy and churches within each parish. The battle continued for many years, even after the division of Canada into Lower and Upper Canada, the opposition to the Church of Scotland's claims in the latter province being led by Bishop John Strachan, a former licentiate of the Kirk. But in 1854 the matter was finally settled by the abolition of all ecclesiastical establishment and the granting to the Church of England the largest share of the endowment, a somewhat smaller amount to the Church of Scotland and smaller sums to some of the other denominations. The stubborn opposition of the Scots led by such men as the Hon. William Morris, George Brown of the *Globe* and William Lyon MacKenzie was one of the principal factors that guaranteed that there would be no state church in Canada.[15]

Meanwhile Scots had continued to migrate to the Canadas, some settling in the Eastern Townships of Lower Canada and others, not infrequently disbanded soldiers, in the Glengarry district of eastern Ontario and others to the west and northwest of York (Toronto) as far as Goderich on Lake Huron and Windsor across from Detroit. Although many of the churches, particularly along the St. Lawrence and the lakes, were frequently ministered to by clergy from the United States, the bulk of the congregations were made up of Scots, farmers, artisans and businessmen who sought to call men from Scotland when they had the opportunity. It was, however, the seceders who again took the first step in organizing as a denomination, for in 1818 the Presbytery of the Canadas was brought into existence by the authorization of the Associate Synod of Scotland. Although the Canadian ministers, who were led by Rev. Alexander Smart of Brockville and Rev. William Bell of Perth, sent out invitations to all Presbyterian ministers throughout the Canadas inviting them to join the presbytery, the Church of Scotland clergy did not even bother to reply. They were apparently content to remain attached somewhat loosely to the Kirk in Scotland.[16] Furthermore, as Rev. William Proudfoot, the founder of the Associate Church in London pointed out, the Church of Scotland men did not seem to have very much zeal for pioneer work and consequently they probably felt that eventually they would return to Scotland to take up charges there.[17]

A change in outlook in Scotland was now beginning to take place. The United Associate Synod of the Secession Church began to display increased interest in sending out men to minister to the needs of the Scottish settlers. To fulfill this plan in 1832 they commissioned three men to act as

123

pioneers. More important, however, was the action of the evangelical wing of the Church of Scotland. Deeply conscious of the responsibility of the Church of Scotland for the spiritual welfare of the Scottish emigrants to British North America, they recognized that the Established Church had not done its part in meeting the settlers' spiritual needs. Therefore, under the patronage of the Earl of Dalhousie, the Governor-General of British North America, they organized in 1825 "The Society (in connection with the Established Church of Scotland) for promoting the religious interests of the Scottish settlers in British North America," often known as the "Glasgow Colonial Society." Led by the Rev. Dr. Robert Burns of Paisley, one of the secretaries, the Society immediately sought to send men to both the eastern provinces and the Canadas. The results, however, were not always happy, for the representatives of the society set up a synod in connection with the Church of Scotland separate from the one established earlier in the Atlantic region. The work of the society, on the other hand, did lead to a considerable expansion of the Kirk's activity throughout the area.[18] Simultaneously, Church of Scotland ministers were coming in larger numbers to Lower and Upper Canada with the result that in 1831 they formed a synod in connection with the home church and shortly afterwards told the members of the United Synod of the Canadas, formerly the Presbytery of the Canadas, that they would receive them if individually they submitted their credentials. The Synod of the Canadas, however, refused to join unless they were received as a body and unless the link with the Church of Scotland and the government were broken. As the Church of Scotland synod would not agree to this, the two bodies remained separate despite the government's wish that they would form one church.[19]

But more division was ahead. The Scots in Canada were watching with keen interest the conflict going on in the Established Church in Scotland over the subject of patronage. Soon after the outcome had become clear in 1843, emissaries of the Free Church arrived in British North America led by the redoubtable Dr. Robert Burns, who set forth the issues at stake. Although the problem of patronage did not exist in America, underlying this official reason for conflict was the basic theological disagreement between the evangelicals and the moderates. Dr. Burns, because of his evangelical zeal and his connection with the "Glasgow Society," succeeded in persuading most of the ministers sent out by the society to follow him out of the Church of Scotland to form a "free" church. In this he had the support of a large number of influential laymen such as Peter Redpath, the sugar magnate of Montreal, William Lyon MacKenzie, the "old rebel," and various others. While this may seem to have been a disaster, in another way it helped the Presbyterian cause, for the new church was missionary-minded and side-by-side with the "Missionary Presbytery" of the United Synod of the Canadas began to expand into the newly opened areas of Upper Canada such as the Huron Tract, and thence to the west of the Great Lakes. By 1851 there were some 238,000 Presbyterians in what was now Canada East and Canada West, making that denomination the second largest Protestant body, by far the largest part of which were first or second generation Scottish immigrants. In the Atlantic provinces of Nova Scotia and Prince Edward Island somewhat the same growth had taken place, with Presbyterian numbers rising to 93,000.[20]

From 1812 on Scots had been moving west on to the prairies, the first colony being that set up on the Red River by the Earl of Selkirk for the ousted crofters of Kildonan, Sutherlandshire. Other Scots had already arrived as officials of the Hudson's Bay and North West Companies, but only after Selkirk had successfully established a Scottish settlement at Eldon in Prince Edward Island and had failed to do the same in the southwest of Upper Canada, did he turn his attention to the lands beyond the Great Lakes. The sufferings of the settlers both from the weather and the opposition of the North West Company are mentioned elsewhere in this volume, but they also suffered from lack of spiritual leadership. Although they had been promised a Presbyterian minister on their arrival, owing to Selkirk's early death the promise was not kept and they had to depend upon the services of an elder, James Sutherland, specially commissioned to baptize and marry, but he left in 1818. The only ministrations from that time until 1851, when the first Scottish minister arrived on the scene, were those provided by the Church of England. Although the Rev. John West, the Anglican clergyman, adapted his services to the Presbyterian form, the settlers were still not willing to become Anglicans. Consequently, when the Rev. John Black, sent by the Presbyterian Church of Canada (Free Church), arrived in Kildonan in 1851, three hundred of the colonists immediately became members of his congregation. They then proceeded at considerable sacrifice to erect a stone building which is still in use as a Presbyterian church at Kildonan on the outskirts of Winnipeg.[21] From this church went out many settlers to points farther west, as well as missionaries to the Scottish and Indian settlements in what are now Manitoba, Saskatchewan and Alberta. Thus as the Canadian West as far as the Pacific coast began to come under settlement, the ministers from the Presbyterian Church of Canada, the Missionary Presbytery of the United Synod and, to a lesser extent, from the Church of Scotland, carried Presbyterianism to the Scottish and any other settlers or native peoples who wished their ministry.

While expansion had been taking place in the work of the various churches, moves had also been made to bring them all together to form one Canadian Presbyterian Church. The United Presbyterian Synod in the Canadas, made up of the Associate Secession and Relief Churches, had from the very beginning declared their independence of all Scottish churches. And while the Free Church body, which had come out of the Church of Scotland in 1844 as the Presbyterian Church of Canada, had some connection with its Scottish mother church, it was also virtually independent. These two bodies, therefore, joined together to form the Canada Presbyterian Church in 1861. Similar moves took place in the

Atlantic region. Thus when confederation of the Canadas and the eastern provinces was effected in 1867, to be followed later by the addition of Prince Edward Island and some of the western territories, it seemed only reasonable that the Presbyterians across the land should all come together. The result was that after some considerable discussion, in 1875 at a large gathering in Montreal the Presbyterian Church in Canada came into existence, with Rev. Dr. John Cook, minister of St. Andrew's Church, Quebec, the first moderator of the General Assembly. Of course, Scottish-like there were minorities who refused to enter the union for various reasons, but in general most Presbyterians came in, the doctrinal, organizational and liturgical bases being those of the Westminster Standards adopted by the Church of Scotland in the seventeenth century and held by all the uniting bodies. The one change made was that the concept of an established church was rejected, a move which caused some of the Church of Scotland ministers to refuse to join. The new body, however, by 1881 had some 650,000 members and adherents east of the Great Lakes, being the largest Protestant denomination in Canada until 1925.[22]

With Confederation, the opening up of the West, the laying down of the Canadian Pacific Railway and the government policy of granting land to homesteaders, settlers, not only from the British Isles, but also from Eastern Canada, the United States and all parts of Europe began to flood into the country. The response of the Presbyterian Church was a vigorous effort to meet the spiritual needs of all comers. In this connection one name stands out as pre-eminent, that of Dr. James M. Robertson, who from 1881 to 1902 acted as Superintendent of Western Missions, establishing congregations from the Red River to the foothills of the Rockies. Coupled with the name of Robertson were other Scottish ecclesiastical pioneers – W.G. Brown of Red Deer, D.G. MacQueen of Edmonton, E.D. MacLaren of Vancouver and almost equally well-known as Robertson, Andrew S. Grant, who followed the "trail of '98" in the Gold Rush to the Yukon where as a medical doctor as well as a minister he established in Dawson City both the Good Samaritan Hospital and St. Andrew's Presbyterian Church.[23] It is impossible to refer to all those who took part in the pioneer work in the West. Perhaps one example of what was being done is the present writer's father, W.D. Reid, who was Superintendent of Missions for the Province of Alberta, 1910-1912, during which period the number of Presbyterian preaching stations increased from around 100 to 160. But the fact that many of those ministered to were Ukrainians, Americans, Germans, and Poles as well as Scots shows that the Presbyterian Church in Canada was losing its strongly Scottish character, although even today that has by no means entirely disappeared.

It was at this point that new developments in the church's life began to appear on the horizon. While the Westminster Standards with their strongly biblically-oriented theology had been adopted as the basis of the union in 1875, biblical criticism, Darwinism and rationalism began to have their influence, particularly in the theological colleges. Queen's Theological College, Kingston, which had been founded by Church of Scotland adherents in 1842, was the spearhead of this movement, particularly under the leadership of Principal George M. Grant at the end of the century. Although Principal Sir William Dawson of McGill University, a New Brunswick Scot, and Principal Donald H. MacVicar of the Presbyterian College, Montreal, founded in 1868, and Principals Willis and Caven of Knox College, Toronto, opposed this tendency, it continued to spread with the result that the Presbyterian doctrinal distinctiveness of a Reformed church was being gradually eroded.[24] Added to this, there was the practical problem of attempting to minister to a widely spread Presbyterian population with limited resources in both men and money. Many were, therefore, beginning to feel that only a larger church organization, perhaps a federation of denominations or even an organic union, along the line of some of the big corporations such as the CPR might be the answer to the problem.

The matter of church union was brought to a head in 1903 when the General Council of the Methodist Church sent a formal invitation to the Presbyterian and Congregationalist Churches to enter into conversations concerning organic or corporate union. Almost immediately there was division within the Presbyterian ranks. Scots and those of Scottish origin took positions on both sides, and, as in most cases of Scottish conflict, feelings ran high and antagonism became bitter, dividing not only friends but families. Two successive votes taken on the matter by the Presbyterians showed a diminishing majority in favour of the union, but at the General Assembly of 1923 held in Port Arthur the final decision was made to take the plunge.[25] One commissioner to the 1923 assembly pled for time, but Dr. Charles Gordon ("Ralph Connor") declared that an act of Parliament would force "you rebels" in whether they wanted to go or not. To this the reply quickly came that Dr. Gordon had obviously forgotten the tradition of John Knox and the failure of the Stewarts to force the Covenanters to conform in the seventeenth century, and, the speaker added, "Scottish Presbyterians have not changed overmuch since then."

On June 10, 1925, the union took place between the Methodist, the Congregationalist and about 65% of the Presbyterian membership. Those Presbyterians who refused to enter the new church constituted themselves as the continuing Presbyterian Church in Canada, and under the leadership of its moderator, Rev. Dr. Ephraim Scott of Montreal, reaffirmed its adherence to the Westminster Standards and promised to carry on as the Presbyterian Church in Canada.[26] As one glances over rolls of presbyteries and of congregations since that date, one can see that the Scottish element is still very strong within both the ministry and the membership: Dickie, MacInnis, MacGregor, Lennox, MacBeth, Reid, Campbell, along with MacDonalds, MacLeods and MacLeans galore, as well as many others indicate clearly that the Scottish Protestant and Presbyterian tradition has

127

continued within this body. In the 1931 census of 870,728 reporting as Presbyterians, 245,000 said they were either Scots or of Scottish origin.

Although the United Church of Canada is much more of a mixture of both races and creeds, Scottish influence in its ranks is also quite strong. Names such as Slater, MacDonald, MacLean, Sinclair and MacLeod appear repeatedly in its records. The 1931 census shows about 8% of its members and adherents claiming to be Scots or of Scottish origin. It, however, has moved away from the basic Calvinism of the Scottish tradition, which tends to change its Scottish character. Nevertheless, the same fundamental moral values seem to survive along with the same tendency towards rebelliousness which has characterized Scots of Presbyterian background down to the present, for while it has accommodated itself to many middle class values, it has also been known as the "praying arm" of the Co-operative Commonwealth Federation, now the NDP, of which a number of Scottish minsters such as William Irvine were founding members.[27]

Up to this point we have dealt with the Scottish Presbyterian tradition in Canada, and rightly so, as this has represented the main Scottish Protestant tradition in Canada as well as in Scotland. Yet we must recognize that Scots were by no means limited to the Presbyterian bodies which went to make up the Presbyterian Church in Canada. It is an interesting point that many of those Scots who are to be found in the Anglican, Baptist and other churches came to Canada as Presbyterians, but for one reason or another joined other denominations. One example is John Strachan who when he failed to receive a call from a Presbyterian congregation joined the Church of England, in whose ranks he rose to prominence.[28] Others joined the Methodist or Baptist churches simply because their own church was not providing them with the services that they needed. A good example of this is to be found in the Eastern Townships of Quebec, where the Methodist circuit riders were quite active, while the Presbyterians under the leadership of Dr. Cook of Quebec City would not send out ministers to the Scottish settlements unless they had passed all the academic requirements of a Scottish presbytery. The result was that many Presbyterians, for want of their own church's ministrations, became Methodists, or where there was an English church, Anglicans. One other reason for Scots joining other denominations or groups was that not infrequently, coming from a background where theology was important and "sermon tasting" strong, they found the local Church of Scotland minister bland and not particularly helpful spiritually. Consequently, if there was no other Presbyterian church available they turned to the Methodists, Baptists or Plymouth Brethren.

As one looks over the roll of prominent Anglican churchmen in Canada one cannot but be somewhat surprised at the large number of Scottish names. It is interesting too that some of the most vigorous supporters of the Anglican Establishment came from this group. It is well to note, however, that few if any of the Scottish Anglicans came from the Scottish

Episcopal Church. Most of them came to Canada as Presbyterians, usually Church of Scotland, joining the Church of England shortly thereafter. It is not always easy to explain why this change was made, but it may have been partially the claims of the Church of England to be the Established Church which made the appeal. Or it may have been the influence of the High Church movement of John Henry Newman and E.B. Pusey which was having a certain amount of impact on some Presbyterian circles in Scotland.

The first Anglican of Scottish descent to become important in Canada was Bishop Charles Inglis, the first Bishop of the Diocese of British North America, a somewhat large area to oversee. He came of an Ulster family which had migrated from Roxburghshire some years earlier. Appointed Assistant of Holy Trinity Church, New York in 1765, as a Loyalist he migrated to Nova Scotia at the time of the Revolution, shortly afterwards being appointed to his episcopate. His son later became the third Bishop of Nova Scotia.[29] Most famous or notorious, depending upon one's point of view, of all the Scots who entered the Anglican Church was Bishop John Strachan, to whom we have already referred, a strong defender of the Anglican claims to establishment, the founder of the University of Toronto and one of the dominant political figures of his day. As tutor in his earlier days of the two sons of Rev. John Bethune, founder of St. Gabriel Presbyterian Church, Montreal, and Scots minister at Williamstown, he brought both of them into the Church of England, Alexander Neil becoming the second Bishop of Toronto and his brother, John, Archdeacon of Montreal and first Principal of McGill University. One might refer to many others such as Charles James Stewart who became in 1826 the second Bishop of Quebec. By 1827 the Church of England had thirty clergymen in the Canadas of whom eleven were Scots, most of them having been Presbyterian when they came to the New World.[30]

As we look west beyond the Great Lakes we see much the same type of development. In 1865 the second bishop of Rupert's Land took office. He was a Scot, Bishop Robert Machray, who effectively organized the missionary diocese which had up to this time been no more than a geographical expression. When he divided the diocese, setting up the Bishopric of Saskatchewan, he had his friend John MacLean who had been teaching in St. John's College, Winnipeg, appointed bishop. Machray, who became archbishop, was succeeded on his death by S.D. Matheson, also of Scottish extraction, who had been brought up by an aunt, a Miss Pritchard, who was an Anglican. Although the rest of the family were strongly Presbyterian he eventually became Anglican primate of Canada.[31] One could mention various other Scots who were active in the Anglican Church in Western Canada, but this should suffice to indicate that they played a considerable part in the development of Anglicanism as well as Presbyteriansism in Canada.

As mentioned above, other churches also had their share of Scots. The evangelical movements of eighteenth century Britain resulted in the formation of the Methodist Church, the development of various Baptist groups and the founding of the Christian Brethren (usually known as Plymouth Brethren) by J.N. Darby soon began to have their offshoots in North American colonies. Laying much less stress on academic qualifications than the Presbyterians and Anglicans, but stressing conversion, commitment and "spiritual gifts" in their preachers, these bodies began to have a wide influence particularly in the areas where the more formal churches never seemed to go. The outcome included camp meetings, revival services and the founding of small churches and assemblies in many localities. A considerable number of the Scots became involved in these bodies, playing a large and important part in their development and extension.

The Methodists were one of the bodies which counted a considerable number of Scots in their membership. For years the official paper, the *Christian Guardian*, was edited by two Ulster Scots: W.B. Creighton, father of Professor Donald Creighton, the well-known historian, and William McMullen. Moreover, many of the ministers of the Methodist Church came of Scottish backgrounds: Alexander Sutherland, Lachlan Taylor, James Roy are but three names which stand out in Eastern Canadian Methodism. In the West Rev. George McDougall, of Scottish parentage but born in Grey County, Ont., was one of the first missionaries to the Cree Indians. Rev. John MacLeod was another Scot who held a number of pastorates in the West. Rev. Ebenezer Robson, born of Scottish Presbyterian parentage in County Lanark, Ont., opened the first Methodist church in Victoria, B.C. When in 1925 the Methodist Church went into union with the majority of the Presbyterians and the Congregationlists, Scots Methodists were quite prepared to welcome Scots from the other denominations.[32]

Not many Scots seem to have been active in the Congregational Church, although there were a few. The most outstanding was Rev. Alexander MacGregor of Yarmouth, N.S., who was active in Upper Canada. He later went to the largest Congregational church in the Atlantic region where he also acted as one of the editors of the church's paper, the *Christian Standard*.[33]

Among the Baptists, Scots have always been a very strong element. Many of the members of the Church of Scotland were influenced by the revivalism of Robert Haldane. Some of his adherents came to British North America early in the nineteenth century and established congregations in a number of places. Having rejected infant baptism, they linked up with the existing Baptist groups, but in many cases remained strongly Scottish in orientation, so that in some places such as Dalesville, Que., until rather recent times there were Gaelic-speaking Baptist congregations. This tendency to attract Scots to the Baptist fold, particularly when the Presbyterian ministers were of the dry-as-dust variety, has continued to the present time. One might cite the influence of Dr. J.A. Johnson, originally of Stirling, Scotland, of Westmount Baptist Church, Montreal, in this regard. Scottish Baptists were active, however, beyond the pastorate, for when what is now McMaster University was founded its first principal was Rev. J.H. Fyfe, another Scot.[34]

An indication of what happened in the cases of some Scots of Presbyterian background is the story of the Elliotts and the McAllisters who settled around Molesworth in southwestern Ontario in the mid-nineteenth century. The nearest Presbyterian church which was at some distance did not seem to meet their spiritual needs. Thus when travelling evangelists representing the Plymouth Brethren came through the district holding services, members of the family were converted through their ministry, and have been leaders among the Plymouth Brethren in Canada for many years.[35]

As we have looked at the Scots in the various Protestant denominations and the important parts they have played in these bodies we have talked more in terms of organization than in terms of lifestyle and general outlook. The question then is what part in the development of Canada has the Scottish Protestant tradition played. The Protestants, like their Roman Catholic fellow-countrymen, if they settled on farms usually congregated in family and kinship groups. But the many artisans, businessmen or professional men tended to put down their roots in the burgeoning cities and towns. Moreover, not infrequently after two or three generations on the land, the Scottish Protestants began to move into the urban areas, breaking with their rural and agricultural background. This meant that the Protestant tradition, while often losing much of its specifically Scottish character, e.g. services in Gaelic, has exercised a wider influence than has the Scottish Roman Catholic tradition which tended to keep the people on the land.

At the beginning we can say that there was little or no class distinction in the influence which the Scottish Protestant tradition exerted. Whether the Scots came as farmers, fishermen, labourers, merchants or professional men they all seem to have had very much the same point of view. Furthermore, the Protestant tradition seems to have fostered considerable social mobility. "The lad o' pairts," whatever his background, social and economic origins, felt that he had the right and duty to make the best of himself and to rise in the world. One can think of farming families which have produced ministers, doctors, lawyers, nurses, and school teachers. This was simply carrying on a Scottish Protestant tradition which, as has been shown in another chapter, was not generally as true of the Roman Catholic Scots, although some did follow this pattern. The important thing to be noted here is that Scottish Protestants did not accept any rigid class structure, but stressed the importance of every man developing his God-given gifts to the best of his ability in this life. Class divisions, therefore, were to be ignored.

This meant of course that the Protestant tradition had its influence on every part of the Scottish social spectrum. We can think, for instance, of a man such as Peter Redpath, the Montreal sugar magnate, who founded the Coté Street Church in support of the Free Church of Scotland after the Disruption in 1844. His principles and outlook were very much the same as those of the humbler, working class members of the same congregation. The Marquess of Lorne, the Governor-General, in his metrical version of Psalm 121, expressed the same point of view as that set forth by Burns' "Cottar's Saturday Night" a scene which was re-enacted over and over again across the country from Cape North in Cape Breton to Prince Rupert on Vancouver Island. In the nineteenth century the Scottish Calvinist tradition was all-pervasive among those Protestants who had come from Scotland.

One thing which stands out very clearly in the Protestant tradition is the desire for intellectual and technical training. The home was the basis for the children's education and it began with the Westminster Shorter Catechism. As R.L. Stevenson points out, the Scot was always surrounded with an air of metaphysical divinity from his cradle by this means, and the tradition continued even when transported to Canada. The writer can remember his father telling him that as a boy on the farm in the Eastern Townships every Sunday night the family would gather to recite the Catechism, one-half one evening and the other half the next. But the Church also played an important role in this, particularly in the country districts. Various methods were taken to train the young. In one country congregation a minister, the Rev. James M'Conachie, set an essay topic which was : "In Old Testament times when men's thoughts and sentiments were rough and crude, their religion had to be of the same character. In the light of this, discuss the significance of animal sacrifice." Over a dozen essays were submitted by the young people, the prize production winning the astounding sum of one dollar. With such church training went the stress upon the school where the teachers were not always good or even kind, but where youngsters knew that they had to have the elements of education if they were to accomplish anything in life. While Ralph Connor draws a somewhat romanticized picture, his *Glengarry Schooldays* comes close to reality in many ways. When the budding scholar had gone as far as he could in the one-roomed schoolhouse, he could then take off for Quebec to Morrin College, for Montreal to McGill, for Kingston to Queen's or for Toronto to the University of Toronto, all of which had a large proportion of Scots both in faculty and student body, to obtain training which would make him a lawyer, a doctor, a minister or even a professor. Others might head for some merchant's counting house, a bank or some other business concern where they often rose to places of importance and responsibility.

Yet the Scottish Protestant did not think only of the importance of "making it" in this world. There was a strong sense of divine calling which arose out of his Calvinistic background. From the days of John Knox great stress had been laid in Scottish Protestantism on the importance of one taking his proper place in society where he could work for the benefit and advantage of the commonwealth, wherever his lot might be cast. As Knox and many of those who came after him constantly stressed, he was to seek to do all for the glory of God. His own personal development, therefore, had not merely a worldly stimulus, for he was actually working for eternity. This was impressed upon him from an early age when he learned the first question and answer of the Shorter Catechism: "What is man's chief end? Man's chief end is to glorify God and enjoy him forever." This gave the Scot a sense of objectivity and of purpose which transcended monetary or social advantage.

Along with his feeling of calling and responsibility went the evangelical emphasis upon conversion. The stress upon man's own weakness and sinfulness, forcing him to turn to God, seeking his grace, mercy and forgiveness through Jesus Christ, was basic to much Scottish thinking. True, there might be theological differences among them, but the evangelical influence was extremely strong as can be seen at the Disruption of 1844 which was partially caused by frustration at the lack of truly evangelical preaching in the Church of Scotland. The fact that a considerable number also left the Church of Scotland for the more evangelical denominations, Methodist, Baptist or Plymouth Brethren, points in this direction. Even when such people turned away from the church of their fathers, they carried with them the stress on sovereign grace and the necessity of loving obedience to God's call.

While it is true that all Scots were not Presbyterians and so would not necessarily study the Westminster Shorter Catechism, yet the large majority were, and their attitudes and outlook certainly influenced the whole Scottish culture, with the result that Scottish Protestants generally developed much the same point of view. Furthermore, when we realize that many of the Scots who became active in non-Presbyterian denominations in Canada were originally trained as Presbyterians it is not difficult to understand how Scottish Protestantism helped to develop a very definite type of individual in Canada.

This in turn seems to have resulted in other characteristics. Probably one of the most noticeable was Scottish hard work and thrift even among those who may have rejected the 'faith of their fathers.' Furthermore, the Scots were prepared to take chances in order to advance their fortunes and their work. It is no accident that the North West Company was made up largely of Scots, and that so many of Canada's other large industrial and commercial ventures were fathered by Scots. Donald Smith, Lord Strathcona of the Hudson's Bay Company, Robert Simpson of the Robert Simpson Company and Colonel Robert MacLaughlin of the MacLaughlin Carriage Works, later General Motors of Canada, are but a few of the names one could mention. This all involved independence of thought and heart, which one sees only too plainly if he attends, even today, a Presbyterian church court. Yet along with this went also a strong sense of responsibility in the use of one's wealth, time and talents. It is no accident, for instance, that so many of the universities, hospitals and similar institutions particularly in Eastern Canada, were established through the generosity of wealthy Scots or Canadians of Scottish origin. This again was part of the Protestant emphasis upon the fact that wealth was given by God for the benefit of all, not just for the enjoyment of the few, a point that is constantly made from the other end of the social spectrum by such Scots as the Honorable "Tommy" Douglas, first leader of the national New Democratic Party. To the Scot his religious beliefs have always been something which must lead to action and application in everyday life.

Although today much has changed with growing secularism and materialism, and declining membership in all the Protestant churches, the Scottish Protestant tradition still exercises its influence. In many cases the religious foundation may have been eroded with the result that the individual rejects, or at least neglects, the specifically religious presuppositions of the Scottish Protestant tradition.

The ethical and moral principles, however, have been so imbedded in the individual's personality that they are still operating automatically. Some may feel that it would be well to rid oneself of these characteristics, while others may seek to keep them even though they do not agree with their source and origin. Since the Scottish Protestant tradition in the past has made men strong to do great things, perhaps it is time that Scots began to look back to the rock whence they have been hewn to renew their strength and the spiritual vitality upon which their forefathers drew with such effect.

NOTES

1. R.L. Stevenson, "The Foreigner at Home," *Memories and Portraits* (London: Collins, n.d.); W. Notestein, *The Scot in History* (London, 1947).
2. *Ibid.*, pp. 119f; P. Janton, *John Knox, L'homme et L'oeuvre* (Paris: Didier, 1967), pp. 174ff; W.S. Reid, *Trumpeter of God* (New York: Scribner's, 1974), pp. 150ff.
3. "The Confession of Faith," (1560) in *John Knox's History of the Reformation in Scotland*, W.C. Dickinson, ed. (Edinburgh: Nelson, 1949), II, 266; cf. D. MacLean, *Aspects of Scottish Church History* (Edinburgh: T.&T. Clark, 1927), *passim*, G.D. Henderson, *Church and Ministry* (London: Hodder & Stoughton, 1951), *passim*.
4. J.H. Burleigh, *A Church History of Scotland* (London: Oxford, 1960), pp. 420ff.
5. W.R. Foster, *Bishop and Presbytery, The Church of Scotland 1661-1688* (London: SPCK, 1958), pp. 155ff.
6. *Ibid.*, pp. 12ff; Burleigh, pp. 261ff; D.G. Henderson, *Presbyterianism*

(Aberdeen: University Press, 1954), pp. 53ff; J.G. Vos, *The Scottish Covenanters* (Shanghai, 1940), pp. 137ff. For a more detailed account of the Covenanters cf. J.K. Hewison, *The Covenanters* (Glasgow: Smith & Son, 1908).

7. Burleigh, pp. 263ff; E. Scott, *Church Union and the Presbyterian Church in Canada* (Montreal: Lovell, 1928), pp. 73ff.

8. MacLean, pp. 37ff; Burleigh, pp. 261ff; R. Buchanan, *The Ten Years' Conflict* (Glasgow: Blackie, 1854), I, 123ff, 151ff.

9. MacLean, pp. 134ff; Henderson, *Presbyterianism*, pp. 1ff, 175ff; W.S. Reid, "The Scottish Disruption and Reunion, 1843-1929," *Christendom* (1943), pp. 318ff, 326ff.; Burleigh, pp. 395ff.

10. For an indication of this trend see J.S. Moir, *Enduring Witness* (Toronto: Presbyterian Publications, 1974).

11. Wm. Gregg, *History of the Presbyterian Church in the Dominion of Canada*.

12. *Ibid.*, p. 135.

13. *Ibid.*, pp. 143ff; W.W. Campbell, *The Scotsman in Canada*, (Toronto: Musson, n.d.), p. 308.

14. *Ibid.*, pp. 309ff; Gregg, pp. 155ff; J. MacKenzie, "John Bethune, Founder of Presbyterianism in Upper Canada," *Called to Witness*, W.S. Reid, ed. (Toronto: Presbyterian Publications, 1975). 15. W.S. Reid, *The Church of Scotland in Lower Canada: Its Struggle for Establishment* (Toronto: Presbyterian Publications, 1936); Gregg, pp. 406f.

16. Gregg, pp. 204ff, 359ff.

17. Reid, *Church of Scotland*, p. 65ff.

18. Gregg, pp. 278ff.

19. *Ibid.*, pp. 446ff.

20. *Ibid..*, pp. 587.

21. *Ibid.*, pp. 213ff.

22. Ibid., pp. 600ff; W. Gregg, *A Short History of the Presbyterian Church in Canada* (Toronto: Robinson, 1892), pp. 188ff; W.S. Reid, "John Cook and the Kirk in Canada," *Enkindled by the Word*, N.G. Smith, ed. (Toronto: Presbyterian Publications, 1966), pp. 28ff. *Dominion of Canada Census*, 1881 & 1921. Those claiming to be Presbyterians increased from 663,000 to 1,409,000, while Anglicans increased from 575,000 to 1,408,000.

23. N.G. Smith, "James Robertson and the Churches in the Prairie Provinces," *ibid.*, pp. 43ff; David A. Smith, "British Columbia and the Yukon," *ibid.*, pp. 53ff; G. Bryce, *The Scotsman in Canada* (Toronto: Musson, n.d.), II, pp. 255ff.

24. W.J. Rattray, *The Scot in North America*. (Toronto: MacLear, 1882), III, 821ff.

25. Scott, pp. 59f; A.L. Farris, "The Fathers of 1925," *Enkindled*, pp. 59ff.

26. *Acts and Proceedings of the 51st General Assembly of the Presbyterian Church in Canada* (Toronto, 1925).

27. Cf. J.E. Hart, 'William Irvine and Radical Politics in Canada,' Unpublished Ph.D. Thesis, University of Guelph, 1972.
28. R. Campbell, *History of St. Gabriel Street Church, Montreal* (Montreal: Lovell, 1887), pp. 183ff.
29. *Ibid.*, p. 326.
30. *Ibid.*, p. 327.
31. Bryce, pp. 278ff.
32. Campbell, pp. 331; Bryce, pp. 282.
33. Rattray, III, 902.
34. Campbell, pp. 291ff, 332f.
35. This information was given to the author by Mrs. R.W. Farnworth of Guelph, Ont., who is a descendant of the original MacAllister settlers.

EIGHT

The Scottish
Military Tradition

George F.G. Stanley

I

'S ann as an tir's 'eachdraidh a chineas spiorad cogail
The military spirit comes out of the land and its history

Ever since the first disbanded Highland soldiery and displaced crofters settled on Canada's shores two hundred years ago, in the 1760s and 1770s, Scottish Canadians have borne their full share of the burden of Canada's defence. Soldiers and regiments bearing Scottish names and wearing the bonnet, kilt and feather form a mighty array in our history; they have fought in the snows of Canada, in the mud of Flanders, in the mountains of Italy; they have inspired Canadians with the military traditions of old Scotland, bravery and devotion, fortitude in distress. Today there are over 2,000,000 people of Scottish descent in Canada, although through intermarriage the Scottish blood flows in the veins of many more Canadians than the census returns would suggest. It is, indeed, sufficiently widespread that, despite dilution, it has encouraged that mystic sympathy of Canada for Scotland which unites the two lands in the unity of understanding. The Canadian soldier in World War II was well aware of it, if only because he seemed to feel more at home in Scotland than in the land of the Southrons. Perhaps that understanding derives, in part at least, from the fact that Canadian and Scot live in northern lands, to the south of which there is a powerful, and too often dominating nation. Each knows that his nation has always to be on the watch lest it lose its freedom and its own distinctive nationality.

The Scottish military tradition is generally associated with the Highlands, the country of the chief, clan and cateran. This does not mean that the Lowlands were bare of men of military virtue, of men ready and able to wield a spear or broadsword in defence of their faith and their possession - the achievements of the Cameronians contradicts that - but rather that the Highlands, by the very nature of the countryside and the tribal feudalism it nourished, tended to develop and perpetuate the military characteristics of independence and combativeness more than did the land and society of the Lowlands.

The country north and west of the Highland Line was, and still is, in many respects, a wild, harsh, forbidding land of violent tempests and uncertain climate. It is not a rich luxuriant land, but one of bare mountains, bleak hills, heathered moors, coniferous forests, lakes, streams and fens. There are only isolated and disconnected patches of arable soil[1] located in the sequestered straths, glens and islands which favoured the settlement of family groups under their natural leaders or *ceann-cinnidh*. Such a land was not of the nature to sustain a large and prosperous agricultural population. The men who lived in the Highlands were the sons of Esau. They lived on the fish they caught in the lochs, the deer they hunted in the hills, and the herds they tended on their thin mountain pastures or reaved from their Lowland neighbours. Only the bold, the strong, the hardy and the independent survived in such a land, men nursed in poverty, men whose needs were simple and basic. Geography made the Scottish Highlander, and it made him good soldier material, because it demanded those qualities which make men good soldiers; hardihood, courage, endurance, self-reliance and loyalty to one's leader and one's comrades.[2]

The history of the country, too, added its strength to reinforce the fighting spirit of the men of Scotland. From the day when Calgacus fell at the head of the Pictish host to the Roman, Agricola, at Mons Graupius in 84 A.D., to the flight of Charles Edward Stewart from the field of Culloden in 1746, Scottish history has been one long, bloody brawl. But Culloden was the end – the end of seventeen centuries of strife between warring tribes, warring religions, warring nations. Did anything of value emerge from it beyond an unpopular union with England bought with English gold? Does anything emerge from Scottish history other than bloodshed and violence and sticky sentiment? Beneath the surface will be found virtues as heroic as they sometimes appear irrational, the virtues of independence, devotion and valour. These are the saving virtues of the Scottish story and the backbone of the Scottish military tradition.

II

Na Sassunaich a ghadhail cothrom air spiorad cogail na Ghaidhail
The Southrons exploit the Scottish military spirit

The immediate British reaction to the Jacobite rising of 1745-46 was an effort to break the spirit of the men who had served the Jacobite cause. Rapine, slaughter and torture, all were used with relentless vindictiveness by the king's son who commanded the British government forces.[3] Quarter was given to no straggler or fugitive, except to the select few reserved for the spectacle of a public execution. For the wounded who lay on the field of battle there was no compassion, only the bullet and the bayonet when they were discovered. All men suspected of rebel sympathies were herded into gaols, prison ships, cellars or lofts, and left without food or water, or clothes to hide their nakedness; even the doctor had his lancet taken from him lest he be moved to blood some of the wounded in order to save their lives. To His Grace of Newcastle, Lord Chesterfield wrote, "Starve the country by your ships, put a price on the heads of the chiefs, and let the Duke put all to the fire and sword."[4] That was exactly what "Bloody Butcher" Cumberland did. Through the glens and over the hills, his patrols laid waste the land, plundered the houses, burned the crofts, killed suspected Jacobites, raped the women and drove the Highlanders' cattle to the military posts. When starving creatures sought a handful of oatmeal they were driven away with the butts of muskets; should any soldier or his wife show a little humanity, well, Cumberland had said "they shall be first whipped severely . . . and then put on meal and water in the Provost for a fortnight."[5] Heartless and abhorrent as these reprisals were, the Duke considered them inadequate. To Newcastle he wrote, three months after the battle of Culloden, "I am sorry to leave this country in the condition it is in; for all the good that we have done is a little blood letting, which has only weakened the madness, but not at all cured it; and I tremble for fear that this vile spot may still be the ruin of this island and of our family."[6]

Such methods were not without results; but even more effective in throttling the Highland spirit were the legislative enactments, the laws that destroyed the clan system, that made the playing of the old music and the wearing of the kilt and tartan criminal offences. Every Highlander was required to surrender his arms. Failure to do so might mean transportation for seven years. Restrictions too were imposed upon the Episcopal Church, regarded by the authorities as only slightly less ardent than the Roman Catholics in their support of the House of Stewart. Most effective of all was the Act abolishing the hereditary jurisdictions. For generations the inhabitants of the Highlands had looked to their chiefs for direction and protection. Now there were no more chiefs. Those who had supported the Jacobites in 1745 were, in some instances, executed, in others, outlawed, and in all instances obliged to forfeit their estates. Those who had not been out in '45 were ready to sell out, salvage what they could in golden guineas, as compensation for what they had lost in giving up their rights of "pit and gallows." They moved to Edinburgh and acquired an English veneer. Thus, when he needed him most, the Highland clansman had no chief. He was leaderless in a hostile world.

Two choices were open to him if he were to avoid starvation. He could emigrate, leave the land of his forefathers and find a new home elsewhere, or he could accept German Geordie's shilling and serve in the army of the Hanoverian king. Both were unpalatable. But the will to survive is stronger even than love of home or pride of ancestry.[7]

Poverty was nothing new to the Highlander. Neither was serving in the armies of foreign monarchs. He had been doing it since the days of the Crusades. During the sixteenth century licences had been granted to individuals to raise men in Scotland for service in Denmark, Sweden and the Low Countries, a traffic which increased during the seventeenth century. Donald MacKay raised 3600 men for Christian IV, and Gustavus Adolpus is said to have had 10,000 Scots under his command during the Thirty Years' War. Others served the King of France as Archers of the Guard. At a later date refugees from the forces of Dundee, Mar and Charles Edward fought in the armies of France. The son of a Scottish Jacobite schoolteacher became a marshal of France under Napoleon, Etienne-Jacques-Joseph-Alexandre Macdonald, Duke of Taranto.

There was precedent too for serving King George. In 1725 the British government had raised a number of independent companies to keep watch on the Highland clans and discourage the popular activities of cattle lifting and blackmailing. These independent companies were clad in a black, green and blue government tartan to distinguish them from the regular troops and were known as the *Freiceadan Dubh*, or Black Watch. Several years later, in the hope of discouraging the growth of Jacobitism, the Lord President Duncan Forbes of Culloden suggested to the British authorities that greater scope might be given the natural military attributes of the Highlanders were they to be recruited into several regiments commanded by English or Scottish officers "of undoubted loyalty" and officered by chiefs and chieftains "of the disaffected clans." "If Government pre-engage the Highlanders in the manner I propose," he wrote, "they will not only serve well against the enemy abroad, but will be hostages for the good behaviour of their relatives at home, and I am persuaded it will be absolutely impossible to raise a rebellion in the Highlands."[8] Forbes's advice was followed only in part. Not several but one regiment only was formed, and this by bringing together the various independent companies of the Watch. In 1740 the new regiment, numbered the 43rd (changed in 1749 to the 42nd) but still bearing the name Black Watch, was embodied under the command of Sir Robert Munro of Foulis, and officered by Highland gentlemen, a number of whom were from the clans Munro, Grant and Campbell, whose Whig sympathies met with the approval of the British government.[9]

In 1743 the Black Watch was ordered to England. It was not a popular order, nor a popular move; the Highlanders had no wish to serve so far from their own glens. However, they were told that the move was simply to satisfy the curiosity of the German lairdie who sat on England's throne and who had never seen a Highland regiment. When they arrived in London the soldiers of the Black Watch learned that the king had gone to Hanover and heard rumours that they were to be sent to America. Regarding such deception as intolerable – many of those even in private rank were gentlemen – they set out on their own for Scotland. Overtaken at Northampton by a larger British force, the Scots surrendered and were disarmed. A number of the so-called mutineers were tried; three of them (all sons of Clan Chattan) were executed. Then the expected blow fell, two hundred of the Watch were sent to the West Indies; the remainder joined Cumberland's forces in Flanders, to contribute their decisive strength to the victory of Fontenoy. During the Jacobite rising of 1745-46 the Black Watch warmed their heels on the shores of Kent; to send them north against their blood relatives in the Highland host would hardly have been a politic act. After Culloden, they went to Ireland on garrison duty where they remained, with one short tour in Flanders, until the outbreak of the Seven Years' War against France in 1756.

The bravery of the Watch at Fontenoy had made its impression upon the British authorities. They therefore decided to repeat the experiment of employing Highlanders in the British service. In 1745 Campbell, the Earl of Loudoun, was commissioned to raise another Highland unit.[10] The time, however, was critical, and the devotion of the recruits to the Hanoverian monarchy suspect. There were desertions to the Jacobites, but for the most part the officers and men remained true to their engagement. Nevertheless the regiment did not see service as a unit. Three companies were at Prestonpans only to surrender to Prince Edward when Cope's army was put to flight. Some men of Loudoun's regiment were victims of the Rout of Moy. Three companies were at Culloden. After a brief tour in the Low Countries the regiment was disbanded in 1748.

It was the outbreak of the Seven Years' War with France in 1756 that led to the policy which drained the Highlands by sending Scotsmen to fight England's wars in Europe and North America. William Pitt adopted Duncan Forbes's ideas with enthusiasm, and during the period of the Seven Years' War no fewer than ten line regiments, the 77th (Montgomery's), 78th (Fraser's), 87th (Keith's), 88th (Campbell's), 89th (Gordon's), 100th, 101st (Johnstone's), 105th (Queen's), 113th (Royal Highland Volunteers), and MacLean's, and two fencible regiments (regiments for the internal defence), Argyll Fencibles and Sutherland Fencibles, were recruited in the British interest.[11] From Britain's point of view it was sound military strategy to make the best use of the Scottish military tradition, and good politics to get so many sullen and resentful unemployed men out of their mountain fastness. It was a policy which lesser men than Pitt were glad to continue when later wars broke out in 1775 and 1793. The regiments raised during the American Revolutionary War included 71st (Fraser's), 73rd (MacLeod's), 74th (Argyll Highlanders), 76th (Macdonald's), 77th (Atholl Highlanders), 78th (Seaforths), 81st (Aberdeenshire Regiment), 2nd Battalion, Black Watch. Additional regiments were raised on the outbreak of the French Revolutionary War in 1793. The depopulation of the Highlands may have been largely the result of the Highland clearances and the emigration of the clansmen; but it was the result, too, of the military exploitation of Scotland's human resources for the sake of Britain's imperial ambitions.

Of Britain's new Highland regiments, three saw service in North America during the French war, the 42nd (Black Watch), the 77th (Montgomery's), and the 78th (Fraser's). The two latter were raised in 1757 from the Jacobite clans, Frasers, Macdonalds, Camerons, MacLeans and Macphersons in particular. The 77th was commanded by Lieutenant-Colonel Archibald Montgomery, afterwards Lord Eglinton, and the 78th by Simon Fraser, son of the Lord Lovat who had lost his head after Culloden for supporting Prince Charles.

The 42nd was the first Highland regiment ever to come to North America. It arrived in New York in 1756 and promptly moved to Albany. During the winter of 1756-57 it underwent serious training in bush fighting in the Canadian manner. It was a kind of training much needed by the Scots, for their traditional tactic of firing a volley and then rushing forward with targe and broadsword to engage the enemy hand-to-hand was of limited value against an elusive foe who knew how to make good use of cover. Early in the summer of 1757, the regiment moved to Halifax as part of the large force assembled for an attack upon Louisbourg. Here it was joined by the 77th and the 78th. The Louisbourg assault was not carried through in 1757. The delay in the arrival of the naval component, the lateness of the season, and the arrival of reinforcements in Louisbourg convinced Loudoun that the assault would have to be postponed to a more opportune occasion and, leaving a number of his troops at Halifax, he returned to New York with his three regiments of Highlanders.

All three regiments played notable roles during the campaign of 1758, albeit in three separate theatres of operations.[12] In the spring, Fraser's Highlanders joined Amherst's force for the postponed assault upon Louisbourg, forming part of the brigade commanded by Brigadier-General Wolfe, who, incidentally, had fought at Culloden and had shared in the ruthless and unsavoury "pacification" of the Highlands. But Wolfe, who had formerly distrusted the Highlanders, now recognized their worth, and used them along with the light infantry in every action calling for the employment of shock troops. After a siege of seven weeks the fortress surrendered. The impatient Wolfe would have continued on to Quebec, but he was compelled to limit his military activities to attacking Acadian communities along the Atlantic shore.

On the far western front, Montgomery's Highlanders pushed their way slowly towards Fort Duquesne as the main regular component of Brigadier General Forbes's corps. At Loyalhanna, about 40 miles from their destination, the Highlanders' weakness in bush fighting became all too apparent when a detachment of the 77th, under Major James Grant, was badly cut to pieces by the French and the Indians. But the French at Fort Duquesne, outnumbered and in no position to offer a prolonged resistance to Forbes's men, in November blew up their defences and withdrew. In honour of William Pitt, Forbes renamed the smoking ruin Pittsburgh. Here the 77th spent the winter. In the following May it moved to the central theatre of operations to join the 42nd on Lake Champlain for a second attack upon Carillon (Ticonderoga).

The first assault upon the French position at Carillon had ended in disaster for the Black Watch. With every confidence in the world, the Highlanders had joined the mighty array which was intended to strike north to the St. Lawrence – 16,000 men, regulars, provincials, rangers and boatmen. What was there to halt them? Only a poor stone fort on Lake Champlain manned by a force considerably inferior in numbers. The British commander, James Abercromby, had all the tools necessary for siege or open warfare. A quick look at the French defences convinced him that Carillon could be carried by storm, and, with a singular lack of imagination, he decided upon a frontal attack. On the morning of July 8 the British assault troops, led by the Grenadiers, deployed in the open area in front of the French defences; four battalions, with the 42nd in support. When the Grenadiers failed to penetrate the thick abbatis in front of the French breastworks, the Scots impetuously rushed forward and began hacking their way through the tangled branches. Safe behind their defences the French infantry cut them to pieces with well-directed musketry. Time and again the brave Highlanders surged forward, only to fall back in the face of a murderous fire. A few men did succeed in reaching the French breastworks, but they had no scaling ladders and when, after great exertion, Captain John Campbell and several others forced their way over the French works, they were stabbed to death by French bayonets. For four hours Abercromby kept it up; then, finally, he gave the order to retreat. Despite their losses, the Highlanders still sought vengeance for the death of their comrades, and Abercromby was obliged to repeat his orders three times before he could prevail upon the stubborn Scots to obey. The 42nd, indeed, paid dearly for its intrepidity: 314 officers and men were killed and 333 wounded in the battle, over half the strength of the regiment. Despite its shattered condition Abercromby gave The Black Watch the honour of covering the retirement, although in its weakened state it is questionable whether the regiment could have beaten back a determined attack had Montcalm been disposed to pursue the retreating British. Abercromby may not have been a brilliant tactician, but at least he knew how to humour the spirit of his Highlanders.

1759 was the decisive year of the war, and to the British success in that year the Highlanders made a notable contribution. The Black Watch, reinforced by a strong infusion of new recruits, and Montgomery's Highlanders formed part of the army Jeffrey Amherst led, methodically and laboriously, through the Lake George-Lake Champlain entrance to Canada. Carillon and Fort St. Frédéric (Crown Point) were occupied without a battle. Had Amherst been less concerned with rebuilding what the French had destroyed, he might have reached Montreal and the St. Lawrence. As it was he got no further than Crown Point before going into winter quarters. Thus it was Fraser's Highlanders, not the 42nd or the 77th, which played the major role in the reduction of Canada.

Occupying a position made formidable by nature and by military engineering, Quebec was the key to Canada. Montcalm realized it and chose to remain on the defensive. Let the British come to him. They did, in the spring of 1759, under James Wolfe. But weeks went by and Wolfe made little or no progress. Fraser's men shared in the ill-fated attack on the French and Canadian position at Beauport in July, and in the terrorist raids carried on by General Wolfe during the month of August. Finally, almost as a last resort, Wolfe sought to gain a lodgement to the west of the city on the Plains of Abraham. Fraser's Highlanders were on the heels of the Light Infantry who first climbed the cliff of Quebec in the early hours of September 13. A French-speaking Highlander, Captain Donald Macdonald, a brother of Clanranald, whose men had been out in '45, lulled the suspicions of the French sentry and made possible the seizure of the plains. When the British drew up their battle array, Fraser's were in the front rank. After exchanging shots with the French, the Highlanders reverted to their traditional tactics; they threw away their muskets, drew their broad swords and swept forward, halting only when they reached the walls of the city. Led by Brigadier-General Murray, they returned to the woods on the left flank to oust the Canadians holding up the other pursuing troops. Watching the whole thing with great interest was Montcalm's aide-de-camp, the Chevalier Johnstone.[13] He, too, had been out in '45, fighting alongside the Glengarry Macdonells at Culloden. He would have recognized the names if not the features of those who were killed or wounded at Quebec, such as McNeil of Barra, Macdonell of Lochgarry, Macdonell of Keppoch, Fraser of Inverlochy and Campbell of Barcaldine.

Fraser's Highlanders witnessed the surrender of Quebec on September 18 by de Ramézay, a Frenchman of Scottish descent, and then spent the winter in the ruined city. It was dreadfully cold, cold enough to cause Malcolm Fraser to admit that "the Philibeg is not at all calculated for this terrible climate."[14] Canada was colder even than Scotland. In the spring the 78th marched out with Murray to face the French and Canadian army, led by the Chevalier de Lévis. Murray was defeated at Ste. Foye, a mishap which elicited from Charles Stewart, who had served at Culloden, "from April battles and Murray generals, good Lord deliver me!"[15] Only the walls of Quebec and the timely arrival of British ships of war saved Murray from surrendering in 1760 the fortress Wolfe had gained in 1759.

Following the capitulation of Canada in September, 1760, the Black Watch and the 77th were sent to the West Indies. Subsequently they returned to assist in the suppression of the Indian rising led by Pontiac. Meanwhile, the 78th contributed a detachment to Colonel William Amherst's force, sent to recover St. John's, Newfoundland, from the French in 1762. In 1763 the war was over and the peace was signed. The Watch remained on the regular establishment, but the 77th and 78th were ordered to be disbanded, the officers and men being given the opportunity of settling in British North America if they wished to do so. Rather than face sad memories and unemployment in Scotland, many chose to remain in

Canada, where each officer and man received a grant of land according to his rank. Thus the disbanded solidiery of Montgomery's and Fraser's Highlanders became the first Scots to form an integral part of Canadian life and history. And they were not the last. Others soon arrived in North America; destitute but proud men, who settled in Prince Edward Island through the initiative of John Macdonald, Eighth of Glenaladale; in Pictou, Nova Scotia, through the inducements of a Lowland promoter; and the Mohawk Valley, through the leadership of three Macdonell lairds, Aberchalder, Leek and Collachie. By far the greater number of them were Jacobites: "ged chaidh an sgadpdth air gach taobh, cha chaochail iad an gnaths," sang the Gaelic bard.[16] "Although they were scattered in every direction, they did not change their ways."

III

Spiorad cogail na Ghadhail a tighinn do Chanada
The Scottish military spirit comes to Canada

Vergennes, the astute French ambassador to Constantinople, is said to have predicted that England would quickly repent having insisted upon the cession of Canada by France, if only because it removed the American colonies' greatest inducement to remain within the British Empire, the threat of French invasion. Peter Kalm had said much the same thing twelve years before. Within another twelve years, history proved both good prophets. By 1775 British soldiers and American minutemen were exchanging shots at Lexington and a British garrison was being besieged at Boston by 20,000 angry American militia. In 1776 the American colonies declared their independence.

Once more the British government looked to the Scots for help. More regiments were raised in Great Britain and old ones, like Fraser's, were revived. More significantly, the practice of employing Scotsmen as soldiers was extended to the British possessions in North America. On June 12, 1775, General Thomas Gage issued orders to Lieutenant-Colonel Allan Maclean, son of Maclean of Torloisk, Mull, to raise a regiment consisting of two battalions, each of ten companies, to be clothed, armed and accoutred like The Black Watch[17] and "to be called the Royal Highland Emigrants."[18] Maclean was appointed lieutenant-colonel commandant of the regiment, as well as commanding officer of the 1st Battalion, with Donald Macdonald as his major, while Major John Small, formerly of the 42nd, was placed in charge of the 2nd battalion.

The idea was that The Emigrants should find their recruits among former soldiers who had served in the 42nd, the 77th and the 78th, and in the several Scottish settlements in America. As inducements to enlist, each man was promised a grant of land at the expiration of hostilities, and one guinea levy-money on joining. Even so, recruits came in slowly. The recruiting parties of the 1st Battalion found it difficult to get recruits safely and quietly out of the Mohawk Valley without arousing the suspicions of

Americans, and it was some time before The Emigrants were brought up to strength. To fill the gaps in the ranks, recourse was had to enlisting Irishmen from Newfoundland and prisoners of war who were willing and ready to change sides. Few of these latter were Scots, and few of them made reliable soldiers.[19] Initially, detachments of The Emigrants were posted along the St. Lawrence and in the Richelieu Valley and, under Maclean's command planned to relieve the besieged Fort Saint Jean. With the defeat of Guy Carleton's co-operating force from Montreal, Maclean hurried his Emigrants back to an almost defenceless Quebec where they furnished the bulk of the "regular" (if they could be called that) army of the garrison. During the siege of Quebec by Montgomery and Arnold, The Emigrants played a notable part. Captain Malcolm Fraser, formerly of the 78th, was the first to observe the American signals on the night of December 31, 1775, indicating that an attack was in the offing. Allan Maclean commanded the defenders under Carleton and was, in large measure, responsible for the defeat of the Americans.[20] When General Burgoyne organized his counter-attack force in 1777, Maclean's Emigrants were posted along the line of communications and provided the garrison for Fort Ticonderoga. As an indication of his satisfaction with their services, George III instructed Sir Frederick Haldimand in 1779 to place The Emigrants upon the regular establishment of the British army and to number them the 84th among the British line regiments.[21] During its career the 1st Battalion in Canada was plagued with desertions, mostly among the Americans and Irish who had joined the regiment; it is worth noting that not one native Highlander deserted, and only one man was brought to the halberts during the time the regiment was embodied.[22]

In Nova Scotia, Major Small had less trouble obtaining recruits than Maclean in Canada. The 2nd Battalion was not, however, employed as a unit. Instead, it was broken up into detachments and sent to garrison such posts as Annapolis, Cumberland, Saint John, Windsor and Halifax, where American raiders might be expected to land. The rest of the battalion, five companies, was sent to join Cornwallis in the southern colonies where they fought with distinction at Eataw Springs. The troops, however, resented being used piecemeal. It was with disgust that Captain Alexander Macdonald wrote, "We have absolutely been worse used than any one Regiment in America and have done more duty and drudgery of all kinds than any other Battalion in America, these three Years past, and it is but reasonable, Just and Equitable that we should now be Suffered to Join together at least as early as possible in the Spring and let some Other Regiment relieve the different posts we at present Occupy."[23]

Both battalions of The Royal Highland Emigrants were disbanded at the end of hostilities. Some of the officers and men returned to Scotland, but the greater number took up their promised land grants, the 1st Battalion in Canada and the 2nd in Nova Scotia, and remained in British North America.

There were other Scotsmen who served the King in British North

America during the Revolutionary War besides those commissioned or enlisted in the Royal Highland Emigrants. A considerable number of Highlanders from Glengarry, Glen Urquhart and Strathglass had emigrated during 1773 to the Mohawk Valley and settled on the lands of Sir William Johnson, the Irish baronet, whose name was so closely associated with the league of the Six Nations. Johnson liked the Highlanders, cultivated them, and encouraged them to maintain their customs. The tradition of the clan and the chief was still very much alive among the Highlanders, and it was hardly surprising that Johnson assumed, in the minds of his Scottish tenantry, something of the character of a Highland chief. When Sir William died in 1774, this attachment was transferred to his son, Sir John. This explains why, on the outbreak of the Revolutionary War, when Sir John Johnson fled to Canada early in 1776, he was accompanied by a considerable number of his Highland followers. These were joined a year later by the remainder of the Mohawk Valley Highlanders.

Scarcely had Johnson put a foot in Montreal when he received a commission as colonel in the British army, and was authorized to raise a regiment of Loyalists under the name of The King's Royal Regiment of New York (KRRNY).[24] With his tenantry at his heels he had no problem in finding recruits, particularly when he had the support of the Macdonell chieftains, Aberchalder, Scotus and Leek, as his officers.

The 1st Battalion of the KRRNY saw action with St. Leger's force in 1776 when they defeated the Americans at Oriskany. However the failure to capture Fort Stanwix nullified this victory and St. Leger did not join forces with Burgoyne. In the years which followed, the "Royal Yorkers," as they were sometimes called, took part in several notable raids into the Mohawk Valley. These actions not only brought in additional recruits to the Yorkers, but also stripped the region of supplies useful to the American rebels. Accordingly, Johnson was authorized to form a 2nd Battalion in 1780,[25] despite the fact that Canada's Swiss governor, Sir Frederick Haldimand,was disposed to sneer at Johnson's regiment as "a useful corps with the Ax," but "not altogether to be depended on with the Firelock."[26]

Like the Royal Highland Emigrants, the officers and men of the KRRNY were given land grants on demobilization in 1783. The 1st Battalion settled largely in what is now Glengarry and Stormont counties; the 2nd Battalion, which contained fewer Scots and more Germans, settled in the Bay of Quinte region.

During the American invasion of Canada at the time of the War of 1812, few Scotsmen from Great Britain saw service in this country. With the exception of the Royal Scots, no overseas Scottish units were sent to Canada until the late summer of 1814, when the Glasgow Lowland Division arrived from Ireland. And in the Royal Scots few of the men were, in fact, Scottish-born; most of them were of English, Irish and French nationality. The Scots who fought in the Canadian War of 1812 were, therefore, most of them Canadian Highlanders who lived on the banks of

the St. Lawrence River, where the disbanded Emigrants and Royal Yorkers had settled a generation previously, and where their numbers had been
reinforced by the arrival from Scotland of the disbanded Glengarry Fencibles and their chaplain, Father Alexander Macdonell, in 1803.

Several times during the early years of the nineteenth century, sugges-
tions had been put forward that a regiment of Canadian Highlanders
should be raised as a force to supplement the British regulars. But no one
had heeded this advice until the threat of war with the United States was
so obvious that it could be ignored only with peril. Finally, under the
shadow of invasion, the Glengarry Regiment of Light Infantry Fencibles
was embodied in Upper Canada early in 1812. Father Alexander Macdonell, assisted by "Red George" Macdonell of Leek, fired the heather,
and on May 12 a unit of some 400 men was paraded for duty, just one
month before the President of the United States declared war on Great
Britain and began to move troops towards the Canadian frontier. The
Glengarrians shared in many of the significant engagements of the war,
including Salmon River, Ogdensburg, York, Fort George, Sackett's Harbour, Oswego, Fort Erie, Lyon's Creek and Mackinac, as well as in the
hardest fought battle of the war, Lundy's Lane, where they protected the
right flank of the British force and were accorded the right to wear "Niagara" on their colours. In 1816 the regiment was disbanded at Kingston.

The men from the Scottish counties also saw service in the militia. In
General Brock's opinion the militia along the St. Lawrence, from the Bay
of Quinte to Glengarry, were "the most respectable of any in the province,"[27] a statement borne out by the battle honours awarded the militia
regiments from Glengarry, Stormont and Dundas. The 1st Stormont Regiment was at Salmon River, Ogdensburg, Crysler's Farm, and Hoople's
Creek, and the 1st Dundas at Toussaint's Island, Prescott, Salmon River
and Ogdensburg. Militiamen from these counties were also employed in
garrison and escort duty along the vital highway of the St. Lawrence, the
sole line of communication between Upper and Lower Canada.

The significant role of the Scots in the militia during the War of 1812 is
revealed by a glance at the names of the officers who commanded the
county units.[28] Among them we find Colonel Neil Maclean, a former
Royal Highland Emigrant, of the 1st Stormont; Colonel William Fraser of
the 1st Grenville; Lieutenant-Colonel Thomas Fraser of the 1st Dundas;
Lieutenant-Colonel Alexander MacMillan of the 1st Glengarry; and Lt.-
Col. Allan Macdonell of Greenfield of the 2nd Glengarry. Lieutenant-
Colonel Allan Maclean of the 1st Frontenac became commanding officer
of the Battalion of Incorporated Militia. Lieutenant-Colonel John Macdonell was A.D.C. to General Brock and died at Queenston Heights with
his superior officer. Colonel Archibald Macdonell commanded the 1st
Prince Edward Militia; Colonel John Ferguson, the 1st Hastings; Colonel
Matthew Elliott, the 1st Essex; Lt.-Col. William Graham, the 1st York;
and Captain William Mackay, the Michigan Fencibles. Mackay and Elliott were officers of the Indian Department. The Adjutant-General of the

Canadian militia during the war was Major-General Aeneas Shaw, a former officer of The Queen's Rangers.

The response of the Canadian Scots to the call to arms was reminiscent of the old days in Scotland, and it was repeated with the mustering of the militia during the troubles of 1837 and 1838. If it was a Scot, William Lyon Mackenzie, who set out to establish a Canadian republic in December, 1837, it was another Scot, Sir Allan MacNab, who led the Loyalists who opposed him. In the Ottawa Valley, the last Highland chief ever to play the traditional role, Archibald MacNab, 12th of MacNab, raised the local militia in Lanark and Renfrew; and in Glengarry, Bishop Alexander Macdonell prompted the Highlanders to form four battalions, one each from the townships of Charlottenburg, Lancaster, Lochiel and Kenyon, commanded by Colonels Alexander Fraser, Donald MacDonald, Alexander Chisholm and Angus Macdonell respectively. In November, 1838, detachments of the militia from Stormont, Dundas and Glengarry took part in the Battle of the Windmill, and other detachments from the Glengarry and Stormont regiments formed part of Sir John Colborne's corps employed in supressing the rebellion in Beauharnois. It was not without justification that a British officer wrote in December, 1840, "I beg to state that the County of Glengarry has, on every occasion, been distinguished for good conduct, and will, in any emergency, turn out more fighting men in proportion to its population, than any other in Her Majesty's Dominions."[29]

IV

That 'n fhuil a tanachadh ach tha an spiorad treun
The blood grows thin but the spirit remains strong

Following the War of 1812 a number of Scottish line regiments saw tours of garrison duty in Canada, including The Royal Scots, the 71st Highland Light Infantry, the 70th Cameron Highlanders, the 80th (Glasgow Lowland), and the 93rd Sutherland Highlanders. But the days of the British garrison were numbered and by 1871 the last of the British regiments had been withdrawn from Canada. The old county militia units were also gone. In their place were the new volunteer territorial units, which still form a considerable portion of Canada's present-day military establishment. The Militia Acts of 1855 and 1859 provided for the organization of volunteer regiments, and in November, 1859, the 1st Battalion, Volunteer Militia Rifles of Canada, was organized in Montreal. The following spring another battalion was formed, the 2nd Battalion, Volunteer Militia Rifles, this time in Toronto. Thus began a series of territorial infantry battalions which, prior to 1914, numbered 110.

The volunteer movement coincided, in date, with the movement to eliminate the kilt as part of the military dress of British regiments. Unable

149

to find sufficient recruits in the Highlands, the War Office had been compelled to fill the so-called Scottish regiments with men of other nationalities, and the new recruits were not only indifferent but sometimes hostile to the traditions the kilt implied. With a home government cool towards the kilt it is hardly surprising that few militia regiments in Canada were initially kilted units. It was argued that Fraser's men had complained of the cold and that the Glengarrians had willingly worn the uniform of the British light infantry in 1812. Accordingly only two Highland units were established, as such, in the 1860s and 1870s in Canada, both of them, appropriately enough, in Nova Scotia: the 79th Colchester and Hants or Highland Battalion of Infantry (later the Pictou Highlanders and today the 1st Battalion Nova Scotia Highlanders), and the 94th Victoria Highland Provisional Battalion of Infantry (later the Cape Breton Highlanders and today the 2nd Battalion Nova Scotia Highlanders).[30] But the kilt survived and was revived in Great Britain in the 1880s, and in Canada the enthusiasm for the Scottish military tradition was reflected in the formation of the 48th Highlanders in Toronto in 1891; the 91st Highlanders (later the Argyll and Sutherland Highlanders) in Hamilton in 1903; the 72nd Highlanders (later the Seaforth Highlanders of Canada) in Vancouver in 1910; and the 79th Highlanders (later the Queen's Own Cameron Highlanders of Canada) in Winnipeg in 1910. The 5th Battalion, organized in 1862 in Montreal, was re-designated the Royal Scots Fusiliers in 1880. In 1906 it became the Royal Highlanders of Canada, and in 1930, The Black Watch (Royal Highland Regiment) of Canada.

Between 1899 and 1901 militia units provided men for the Canadian battalions which served under British command during the South African War, but it was not until the Great War of 1914-1918 that Canadian troops were sent abroad in any very considerable numbers. Following the declaration of war between Great Britian and Germany in August, 1914, the Canadian Department of Militia and Defence, ignoring existing militia units and the traditions they had developed, enlisted men into a new series of numbered Canadian Expeditionary Force battalions. Because the kilted units had demonstrated their popularity in Canada, several of the CEF battalions were given Scottish designations. It was almost as if Sir Sam Hughes and Sir Edward Kemp had read the words of Duncan Forbes of Culloden or those of William Pitt. Thus the 13th Battalion CEF carried the name "The Royal Highlanders of Canada," the 15th CEF was the "48th Highlanders of Canada," and the 16th CEF "The Canadian Scottish." These three Scottish units were grouped together in the 3rd Canadian Brigade. The 42nd (Royal Highlanders of Canada) and the 43rd (Cameron Highlanders of Canada) were in the 7th and 8th brigades; the 38th (Cameron Highlanders), the 72nd (Seaforth Highlanders of Canada), and the 85th (Nova Scotia Highlanders) were part of the 12th Infantry Brigade. None of these battalions, although they carried Scottish names and their officers and men wore the kilt, were composed solely of

Canadian Scots or Scots living in Canada. If the 16th Canadian Scottish was anything to go by, they included almost all the nationalities one could find in Canada; Scots, of course, but also English, Irish, French, Americans, Italians, Dutch, Danes, Mexicans and others.[31]

The first major battle involving a Canadian Scottish unit was a trying ordeal. When the French colonial troops broke under the German gas attach at Ypres early in 1915, the 3rd Canadian Infantry Brigade was left dangling at its flank. It was this brigade, with its three Highland units, which bore the initial brunt of the German attack. All three regiments suffered heavy casualties at Ypres and St. Julien, but all proved their worth in battle. They had gone to France green and untried. In the crucible of Ypres they became the veterans who gave the Canadian corps its strength and its reputation.

Manifestly it is impossible to tell the whole story of the Canadian Scottish battalions in World War I within the compass of a few paragraphs. It is sufficient here to record the battle honours worn by the Scottish units on their colours – household names to an earlier generation and all too unfamiliar to those who have followed – Festubert, Mount Sorrel, Somme, Courcellette, Arras, Vimy, Passchendaele, Amiens, Hindenburg Line, Drocourt-Quéant, Canal du Nord, Valenciennes. These names echo through the halls of our history the contribution made by the Canadian Scottish battalions, indeed of all Canadian battalions, which fought under General Sir Arthur Currie's command. And there is further testimony, too, of the prowess of Canadian Scots. Should we forget the name of Sir Archibald Macdonell, that descendant of the Glengarry Macdonells who commanded the 1st Canadian Division? Should we forget the fact that eight of the Canadian winners of the Victoria Cross between 1914-1918 were members of the Highland battalions of the Canadian Corps? Such men as these walk erect among the shades of those heroic Scots who, if not necessarily their progenitors, were the inspiration of the tradition which the Canadians, as members of Scottish units, had willingly embraced.

Perhaps it was the fighting reputation which the Highland units earned during World War I; perhaps it was the strong pride Canadians had in the kilt; perhaps it was the affection which our people generally have had for the pipes; whatever the explanation, there was a remarkable increase in the number of Scottish-named units when the Canadian militia was reorganized after peace had been established in 1919. Not that new units were established, but a considerable number of old infantry militia regiments were redesignated as Scottish units. In this way the 20th Regiment (1866) became The Lorne Rifles (Scottish) in 1931 and, after amalgamation with the Peel and Dufferin Regiment, The Lorne Scots in 1936; the 21st (1885) became The Essex Scottish in 1927; the 29th (1866) became The Highland Light Infantry in 1915; the 42nd became The Lanark and Renfrew Scottish in 1927; the 43rd (1881) became The Ottawa Highlanders in 1922 and, in 1933, The Cameron Highlanders of Canada; the 50th

(1913) and the 88th (1912) amalgamated to become The Canadian Scottish in 1920; the 59th became The Stormont, Dundas and Glengarry Highlanders in 1922; the 82nd became The Prince Edward Island Highlanders in 1927; and the 103rd became The Calgary Regiment and later The Calgary Highlanders in 1924. The Mississauga Regiment lasted a year before becoming The Toronto Scottish in 1921. A whole new array of kilted units (only The Lorne Scots were trewed) was thus added to the *Canadian Militia List.*

But the new regiments, as well as the old, had their problems in the between-wars years. These were not propitious years in Canada for things military; indifference and hostility towards the militia and towards military training were characteristic attitudes both in Parliament and out. The 1920s were the years of pacifist idealism and the 1930s of economic realism. Short of men, short of equipment, working with hand-me-down uniforms and hand-me-down weapons, the officers and men who devoted their time, effort and money to the militia performed a service for their country which was ill-appreciated at the time.

Then everything changed. War broke out in 1939. Men and money were readily available, and the military virtues, for nearly 20 years derided or ignored, became a source of popular admiration. On this occasion the Defence Department did not repeat the blunder of ignoring the militia units. The regiments mobilized in 1939 and 1940 were those which already existed in the peace establishment; and they included a considerable number of Canadian Highland units. Among those which served overseas in Italy and Northwest Europe between 1939 and 1945 were the 48th Highlanders (1st Canadian Infantry Brigade), The Seaforth Highlanders of Canada (2nd Brigade), The Essex Scottish (4th Brigade), The Black Watch (Royal Highland Regiment) of Canada, and The Calgary Highlanders (5th Brigade), The Queen's Own Cameron Highlanders (6th Brigade), The 1st Battalion Canadian Scottish (7th Brigade), The Highland Light Infantry of Canada, The Stormont, Dundas and Glengarry Highlanders, The North Nova Scotia Highlanders (8th Brigade), The Argyll and Sutherland Highlanders (10th Brigade), The Cape Breton Highlanders and the Perth Regiment (11th Brigade), and The Lanark and Renfrew Scottish (12th Brigade). The Toronto Scottish and the Queen's Own Cameron Highlanders of Canada served as divisional troops in the 2nd and 3rd Canadian Infantry Divisions. The Lorne Scots provided defence and employment units at formation headquarters in Italy and Northwest Europe. In the North American zone, we find The Renfrew Scottish, the 2nd Battalion Black Watch, the 2nd Battalion Canadian Scottish, The Prince Edward Island Highlanders and The Scots Fusiliers.

The blooding of General Andrew McNaughton's Canadian Army in World War II began in August, 1942, when the Essex Scots returned with only two officers and forty-nine other ranks from the blood-stained beach of Dieppe. In the following year the 48th and the Seaforths of the 1st

Canadian Division landed in Sicily and, joined later by The Cape Breton Highlanders of the 5th Armoured Division, began the long, slow, push up the boot of Italy, through the Hitler and Gothic Lines almost to the gates of Bologna. Finally, after twenty months of separation, they rejoined the other Canadian divisions in Northwest Europe. In June, 1944, the 3rd Canadian Infantry Division landed on the channel coast of France to be joined subsequently in the Normandy bridgehead by the 2nd Infantry and 4th Armoured Divisions. Under the command of General H.D.G. Crerar, they broke through the German defences between Caen and Falaise, pursued the retreating foe across France and Belgium into Western Holland, and secured a winter position on the river Maas. The Scottish units in these three Canadian divisions, like the other Canadian regiments, paid heavily for their victories, but none perhaps so heavily as The Black Watch, which experienced near disaster at the Verrières Ridge on July 25, thus imposing upon the Calgary Highlanders the heavy and almost intolerable burden of carrying out not only their own responsibilities but those of The Black Watch, until the Royal Highlanders could recover. That the Calgaries were able to do this speaks volumes for their grit, training, and loyalty to their trust, and the determination of their commanding officer, Donald MacLauchlan. Early in 1945, the final offensive against the Germans began in the Reichwald. It continued, in the face of determined and often suicidal opposition, until the crossing of the Rhine. The final stage of the war saw the Canadians of both the 1st and 2nd Corps co-operating in the liberation of the whole of Holland.

When we read the battle honours of the Scottish regiments which formed part of the Canadian First Army, we read, in effect, the battle honours of all Canadian overseas regiments – Moro River, Ortona, Liri Valley, Hitler Line, Gothic Line, Coriano Ridge, Savio Crossing, Caen, Bourguébus Ridge, the Scheldt, Walcheren, Breskens Picket, Hochwald, Zutphen, Kusten Canal, Apeldoorn – these are only a sampling of the names inscribed on the colours of the various units which served in the Canadian army during World War II. These and other names are today part of Canada's military history, part of Canada's military tradition. It is a tradition which has been purchased at a high price in torn bodies and mutilated minds, and in determination, heroism, valour and self-sacrifice. It is a tradition of which we can be proud.[32]

The immediate post-war period has witnessed the organization of only two new Scottish regiments in Canada, or rather the conversion of three infantry regiments into Scottish regiments, the Lake Superiors, and the New Brunswick Rangers, which became respectively, the Lake Superior Scottish and The New Brunswick Scottish, and The Perth Regiment which became kilted in 1946. But other changes were in the offing. Three Canadian Highland regiments, The Cape Breton, The Pictou and The North Nova Scotia Highlanders were amalgamated into a single regiment, The Nova Scotia Highlanders, with two battalions – in New Brunswick, the New Brunswick Scottish and The Carleton and York became the 1st Battalion of The Royal New Brunswick Regiment. Today some eighteen Canadian regiments out of fifty-five in the post-war *Canadian Army List* bear Scottish names.[33] One of these, The Black Watch, was activated as a regular regiment between 1953 and 1969. On the reduction to nil strength of the regular battalions of The Black Watch, the militia battalion became once again the perpetuating unit of what is the senior Highland regiment in the Canadian armed forces.

V

Mairidh an cliu gu brath
May their names live forever

But there are clouds of doubt gathering on Canada's military horizon. With the unification of the Canadian armed services and the acceptance of the principle of uniformity, the question arises as to what may be the future of Canada's Scottish regiments. To some Canadians, these regiments appear as anachronisms, relics of a past that is dead and gone. It is said that they no longer possess any ethnic significance, since officers and men alike are drawn from all the nationalities which now make up the composite Canadian population. Others point out that active service had denationalized the Scottish units in uniform as well as in personnel. They take the view that the unsuitability of the kilt in modern warfare, apparent when the khaki apron had to be introduced during the South African War and continued during the War of 1914-18, became obvious even to the most stubborn Scot when it had to be dropped entirely during World War II. Modern combat uniform has no place for a tartan kilt or a Glengarry bonnet. Efficiency must replace tradition, whether it be on the field of battle or in the counting house.

Undoubtedly efficiency will have its way, if only because it represents the future while tradition represents the past. But if we ignore tradition, will we not lose those qualities which tradition brings to us? Will we not sacrifice to the computer the virtues which have been the strength of our military history? Can efficiency provide an inspiration as moving and powerful as the memories of the achievements of those who have gone before us? Does the skirl of the pipes, the beat of the drum and the swing of the kilt no longer stir the sluggish blood of the young Canadians, whether they be of Scottish origin or not?

The end of the Scottish military tradition in Canada will mean the end of an era that began centuries ago in the mountains and glens of Scotland, that came to this country in the eighteenth century in the haversacks of Fraser's and Montgomery's Highlanders, and in the wooden trunks of those unhappy displaced Scotsmen seeking in Canada the freedom and future their own land could not afford them after "Butcher" Cumberland's "pacification."

NOTES

1. There is a further similarity between Canada and Scotland. It is not always realized that Canada has only 3.9% of its total area in arable land; 34.4% is in forest; 2.2% is in pasture; and the remainder is in city, mountain, waste and water areas. This is in contrast with the United States where 23.5% of the land is arable and 34.2% is pasture, with only 10% in city, mountain, waste and water areas.

2. David Stewart of Garth, *Sketches of the Character, Manners and Present State of the Highlanders of Scotland* (Edinburgh: Constable, 1822) I, 218.

3. Lord Mahon, *History of England from the Peace of Utrecht to the Peace of Versailles* (London: Murray, 1853) III, 324-327.

4. Quoted in John Prebble, *Culloden* (London: Penguin, 1967),163.

5. *Ibid.*,184.

6. Quoted in Mahon, III,327.

7. Gordon Donaldson, *The Scots Overseas* (London: Hale, 1966),32.

8. Quoted in Frank Adam and Sir Thomas Innes of Learney, *The Clans, Septs and Regiments of the Scottish Highlands* (Edinburgh and London: Johnson, 1952), p.440.

9. The colonel of The Black Watch was a Lowlander, the Earl of Crawford and Lindsay, who had been raised in the Highlands by the Duke of Argyll. For a list of the original officers of The Black Watch see Stewart of Garth, I, pp. 227-228.

10. The Lieutenant-Colonel of the regiment was John Campbell, later Duke of Argyll.

11. According to *The Scots Magazine*, 1973, 65,000 Scotsmen were enlisted, of which by far the greater number were from the Highlands. See Adam and Learney, p.441.

12. See for instance A.G. Wauchope, *A Short History of The Black Watch Royal Highlanders 1715-1907* (London and Edinburgh: Blackwood, 1908), and B. Fergusson *The Black Watch and the King's Enemies* (London: Collins, 1950).

13. For James Johnstone's story see *Memoirs of the Chevalier Johnstone*, trans. C. Winchester, (Aberdeen: 1871).

14. "Malcolm Fraser's Journal of the Operations before Quebec, 1759," (Quebec Literary and Historical Society), 27. Quoted in G.F.G. Stanley, *New France: The Last Phase* (Toronto: McClelland and Stewart, 1969), p.243.

15. Stewart of Garth, I, 319. The battle of Culloden was fought on April 16, 1746. The commander of the Highland host was Lord George Murray.

16. C.W. Dunn, *Highland Settler: A Portrait of the Scottish Gael in Nova Scotia* (Toronto: University of Toronto Press, 1953), p.64.

17. The sporrans were of raccoon rather than badger heads, thus giving the unit a distinctive North American feature of dress.

18. *The Quebec Gazette*, August 10, 1775. For various documents relating to

The Royal Highland Emigrants and the KRRNY see *A History of the Organization, Development and Services of the Military and Naval Forces of Canada* (Historical Section of the General Staff, Ottawa, 1919-1920), Volumes II and III.

19. *A History of the Organization etc.*, II, 167, 172: Caldwell to Murray, June 15, 1776.

20. *Ibid.*, II, 143: Memorial of Malcolm Fraser, March 31, 1791.

21. *Ibid.*, III, 103: Germain to Haldimand, April 10, 1779.

22. John Keltie, *A History of the Scottish Highlands, Highland Clans and Highland Regiments* (Edinburgh: Fullarton, 1879) II, 566.

23. Quoted in J.P. MacLean, *An Historical Account of the Settlements of Scotch Highlanders in America prior to the peace of 1783, together with Notices of the Highland Regiments and Biographical Sketches* (Baltimore: Genealogical Publishing Co., 1968),318. Captain Alexander Macdonald's letter book will be found in *The Collections of the New York Historical Society*, 1882. For an account of the 2nd Battalion, R.H.E., together with the muster roll, see Jonas Howe, "The Royal Emigrants," *Acadiensis* (Saint John, N.B., 1904), pp. 50-75.

24. *A History of the Organization etc.* II, 179: Carleton to Germain, July 8, 1776.

25. *Ibid.*, III, 162: Haldimand to Johnson, July 13, 1780.

26. *Ibid.*, III, 109: Haldimand to Clinton, May 26, 1779.

27. Quoted in G.F.G. Stanley, "The Contribution of the Canadian Militia during the War of 1812," in P.P. Mason, ed., *After Tippecanoe – Some Aspects of the War of 1812-15* (Toronto: Ryerson, 1963), p.31.

28. See L.H. Irving, *Officers of the British Forces in Canada during the War of 1812-15* (Welland: Tribune, 1908).

29. Quoted in R.M. Barnes (In collaboration with C.K. Allen), *The Uniforms and History of The Scottish Regiments 1625 to the Present Day* (London: Seely Service, 1956), p.316.

30. For the various changes in names and organization of Canadian regiments, see C.E. Dornbusch, *Lineages of the Canadian Army, 1855-1961* (Cornwallville: Hope Farm Press, 1961).

31. H.M. Urquhart, *The History of the 16th Battalion (The Canadian Scottish) Canadian Expeditionary Force in the Great War 1914-1919* (Toronto: Macmillan, 1932), p.15.

32. Among the various regimental histories of Canadian Scottish regiments are E.J. Chambers, *The 5th Regiment Royal Scots of Canada Highlanders* (Montreal: Guertin, 1904); K. Beattie, *48th Highlanders of Canada 1891-1928* (Toronto, 1932); and Dileas, *History of the 48th Highlanders 1925-1956* (Toronto, 1957); W. Boss, *The Stormont, Dundas and Glengarry Highlanders 1783-1951* (Ottawa: Runge Press, 1952); F. Farran, *The History of The Calgary Highlanders 1921-1954* (Toronto, 1955); D.W. Grant, *Carry On – A History of The Toronto Scottish* (n.p., 1949), H.M. Jackson, *The Argyll and Sutherland Highlanders of Canada* (Montreal, 1953); R. Roy, *Ready for the Fray, The History of the Canadian*

THE SCOTTISH MILITARY TRADITION

Scottish (Vancouver, 1958); C.B. Topp, *The 42nd Battalion CEF* (Montreal, 1931).

33. See *The Regiments and Corps of the Canadian Army prepared by the Army Historical Section, Volume* I of the Canadian Army List (Ottawa, 1964).

Scottish Regiments in the current Canadian Army List

1. The Black Watch (Royal Highland Regiment) of Canada
Tartan	Black Watch; Royal Stewart for pipers
Regimental march	Highland Laddie
Regimental motto	*Nemo Me Impune Lacessit*
Order of precedence	5
Headquarters	Montreal

2. The Lorne Scots
Tartan	Campbell of Argyll
Regimental march	The Campbells are Coming
Regimental motto	*Air Son Ar Dutchchais*
Order of precedence	14
Headquarters	Brampton, Ontario

3. The Perth Regiment
Tartan	Douglas
Regimental march	Kenmure's On and Awa
Regimental motto	*Audax et cautus*
Order of precedence	15
Headquarters	Stratford, Ontario

4. The Highland Light Infantry of Canada
Tartan	Mackenzie
Regimental march	Seann Triubhas
Regimental motto	*Defence, not Defiance*
Order of precedence	16
Headquarters	Galt, Ontario

5. The Lanark and Renfrew Scottish
Tartan	The Black Watch
Regimental march	Highland Laddie
Regimental motto	*Fac et Spera*

	Order of precedence	18
	Headquarters	Pembroke, Ontario

6. The Stormont, Dundas and Glengarry Highlanders

	Tartan	Macdonell of Glengarry
	Regimental march	Bonnie Dundee
	Regimental motto	*Dileas gu Bas*
	Order of precedence	19
	Headquarters	Cornwall, Ontario

7. The Nova Scotia Highlanders

	Tartan	Macdonald
	Regimental march	1st Battalion – Sweet Maid of Glendaruel
		2nd Battalion – Highland Laddie
	Regimental motto	*Siol Na Fear Fearail*
	Order of precedence	28
	Headquarters	1st Battalion – New Glasgow, Nova Scotia
		2nd Battalion – Sydney, Nova Scotia

8. The Cameron Highlanders of Ottawa

	Tartan	Cameron of Erracht
	Regimental march	The Piobaireachd of Donald Dhu
	Regimental motto	*Advance*
	Order of precedence	30
	Headquarters	Ottawa, Ontario

9. The Essex and Kent Scottish

	Tartan	MacGregor
	Regimental march	1st Battalion – Highland Laddie
		2nd Battalion – Hundred Pipers
	Regimental motto	*Semper Paratus*
	Order of precedence	32
	Headquarters	1st Battalion – Windsor, Ontario
		2nd Battalion – Chatham, Ontario

10. 48th Highlanders of Canada

	Tartan	Davidson

Regimental march	Highland Laddie
Regimental motto	*Dileas gu Brath*
Order of precedence	33
Headquarters	Toronto, Ontario

11. The Argyll and Sutherland Highlanders of Canada

Tartan	Black Watch
Regimental march	The Campbells are Coming
Regimental motto	*Albainn gu Brath*
Order of precedence	35
Headquarters	Hamilton, Ontario

12. The Lake Superior Scottish

Tartan	MacGillivray
Regimental march	Highland Laddie
Regimental motto	*Inter Pericula Intrepidi*
Order of precedence	36
Headquarters	Lakehead, Ontario

13. The Queen's Own Cameron Highlanders of Canada

Tartan	Cameron of Erracht
Regimental march	The Piobaireachd of Donald Dhu
Regimental motto	*Ullamh*
Order of precedence	43
Headquarters	Winnipeg, Manitoba

14. The Calgary Highlanders

Tartan	Black Watch
Regimental march	Highland Laddie
Regimental motto	*Onward*
Order of precedence	45
Headquarters	Calgary, Alberta

15. The Seaforth Highlanders of Canada

Tartan	Mackenzie
Regimental march	The Piobaireachd of Donald Dhu
Regimental motto	*Cuidich'n Righ*
Order of precedence	47
Headquarters	Vancouver, British Columbia

16. The Canadian Scottish Regiment

Tartan	Hunting Stewart
Regimental march	Blue Bonnets over the Border
Regimental motto	*Deas gu Cath*

	Order of precedence	48
	Headquarters	Victoria, British Columbia

17. The Scots Fusiliers of Canada

	Tartan Trews	Black Watch
	Regimental march	Highland Laddie; The British Grenadiers
	Order of precedence	50
	Headquarters	Kitchener, Ontario

18. The Toronto Scottish

	Tartan	Hodden Grey
	Regimental march	Blue Bonnets over the Border
	Regimental motto	*Carry on*
	Order of precedence	53
	Headquarters	Toronto, Ontario

NINE

The Scot
as Farmer and Artisan

J. A. McIntyre

The objective in this chapter is to show the part played by Scottish farmers and artisans in the shaping of Canada in its formative years. Two periods of time will be discussed: the early years of settlement and the years from 1800 to 1867, the later period receiving most attention. Even for this period, however, it is possible at this juncture to present only an impressionistic picture for lack of data: a broad, sweeping sketch of where the immigrants came from, where they settled, what conditions they met and how they responded to those conditions. The study in detail and the precise measurement of their contribution will have to await the assembling of such material as family histories, collections of correspondence and corporate histories.

THE SEVENTEENTH AND EIGHTEENTH CENTURIES

In the seventeeth century, although the Scots made attempts at colonization in North America, no settlement of any importance was established. Scotland at the time possessed neither the financial, military and naval support, nor the independent foreign policy needed for such an enterprise. The Scots who went to North America during this century went more often as a consequence of compulsion of one type or other than of their own free will: transportation, penal as well as political, or outright abduction. Such forced movement is said to have continued well into the eighteenth century.

During the eighteenth century the foundations were laid for the substantial immigration of Scots to British North America that was to occur in the following century. The first major emigration began during the middle years of the century, principally following the '45. Substantial social change was under way in Scotland. The alterations in clan organization, hikes in land rents, and innovations in agricultural methods all contributed to a profound altering of an inefficient and archaic social system.

The first to respond to the changes by emigrating were families of social standing, trying to transfer their whole social system to the New World. They were tacksmen, semi-aristocratic tenants of large acreage, who sublet their holdings to crofters and small farmers. Many had substantial capital, although some may have been poverty stricken.[1] In the last quarter of the century, they were followed by more humble emigrants.[2] Some were clansmen with families, of modest financial resources and sometimes unskilled, who had known the semi-agricultural life of the Highlands or Islands. Others were discharged members of the military, settled upon small holdings in North America by a grateful government in lieu of being transported home, and intended to serve as part of a buffer of military capacity north of the troublesome North American colonists who had dealt the first revolutionary blow to the Empire.[3]

In addition to those who came directly from Scotland to Canada, it must not be overlooked that the triumph of the American colonists' revolution resulted in driving northward, into what would become Canada, a substantial number of colonists, many of them Scots, who, loyal to the Crown and its established political institutions, saw only disarray in the constitutional forms emerging in the rebellious colonies. For the most part, these United Empire Loyalists were of the tacksmen class, still possessing substantial wealth even though in some instances they had lost much because of their hurried departure. As established entrepreneurs they quickly regrouped to make a substantial contribution to their newly adopted country. Only in rare instances were they farmers or artisans. The massive immigration of farmer and artisan was still in the future: it would characterize the Scots emigration of the nineteenth century.

THE NINETEENTH CENTURY

Settlements begun in Pictou County, Nova Scotia, and Prince Edward Island in 1773 and 1777 served to attract other Scots after the American war was over. The disbanded regiments served as nuclei for immigrants, attracting them to Quebec, Montreal, and the Ottawa Valley. It was not, however, until the social and economic upheaval characterizing Scotland during the nineteenth century encouraged substantial emigration, and until both government and free enterprise undertook commercial ventures in emigration, that peasants began to reach North America in substantial numbers:

> Between 1815 and 1820 many went overseas from Sutherland and other parts of the West Highlands . . . by the 1820s the clearance or eviction of tenants for the sake of sheep farming was well under way, and emigration began to be looked upon with a fresh eye. Many thought it desirable, as providing an outlet for over-numerous tenants who were a burden on the estates. Much of the clearance involved nothing more than resettling tenants on new holdings within the same county, sometimes within the same parish, and the notion

that scheming landlords, for their own financial profit, shipped to America tenants who were living in plenty, or even in comfort, at home, is preposterous. The truth is that people who had experienced the miseries of life in the Highlands in the 1840s clamoured for assistance to enable them to leave the country ... When the next highland crisis came, in the 1880s, emigration was once more regarded as the obvious remedy. Again there was private enterprise ... But it was also true that the Napier Commission which investigated crofting conditions and made recommendations so favourable to the tenants, reported in favour of emigration, aided and directed by the state, as the only remedy for the overpopulation of certain areas.[4]

Changes in Lowland agriculture, beginning in the eighteenth century, ultimately revolutionized this aspect of the Scottish economy. Root crops and new types of grasses, in combination, created an improvement in the feed, hence in the animal stock. By more careful fertilization practices, coupled with a careful rotation of crops, soil productivity was increased. Implements underwent improvement; for example, a lighter plough was developed and came into use. Farms gradually became larger with fields being enclosed by dikes and tenant farmers being granted long leases to enable them more readily to recover their investment in any improvement they introduced. In short, Scottish agriculture became more efficient, and this, coupled with a substantial increase in demand for agricultural produce, led to growing prosperity among Scottish farmers.[5] But the new methods of farming often led to surplus labour. Tenants whose leases expired without hope of renewal therefore had an understandable desire for emigration, supported by the widespread belief that departure was no longer exile but potentially beneficial.[6]

Vitality was evident also in the industrial sector of the Scottish economy during the late eighteenth and the nineteenth centuries. Indeed, the substantial development and expansion of industry had the inevitable consequence of altering a predominately rural country into a labour-saving machine-oriented industrialized one. While it is said that "the general pattern of Scottish industry in the nineteenth century was one of progress and prosperity and of opportunities for Scotsmen of capacity,"[7] and that this was equally true for those working in agriculture as well up to the middle of the century, the general trends tend to obscure the effects of slumps, depressions, financial crises, bad harvests, and altered legislation, such as the Corn Laws. All of these together with the application of mechanization had important influences upon another general trend, namely, the displacement of people from productive employment on the land and in the factory. Weavers were among those particularly affected, and former weavers made up a significant part of the emigration from Scotland.

An additional factor influencing the development of a desire to emigrate overseas was the widespread belief that less social and political inequality as well as better economic conditions existed in British North America.[8] The belief was probably well grounded as far as the frontier areas were concerned. The necessity for all to labour at the same chores had a powerful levelling effect in the backwoods, further strengthened by the egalitarian ideology that wafted northward from the United States. In the towns, however, the situation was otherwise, with small cliques of office-holders in government, church and army jealously guarding their privileges.

Lower class Scots during the nineteenth century thus seem mainly to have emigrated in order to escape destitution at home; they came from the Highlands and the Lowlands but also from the major cities to which they had previously moved as a response to unfavourable economic conditions. They arrived with intelligence, shrewdness, and adaptability, but often with few skills which could qualify them as farmers, let alone artisans.[9] In some instances, however, they had and could use basic skills, long in use in the Highland and Lowland areas from which they had come:

> Even in the most primitive communities in the Highlands and Islands the people had employed local handy men who specialized each in some craft. As society stabilized itself in the New World, the settlement gathered around itself a clergyman, a doctor, a teacher, a storekeeper and a group of artisans. Each district was provided with a shoemaker and a tailor, who often travelled from house to house in the traditional Scottish manner. Each district had its own grist-mill and saw-mill. Villagers often had both a cabinet-maker and a carriage-maker, sometimes a boat-builder, and always a blacksmith .... An occupational directory of Nova Scotia for the year 1864 presents a very different picture of the Highland communities from that of today. In Whycocomagh, for instance (which at that time had a population of about 1,800), besides the inevitable teacher, innkeepers, and merchants, we find a shipwright, a carriage-maker, a wheelwright, a tanner, two millers, two blacksmiths, and two tailors. A later directory for the year 1868 shows the village still as well provided and enumerates, in addition to the previous list, one dyer ....
>
> Other districts were all once well supplied with the service of the local craftsmen. Sometimes one craft predominated, sometimes another. In North Gut St. Ann's, for instance, we find no less than five weavers listed for the year 1864. On the mainland of Nova Scotia during the same period we find in the St. Andrew's district seven carpenters, six shoemakers, three ship-carpenters, three tailors, two masons, two millwrights, two carriage-makers, two tanners, and a surveyor.[10]

For the most part, the problem lay in adapting to the newer conditions

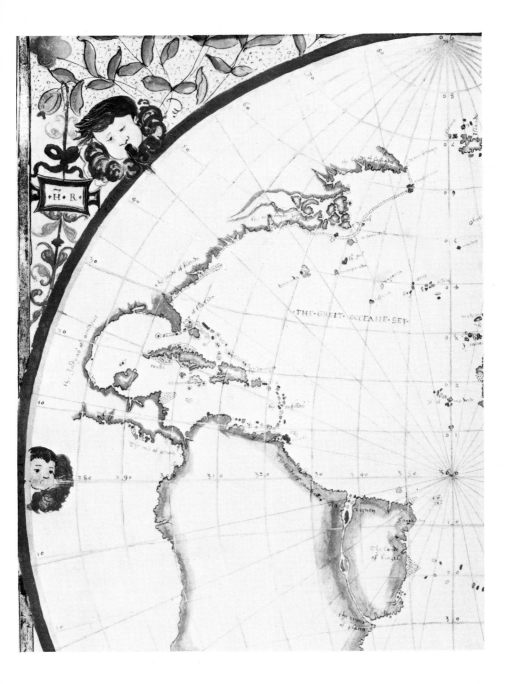

An early map of the Americas. Scots were active explorers at the time this map was drawn. (Courtesy the British Museum)

St. Gabriel's Street Church, the first Scots church in Montreal, built by John Bethune.

William Notman and his sons, William McFarlane, George and Charles, 1890. (Courtesy Notman Photographic Archives, McGill University)

Sergeants of the 78th Highlanders, 1867. (Courtesy Notman Photographic Archives, McGill University)

Master Frank Meighen, 1874. (Courtesy Notman Photographic Archives, McGill University)

Followers of Rev. Norman McLeod, who emigrated from Cape Breton to New Zealand in the 1850s.

Royal Montreal Golf Club Composite Key, 1882. (Courtesy Notman Photographic Archives, McGill University)

William McLennan, 1890. (Courtesy Notman Photographic Archives, McGill University)

Scottish immigrants on board train, Quebec City, Quebec. (Courtesy Public Archives of Canada)

A party of Scots boys taken on arrival in Canada. (Courtesy Public Archives of Canada)

Curling on the St. Lawrence, Montreal, Quebec. Composite photograph, 1878. (Courtesy Notman Photographic Archives, McGill University)

by W. Notman and H. Sandham - 1878

17. Theo Lyman (?)
18. Sir E. Selby Smith
19. Captain Sheppard
20. A. M. Stewart
21. C. A. Boxer and friends
22. Rev. Mr. Norman
23. Alex Barnston
24. Sir A. T. Galt

25. Sir Hugh Allan
26. Rev. Mr. Elligood
27. Mr. Cummings (?)
28. Rev. J. S. Black
29. Lord Dufferin
30. Lady Dufferin
31. Lady Dufferin's dogs

J.M. Mathewson (Piper), 1891. (Courtesy Notman Photographic Archives, McGill University)

A.C. Pittendrigh and family. Scottish settlers near Rapid City, Manitoba. (Courtesy Public Archives of Canada).

*Mrs. Duncan MacLachlan of Kitchener, Ontario, does a Highland dance accompanied by her husband (left) and James Nowlan. (Copyright and photo:*Kitchener-Waterloo Record)

Highland stepdancers, Highland games, Antigonish, Nova Scotia. (Buckley's Studio)

Tug of War, Highland games, Antigonish, Nova Scotia. (Buckley's Studio)

Tossing the Caber, Highland games, Antigonish, Nova Scotia.
(Buckley's Studio)

Throwing the Hammer, Highland games, Antigonish, Nova Scotia.
(Buckley's Studio)

Bringing in the haggis, Highland banquet. (Buckley's Studio)

characterized by an initially hostile environment that could by hard and persistent work be coaxed to fecund response.

Although the early emigration attracted much opposition, by the first decades of the nineteenth century public opinion in Scotland had swung completely around. Through the assistance of kinsmen and emigration associations, and with substantial overseas encouragement through correspondence, a thriving passenger service developed for those who could pay their passage. It is said that "by 1820, small tradesmen, mechanics, men of every occupation were joining the throngs of emigrating small farmers, and every port in the north and west was sending hundreds annually to Nova Scotia and Quebec."[11]

Even though many emigrants were disaffected politically, were relatively unskilled and by no means members of the 'proprietory class,' they exhibited no lack of knowledge, initiative, capacity for work or adaptability upon their arrival in the New World. They brought with them not only a desire for a less definitively ordered class structure, but also the willingness to try new methods and new means for wresting a livelihood from the climate and the land. By no means all were destitute, but most had to husband their resources with care.[12]

They came to Nova Scotia or Quebec. For the most part, however, their objective was farther west. Nova Scotia and the St. Lawrence lowlands were settled; the Eastern Townships of Lower Canada near the American border and Upper Canada were being opened up, and promised most to the industrious immigrant. Since by no means all possessed funds for buying land from local land boards, individuals like Colonel Talbot, or land development companies such as the Canada Company, the initial step was frequently to make a down payment or accept employment on the land with the intent to save capital for ultimate purchase.

Appearing before the *Select Committee on Emigration, Scotland*, Dr. Thomas Rolph from Upper Canada commented concerning one Scot who emigrated to Canada:

> Under judicious management the expense might be very much abridged. I will give you proof of one from Aberdeen whom I hired at $16.00 a month as a farm labourer. I had an Englishman at the same time to whom I paid the same wages. I was astonished that the Scotsman never came to me for his wages; he said he wanted to accumulate them for a certain purpose; at the end of three years he took nearly $100 off me and went and purchased land of his own.[13]

Where did these newcomers tend to settle? Frequently they were attracted to locations where fellow clansmen, relatives or other Scots had already established themselves. If they came out under the auspices of one of the developers, whether an individual or a company, they settled on their lands. In some cases, one cannot but suspect that even the scenery which reminded them of their Scottish homeland may have exercised a determining influence. Even today, a traveller through the Eastern

Table I: Arrivals at the Port of Quebec from the British Isles, Europe and the Maritime Colonies, 1829-1859

Year	England	Ireland	Scotland	Europe	Maritime Provinces	Total
1829	3,565	9,614	2,634	–	123	15,945
1830	6,799	18,300	2,450	–	451	28,000
1831	10,343	34,133	5,354	–	424	50,254
1832	17,481	28,204	5,500	15	546	51,746
1833	5,198	12,013	4,196	–	345	21,752
1834	6,799	19,206	4,591	–	339	30,935
1835	3,067	7,108	2,127	–	225	12,527
1836	12,188	12,590	2,224	485	235	27,722
1837	5,580	14,538	1,509	–	274	21,901
1838	990	1,456	547	–	273	3,266
1839	1,586	5,113	485	–	255	7,439
1840	4,567	16,291	1,144	–	232	22,234
1841	5,970	18,317	3,559	–	240	28,086
1842	12,191	25,532	6,095	–	556	44,374
1843	6,499	9,728	5,006	–	494	21,727
1844	7,698	9,993	2,234	–	217	20,142
1845	8,883	14,208	2,174	–	160	23,375
1846	9,163	21,049	1,645	896	–	32,753
1847	31,505[a]	54,310	3,747	–	–	89,562
1848	6,034[a]	16,582	3,086	1,395	842	27,939
1849	8,980	23,126	4,984	436	968	38,494
1850	9,887	17,976	2,879	849	701	32,292
1851	9,677	22,381	7,042	870	1,106	41,076
1852	9,276	15,983	5,477	7,256	1,184	39,176
1853	9,585	14,417	4,745	7,456	496	36,699
1854	18,175	16,156	6,446	11,537	857	53,183
1855	6,754	4,106	4,859	4,864	691	21,274
1856	10,353	1,688	2,794	7,343	261	22,439
1857	15,471	2,016	3,218	11,368	24	32,097
1858	6,441	1,153	1,424	3,578	214	12,810
1859	4,846	417	793	2,722	–	8,778

Source: Parliamentary Paper, 1836, XL (76), 8; 1837, XLII (132), 9; XXXIII (613), 74; 1843, XXXIV (109), 11; 1847, XXXIX (777), 19; 1847-8, XXVI (961), 38-9; 1849, XXII (1082), 16; 1854, XLVI (1763), 30; 1857-8, XLI (165), 20; 1860, XLIV (606), 17.

a. From British sources. In the famine year, the Emigration Commissioners were handicapped by the lack of a report from A.C. Buchanan, emigration agent at Quebec, who was seriously ill of the emigrant fever. From Cowan, p. 289.

Townships of Quebec or the Grey and Bruce Counties in Ontario cannot but be impressed with the fact that the appearance of the land is very similar to that of Scotland, which may well have attracted the homesick colonist.

One example of the interaction of a number of these factors is to be found in the settlement of a part of the Eastern Townships where many Scots established themselves, i.e. the Township of Leeds, Megantic County. During the mid-1820s a number of Scottish families moved on to the back concessions: Allans, Olivers, Gillanders, Nugents and others. In 1828 William Reid and his family arrived from New York where they had located the preceding year, but for a number of reasons had decided to return to British rule in Canada. At first they had visited the Township of Hinchinbrook, Beauharnois County, but it was too flat for their liking, and hearing of the Scottish settlement at Leeds, an area geographically very similar to the Perthshire from which they had come, they obtained land in that township. Soon afterwards they were joined by Andrew Dunn, a distant relative, who had originally planned to settle in Nova Scotia.[14]

Meanwhile other Scots, usually related to each other in some way, had received grants in the Township of Hinchinbrook, which the Reids had scorned. Out of 225 families settled there in 1831, Scots formed 79, located mainly on the land as farmers, while the Irish, the next largest group (78), moved into the village of Huntingdon.[15]

One group of Scots made up of between 60 and 80 families settled in the parish of St. Anne Desplaines in the 1820s, in the Seigneurie of Blainville on the mainland north of Montreal. This caused some surprise among the French-Canadian habitants, for the land was not particularly good, which we can see from the fact that the local curé referred to the parish as "mon désert." But what was perhaps the principal reason for the surprise was that the new arrivals would hold the land *en roturier*, which would mean that they would have to pay *cens et rentes* and fulfil other seigneurial obligations. This was quite unusual since the Scottish settlers, like the English and the Irish, usually sought to obtain land in free and common socage. Indeed, Joseph Bouchette, in his *Topographical Dictionary of Lower Canada*, explains that the principal reason for the immigrants from the British Isles and the United States settling in Megantic County was that free and common socage was the only form of landholding in that area. He points out that since none of the land was held by seigneurial tenure, there were no French Canadians in the county.[16]

In Upper Canada much the same pattern of settlement was followed, as is indicated by what happened in and around Guelph at the same time as the settlement of the Eastern Townships (1827-30):

> Another party of emigrants arrived later in the summer, and being mostly farmers, they settled on what has since been known as the Scotch Block, on the Elora Road. Among them were Alex McTavish,

167

Donald Gillies, Alex Reid, McFie, Peter Butchart, Angus Campbell, Halliday, Joseph McDonald (who was an uncle of the present Lieu-tenant-Governor of Ontario, and who died a few years ago upwards of 90 years of age), Jas. Stirton, Jas. McQuillan, Wm. Patterson, Rose, the Kennedys (three families) – most of whom, however, afterwards sold out, when they had made some improvements and removed elsewhere . . . While on the other hand, all of those who retained the farms they themselves had cleared afterwards became more or less wealthy, and many of them were in after years able to purchase eli-gible land in other places. A third party arrived at about the same time and settled in the Paisley Block, among them were – Jas. Inglis, Jas. Laidlaw, J. McCorkindale, Drew, Campbell, Alexander, Gideon, Hand-Boyd, McKersie, John Speirs, Thos. Jackson . . . most of whom became wealthy and influential citizens. Most of these early settlers had families, and the sons of some of them have since held prominent positions in the various councils and in the legislative halls of the country.[17]

We observe the essential Scottishness of the emigrants, their tendency to settle together, the nature of their enterprise of hard work, risk-taking, and ultimately their upward mobility. Another author summarized: "Like the sheep on their Scottish hills, as far as possible, they settled together in flocks, and it was uncommon to find one of them located alone among people of other origins."[18]

In all of this settlement and ensuing development, the Scot, and in particular the Highlander, was a sought-after immigrant. For example, the British American Land Company made special appeals to Scottish Highlanders who are said to have arrived in numbers greater than the Company could employ.[19] At an earlier period, when the Huron Tract was under development, Dr. Alling of Guelph, in presenting testimony before the British Parliamentary Select Committee, urged the virtue of Scotch emigrants over others.[20] Not all observers, however, found the Highlander the most satisfactory of farmers. John McGregor mixed praise and blame:

The Scotchman, habituated to greater privations in his native coun-try has probably left it with the full determination of undergoing any hardships that may lead to the acquisition of solid advantages. He therefore acts with great caution and industry, subjects himself to many inconveniences, neglects the comforts for some time which the Englishman considers indispensable, and in time certainly succeeds in surmounting all the difficulties, and then and not till then, does he willingly enjoy the comforts of life . . .

The Highland Scotch, unless intermixed with other settlers, are not only careless, in many particulars, of cleanliness, within their houses but are also regardless of neatness and convenience in their agricul-tural implements and arrangements. All this arises from the force of habit, and the long prevalence of the make-shift system; for whenever a Scotch Highlander is planted among a promiscuous population, no one is more anxious than he to rival the more respectable establishment of his neighbours.

The Scotch settlers from the Lowland countries, although they generally know much better, yet remain from a determination first to accumulate property, for some years regardless of comfort or convenience in their dwellings; but they at last build respectable houses, and enjoy the fruits of industry . . . Few people, however, find themselves sooner at their ease than the Highland Scotch; no class can endure difficulties or suffer privations with more hardihood, or endure fatigue with less repining. They acquire what they consider an independence in a few years; but they remain, in too many instances, contented with their condition, where they find themselves possessed of more ample means than they possessed in their native country . . . I have observed, that whenever the Highlanders inhabit a distinct settlement, their habits, their systems of husbandry, their disregard for comfort in their houses, their ancient hospitable customs, and their language undergo no sensible change.[21].

Adam Fergusson, on his journey throughout Upper Canada during the 1830s, commented acidly:

One of the first settlements we meet with is the Glengarry district, an extensive tract of good land enjoying the advantage of water carriage. The language, the customs, the native courage of their Celtic sires still distinguishes the Clans, though at the same time we are afraid accompanied by some of those less profitable traits which stamp the Highlander as more at home wielding the claymore or extracting the mountain dew, than in guiding the plough-shares to slow but certain results. The farms are but indifferently improved, considering the advantages they have enjoyed; and much valuable time is expended in the depths of the forest in a semi-savage life, cutting and preparing timber for the lumber merchant, which if steadily devoted to the cultivation of the land would certainly be attended with infinitely greater benefit, both in a physical and mental point of view.

and again:

The Canadian farmers pursue the old Scottish practice of infield and outfield taking crop after crop of grain from their fields until nothing but weeds remain and looking to nature for the renovation which their own industry ought to have effected.

These are comments and observations of a Lowland agricultural specialist who might be expected to have an extremely critical eye for Highland practices. Not all his comments were acerbic, however:

My Angus friend who seemed to be in the enjoyment of very easy circumstances, affords a proof, among hundreds, of what an industrious and steady man may do for himself in Canada. He came out in 1817, was wrecked in the Gulf of St. Lawrence, suffered many hardships, and finally landed in Montreal, devoid of every resource, save his own hands and good spirits. He soon found employment and in due time took a lease of a farm which he finds to succeed extremely well. His wheat and potatoes he says are excellent: oats inferior. He cultivates green crops, taking mangel wurzel instead of turnips which suffer from the fly. He uses horses in preference to oxen: has iron plows, and follows what he called a sort of rotation – 1st wheat; 2nd green crop; 3rd clover; 4th timothy for hay; and 5th pasture.[22]

Fergusson's favourable comments are borne out by the evidence of other of his contemporaries as well as by later historians. According to one recent French-Canadian work, the habitants' agricultural methods were very backward at the opening of the nineteenth century, and it was the advent of "les Yankees et les Ecossais" which improved the situation.[23] Bouchette when describing the Seigneurie de Blainville, after he had referred to the Scotch Church in Ste. Therése, added this comment in the next sentence:

The Protestants who are all cultivators, cannot but be advantageous to the improvement of agriculture for the system they practise is so good that their Canadian neighbors cannot long delay to adopt it, at least in part.

When we consider the context in which this is stated and his later reference to the 60 or more Scottish families in Ste. Anne Desplaines, it is clear that he is referring to the predominantly Scottish element in the area. In discussing the Eastern Townships, particularly Megantic Country where so many Scots settled, he remarked:

Labouring under the weighty disadvantage of the want of good and convenient roads communicating with the principal market-towns of the province, the prosperity of the eastern townships can only be attributed to the enterprise, industry and perseverence of the inhabitants, who, considering merely the mildness of the climate, the advantages of the soil, and the locality, boldly entered the wilderness originally, and have now the gratification of seeing around them corn-fields of unrivalled luxuriance, thriving farms, and flourishing villages.[24]

Modern historians agree with this estimate of the situation, holding that "Les colons anglophones y sont ouverts, actifs entreprenant." Since they found it easier to sell their produce on the adjacent American market, however, the only thing which kept them from seeking annexation to the United States was their very strong British loyalty.[25] But not all emigrants possessed skills essential to effective survival, although officialdom tended to anticipate fairly rapid self-sufficiency. Less than one year after one of the settlements had begun, "most of the people at Drummondville, inexperienced even in agriculture, let alone pioneer agriculture, were plunged in abject misery."[26]

It is difficult to ascertain with any precision what industrial skills the Scots possessed on coming to British North America. Records were kept not only of the sources of immigrants who arrived at Quebec and other ports, but also of the trades and callings of the immigrants; however, no cross-classifications were made. Information about Scottish artisans must therefore be gleaned from such sources as family histories, local histories and travellers' journals.

From these, it appears that immigrants brought a variety of skills with them. Guillet noted:

> A list of 24 Scots settled at Perth in 1816 shows that one had been a farm grieve (manager) in Scotland, and seven others farmers or farm labourers. The other 16 included the following occupations: weaver, dyer, shoemaker, ship-master, mason, millwright, ship carpenter, schoolmaster, whitesmith, widow, shopkeeper, gardener, clerk.[27]

Even among the farmers, many had acquired skills by the practice of which they could supplement the yield of their fields.

But more significant are the occupational activities in which the Scots engaged in Canada. In addition to farming, and to business and finance, in which Scottish participation has been so notable as to warrant detailed discussion, Scots in the nineteenth century exercised skills acquired before migration or newly learned in British North America as millwrights, distillers, coopers, smiths, sawyers, masons, builders, tanners, cobblers, weavers, dyers, tailors, iron workers, bakers – in short, as mechanics or artisans in all of the callings of which their young communities had need. The number of cheese factories, sometimes one-man operations, established by Scots[28] was notable, as was the number of flour mills, fanning mills, sawmills, paper mills and carding mills.[29] Distilleries also, not unexpectedly, were set up in quantity.[30]

Many of the Scottish artisans enjoyed only local fame; others, however, won wider renown. For example, Adam Fergusson was not solely a gentleman farmer and keen observer; he possessed an alert imagination, progressive ideas, and a capacity for persuasion which resulted not only in the founding of a community, now the town of Fergus, but also in the training of veterinarians, the breeding of Durham bulls, and indeed, the founding of the Ontario Agricultural College.[31] Red Fife, the first hard spring wheat developed in North America, owes its origin to David Fife of Otonabee Township who enterprisingly secured the original European Northern wheat from which he developed this ultimately widely approved strain. Patrick Bell's reaper, which he did not patent, was widely used in the 1830s and was considered "a beautiful piece of mechanism, (which) cut the grain . . . and by an endless conveyor belt of canvas laid it in a swath

171

on one side of the machine."[32] Peter McKellar and another man in the Talbot Settlement in 1819 invented a handmill which they called a 'bragh' which was widely used among the settlers in that district. "It consisted of granite stones fitted into a framework, the smaller stones on top and a large bolt passing through the centre of both to fasten them together. A large eye at the top of the bolt made it possible to insert a hand spike and carry the mill from place to place."[33] Finally, the founder of Hull, Philemon Wright, was considered one of the most enterprising, resourceful and successful of Canadian settlers. Sometimes referred to as the "white chief of the Ottawa," he owned and operated a mill and tavern at Chaudiere Falls; in 1840 his financial worth was estimated at £100,000.[34]

In Montreal as industry began to develop, particularly in engineering and similar fields, Scots from the Clydeside shipyards, from the engine-building works in Motherwell and various engineering firms in other parts of Lanark, Renfrew and the Glasgow area, began to emigrate to Canada, some to carry on their trades and crafts in the Maritime provinces, but most to obtain employment in the CPR Angus Shops in the east end of Montreal or in the Grand Trunk shops in the St. Henry district. Even in the first decade of the present century either first or second generation Scottish immigrants still dominated the skilled personnel employed in these two large plants.

In the category of artisan, we should perhaps also include Sandford Fleming, an engineer. His career embraced much more than railroading, although it is worth noting that the Great Western Toronto-Hamilton (1854), the Canada Southern (Hamilton-Port Dover), the Inter-Colonial, and finally the Canadian Pacific Railroad all bore his imprint. He also initiated the first Canadian postage stamp (1851), and pioneered in the establishment of Standard Time in 1884. He was instrumental in the construction of the Dundas Canal; before he died in 1915 he had also served as Chancellor of Queen's University. This was an impressive record for any person in any country.[35]

An indication of the role of the Scots may be found in the description of a community founded and largely populated by Scots, such as Guelph, Ontario. In 1843 Guelph had

Jail and Court House	1	Coopers	2
Houses	234	Brickyard	1
Grist Mills	3	Stone masons	15
Saw Mills	1	Bricklayers and plasterers	7
Distilleries	4	Watchmakers	1
Churches with spires	3	Confectioner	1
Plain churches	2	Carpenters	20
Chapel buildings	2	Breweries	3
Stores	14	Painters and glaziers	2
Bakeries	3	Cabinet makers	4

Saddlers and harness makers	2	Nurserymen and gardeners	2
Coach makers	1	Tailors	8
Wheelwrights	4	Dressmakers	7
Blacksmiths	6	Hatter and furrier	1
Tinware factory	1	Tanneries	1
Butchers	3	Chairmakers	4
Lawyers	2	Upholsterers	1
Surgeons	4	District grammar school	1
Druggist	1	Common schools	2
Taverns	7	Taverns (temperance)	2[36]

It will be recalled that Guelph was founded in 1827. At the time of the above analysis the community was the capital of Wellington County and contained a population of 703 persons. It would be extremely valuable to be able to identify all the persons classified in these respective occupations. By name we could obtain perhaps some meagre indication of national origin. At this time the following persons are identified as living in Guelph and employed in the cited occupations: architect, Victor Stewart; master builders, David Kennedy, Thomas Dobbie, Robert Grierson, Robert Emslie, James Davidson, James Barclay, George and Alexander Bruce, James Dobbie.[37] It seems a reasonable assumption that all were Scots.

William Allan, born in Killochan, Ayrshire, arrived in Canada in 1830. An engineer and specialist in the erection of saw and flour mills in Sweden, he acquired property from the Canada Company in the Guelph area and proceeded to construct "a mill proper, a cooper shop to make the barrels, a blacksmith and a metal-working ship, a planing mill and a wood-working shop."[38] His eldest son, David, became owner and manager and he, "being an architect, maintained a fully equipped drafting room above his business office."[39] Son James, who was a competent miller, looked after flour production, while son John, who was a qualified millwright, kept the machinery running. Son William completed schooling at Rockwood Academy and afterwards at Tassies in Galt, ultimately becoming office manager. In a sense this is a not unusual series of events and illustrates the cumulative human component in a specific Scots family brought to the New World even though the illustration may only be tenuously artisan.

Alex (Sandy) Glass and John Busby, head and assistant gardener respectively at the Priory when owned by William Allan, would have to be considered specialists in agriculture. It is said that:

These two men kept the grounds always in excellent order. There was the green-house, in the centre, in which many rare plants were propagated, as well as some choice varieties of grapes, the roots or seeds for which were imported from Spain; then, out in the garden, were some varieties of gooseberries which attained large size, apples and plums also of choice varieties, which yielded luscious fruit, many of them prize winners in the horticultural show in the Fall. 'Sandy' developed some choice varieties himself, including what was afterwards "the Glass seedling plum", which some years later (after he had moved to St. Catharines), became a staple and much sought for fruit in that district.[40]

This is surely an example of substantial and significant contribution, not only to the lifestyle of the times but to its life content as well. The degree of sophistication of the agriculturalists cited, their contact with and dependence upon other parts of the world, particularly Europe, clarifies a little of the 'actual lifestyle' occasionally to be discovered, in 'life in the bush.' It suggests also that one of the critically important ingredients permitting 'contribution' is the human's perception of the type and variety of opportunity.

Mr. Alex McKenzie, who worked in the office of the Allan mill, later became clerk of the surrogate court in Guelph.[41] James Mays settled on 100 acres in 1830; later he built a fanning mill; still later he moved to Guelph and built a stone residence and a stone business block. Robert Crowe arrived in 1832 and started a foundry for the production of stoves and general castings. Messrs Harley and Heather set up an iron and brass foundry. Mr. Thain in 1862 opened a blacksmith and wagon shop; Mr. Stewart in 1854 opened a wood products business; Mr. Clarke built the first bridge on Dundas Street for the Canada Company, later returning to Guelph to open a tannery. Two tanneries were also opened in 1869, one by a Mr. Harvey who later became town clerk, and another by a Mr. Gow who later became sheriff of the community. In 1864 a Mr. Bell established a business to manufacture melodeons, which business was later taken over by McLeod, Wood and Company, still later by John Jackson and Company.

The Mechanics Institute in 1850 had as the principal officers president, C.J. Mickle, secretary, T. Sandilands, and librarian, Edwin Newton, and members with the names of McDonald, Torrance, Scott, Gow, Ferguson, Watt, Savage and Armstrong. The precursor of the organized public library system, the Mechanics Institute represented an important contribution to informal education, principally for the working man. It is interesting that some of the key people in the endeavour were Scots, continuing the tradition of a concern for learning.[42]

What could one conclude from the following list of 'firsts' in the town of Guelph except that the Scots had impressively made their presence felt in that community, contributing significantly to the emerging social structure?

1827	first baker	Wm. Gibbs
1827	first blacksmith	John O. Lynch
1827	first carpenters	Wm. Collins and James Anderson
1827	first shoemaker	Thomas Stewart
1827	first wagonmaker	Wm. Holmes
1827	first tavern opened by	Reid who became the first postmaster
1828	first weaving loom	James Hodgert
1830	first flour mill – sold by Canada Company to	Wm. Allan
1832	first public library	Thos. Sandilands
1841	first carding mill	Wm. Allan
1845	first branch bank – 'Gore Bank' Manager	T. Sandilands
1843	first Court House (present) contractor	Wm. Allan, architect his son David.[43]

James Logan, a Scottish advocate who visited Canada in 1836, noted that David Allan of Guelph, an ingenious mechanic, had erected a distillery with his own hands.[44]

The main portion of Scots coming to British North America after the beginning of the nineteenth century were artisans or farmers or those who in the absence of such skill or knowledge took up work on the farm, in the factory, or in the store with the confident intention of self-improvement. For the most part their first move in the new environment was to obtain land, either to farm or to use as a base of operation. Frequently they cleared it, sold it and moved on to repeat the process; served, that is, as openers of land rather than developers of it. Others came with particular and specific skills which they were not always able to use immediately to personal advantage in the new country. The skilled carpenter was not always able to obtain work at his trade, but frequently transferred his skill to clearing the land and building a dwelling place; in short, there seems to have been substantial capacity, adaptability, and initiative which as time passed flowered under the stimulus of a variety of social and economic stimuli.

This tendency continued even after the new arrivals were well and comfortably settled. As one traces the fortunes of the Scots who took up their residence in the Maritime provinces, the Eastern Townships, Glengarry and western Ontario, one soon finds that they were often not content to remain merely as farmers or artisans. If they did desire to continue on the land they were usually on the constant lookout for new and better locations in places such as the Prairie provinces and British Columbia, with the result that the Scottish settlements in Eastern Canada were often depleted by the adventurous who were caught up in the movement to the

West in the late nineteenth century. Others left the farms or the factories to obtain an education and to enter the professions. The Township of Leeds, for instance, of which mention has been made earlier, for the period of a century after its first settlement put forth over 100 school teachers, about the same number of nurses, some 25 clergymen (mostly Presbyterian), fifteen doctors, one of whom was the first woman psychiatrist in the United States, an equal number of lawyers and smaller numbers in other professions; and Leeds was by no means exceptional.[45]

An important ingredient in this flowering was the social environment, and more particularly the feeling the immigrant had about it. The majority of the immigrants, although they may have been short of funds, were trying to escape not so much from poverty as from lack of opportunity in Scotland. As McColl states:

> In warm houses sheltered by the great woods, in homes they could for the first time call their own, with no pompous aristocrat to collect rent, or threaten eviction, or compel obeisance, they were comparatively comfortable and contented, and from the outlook of the future received both cheer and stimulus.[46]

It is sometimes said that the effect of 'open opportunity' upon the emigrant has been overemphasized, that the whole notion of 'open opportunity' is romantic, and not a 'hard, scientific fact.' However, although no quantification is possible, the growth and development of the nation called Canada offers strong evidence that the ' definition of the situation ' formed a profound and critical part of the circumstances requisite to the survival of immigrants and their ultimate success. In the early pioneer stage on the land, the freedom to fail was a powerful stimulant to concerted effort towards achievement. This appears no less true at later stages in the development of the country, although with the emergence of organized economic activity some of the flavour of independently co-operating with one's neighbours in the 'Scotch Block' for one's own profit may have appeared ephemeral or possibly non-existent to the immigrant employed as a mechanic in a railway shop at an hourly wage. Then the circumstances may well have seemed little different from those they had left, although the difference seems still to have been perceived as significant. Certainly in aspiring towns and cities, Scottish enterprise was no less evident than in rural communities, among artisans and craftsmen as well as among businessmen, financiers, politicians and scholars.

NOTES

1. Margaret I. Adam, "The Highland Emigration of 1770," *The Scottish Historical Review*, 15/16 (1918-19), 282-84.

2. *Ibid.*, 17/18 (1920-21), 74.
3. *Ibid.*, 284-290.
4. Gordon Donaldson, *The Scots Overseas* (London: Hale, 1966), pp. 74-75, 79.
5. *Ibid.*, pp. 82-83.
6. Helen I. Cowan, *British Emigration to British North America* (Toronto: University of Toronto Press, 1961), Chapter V.
7. Donaldson, p. 85.
8. *Ibid.*, p. 88.
9. *Ibid.*, pp. 205-206.
10. Charles W. Dunn, *Highland Settler* (Toronto: University of Toronto Press, 1953), pp. 120-121.
11. Cowan, p. 52.
12. *Ibid.*, p. 53.
13. Z 2009 (1841), 173, V 1-8, *British Parliamentary Papers*, paragraph 1548.
14. McKillop, *The Annals of Megantic* (n.p., 1902), pp. 135, 148; W.D. Reid, The Genealogy of the Reid Family (Unpublished).
15. J. Bouchette, *The British Dominions in North America* (London: Colburn & Bentley, 1831, repr. N.Y., AMS, 1968) I. Topographical Dictionary of Lower Canada: "Hinchinbrook."
16. *Ibid.*, II, "Megantic County," "Mille Isles, Seigneurie of."
17. C. Acton Burrows, *The Annals of the Town of Guelph* (Guelph: Herald Steam Printing House, 1877) p. 15.
18. H. McColl, *Sketches of Highland Pioneers of the County of Middlesex (1901)*, in Public Archives of Canada, Ottawa. See also James M. Cameron, "An introduction of the Study of Scottish Settlement of Southern Ontario: A Comparison of Place Names." *Ontario History*, LXI (1969), 167-172.
19. Cowan, p. 137.
20. Z 2009 (1842), 173, V 1-8, *Brit. Parl. Papers*, para. 1561.
21. John McGregor, *British America* (Edinburgh, 1833), Vol. II, pp. 445, 447-50.
22. Adam Fergusson, *Tour in Canda*, 11th ed. (Edinburgh: Blackwood, 1833), p. 263.
23. J. Hamelin & Y. Roby, *Histoire économique de Québec, 1851-1896* (Montreal: Fides, 1971), p. 9.
24. Bouchette, I, p. 308.
25. Hamelin & Roby, p. 21. F. Ouellet [*Histoire économique et sociale du Quebec, 1760-1850* (Montreal: Fides, 1966), pp. 81ff] points out that the first English-speaking governor of Quebec, General James Murray, a Scot, did everything he could to improve agriculture but that the real drive for advance came from the British merchants and settlers, most of whom were Scots. Lord Elgin, also a Scottish governor in the mid 1850s distributed 50,000 copies of a tract to give guidance about agriculture, while Governor Dalhousie, another Scot, endeavoured to organize agricultural societies, presumably along the pattern of the Scottish agricul-

tural bodies of the time. [M. Seguin, *La "Nation Canadienne" et l'Agriculture, (1760-1850)*, (Montreal: Boréal, 1970), pp. 137ff].

26. *Ibid.*, p. 41.

27. E.C. Guillet, *The Pioneer Farm and Backwoodsman* (Toronto: The Ontario Publishing Co. Ltd., 1963), p. 87.

28. Norman Robertson, *History of the County of Bruce* (originally published in 1906 by William Briggs of Toronto, reprinted, Toronto: J.M. Dent and Sons, 1960), p. 332; Robert J. Fraser, *As Others See Us* (Beamsville, Ont., Beamsville Express, 1959), pp. 112, 235-239.

29. F.H. Dobbin, *Our Old Home Town* (Toronto: J.M. Dent and Sons, 1943), pp. 12, 226, 227; Norman Robertson, *History of the County of Bruce* (originally published in 1906 by William Briggs of Toronto, reprinted in Toronto: J.M. Dent and Sons, 1960), pp. 328-0, 339, 374; Claire Thompson, *Township of Lanark 1820-1970* (Lanark, Ont., The Lanark Era, 1970), p. 25; Andrew F. Hunter, *A History of Simcoe County* (Barrie, Ont., Historical Committee of Simcoe County, 1909), pp. 211, 237, 247.

30. E.A. Owen, *Pioneer Sketches of Long Point Settlement* (Originally published in 1898 by William Briggs of Toronto, reprinted in Canadian Reprint Series, No. 17, Belleville Ont., Milca Silk Screening Ltd., 1972), pp. 400, 401; Dobbin, *Our Old Home Town*, pp. 13-14, 227.

31. Fraser, p. 64.

32. *Ibid.*, p. 148.

33. *Ibid.*, p. 216.

34. *Ibid.*, p. 46.

35. Thomas Melville Bailey, *Traces, Places and Faces: Links between Canada and Scotland* (Hamilton, 1957).

36. D. Allan, "About Guelph, its Early Days and later," (Unpublished typescript, 1939, in Guelph Public Library), p. 37.

37. *Ibid.*, p. 38.

38. *Ibid.*, p. 9.

39. *Ibid.*, p. 10.

40. *Ibid.*

41. *Ibid.*, p. 11.

42. Burrows, p. 63.

43. Allan, p. 61.

44. A.C. Byerly, *The Beginning of Things* (Guelph: The Guelph Publishing Co., 1935), p. 26.

45. Personal recollections of the late Rev. W.D. Reid who himself was one of the first natives of Leeds Co. to leave home.

46. McColl, p. 4.

TEN

The Scot
as Businessman

David S. MacMillan

When a rigid structure collapses the pieces can be put to use. This was a
tenet of the old engineering theory as propounded in the early nineteenth
century, but it also has validity in the field of "social engineering." There
are few more striking examples of its applicability than the way in which
the Scottish society, in increasing flux from the early eighteenth century
onwards, provided a class of men of enterprise that played a role, entirely
out of proportion to its small numbers, in the promotion of mercantile and
industrial concerns not only in Scotland, but also in North America, the
West Indies, and the East.

Until the end of the seventeenth century, Scottish society was much
more static than that of England, Holland, and France. The middle class
of traders was small, and lacked political influence in a country dominated
by landed and semi-feudal magnates. Economically, Scotland lagged far
behind Western Europe, and even in the first two decades of the
eighteenth century showed little sign of fulfilling the destiny that lay in
store – the achievement within years of a new role in the forefront of
European culture, commerce, industrialization, finance and economic
thought. It was a remarkable transformation, and in no field can its work-
ings be observed more clearly, and in such illuminating detail, than in the
British North American colonies which were eventually to confederate.
That is one reason why the role of the Scot as businessman in the early
phases of Canadian history is so important. These colonies were an easily
available laboratory for early Scottish mercantile experimentation, and
the specific character of Scottish enterprise is clearly revealed in its colonial application.

For Canada, just as much as for Scotland, investigation of these "mercantile men" who came out from their homeland in the eighteenth and
early nineteenth centuries is valuable and important, for the Scots were to
imprint indelibly their methods, "mores" and outlook on the whole commercial and economic life of these colonies. Recent studies in Canadian
business and entrepreneurial history have shown clearly that they were

179

predominant and pre-eminent in trade, commerce and industry, and their influence as well as that of their descendants has largely moulded the economic outlook of Canada.[1]

Yet in this business role the Scot has been surprisingly neglected. With the exception of the fur trade, the only aspect of Scottish enterprise to attract the attention of historians, little basic work has been done on the work of Scottish entrepreneurs in the general trade of importing and exporting, in banking, in ship-building, the vitally important timber trade and the establishment of manufactures.[2]

This chapter will attempt to survey, in brief form, the activities of mercantile Scots in the whole area to 1900 and to elucidate the motivations of the men concerned. It will also attempt to gauge the characteristics which they brought with them, and their operating methods and techniques. The subject is a two-sided one, for it investigates not only Scottish influences in Canada, but also the effects which these Canadian activities had on the attitudes, aspirations, and the various regional economies of the homeland. If the Canadian experience reflected strong Scottish influence, it also exerted a "counter influence" on Scotland itself.

The main problem facing the traders and merchant burgesses of the small cities and towns of Scotland in the seventeenth century was the lack of overseas markets for their hides and fish and other primary products. As Professor S.G. Lythe has shown, marketing was difficult, with demand constantly fluctuating on the continent. In the later part of the century, as the standard of living, at least for nobility, gentry and burgesses, began to rise, there developed a demand for colonial produce and for trade with colonial areas. This demand was difficult to meet, since Scotland, with no colonies of her own, was precluded from trade with the flourishing English colonies in North America and the West Indies. The Scottish social system in the seventeenth century was fairly rigid and static, as far as the lower groups were concerned, but an interesting change in the pattern of land ownership had begun well before 1650. Small estates, all over the country, and particularly in the Lowlands, were tending to be absorbed into larger estates, and numerous members of the lesser gentry, faced with rising living costs and fixed returns in rentals from their lands, were selling out to the greater gentry or the landed nobility. This "displaced gentry" frequently sought employment in the armies of Sweden, Holland, Muscovy, and the German states as mercenaries, or settled in the "Plantation" of Ulster. A considerable number also took up various lines of trade, manufacture, or the professions in the towns, thus augmenting the embryo middle class of merchant burghers.

This early period saw the first glimmers of Scottish interest in North America, as the Scots sought for outlets for their produce and a share in England's promising colonial ventures. In 1620 a group of seven of the "principal merchantis" of Glasgow put together a fund of money, which they invested in an English North American venture, the Newfoundland Company, established in Bristol and London in 1609, and chartered by the Crown in 1610.[3] The Scottish investment in this joint stock company brought slight return, the major beneficiaries being the shipowners of London and Bristol, but the Scots continued to be interested in Newfoundland and its fisheries, seeing in the island a loophole in the tight English colonial system, for there was great legal uncertainty regarding the exact status of the area. Some English authorities-at-law held that Newfoundland was "no true plantation, but a part, nay, a mere extension of His Majesty's good realm of England," and since Scots were, in fact, allowed to trade openly with England, though not with its colonies, the island seemed to afford a useful outlet for budding Scottish enterprise.[4]

Yet the weakness of Scotland as a potential trading and colonizing power was shown by the failure and confusion which resulted from the ambitious schemes of Sir William Alexander, later Earl of Stirling, who projected the feudal domain of "New Scotland" or Nova Scotia, and of Lord Ochiltree, with his even more remarkable scheme for a "Scots Barony or Stewardry" in Cape Breton Island. These projects broke down because a basis of financial backing, of adequate shipping and a well-developed mercantile class was lacking to support them.[5] It was only as the pattern of ownership of land – the sole real source of wealth in the country – changed in the course of the seventeenth century that the accumulations of capital necessary for mercantile and overseas investment came to exist in private hands. It is significant that the financial magnate and educational benefactor, George Watson, who flourished in the latter years of the century, made most of his money from "Wadset" or mortgage transactions, or from loans against rentals.[6]

Despite all these difficulties, weak and undercapitalized, the merchant burghers of Glasgow pushed on their "interloping" activities in the English colonies, especially in Virginia, with its attractive tobacco trade. These ventures, commenced as early as the mid-1660s under the useful cover of the Newfoundland fisheries, started the popular national game of evading the English Navigation Laws and the London-centred English colonial system. In June, 1680, Edward Randolph, "Surveyor General of Customs for the American Plantations," complained bitterly to the commissioners of customs in London that "many vessels full laden with tobacco" gave in bond at the Naval Office in Boston that they were bound for Newfoundland, but proceeded in fact to Scotland, Canada, and other countries.[7] This interesting practice, together with the ruse of registering their ships at Whitehaven, just across the Border in Cumberland, England, enabled the Glasgow merchants to break into the tobacco and plantation trades long before the Union Act of 1707 gave them a right to participate. The Board of Trade raged in the 1690s against the "dubious legality" of the Scots' expedient of dispatching convoys of cartloads of tobacco by road from Virginia to Massachusetts, whence it was shipped to Newfoundland in colonial vessels and there transhipped into Scottish ships for dispatch to the Clyde; but the Newfoundland coastline and waters were difficult to police and patrol. In 1701, Randolph reported the "audacity" of a combine of Scottish merchants in setting up a "factory" on the Newfoundland coast. Ostensibly a "fishing station," this establishment was in fact a "front" for a point of transhipment for Virginian tobacco and West Indian sugar for dispatch in Scottish vessels to the Clyde, Holland, the Baltic, France, and Scandinavia.[8]

The remarkable display of ingenuity on the part of the handicapped Scottish merchants is significant, for it helped to set the "tone" of Scottish mercantile activity throughout the eighteenth century. The disregard for rules and regulations that had been inculcated in the period before 1707 as a national necessity if Scottish overseas trade was to develop continued to be characteristic of the Scottish traders. After the union they had little compunction in breaking the law if the law hampered the plying of their trade. As smuggling was given more countenance by all classes in Scotland than in England, there seems little doubt that the debut of the Scots on the Canadian mercantile scene was made by those merchants of Glasgow and the Clyde ports who engaged in the "Newfoundland trade" from the 1680s throughout the eighteenth century.

There is also no doubt that the trade was a "cover" for the shipment to Scotland and the continent of enumerated colonial products (which could only be shipped legally from the colonies to England before 1707), and of sugar and other French and Spanish colonial produce thereafter. The transhipment of vast quantities of French brandy, laces and silks, Dutch spirits, and German and Russian linens also went on, the goods being smuggled into Scotland as well as to the British West Indian and North American colonies.

Before 1759-60, when the first Scottish merchants secured a foothold in Quebec and Halifax, and long before 1783, when the "grand period" of Scottish mercantile enterprise in Canada and the Maritimes began, there were Scottish factors, agencies and firms in the "fishing" settlements of Newfoundland. By the 1770s the firms of Johnstone and Co., Lang and Co., and Graham and Co., and several lesser concerns were operating in and around the island. Little is known about the activities of these companies prior to the 1790s for of their records only a few fragments of the archives of Lang and Co. survive. We can, therefore, only guess at the scope and scale of their activities.[9] All of the Newfoundland firms were based on or had strong connections with the Clyde, which was, from the 1680s through to the first half of the nineteenth century, the hub and focus of Scotland's trade with Canada and of Scottish emigration to Canada, and the chief supplier of Scottish merchants and businessmen to the colonies.

By 1807, Greenock, down the Clyde from Glasgow, alone had thirty-nine sizable vessels engaged in Newfoundland, coming third on the list of British ports involved in the "fishery."[10] By 1785, practically all commerce with Canada, Nova Scotia, and New Brunswick was conducted through this port, which was well-described by a contemporary as "the throat, as it were, of the principal manufacturing district of this nation."

The population rose from 15,000 in 1783 to 25,000 in 1800, and by the latter date no fewer than 377 ships were owned there.[11] In this thriving town were situated sugar refineries and rum distilleries, ropeworks, and sailcloth manufactories, and most important, a number of excellent shipyards, some of which had by 1780 gained the reputation of being among the best in the United Kingdom. There were also numerous mercantile and ship-owning firms, and from their counting houses men would go out to Canada and the Maritimes to create a vast, informal, commercial empire.

Even more important were the developments in the Clyde's hinterland, as between 1750 and 1800 Scotland experienced a radical and amazing change in its social and economic life. The country "took off," in the economists' phrase, into the first stage of its industrial revolution with dramatic suddenness, principally in Glasgow and the surrounding area. Linen and cotton mills, ironworks, coal mines, shipyards, and numerous other industrial enterprises sprouted around what had been a quiet little cathedral city in the seventeenth century. By 1800 Glasgow rivalled Edinburgh in population, with over 100,000 inhabitants, and Glasgow's chief port, Greenock, was surpassing Scotland's ancient "metropolitan and paramount port" of Leith in trade, shipping, and initiative.

Within the hub of commerce a new breed was appearing – the commercial Scot, a creature very different from the ultra-cautious seventeenth century merchant burgher with limited objectives and willingness to leave affairs of state to his betters. The "new men" were ambitious, and increasingly determined to have a say in matters of church and state, especially in those which touched their own interests. Since this class provided the men who spearheaded the Scottish commercial advance in what was to become Canada, its characteristics are worth examining in some detail.

The career of William Forsyth of Cromarty, and the writings of another veteran Scottish merchant, David Lock of Over Carnbie, who flourished in the 1760s, show how aware they were of the gap that separated English affluence from the old Scots penury, and how determined they were, by every effort in their power, to rectify this imbalance, which they felt to be unjust and discriminatory.[12] Men of this stamp felt that their country had lagged behind, and that now, at last, the chance was afforded them to "catch up." After 1750 a new vigour, a new breadth of vision, had entered into the bodies and minds of Scottish businessmen. This was clearly seen in the midst of the frantic controversy that raged in Britain following the taking of Quebec, as to whether Canada should be retained. Many Scots felt acutely that *here* lay the field for enterprise, the markets for manufactures and the sources of raw materials that their country so badly needed, and they threw their full weight on the side of the "Retentionists." In January, 1760, a merchant, signing himself "Britannicus," stated in a letter to the *Glasgow Journal*: "Of all our acquisitions, the conquest of Quebec and consequently, of the country of Canada is the most important and most beneficial . . . for such a source of trade and commerce will be opened to us here, as will be fully sufficient, had we no other, to employ all our trading and commercial people, and find a vent, or constant consumption, for all our goods, products, and manufactures. It is therefore above all things to be wished that the country of Canada may never be relinquished."

This especially strong desire for the possession of Canada as a solution to Scotland's economic and social problems was further evinced by an editorial comment in the same newspaper (editorial comments were then rare, and only provoked by especially weighty issues). It ran: "The expense of this Conquest (i.e. of Canada) is the most thrifty disbursement ever made – an exclusive fishery! A boundless territory! The fur trade engrossed! and innumerable tribes of savages contributing to the consumption of our staple! There are sources of exhaustless wealth! Ignorant and designing men have called this a quarrel for a few dirty acres of snow, but the public will soon have feeling [sic.] proofs that Britain must sink or swim with her colonies."[13] A further proof of the particular interest in the Glasgow-Greenock area in ensuring that Canada be not restored to the "Papistical Bourbon Tyranny of the House of France," but kept British "regardless of our outlay in moneys and blood," was seen in the deputations of Glasgow and Greeock merchants to the Provost, the baillies, the local nobility and gentry, and to the local Presbytery, asking that they use their influence to ensure that "the French should be totally cleared out of North America."[14]

With this new awareness went a rapidly developing combativeness. Many of the "new men" were increasingly dissatisfied with the religious establishment in Scotland, where Queen Anne's Acts of Patronage left the right of nomination of parish ministers in the hands of the heritors, i.e. the local aristocracy and gentry. Since the parish schools were run in conjunction with and under the supervision of the Kirk, this was a matter of more than simple religious significance. Consequently, the majority of the mercantile Scots were Dissenters, supporters of various "breakaway" groups, such as the "Anti-Burghers" and the United Secession Synod. Their role in organizing and leading such dissident bodies undoubtedly gave them valuable experience which increased their growing confidence as men of business and as participants in politics.

In politics, they were also exponents of the cause of Reform – not only of Parliamentary Reform, but of the much more vital cause of Burgh Reform, particularly important in Scotland because of the peculiarly corrupt system of parliamentary election by nominated town councils, which made the country an easily-managed electoral appanage of the Dundas family and its connections. Adherence to reform as a good cause was another characteristic that the Scottish businessmen brought to their new North American environment.

These were all admirable qualities under the circumstances, but other features of the class were, perhaps, less attractive. Reference has already been made to their ingenuity in evading the law and the trade regulations.

This was to be a continuing trait, as we can see in the "trading on the line" activities of Christopher Scott, in the "prize-purchasing operations" of the Scottish Halifax circle, and in the utter high-handedness in taking the law into their own hands displayed by the leading partners of the North West Company, to which reference will be made later. From the most charitable point of view it can be regarded as an attitude bred of English discrimination against the Scots in the period following the union of the crowns in 1603. In support of this contention it must be remembered that as late as the 1760s it was still possible for an "anti-Scottish campaign" to be launched by Wilkes and others in London.

Another less admirable feature of the new Scottish commercial class was its intense, narrow localism. Despite the rapid social and industrial change of 1750-1800, Scotland was still essentially a country of regions – not only of "Highlands" and "Lowlands" but of subdivisions within each, among which population movement was still comparatively slight. "Clannishness," "parochialism," "favour to kin," and the nursing of prejudice, not only against the English and the Highlanders, but also against Scots from other areas of the Lowlands (most of the businessmen, because of the different social and economic structure of the Highlands and Lowlands, were Lowlanders), were charges that were absolutely valid when directed against Scottish businessmen of the time, whether at home or abroad. Scottish merchants in Canada, Newfoundland, and the Maritimes tended to trade with their home ports (mostly with Greenock) and to congregate in their colonial settings with Scots from their own regions, if they were available. They also recruited clerks, craftsmen, and labourers from their own districts back in Scotland – and kinfolk wherever possible, often to the detriment of the colonial population seeking employment. It is not surprising that in Quebec and Montreal, the Scottish paramountcy in trade, commerce, and industry came to be bitterly resented by some of the local population.

The high hopes held by Scottish merchants that Glasgow might "engross" the fur trade of Canada, and thus replace Paris as the main emporium for the peltries of North America, were not fulfiled. The dominant part that the Scots of the North West Company were to play in the trade after the 1780s is considered elsewhere in this volume, but the fact is that London, always the centre of Britain's fur importations from the time of the establishment of commercial links with Muscovy in the 1550s, went on to be the principal market for North American furs as well. As London had the specialized manufactures, and the experienced dealers and processers, accustomed to handling shipments of furs from Russia and Hudson's Bay, Scotland never became a major importer of peltries. Between 1764 and 1778 only four small consignments of furs are recorded as arriving in the Clyde; and of the total of 152 ships listed by the Colonial Office and the Board of Trade as sailing for Britain from Montreal and Quebec with full cargoes of furs between June, 1786, and January, 1814, only seven were destined for Scottish ports.[15]

It was in the field of general trade (importing and exporting a wide range of commodities) that they were active at first. There were scores of Scots among the "four hundred and fifty contemptible sutlers and traders" to whom their countryman, General Murray, made such scathing reference as being an embarrassment to him in newly conquered Canada.[16] Many had been attracted by the lucrative trade in supplies for the large British and colonial armies engaged in the conquest. Several of the Scottish-Newfoundland traders shipping flour, salted beef and other supplies from the Clyde and from Cork in Ireland to the St. Lawrence, to judge by references in the contemporary Scottish press, were obviously making considerable profits. In the years 1759, 1760 and 1761, no fewer than thirty-three full shiploads of provisions for the conquest armies sailed from Greenock alone.[17]

Many Scots "sutlers" stayed on in Halifax, Montreal, and Quebec after 1763. In 1768 in Halifax they were already numerous enough to form a "North British Society," which flourished and grew from its inception. In Quebec, the Scots soon dominated the trade of Canada. Unfortunately little is known in detail about these Scottish merchants in the early phase between 1759 and 1783, but from the Scottish and colonial press some "reconstruction" can be done to offset the lack of archival material.

Most prominent of the early Scots merchants was James Finlay, who headed the Canadian side of a joint concern, based in Greenock. From this latter point, his elder brother Robert, one of the most powerful and enterprising of the "new breed" of commercial men in the port, directed operations. By 1764, the Finlay brothers had established what constituted, in effect, a regular shipping service between Quebec and the Clyde. They shipped out Scottish linens, woollens, spirits, and ironware, bringing back to the Clyde colonial lumber, potash for glass-making and textile processing, and scant quantities of furs. More important, they organized a primitive emigration service based on the "indenture" principle already practised on the Clyde for the securing of slave overseers and craftsmen for the West Indies plantations. In Greenock, Robert Finlay advertised on behalf of his brother and his brother's Scottish mercantile associates in Quebec for "masons skilled in building, gardeners, quarriers, and millers, fabricators of dry stone dykes, and good and sober men skilled in the management of flour and saw mills."[18] Applicants were offered free passage in the Finlay ships and well-paid employment. These Scottish craftsmen brought out by the Finlays and other operators who speedily emulated them played an important part in the building of stores, warehouses, and residences for their fellow countrymen in Quebec's building booms of the 1760s, 1770s and 1790s.

As with the Quebec/Montreal Scottish mercantile circles, that of Halifax, largely drawn from Glasgow, Greenock, and the Clyde area maintained the closest of links with Scottish west coast ports in trade and the fostering of emigration. This was natural enough, for several of the earliest merchants to find lodgement in Halifax, during the Seven Years' War, were Scots from Newfoundland, attracted by the rapidly-developing fisheries of Arichat and by the chance of sharing in contracts for the supplying of the conquest army. The three most notable of the early arrivals were John Geddes of Glasgow, who appeared in 1755, Peter McNab of Inverness, who came out in the same year, and Alexander Brymer, a successful Glasgow merchant, who ventured to settle in Halifax in 1760 with the fruits of his commercial activities in Glasgow, the then-sizable capital of £4000.

Brymer, a remarkably able merchant, was intent on encouraging other Scots to come out to join the circle. He became known as "Father of the Community of Scottish Merchants" in the town, the group which Harold Innis described as "the little commercial group which dominated Nova Scotian behaviour." The North British Society, which he helped to found in 1768, was essentially a Scottish commercial club, though it also had benevolent and charitable aims.[19] Brymer prospered exceedingly from the trade in fish to the West Indies and from the import trade, especially in rum and other spirits from the Clyde, and by the 1770s was regarded as a merchant prince. Like many of his type and nation, however, the merchant had a strong philanthropic streak. He not only personally paid for the return passages to Scotland of many emigrants who were unable to cope with colonial life, but also lent large sums without interest to encourage merchants in Glasgow and Greenock to come out and join the "circle" in Nova Scotia.[20] Since by 1777 the North British Society had over one hundred members, nearly all merchants, it was necessary to employ a full-time messenger to maintain communications among them. It may be guessed that the purpose of these messages was largely commercial, pertaining to shipping arrivals and departures, prices and cargoes.

The St. Lawrence trade became in the period between 1764 and 1800 one of the principal strands in the complex commerce of the Clyde. In the 1760s some sixteen owners were recorded as sending out vessels to Quebec, including the owners of ships who employed them from time to time as well in the West African-West Indian slave traffic. By 1800 there were at least thirty-five firms in Greenock and Glasgow which were largely concerned with the St. Lawrence trade. It would be no exaggeration to say that Scotland's share of the trade with Canada in the last forty years of the eighteenth century was far out of proportion to the country's population or shipping and mercantile strength. It was dominated by the Clydeside Scots and their kinfolk, agents and representatives on the other side of the Atlantic; and the same situation was intensified in the Nova Scotian and New Brunswick trades in the period of intense economic development after 1783.[21] To draw together, however, the widely separated threads of Scottish enterprise in the newly conquered colony of New France, in the Province of Nova Scotia and, after 1784, in the new territory of New Brunswick, is not an easy task, for these places were far apart, not only geographically, but in outlook and background. Still, as far as the Scottish mercantile connection was concerned, there is a common factor which applied to them all. It was the utterly disruptive but still creative effect of the American Revolution. There can be no doubt that this phenomenon led to a vital change of direction in the economic life of Nova Scotia and Canada, while it created the economic life of New Brunswick. To all three areas, the Revolution brought a further Scottish wave made up of the dispossessed Scottish Loyalist businessmen and merchants, many of them bringing valuable experience of colonial trading conditions, and useful expertise in the pioneering of new lines of commerce. A few, such as James Dunlop of Montreal, even managed to bring with them some capital which they had contrived to save from the wreck of earlier careers.

The change in the direction of the Scots' trading interests after 1783 was towards the timber trade and its ancillary, the ship-building industry. True, other types of trade did not disappear, but the shipping of timber to Great Britain and the building of West Indian ships in North America began to loom ever larger in the general trade pattern. With the outbreak of the wars with France in 1793 the need for supplies of timber and ships became very pressing. Furthermore, with Napoleon's institution of the Continental System as an attempted blockade of the British Isles, other commodities such as sugar and grain were in great demand. Of all this the British North American-based merchants took quick advantage, and none more quickly than the Scots. Timber, however, remained basic as the foundation for many of the fortunes made before the mid-point of the nineteenth century.

William Forsyth, who possessed a combination of daring, caution and vision, was the classic type of Scottish entrepreneur. He arrived in Halifax in 1782, and as a partner in the important Greenock firm of Hunter and Robertson, rapidly made his mark in the West Indies fish trade and in ship-owning. By the mid-1780s he was the owner of two fleets of vessels – one made up of eight large ships which he employed in the trans-Atlantic trade, the other consisting of a score of smaller ships which were engaged in the coastal and West Indies trades. Judged by the standards of the time, the supply of salted fish, often of the poorer or "refuse" quality, sent to the West Indian plantations as food for the slaves, was the basis of all his commerce. These were shipped from Halifax in Forsyth's larger coasting vessels to Jamaica, Grenada and Antigua.

The proceeds of the fish cargoes were invested in rum, sugars, and salt from St. Ubes, which were then shipped back to Halifax, where the rum and salt went out to supply the fisheries, and the sugars were consigned to the Clyde. Because prices of salt fish in the West Indies and of quality sugars in Britain rose steeply during the Wars of 1776-83 and 1793-1815, Forsyth profited greatly.[22] On the basis of this success, he then launched into a variety of other lines of business, acting as Halifax agent for numerous Scots, American, Dutch and German shipowners, exporting New Brunswick timber to the West Indies and masts to Britain, and acquiring large vessels in New Brunswick which in the 1790s made his fleet the largest in Nova Scotia. After war with revolutionary France broke out in

1793, he saw that ships and ship-building timber would shortly be at a premium because of wartime losses, and if a trade in lumber with Britain could be built up in wartime, it might well continue profitably when peace came.[23]

He also pioneered in other lines of trade, including importing from Liverpool vast quantities of prime Cheshire salt for the fisheries, of which he obtained a virtual monopoly.[24] Also, through relatives established in trade in Montreal from 1790, he speculated in furs, potash, Canadian timber and colonial grain, the latter a commodity in increasing demand in Britain in the 1790s. Contracts with the Admiralty for the supply of masts to British and West Indian naval dockyards, the importation of wines from Madeira, Spain, Portugal and the Mediterranean, the export of Cape Breton coals to Newfoundland, and the importing of entire shiploads of cottons, linens, and woollens from the Clyde also swelled his business. By these means he helped to raise Halifax to the key position as an entrepot of the North Atlantic trade by 1800.

Forsyth also joined in a lucrative practice that grew up in Halifax in wartime – that of speculating in prize ships and cargoes seized by the navy and auctioned by order of the Vice-Admiralty Courts. Many Scottish naval and military officers, professional men and merchants made large fortunes by forming syndicates for such dealings. The system is well described by James S. MacDonald when he states that "although Halifax had a small population at this time, the enterprise of her Scottish merchants was known to all mercantile centres of the trading world."[25] In bidding for prize ships and cargoes knowledge of their character was invaluable. This the Scots were often able to obtain through collusion with their countrymen in high positions in the naval establishment. There seems little doubt that there was a good deal of sharp practice, verging on illegality, in these proceedings.

Forsyth, however, saw that the seizure of neutral vessels, if overdone, could only dislocate trade and generate bad feeling among the victims. On many occasions, he acted as agent for the owners of captured ships, managing to secure their release. As he put it in a letter to an American correspondent (needless to say, a Scot), James Crawford of Philadelphia, in September, 1796: "We shall upon all occasions afford to American citizens every protection and assistance in our power to obtain justice, it being no more than we should expect of others were our property in the like situation."[26] This attitude was a remarkably advanced and civilized one for the time, especially considering that Forsyth lost several vessels to French privateers. But there can be no doubt that Forsyth's assistance to neutrals helped to strengthen his network of useful contacts in foreign ports, in many ways the true foundation of his prosperity.

Other Scots were of key importance in Nova Scotia, but they are little more than names today. One such was the industrious partnership of Fraser and Thom, who came out from Scotland in 1786 with the backing of the Greenock firm of Alan Kerr and Co. They established a fisheries and general trading base at Beaubair's Island, which became the central point for the commercial development of the Northumberland Strait and the Gulf of St. Lawrence. In typical Scots fashion, they did business with William Forsyth in Halifax. They also brought out ship-builders and other craftsmen from the Clyde, from whose activities sprang the later flourishing ship-building centres of Pictou, New Glasgow and Antigonish.

Another dim figure of whom there is little record is Captain Lowden, also from the Clyde area, who set up the first shipyards in Pictou County in 1788-92. William Davidson and John Cort, Scottish partners with experience in the large scale salmon fisheries of their native land, established themselves about 1762 at the mouth of the Miramichi River, in an area abandoned by the French. By 1766-70 they were exporting annually, to Britain, Boston, Philadelphia, New York, the Mediterranean, and the West Indies, no less than 1800 tierces of salted salmon, or about twelve hundred barrels. By the mid-1770s they had secured a vast grant of 100,-000 acres on the river and had launched out into lumbering on a large scale, ship-building and general trade. Little is known in detail of these operations, as is the case of Edward Mortimer, the Scot from Banff, who became known as "the King of Pictou" and the "master trader" in the 1790s, or of Alexander Walker, who built up from Bathurst harbour a flourishing commerce in fish, furs, walrus tusks and hides, oils and other local products. All of these men looked to Halifax and its Scottish mercantile community as their natural base of supply and source of provisions and trade goods. But because of the loss of their records, our knowledge of the foundation era of Canadian commerce is the poorer.

The centre of the economic life of the Province of Canada from the 1770s on was Montreal. Fortunately here there is more evidence to go on, partly because of the interest that has been taken in that predominantly Scottish concern, the North West Company of fur traders. Yet our detailed knowledge of such men as James McGill and the remarkable Simon McTavish (alias "the Marquis") is really very slight. In the case of James Dunlop, Loyalist refugee from Virginia, a merchant trained in Glasgow and linked with several Greenock firms, we are fortunate that his letters to his Scottish kinfolk have survived.[27]

Dunlop was intensely ambitious, rather ebullient, very convivial, loved social life and liked to operate on a large scale. He was, in fact, very different from the balanced, rather self-effacing, cautious and sagacious William Forsyth of Halifax. Yet what the two men did have in common was a keen perception of trading trends, coupled with an ability to grasp the main chance when it offered. Commencing operations as a "general trader" in Montreal in 1776, he built up by 1791 a thriving business as an importer of textiles, liquors and groceries, based on his large warehouse – the most extensive in town – on St. Paul Street. On the outbreak of war with revolutionary France in 1793 he was quick, like Forsyth in Halifax and numerous other Scots merchants in colonial centres, to see the opportunities afforded by the new wartime conditions. He launched out into the West Indian trade, taking advantage of the Act of Parliament of 1788 which allowed vessels carrying lumber, provisions and livestock to ply directly between Canada and the British West Indies, and to bring back from the islands sugars, rum and other commodities. As a result of this trade, between 1793 and 1815, Dunlop became one of the colony's largest shipowners. Dunlop also exported cargoes, in both his own and chartered vessels, of choice Canadian oak to Leith and to the Clyde, where they fetched unprecedented prices due to wartime demand, profits of several hundred per cent being made from some of these voyages. He invested heavily and profitably in the export of Canadian grain and potash, for cereals were scarce in the West Indies, England and Scotland while potash was in strong demand for industrial purposes.

Unlike Forsyth, who operated his far-flung trading empire from his Halifax counting house, Dunlop was a traveller par excellence, devoting much of his time and energy to wayfaring through Lower and Upper Canada seeking out grain, timber and potash and bargaining with the producers. The goods purchased were paid for largely in imported Scottish manufactures or West Indian rum, so that Dunlop benefitted from both sides of the trade.[28] He was also a dealer in treasury and other bills, and an acute manipulator of the colonial money market. According to the historian of St. Gabriel Street Presbyterian Church, in which Dunlop worshipped, he was by far the largest operator in bills in British North America, negotiating as much as fifty thousand pounds of government and private paper on occasion.[29] The proceeds from these transactions were used to build larger and finer vessels, and to stockpile vast quantities of wheat, potash and timber for speculative export to the British market. On several occasions between 1891 and 1812 he was almost able to corner the market in these commodities – an exciting game, which he played with verve, and steadiness of nerve.[30]

The ships which he built in his own yards, using imported Scottish ship-designers, shipwrights and craftsmen, and manned on completion entirely by Scottish crews, were among the largest built up to that date in Quebec and Montreal. Named after members of the Dunlop family, they were ships of over 400 tons – large sea-going vessels judged by the standards of the time. By 1810 he owned three such ships and was building two more in Montreal. In addition he owned, or had shares in, more than thirty smaller vessels engaged in the coasting or St. Lawrence River trade.

Dunlop's aim, in his own words, was to have "the largest mercantile establishment in the colony." Therefore in the early 1800s he purchased extensive water frontages on the St. Lawrence River, where wharves, houses, stores and other facilities were constructed, achieving this high ambition.[31] The climax of his success came in the War of 1812. He had already made large profits by shipping barrelled beef and flour to Wellington's armies in the Peninsula, and he was a past master at securing supply contracts from commissary officials. He now calculated that there would be bonanza profits from treasury, army and navy bills, from an even greater demand for Canadian ship-building timber, flour and potash, owing to the fact that there were no longer competing United States goods on the British market, and that rum and other provisions had to be supplied to the augmented British land and naval forces in North America.

He also embarked on the project of taking out "letters of Marque" for his finest ships so that they could operate against the Americans as privateers. Remarkably, every single one of his ventures, including the privateers, bore fruit. By 1814 he could declare, "I have done more good business since the War began than ever I did in the same space of time, but I also have been more bold in my speculations than any other person or Company in this Province." [32] The claim sounds rather vainglorious, but it was no less than the truth.

Active in the militia (he served as a Major of Volunteer Artillery), Dunlop was a "hard-liner" on the issue of the American war. Unlike his countryman Forsyth in Halifax, who wished to conciliate the Americans, Dunlop held that the War should be waged to the bitter end, since "we will never again have the same good opportunity of bringing the United States to our own terms." [33] It is interesting to speculate about what further heights of success this brilliant businessman might have attained, had he not died suddenly in August, 1815, probably due to overmuch "conviviality" in the celebration of Waterloo.

From the time of the foundation of St. John, New Brunswick, by United Empire Loyalists in 1784, Scots had been predominant among its traders. The principal commercial street of Saint John in the 1790s was known as "Scotch Row," and McPhail's Tavern thereon was a sort of unofficial commercial exchange in which goods were advertised or "cried" and auctioned, and deals made. By 1790 there were at least fifteen mercantile houses operated by Scots in the town. These firms dominated the trade of New Brunswick, especially those headed by the Black, Pagan and Johnston families, and by the enterprising Andrew Crookshank. By 1798 there was also a flourishing Saint Andrew's Society.

Timber and fish were the principal staples in which these houses specialized, the former becoming increasingly important with the onset of the great revolutionary wars in Europe in 1793. Hugh Johnston, founder of the house of Johnston and Company, the largest mercantile concern in Saint John, came out from Morayshire in 1784 in his own ship, with a cargo of Scottish manufactures. He rapidly built up a flourishing business, based, like that of William Forsyth in Halifax, on the trade to the West Indies, in exported fish and imported rum and sugar. On this foundation he launched out in the late 1790s and early 1800s into a variety of other lines, most of them highly profitable, but involving illegal smuggling activities on the border and the coastal waters of the Bay of Passamaquoddy. From 1812 he played a leading part in the highly illegal but most lucrative

"Trading on the Line" with the Americans. Like many of his country-men, he was keenly interested in that revolutionary maritime innovation, the steamboat. As a leading member of the consortium which owned the *General Smythe*, New Brunswick's finest steam vessel, plying on the Saint John River, Johnston took the lead in operating steam vessels in the Bay of Fundy, being half-owner of the *Saint John*, the first steamship to sail those waters.[34]

So large did these early Scots businessmen loom in the Maritimes that only passing reference can be made to the more outstanding figures such as John Black, from Aberdeen, *via* Glasgow, who arrived in Saint John in 1786 as purchasing agent for the important firm of Blair and Glenie, a Scottish concern based in London, which was interested in securing masts and yards from New Brunswick's virgin forests. He soon built up a vigor-ous trade in shipping, general importing and timber exporting by having his own agents in Scotland. In 1802 he moved to Halifax where he took a leading part in organizing the Halifax Committee of Trade (1804) and five years later promoted the foundation of the Quebec Board of Trade which, like the Halifax Committee, was formed to put pressure through the London Committee on the home government to grant privileges to the British American ports.[35]

Another interesting personality was John Young of Glasgow, merchant and agricultural reformer, better known under his *nom-de-plume* of "Agricola." Young was an active trader "on the Line" during the War of 1812, and a devoted champion of the commercial interests of the Mari-time provinces and of his countrymen there. Indeed, the two causes were so closely identified as to be well-nigh identical.

The case of Christopher Scott, another leading Scottish merchant, is an unusual one, because of the circumstances in which he came out to New Brunswick. In 1797 the Scotts, already in the first rank of British ship-builders, faced a desperate situation due to the lack of ship-building tim-ber. Supplies from the Baltic were scarce and expensive because of the restrictive policies of the Russian government regarding exports. Conse-quently it was obvious to the senior partners, James and William Scott, that new supplies must be secured speedily. They conceived the plan of sending out their younger brother Christopher, an experienced ship-builder and master mariner, with tools and metal fittings, cordage and sails, as well as a number of skilled craftsmen from their yard, to set up a completely new ship-building installation on the Saint John River. This was a remarkable project for the time, and one that proved an immense success for the Scotts, as well as a boon to the infant ship-building industry of the colony, for the Scott craftsmen who settled there taught their crafts and expertise to the locals.[36]

Within two years Christopher Scott sent nineteen new vessels to the Clyde with timber, not only oak and pine for ship construction, but also large quantities of black birch, which found a ready market among the cabinet-makers of the growing furniture industries of Paisley and Beith.[37]

The shipping of copper fastenings and other metal fittings from the Clyde to the firm's New Brunswick yards was illegal, prohibited by British orders-in-council, but, as in so many other cases where evasion of the law was necessary for Scots to achieve their commercial ends, the law was breached continuously.

Christopher Scott settled permanently in the colony, in the border town of Saint Andrews in 1805, and became an expert "Trader on the Line," privateer, smuggler, speculator in prize ships and cargoes, and architect of a considerable fortune which he invested in landed estates in New Brunswick and in his native land. He was responsible for building the superb "Greenock Church" in the town, providing financing, craftsmen and plans from Scotland; he also built the fine blockhouse which still stands as a memento of the War of 1812.[38]

The activities of Johnston, Black and Scott helped to usher in what has been called "the golden age of the New Brunswick timber trade," as well as the apogee of Scottish mercantile influence in that colony. In 1807, 156 ships sailed from its ports with almost 24,000 tons of timber. More than one-third of the vessels engaged in the trade between 1800 and 1825 were Scots' ships, a number out of all proportion to the country's relative shipping strength.

In the latter stages of the Napoleonic Wars, industrial over-production, exclusion from continental markets, and a glut of tonnage brought difficulties for Scottish manufacturers, merchants and ship-owners. To many ship-owners, the Saint John and Miramichi timber trades seemed the last resort if their vessels were to have employment. The emigration traffic from Highlands and Lowlands was also attractive in providing some return for outward voyages. This led to a razor-keen competition among Scottish ship-owners, and, for the first time, the ports of the east coast – notably Aberdeen, Alloa and Grangemouth – began to participate in the trade, but Greenock, backed by Glasgow, held on to its leading place.

Freight rates sank so low in this post-war period that some Scottish merchants in the Newfoundland and Quebec trades sold off most of their vessels, since low rates in the ships of others were so readily available. Peace-time timber gluts on the Thames, the Mersey, the Clyde and the Forth, with a new emphasis on quality and a need for larger vessels specially built for the trade, soon led to the emergence of large scale timber firms, who operated their own concessions on contract systems rather than extending credit for goods to settlers and taking timber in return. These new firms maintained their own sawmill establishments and fleets of timber ships. Now a new phase opened in the commercial relations between Scotland and British North America.

The four principal firms of the "new wave" of large scale operations were all Scots' concerns, though two of them, Richardson Forsyth and Co., and Scott, Idles and Co., were based in London and Montreal, and another, Duncan Gibb and Co., operated from Liverpool. The fourth of these leaders in the timber trade was the firm of Pollok, Gilmour and Co., which revolutionized the industry in the colonies.

The key figure in conceiving this giant among contemporary companies was Allan Gilmour. Temperamental and adventurous, he began his business career as a small importer of lumber from the Baltic area.[39] In 1804, however, he went into partnership with the Pollok brothers, grocers and sons of a Renfrewshire farmer. The new firm was capitalized at £1500 of which Gilmour provided £1,000. During the latter years of the Napoleonic Wars, Pollok and Gilmour gradually expanded their business by turning to the Canadas and New Brunswick for their timber and by pressuring the British government into imposing duties on Baltic imports. As one of the first Scottish timber merchants to recognize the advantage of importing North American wood, Gilmour moved his headquarters from Grangemouth at the mouth of the Great Canal to Port Glasgow on the Clyde. In 1804 he established a branch in Quebec City and in 1812 another at Miramichi, and from that time on the firm grew rapidly. In the late 1820s they were operating eleven shipyards in the North American colonies, and between 1822 and 1832 their fleet increased from 54 to over 100 vessels. In the 1830s, apart from the 5,000 men employed in the ships and shipyards, over 15,000 were working in the forests of New Brunswick to obtain the timber, although in Canada they bought directly from the lumbermen as they rafted their logs down the St. Lawrence and Ottawa Rivers. In 1834 alone the firm exported 300 shiploads from Miramichi, St. John, Quebec, Montreal and Bathurst, probably amounting to some 150,-000 tons if the average ship's capacity was 500 tons, although some were much larger. Pollok and Gilmour also acted as agents for ship-builders in the Maritime colonies, selling large numbers of their vessels on the London market. We may gain some idea of the way in which the wealth of the partners increased during this period by the fact that Gilmour between 1815 and 1836 bought a number of country estates and finally in 1838 sold out his share to the Polloks for £150,000, not a bad capital gain on his original £1,000 investment.[40] The Polloks then moved the headquarters of the firm to Liverpool where capital was more easily obtainable and the port facilities had been greatly expanded. From then on, the firm became English, although its fortunes had been made by Gilmour.[41]

Pollok and Gilmour was only the most prominent of a cluster of Glasgow, Greenock and Port Glasgow firms which were followed by others in Aberdeen, Leith, Dundee and Dumfries, and which grasped at the new sources of timber supply. James Scott of Glasgow had sixteen ships in the Quebec-Miramichi lumber trade by 1823, while John Mitchell of the same city had eleven vessels constantly plying from the Clyde to the Miramichi by the same year. The squared pine of that river, so easily worked, appealed to carpenters, joiners, house-builders and shipwrights all over Scotland in the years of the wars and their aftermath, marked by prosperity, temporary setbacks, but population growth at an unprecedented rate.

When peace came, the timber trade continued to flourish, and the Scots were predominant in it. Though Brougham might rail in parliamentary debate in 1817 against the "Canadian and shipping interests" and the "mercantile school" with its "inferior timbers from the North American Colonies," the ship-owners and lumber merchants whose interests were bound in with the Quebec, Miramichi and Saint John trade were now so influential that there was no question of reversing the policy of preference instituted in 1810.[42] It is significant that Kirkman Finlay, member for Glasgow, and a leading exponent of freedom in trade, who was presenting petitions for his city's Chamber of Commerce at this time urging an end to all restrictions, did nothing to support Brougham on this issue. His constituents and their Greenock, Leith, Aberdeen and Dumfries associates were doing too well out of the trade.[43] Arguments like that of the able shipowner Joseph Marryat, member for Sandwich in 1820, that the Canadian lumber trade employed 340,000 tons of shipping in 1819 as against 80,000 tons in 1811, were bound to be conclusive.[44]

The dominant role of the Scots in every department of the commercial life of British North America up to 1825 is so vast a topic that it has been possible only to indicate some of the major lines of development. The period between 1759 and 1825 saw the Scots secure not only a foothold, but also a commanding position in the economic life of the country, and this trend continued unabated as emigration from Scotland increased at an unprecedented rate in the hard decades of the 1820s, 1830s and 1840s. The new waves of emigrants showed the same characteristics as their forerunners, and as James MacGregor, an acute observer, put it when he described the influx into the Maritimes: "The lessons of early life infuse among the lower and middle classes in Scotland a spirit which will endure the greatest hardships without repining whenever a manifest utility is to be attained."[45] To the founding of banks, insurance companies and industrial and trading concerns of all types great and small, the Scots brought tenacity, shrewdness, industry and expertise.

The Scots' prominence and leadership in the Canadian business world after 1825 appears most clearly in Montreal where men such as James McGill, Simon McTavish, Peter Redpath, and many others too numerous to name dominated the scene. The North West Company was made up largely of Scots, as is pointed out in another chapter of this book. The Bank of Montreal, founded in 1817, had Scots as five of its first directors and the following year three more Scots or Scottish Canadians joined the board.[46] As the nineteenth century wore on other Scottish names appeared. George Stephen, Lord Mount Stephen, and his cousin, Donald Smith, Baron Strathcona and Mount Royal, both played important parts in the financial world of Montreal and were the two men responsible, along with the engineer Sandford Fleming, another Scot, for the successful completion of the Canadian Pacific Railway.[47] Many of these Scots were the leading philanthropists of the city, being responsible for the founding of institutions such as McGill University, the Royal Victoria and the Montreal General Hospitals, the building of churches and the establishment of commercial organizations such as the Board of Trade and even the Mercantile Library Association, a kind of merchants' mechanics' institute. While there were other ethnic groups involved in the business life of Montreal, Professor Tulchinsky's view that in Montreal, "the Scots comprised the dominant group in most forms of commerce," is amply born out by the facts.[48]

If one looks to the Atlantic provinces one finds that much the same state of affairs prevailed there during the mid and latter part of the nineteenth century. When the Charlotte County Bank was set up in St. Andrews, New Brunswick, in 1825, out of a total of twenty-five directors, fourteen were Scots. Forty-four years later, William Jarvis wrote a description of the launching of a commercial bank in St. John in 1832, in which he emphasized that the organizers were anxious that "the Scotch system of banking should be brought into operation in the Province . . . ."[49] The early Canadian banks were modelled on those of Scotland, with their wide distribution of shares among the public, their establishment of branches and their novel idea of lending money to well-recommended individuals. Other forms of business in the Atlantic provinces usually followed the Scottish patterns of operation.

To the west of Montreal from Toronto and Hamilton as far as Fort William and Port Arthur at the Lakehead, the same phenomenon was observable. Whether it was Sir Alan MacNab, who with J.B. Ewart and Peter Buchanan pushed through the construction of the Great Western Railway, or Robert Simpson, the originator of the chain of retail departmental stores, Scots seem to have dominated the business world.[50]

If we leapfrog over the prairies to Victoria – founded by a Scot, James Douglas – on the west coast we find that the eastern pattern tends to repeat itself. Although many different ethnic groups were represented in the thousands of people who came in with the Gold Rush in the Fraser River Valley, Scots soon made their appearance and gradually became some of the most important and influential businessmen in the area. Thomas and James Lowe were two of the first to come, arriving in 1861-2, and eventually became leaders of the business community. Other Scots who came about the same time were J. Robertson Stewart and Gilbert M. Sproat, president of the local St. Andrew's Society in 1863. Sproat represented Anderson and Co. which was interested in ship-building and the lumber trade. In 1859 the first private bank was established by Alexander Macdonald who was ruined, however, by a burglary. Gradually more Scots, with names such as Dickson, Campbell and Haliburton, moved in. One of the most important was Robert Dunsmuir who had been selling coal from Nanaimo since 1855. In 1869, he discovered the Wellington mine which enabled him to form a large coal mining company. In the 1860s men such as William Irving and Alexander Murray operated the first steam ships in the area. A little later another Scot who was to wield a great influence settled in Victoria: Robert Paterson Rithet, who in 1868 was working for

Sproat and Co. but later joined J. Robertson Stewart. When Robertson retired Rithet formed a partnership with an Andrew Welch and bought the firm. Gradually his interests expanded in the '80s to wholesaleing, shipping, insurance, lumbering, canning, groceries, and sugar plantations in Hawaii. In 1890 he was a member of the legislature, and subsequently became involved in railway-building and the developing of port facilities.

In this connection we should mention the activities of John Irving, son of the aforementioned William Irving, who along with Rithet established the Canadian Pacific Navigation Co. which was eventually bought out by the Canadian Pacific Railway in 1900. Robert Dunsmuir also continued to expand his interests, buying more mines and finally building, with the help of government subsidies, the Esquimalt and Nanaimo Railway. While extensive statistical studies of the situation on the west coast have not been made, it is clear from what has been said that the Scots operated in much the same way wherever they located.[51]

The statistics provided by Professor T.W. Acheson confirm the impression which one receives from accounts of individual Scots. In dealing with the question of the origins of the industrial elite during the period 1880-1885, he points out that 38% of the country's population lived in the Quebec to Kingston area, and a similar percentage in the area from Kingston to the Lakehead. The Maritimes had 20% and the West, principally British Columbia, 4%. Of what he counts as the industrial elite 40% were in the St. Lawrence (Quebec to Kingston) region and 37% in the Lake Peninsula (Kingston to the Lakehead) region while the other two regions had about the same percentage as their proportion of the total population. When recording the birthplaces of the elite, 20% came from Scotland, the highest percentage of any group, Canadian or non-Canadian, and it is interesting to note that at this period the Scottish elite formed only 3% of the population. Carrying this somewhat farther, however, we find that 28% of the elite's fathers were born in Scotland, a percentage larger than that of all the native-born and almost twice as large as the next percentage of "foreign-born" who were Americans. Moreover it is well to note that while only 10% of the elite with Scottish fathers were located in the Maritimes, 31% were in the Lake Peninsula region and 40% in the West. While these figures are based upon a sampling, it would seem that they give a fairly accurate picture which certainly indicates that the Scots tended to be the predominant element in Canadian industry before 1900, and undoubtedly this would also hold true for their activities in finance and commerce.

One further fact which should be considered is that of the industrial elite who had Scottish fathers, 46% of the fathers were farmers, 14% were craftsmen, 11% were in management and 21% in manufacturing. The predominance of men with agricultural backgrounds may explain in part their frugality, their usual strong religious convictions and their industry. Farming either in Scotland or in Canada was no easy life and tended to breed hard-working and rugged individuals. This same background may also, partially at least, explain their high degree of adaptability and the capacity of Scottish businessmen to assimilate easily to their environment.[52]

This chapter has barely scratched the surface of a very large topic which can be fully examined only when hundreds of case studies of individual Scots have been made on the basis of research into business records. Yet from the work which has already been done it is clear that the Scots' contribution to Canada as traders, businessmen, manufacturers and financiers was extremely important. Their initiative and their energy, backed by a network of business connections at home and throughout the country, had most important long term implications for the colonies which eventually became the Dominion of Canada.

Pierre Berton in *The National Dream* states the Scots' accomplishments most clearly. He quotes from Lord Mount Stephen's address when the latter received the freedom of the City of Aberdeen:

> Any success I may have had in life is due in great measure to the somewhat Spartan training I received during my Aberdeen apprenticeship, in which I entered as a boy of 15. To that training, coupled with the fact that I seemed to have been born utterly without the faculty of doing more than one thing at a time is due that I am here before you today. I had but few wants and no distractions to draw me away from the work I had in hand. It was impressed upon me from my earliest years by one of the best mothers that ever lived that I must aim at being a thorough master of the work by which I had to get my living; and to be that I must concentrate my whole energies on my work, whatever that might be, to the exclusion of every other thing. I soon discovered that if I ever accomplished anything in life it would be by pursuing my object with a persistent determination to attain it. I had neither the training nor the talents to accomplish anything without hard work, and fortunately I knew it.

And Berton then adds:

> It was this hard ethic, so forcefully expressed by Stephen, that explains the dominance of the Scot in pioneer Canada. The Irish could loll in the taverns, sing, brawl, engage at ward level in the game of politics and otherwise disport themselves with the religious bickering that so engrossed their time and energies. For the Scots it was work, save and study; study, save and work. The Irish outnumbered them, as they did the English, but the Scots ran the country. Though they formed only one-fifteenth of the population they controlled the fur trade, the great banking and financial houses, the major educational institutions and, to a considerable degree, the government. The CPR was built to a large extent by Irish navvies and Irish contractors; but it was the Scots who held the top jobs. Almost every member of the original CPR syndicate was a self-made Scot. In the drama of the

199

railway it is the Scottish names that stand out: Macdonald and Mackenzie, Allan and Macpherson, Fleming and Grant, Stephen, Smith,
Kennedy, McIntyre, Angus and Hill – (who was half Scottish) –
living embodiments of the popular copybook maxims of the time.
Waste not, want not . . . Satan finds more mischief still for idle hands
to do . . . . God helps those that help themselves . . . . A penny saved
is a penny earned . . . . Remember that time is money . . . . Early to
bed, early to rise . . . Keep your nose to the grindstone . . . . See a pin
and pick it up . . . . [53]

NOTES

1. David S. Macmillan, ed., *Canadian Business History: Selected Studies,
   1947-1971* (Toronto: McClelland and Stewart, 1972); W.J. Rattray, *The
   Scot in British North America*, 4 vols. (Toronto: Maclear, 1880); John
   Murray Gibbon, *Scots in Canada* (Toronto: Musson, 1911).
2. For the role of the Scots in the fur trade, see Mrs. W.F. Mitchell's chapter
   in this volume, as well as such earlier works as G.C. Davidson, *The North
   West Company, 1818* (Berkely: University of California Press, 1970): W.
   Stewart Wallace, *Documents Relating to the North West Company* (Toronto: Champlain Society, 1934); John Gray, *Lord Selkirk of Red River*
   (London: Macmillan, 1963). Harold Innis' classic study of the trade also
   contains valuable material on the Scottish participation.
3. R.G. Lounsbury, *The British Fishery at Newfoundland* (Hamden: Ar-
   chon, 1969), p. 44.
4. *Ibid.*, p. 401.
5. For these early Scottish schemes, see the works of George Pratt Insh.
6. For Watson's financial career, see the chapter by Dr. Ian Nish in the
   history of George Watson's college, recently published.
7. Lounsbury, pp. 198-9.
8. *Ibid.*, p. 201.
9. *Ibid.*, p. 203-6. For Scottish attitudes to smuggling or "free-trading" in
   the eighteenth century, see P.W.J. Riley, *The English Ministers and Scotland* (London: Athlone Press, 1964), University of London Historical
   Studies No. 15.
10. A.C. Wardle, "The Newfoundland Trade," in *The Trade Winds: A
    Study of British Overseas Trade During the French Wars, 1793-1815*,
    C.N. Parkinson, ed. (London: Allan, 1958), pp. 243-4.
11. Daniel Weir, *History of the Town of Greenock* (Greenock, 1829), pp. 11-
    18; "Note on the Progress of Greenock," *The Scots Magazine*, January,
    1805; David Macpherson, *Annals of Commerce, Manufactures, Fisheries
    and Navigation* (Edinburgh, 1805) 4 vols. For the best account of the
    Industrial Revolution in Scotland, see Henry Hamilton, *An Economic*

History of Scotland in the Eighteenth Century (Oxford: Clarendon Press, 1963), Chapters 5-7.

12. Hugh Millar, *William Forsyth of Cromarty* (Cromarty, 1844); David Loch of Over Carnbie, *Letters Concerning the Trade and Manufactures of Scotland* (Edinburgh, 1774).

13. *Glasgow Journal*, January 28, 1760.

14. *Ibid.*, January 8, 1761.

15. Colonial Office Records, Series 47, Vols. 80-83, and Board of Trade Records, Series 5, Vol. 8 (London, Public Records Office).

16. W. Stewart Wallace, *The Pedlars from Quebec and other Papers on the Nor'Westers* (Toronto: Ryerson, 1954), p. 21.

17. Shipping lists and "Plantation News," *Glasgow Journal*, 1759-1761.

18. *Glasgow Journal*, February 2, 1764, *et passim*.

19. *Ibid.*, shipping lists, shipping advertisements and "Plantation News," 1765-1805.

20. For a full account of the North British Society of Halifax, and its early worthies, see James S. MacDonald, *Annals of the North British Society* (Halifax: Alpine, 1905), *passim*.

21. *Ibid.*, p. 27.

22. Letter book of William Forsyth, 1796-8, Public Archives of Nova Scotia.

23. Forsyth to Messrs. J. Petrie Campbell, London, November 12, 1796, Forsyth letter book.

24. *Ibid.*, *passim*, 1797-98. See also numerous entries in Forsyth's account books.

25. MacDonald, p. 63.

26. Forsyth's letter book, pp. 83-4 ff.

27. Letters of James Dunlop, G.D./1/151 (Scottish Record Office, Her Majesty's General Register House, Edinburgh).

28. Dunlop to his brother Alexander Dunlop, Glasgow, April 15, 1798, and December 29, 1799, and to his sister, Mrs. Janet McNair, Greenock, July 1, 7 and 24, 1800, Dunlop Correspondence.

29. Robert Campbell, *A History of the Scotch Presbyterian Church, St. Gabriel Street, Montreal* (Montreal: Lovell, 1887), pp. 96-7.

30. Dunlop to Mrs. Janet McNair, Greenock, June 1, 1811 and November 9 and 30, 1811, Dunlop Correspondence.

31. *Ibid.*, Dunlop to Alexander Dunlop, Glasgow, December 29, 1799.

32. *Ibid.*, Dunlop to Mrs. Janet McNair, Greenock, May 17, 1814.

33. *Ibid.*, same to same, March 27, 1815.

34. Cf. Johnston-Fulton Correspondence, New Brunswick Provincial Museum, St. John, New Brunswick; also *Royal Gazette and New Brunswick Advertiser* 1885-95; 1797-1814; 1816-1821.

35. For Black's early career, see *The Judges of New Brunswick and Their Times* (St. John, 1912), pp. 223-4.

36. Letter book, September 1798-August, 1800 (Archives of Scotts, Ltd., Greenock).

37. *Ibid.*, John Scott to Messrs. Hunter and Walkinshaw, Paisley, August 23, 1798.

38. For further details of Scott and his career, see David S. Macmillan, "Shipbuilding in New Brunswick: From the Clyde to the St. John River, 1798," in *The Canadian Banker*, 77 (1970), No. 1; and "Christopher Scott: Smuggler, Privateer and Financier," *ibid.*, 78 (1971), No. 3.

39. Correspondence, June, 1819, Lang Papers (Business Archives Collection, Glasgow University); *Parliamentary Papers*, Proceedings of the Select Committee on Foreign Trade, 1812 (186), vi, Evidence and Submissions.

40. John Rankin, *A History of Our Firm* (Liverpool, 1921). This book is obviously based on valuable business records which have since disappeared. The "Pollock and Gilmour Papers" held in the Business Archives Collection of the University of Glasgow consist mostly of eighteenth century Scottish estate papers.

41. *Ibid.*, p. 110. For details of the timber firms and their relative importance see Louise Dechène, "Les Enterprises de William Price," *Histoire Sociale – Social History*, 1 (1968), pp. 16-52; R.G. Albion, *Forests and Sea Power* (Hamden, 1965), pp. 355-6.

42. J. Smart, *Economic Annals of the Nineteenth Century* (New York, 1964), pp. 596, 599-600, 757.

43. Rankin, pp. 188-9.

44. David M. Williams, "Merchanting in the First Half of the Nineteenth Century: The Liverpool Timber Trade," *Business History*, VIII (1966), 106, 110, 111.

45. J. MacGregor, *Historical and Descriptive Sketches of the Maritime Colonies of British North America* (1828) (Toronto: Social Science Research Council, 1968), p. 72.

46. MacMillan, "The New Men in Action," in MacMillan, *Canadian Business History*, p. 101.

47. J.L. MacDougall, "The Character of the Entrepreneur: The Case of George Stephen," *ibid.*, pp. 192ff.

48. G. Tulchinsky, "The Montreal Business Community, 1837-1853," *ibid.*, pp. 135f.

49. "Second Letter of William Jarvis to the Shareholders of the Commercial Bank," Jarvis Papers, 16/19, New Brunswick Museum, St. John.

50. D. McCalla, "Peter Buchanan, London Agent for the Great Western Railway of Canada," in MacMillan, pp. 197ff.

51. J.M.S. Careless, "The Business Community in the Early Development of Victoria, British Columbia," *ibid.*, pp. 104ff.

52. T.W. Acheson, "The Social Origins of the Canadian Industrial Elite, 1880-1885," *ibid.*, pp. 144ff.

53. MacMillan, pp. 44ff.

54. Pierre Berton, *The National Dream*, (Toronto: McClelland and Stewart, 1971), pp. 319f. Reprinted by permission of the publishers.

ELEVEN

The Lowland Tradition in Canadian Literature

Elizabeth Waterston

The parallels between Scotland and Canada, both physical and social, are striking and important. The new country is larger, but it sprawls along the same inhospitable latitudes. To the south in both cases there is a large, powerful, and domineering neighbour. In Canada, as in Scotland, two languages, two religions, and two cultures have co-existed.

Little wonder that in the nineteenth century Scottish cultural models transplanted so easily. Given our climate, Burns made more sense than Wordsworth. In the brief Canadian springtime, Canadians could relish the small detail of flower or stream, rather than the Wordsworthian vista of lake or mountain. Given the need for energetic social interaction as a defence against isolation, Canadians responded to Scott's eventful bustling plots, rather than to the misty paradoxes of Poe or Hawthorne. As the century moved on, Canada remained the scene for manly action, sport, physical adventure: Robert Louis Stevenson's tales of adventures and escapes, of hardy travel and daring encounters, were closer to Canadian reality and Canadian dreams than were the spidery finenesses of a Henry James or the depressing naturalism of a George Moore or a George Gissing. And for those Canadians not facing the frontier, but settling into the quieter patterns of Brantford or Orillia, Ormstown or Fredericton, there was more to be admired and recognized in a Kailyard novel, an "Auld Licht Idyll," than in the bleaker negativism of American novels about dusty main streets or about the dreary main-travelled roads of the countryside.

In 1911 George Bryce proclaimed the creed of many Canadians, including many not of Scottish origins: "The world's greatest lyric singer [was] Robert Burns; the world's greatest novelist, Sir Walter Scott; the two greatest historians, Macaulay and Carlyle." He might have extended the credo, and still expressed a Canadian consensus in the early twentieth cenutry, by adding: "The greatest writer of adventure stories for young people was Robert Louis Stevenson; the greatest writer of sentimental regional idylls, and the most tender and whimsical of dramatists was J.M. Barrie."

The Canadian education system and Canadian publishing houses, largely dominated by Scots in the nineteenth century, promulgated and perpetuated this creed. The results are clear in nineteenth century Canadian poetry and prose, arts and architecture. Love for Burns set the bounds of theme, metre, tone, and length of Canadian poems from McLachlan to Carman. Devotion to Sir Walter established the dominance of historical romance in Canada, from Richardson and Kirby to Gilbert Parker, at the expense of other possible models such as Dickens or Hawthorne, George Eliot or Melville. "Great Man" history, thesis history, following the examples of Macaulay and Carlyle, flourished in Canada – witness the tremendous acceptance of works like the "Makers of Canada" series – though again at the expense of more scientific or sociological approaches that might have been learned from German, French or American models. The influence of Stevenson and Barrie in the later part of the century produced an over-abundance of children's books and of regional idylls. Canadian names on this list of later Scottish-dominated romancers would include Ralph Connor, Marshall Saunders and L.M. Montgomery.

Lowland influences should also be similarly noticed as predominant in the graphic arts. Wilkie and Landseer rather than Constable or Whistler in turn dominated the style of the Canadian academies. Abbotsford inspired the worst of our architecture, and the Adams' influence perhaps generated our best. In theatre, in choral music, in folklore and dancing, the pressure of Scottish models has been constant. Study of the reasons for this preponderance of influence by a single culture, imported as one among many, clarifies many facets of the needs and nature of the importer.

The physical, social and economic similarity between Canada and Scotland, added to the large number and the power of the Lowland immigrants, made the Scottish strain in Canadian art appropriate as well as pervasive and persistent. I propose to examine the extent of this borrowing and adaptation, first in early Canadian poetry and in pre-Confederation fiction, and later in the early productions of the Dominion after Confederation and during the extended national growth in the railroad era. Such an examination will lead to speculation as to the price paid by Canadian culture for this century-long habit of importation.

BEFORE BURNS

A glance at any Canadian song-book or keepsake album or literary anthology of the nineteenth century will show how great was the influence of Burns on Canadian writers. But in Canada as in Scotland the love for Burns came as culmination of a taste developed earlier in the eighteenth century. Ramsay in 1724, Fergusson in 1774, had revived the native tradition of the "makaris." In the years after 1707, although Scotland's political and economic autonomy had been ended, her literary and intellectual life had taken on new lustre. Now vernacular poetry achieved new respect, joining the folk songs which had been kept alive in the Lowland dialect. Scotland in the late eighteenth century contributed three major works to the popular literature of all English-speaking people, on both sides of the Atlantic: Bishop Percy's *Reliques*, Henry Mackenzie's *Man of Feeling*, and James Macpherson's *Ossian*.

Scots who came to the Canadas or the Maritimes in the eighteenth century brought a taste for the austere border ballads, for the occasional verse cleverness of mock elegies and last testaments, and for satiric lovers' oaths in the Ramsay-Fergusson manner. They brought a liking for the misty grandeurs of Ossian, and for the sentimentalities of *The Man of Feeling*. They also brought a pride in the intellectual glories of the Edinburgh schools, in philosophers like Hume and Reid, economists like Adam Smith, Blair and Kames and Robertson. Scottish culture centres in the Maritimes predated the American Revolution: Windsor, Saint John, Moncton, Saint-Andrews-by-the-Sea flourished as "little Edinburghs" with interest ramifying into history, theology, and belles-lettres, long before the New England Loyalists added their store of bookish interests in the 1780s and 1790s.

Eighteenth century Montreal merchants also built a culture similar to Edinburgh's: neighbourly, bourgeois, bastioned against both a wilderness to the north and an alternative culture to the south. These Quebec-based businessmen sent fellow Scots into the commercial network being cast westward. From 1670 the Hudson's Bay Company had been placing hardy Scots among its factors, and Scots continued to dominate fur trade and exploration throughout the century, climaxing the dominance with the formation of Montreal-based groups rivalling the HBC and dominated by the Frasers, the McTavishes, and the Mackenzies. These men had brought with them from their Scottish schools a taste for science. They moved through the northwest as amateur geologists, ornithologists, and anthropologists, making notes as if in preparation for delivering a paper at some literary and historical society back in Ayrshire or Paisley. The American frontiersman – the Davy Crockett type – is pictured in legend as illiterate, almost inarticulate except in tall tales and bawdy anecdotes. The Canadian frontiersman could be correctly pictured as serious, cautious, observant, a man simply but sensibly educated, keeping his journal in clear, statistical order. Early in Canadian records appear not tall tales but the travel narratives of Mackenzie, Fraser, Henry. All reflect the impact of the Scottish renascence on Canadian style, tone, and content.

Besides the fur traders, Lowland Scots had come as tradesmen and independent farmers throughout the eighteenth century, many of them in the wake of economic or military failure at home. They brought conflicting attitudes: a sense of recent defeat, of present difficulties, plus a national pride, a belief in free enterprise and an insistence on education and theology as prerequisites of each new community. The basis of their culture was carried over from the Scottish "moral sentiment" school: "sentiment as a principle, rationality as a method" – leading to the warmth of Scottish family life, and the hard-headed enterprise of Scottish business. The villages they clustered into were tribal, not feudal or hierarchic. Kinship led to family bluntness in speech as well as to hovering concern over courtships and illnesses. The family feeling was no doubt strengthened when the Scots came up against the prejudice and disdain carried from England by the Johnsonian English administrators.

In the older Canadian towns and the new frontier settlements, then, the Lowland presence was strong, distinct, colourful and conspicuous.

THE CULT OF BURNS AMONG CANADIAN PIONEERS

Burns's themes and assumptions, as well as the forms of his poetry, became a powerful part of Canadian pioneer art and life. They may have blocked the growth of alternative styles as the country moved toward Confederation. In the hands of Scottish-Canadian poets of the 1830s to 1850s, Burns's themes undergo interesting modifications, but the phenomenon of McLachlan's poetry, for instance, is one of many examples of the essential survival of a poetic tradition, after the cause and manner of its emergence are no longer relevant.

Burns himself at one time contemplated emigrating to America. This was a nearly inevitable choice facing men of his time and place. Of his contemporaries in Ayr and Paisley, Tweeddale and Dumfriesshire, many of the liveliest, most patriotic, most enterprising, were being forced by pressure of competition to leave home. By the 1820s, emigration societies, mostly operating in the Lowlands, were arranging mass export of manpower. In the chattels on those emigrant ships went many a copy of Burns; and in the emotional baggage went many an attitude that guaranteed transplanted fondness of Burns's work. The Lowland workers brought with them the tensions, the habits, and the aspirations from which Burns's songs had sprung, and which had reached their apotheosis in his songs.

"Bad habits," for instance those of gambling, drinking, nostalgic inertia, and shiftlessness, had been among the legacies of hard times in the border counties. These were among the major stimuli of Burns's songs. They were carried to Canada, all too often to intensify there. Brandy and whiskey continued necessary for endurance, for survival. The convivial "drappie" carried with it to Canada the poetic ratification of Burns. So did the social energy, manifest in fighting, brawny sports contests, vigorous dances, raw jokes.

Humour was another defence against the indignities of the new life. Again Burns provided the wry tone, the mock-heroic note, that had helped overcome melancholy in the Old Country, and would keep the exile's melancholy in proper perspective.

206

Family warmth, combined with intense personal independence, expanding into a rich sense of national identity – these good elements too were imported in augmented strength into the Canadian frontier. In particular, the kind of patriotism that Burns had hymned – defiant, irrational, surviving the absence of state help or sympathy – became the basis of a fondness for the new country blending easily with the tenderness for the Scot's "ain countree."

Lowland settlers moved into the new Canadian terrain, finding at every point a snatch of Burns's song that could release the tensions of experience. Here, as at home, flowers were frail and precious, winters sudden and cruel. As at home, men and animals lived close together, dogs, cattle, horses almost becoming part of the family, and certainly felt as personalities. As at home, the warmth of the house, the shelter of love, was in sharp contrast with the "cauld blast" outdoors. When it came to putting these things into song, Burns's tight forms were appropriate channels for the brief creative gusts possible in an energy-draining life. Burns's forms, as well as his themes, made appropriate transplants.

By the 1820s, Lowlands Scots in the Maritime provinces were producing and publishing verse strong in "pith and realism" (to quote Fred Cogswell's account in the *Literary History of Canada*). Andrew Shields, "the Cape Breton Blacksmith," William Murdoch of Partridge Island, John LePage of PEI, Robert Murdoch, John Steele – all produced direct, clear verse, humorous, much of it, though with a melancholy undercurrent. The same simple strength appears in imitations of Burns produced in Lower and Upper Canada by such poets as McQueen, 1836. Numbers of these poems were printed in local journals whose presses as well as editorial desks were largely manned by Scots: Hugh Thomson of Kingston, David Chisholme, A.J. Christie, Andrew Armour of Montreal.

Early Canadian poets made simple local substitutions in Burns's flora and fauna. "To a Dandelion" supplements "To a Daisy" in a poem by Miss Johnson, and the owl replaces the mousie in John Massie's "Hoot awa, hoolet, alane in the tree." Bonnie Doon gives way to innumerable Canadian banks and braes, in acceptable lyrics written with one eye on the stream and the other on the standard Habbie verse form of Burns.

These poems are not merely harmless imitations; they are a healthy transplant of a vital tradition. In these early days such poetry, unsubtle as it was, served well to reflect and to entertain all settlements in the Canadian bush, whether or not dominated by Scots. The presence of such verse, and of a press to purvey it, must be considered a major contribution made by Lowland Scots to the emerging Canadian nation. Burns was a valuable and appropriate model in early days in Upper and Lower Canada and in the Maritimes, wielding an influence which would differentiate all early Canadian literature from contemporary work in the United States. The yearning for a lost homeland was a note that could be struck within the empire's bounds in a way impossible in the republic. So the sentimental imitations of Burns's patriotism could be appropriately entwined into *all*

Canadian song. There is nothing in republican literature to equate with the plethora of Canadian publications with titles like "My auld Plaid," "My Birth-place," "Our Mither tongue," "White Heather," "The Old Scottish Songs," "The Burn's answer." Songs thus titled would stir fellow-feelings in exiles from other parts of the British Isles, as well as in Burns's compatriots. Yearning for a lost homeland was a shared sentiment; "Strange earth we sprinkle on the exile's clay" (in the words of McGeorge, 1858). The sense of enduring a life-long exile was a strong, and a strongly-shared, Canadian sentiment.

Voicing the sense of exile was not the only way in which Burns's imitators served to release Canadian feelings. The immediate contact with details of environment – single flower or animal – was a natural topic for the consciousness harshly limited by the monotonous, pressing forest. Poems titled "To – – – ", with their assumed convention of personal song, overheard by a small intimate circle of friends, would be appropriate poems for a village audience in Burns's own society. They would also be appropriate for what was virtually an extended village – the thin-spread settlements of the frontier. The author's stance of familial intimacy, so much a part of Burns, was a tenable convention for the small though scattered coterie of readers and listeners in Canada. Burns's subjects served to catch and record central, simple Canadian social occasions – church meetings, drinking parties, funerals, courtship-directed dances.

Burns's stance suited the early Canadian taste too well perhaps. The ironic downrightness of "a man's a man for a' that" permeated the working class, spreading from the nucleus of Scottish artisans into the whole early Canadian community. Its acceptance curtailed the desire for subtlety and elegance, and made laughable the finer social forms and conventions. In poetic form, downrightness resulted in simple adherence to Burns's simple forms: Standard Habbie, for instance, with its rigid rhyme scheme (a, a, b, a, b, with the last line curtailed) has a kind of blunt reductiveness, a refusal of any expansiveness in the concluding movement. The refrains many of them inherited by Burns from Ramsay, Fergusson, and even older models, are simple and blunt: "He's dead;" "That day." Such refrains have a finality, a tight-lipped honesty that inhibits subtlety or fantasy.

In general, early Scottish poets in Canada wrote more patriotic songs but fewer love songs than Burns, more egalitarian songs but fewer drinking songs; more on nature's details (flowers, animals, waterways), but fewer satires on people; more songs of sentiment, fewer of passions. But in all these categories there is an amazing bulk to be noted. In all, the influence of Burns is very strong, in rhythm, rhyme scheme and phrasing, as well as in tone and content.

The climax of the Burns tradition in Canada is the work of Alexander McLachlan, a poor boy who came from Glasgow in 1840, and became the best known of the Scottish poets before Confederation. He published *Lyrics* in 1858, *The Emigrant* in 1861, *Songs and Poems*, 1874. His work appears in all early anthologies as a major representative of Canadian poetry in the early nineteenth century. Dewart, in *Selections from Canadian Poets* (1864), called McLachlan "the Burns of Canada" both for "his racy humour" and for his "moral grandeur and beauty." McLachlan himself reports the pioneer love of the Lowland poet. On the Sabbath, McLachlan says, writing of a pioneer's life,

> Even Burns he puts aside
> Burns! his weekday joy and pride
> Burns! so human, wild and wide . . .

The Canadian Scot, like his Lowland cousin, adds a greater literary idol:

> And he brings from out its nook,
> That great Book of Books, the Book!

The Pioneer's prayer is Burnsian:

> Break! O Lord! the spell of birth,
> Haste the time when moral worth
> Shall take highest rank on earth. (96)

A brief look at McLachlan's *Songs and Poems* (Toronto: Hunter Rose, 1874) shows how widely the range of Burns has affected his Canadian follower. Best known of his poems is, "We live in a Rickety House," with its sardonic attack on the Holy Willies of the new country:

> Ye clog the soil of nature
> With your wretched little creeds,
> Then hold up your hands in wonder
> At the dearth of noble deeds.

Another Burns theme, manly independence, sings in "Acres of your own." The "cauld blast" note of realism in "The rain it falls" presents dour recognition of the incomprehensible harshness of nature, fate, and death. McLachlan can also sing blithely of the flowers and buds in "May." He is nostalgic on love:

> The faith and the friendship
> The rapture of yore
> O shall they revisit
> This bosom no more?

Some of McLachlan's poems integrate echoes of Burns into more Victorian notions. "Britannia," for instance, strikes an imperial note – but even here the rhythm is derived from "Scots wha hae":

> Great mother of the Mighty Dead,
> Sir Walter sang, and Nelson bled
> To weave a garland for thy head,
> Britannia . . .

And Bacon's head and Burns's heart
Are glories that shall ne'er depart,
Britannia.

McLachlan extends some of Burns's themes in adapting to the new country. To the satire of the "unco guid" he adds the satire of new butts – Americanized Scots, the "unco money-minded:"

Talk not of old cathedral woods,
Their gothic arches throwing,
John only sees in all those trees
So mony saw-logs growing.

He laughs at all our ecstasies
And he keeps still repeating
You say 'tis fair, but will it wear?
And is it good for eating? (103)

Some of the ironies of "rising in the world" are Burnsian in spirit though not echoing any particular Burns song.

Burns's melancholy strain is given a new twist by the absence of continuity with the past: In "pic-nic," McLachlan muses by the stream,

Still at the song, it sang so long
To Red Men gone for ever!
And it will leap and laugh along
As gay and happy-hearted
And it will sing this happy song
When we too, have departed.

Elsewhere McLachlan speaks of the "deeper joy of sadness" in a new world. The sense of discontinuity leads from nostalgia to terror, the terror of finding change everywhere, even in the beloved remembered scenes of home: "I'll no gae back, I'll no gae back."

In McLachlan, Burns's love of animals is directed to new fellow-creatures: Buck and Bright the oxen, or Old Hoss and Young Hoss. Independence can become the restlessness of the frontier: "This settlement is getting old, and just a leetle crowdy" (135). "Heroes!" cites intellectuals, teachers and preachers in a new pantheon. Burns would hardly worship at these shrines, but certainly McLachlan's reverence is in keeping with the Lowland values of his own day.

The Canadian poet, as has appeared in all these quotations, imitates Burns's metres as well as his themes. He loves a rollicking rhyme:

If roughs assembled at a bar
And steaming with the barley-braw
They raged and roared and staggered,
As soon as e'er his face they saw,
It held in reverential awe

The most regardless blackguard.

McLachlan's intricate rhyme schemes, and the craft of his internal rhymes as well as the rollicking swing of his metres, all show the influence of Burns. They show too the resistance to alternatives; to, for instance, the slower dignity of Wordsworth's metres. The Scottish poet sufficed. Burns' simple, independent vigour and his tight crafted verses served as a useful, expandable model for McLachlan in particular; they served with equal dominance for the vast majority of early Canadian poets including many not of Scottish extraction. In all we see the dangers of a too-exclusive response to the single model. Burns suited Canadian needs too well. Loving his work, finding it applicable, Canadian poets settled for his range, and sent out few feelers into the realms of experience more complicated than his.

THE AGE OF WALTER SCOTT

The same sort of story can be told about fiction in Canada before Confederation. Here the first powerful name is that of Sir Walter Scott. Like Burns, his influence fell on ready soil here; unlike Burns, it was closely followed by the influence of a second major Scottish novelist, John Galt. From 1814 to 1832, the author of *Waverley* dominated popular sales in Canada as in the United States and the United Kingdom. His work was particularly acceptable in Canada because of its moral tone, its sense of the tissue of the past (dear to an exiled generation), and its heroic action and pageantry (vicarious enrichment for the bare life of subsistence in the settlements).

Scott avoided Burns's bawdry, but maintained Burns's feeling of homeliness and warmth, humour and gusto, especially in the treatment of Lowland characters such as Baillie Nicol Jarvie. For the settlers in farms and villages in the Maritimes, in English-speaking areas of Lower Canada, and in Upper Canada, Scott's border farmers, his fishermen, his gypsies were a reminder of home: Dandy Dinmont, McAulay, Dalgetty, and Edie Ochiltree aroused affection, sentiment, and laughter. Their qualities were much like those that the new colony fostered and intensified: eccentricity, doggedness, ingenuity. Even when, back home in Scotland, these qualities had begun to blur under the impact of increasing industrialization, they endured in the newer, more open economy of Canada.

And for those (fewer) members of the Canadian audience who were striving for garrison gentility, Scott offered a second level of characters in most of his novels – those rather wooden heroes and maidens and fine old gentlemen, whose imagined company must have sweetened many a lonely evening for the legion of Mrs. Moodies, "roughing it" in the 1820s and 1830s. The stiff "unreal" conversation of Scott's ladies and gentlemen served as a pattern for writing and speaking among those desperately clinging to propriety and decorum.

Scottish critics of Scott remind us that the bulk of his readers at home in the United Kingdom were neither fisher-folk nor aristocrats, but rather the new urban bourgeoisie of Edinburgh, and Glasgow, Manchester, and London. Such a mercantile middle class represented a much smaller proportion of Canada's population and of her reading public. The audience here perhaps read more for a sense of identification than for a sense of illusion and escape. What could be read in Scotland and England as romance could be read in Canada as realism. Scott's ineffectual heroes, those innocent travellers on whom the wilder natives act, became an obvious prototype for the Canadian gentleman, travelling through a strange uncivilized land. A characterization that seemed to European critics an imaginative ideal becomes a realistic report on a normal state of mind, a role being acted out everywhere in Canada in the first decades of the century. Scott's "hero" – whether he was Waverley, Lovel Brown, or Osbaldistone – would be swallowed by British readers as a helpful device for getting the story going. For Canadian readers, these portraits were a report on a very present reality: the genteel traveller, the man who had lost his identity, the young fellow who had been set against an older generation back home. This was not a fantastic fairy tale but an exciting report on a commonplace of Canadian experience.

When early Canadian writers copied – and over-copied – Scott's plots and characterizations, they were copying not for the romantic escapist qualities but as a response to realities effectively and accurately captured. Scott recreated an imagined border country filled with uncertainties about law and duty; he presented melodramatic contrasts of old and new ways of life. In Canada, these fantasies were observable as fact. Physical pain and torture scenes were used by Scott to give a *frisson* of terror to his safely-housed Edinburgh friends; travel books on Canada show how close was the anguish of cold, hunger, fire in real life here. Again Scott's fiction fitted in with the life of his Canadian readers, not as illusion, but as confirmation, report, documentary.

Scott's real world was an urban one; his imagined world is half wilderness. But the reader who had vicariously experienced this imagined world was prepared to cope with a world full of events such as Fergus's gathering, of places like Bane Lane cave, a world literally of smugglers and caves and brigand-infested marshland.

Did having a "literary prototype" help soften travellers' feelings? Did the presence of a surrogate – a "genteel young man, of genteel appearance travelling" – run through one's mind as one found a place in the Montreal coach, or the bateau at Coburg, or the canoe at Les Chattes? Scott's fiction seemed peculiarly relevant to the deep facts of Canadian life, to the mythic pattern, as well as the daily drift. Scott's fiction was accepted by Canadian readers, so powerfully accepted as to become an all-pervasive influence on Canadian writers, over-exclusive of other points of view, and almost exclusive of native experiments.

In the first chapter of *Waverley*, Scott lists the kinds of novels he could have written. It is an amusing catalogue of all the sub-species of fiction in vogue in 1814: the Gothic, the German romance, the sentimental tale, the fashionable sketch of society. *Waverley*, of course, was to add a new sub-species: the romance, in which historical fact could be intertwined with adventure and homely comedy, all set against a landscape of strange and rugged grandeur.

Titles of the Canadian novels published in the post-*Waverley* period may suggest that the novelists had early, pre-Scott models in mind. For instance, Hart's *Saint Ursula's Convent* (1824) sounds as though it would be more indebted to "Monk" Lewis than to Scott; Lane's *The Fugitives* in 1830 suggests a romance plot of disguised identities; Cheney's *Rivals of Acadia* (1827) conjures the sentimental vein. But examination of any of them shows the power of Scott's manner to overflow into every category of fiction.

When Scott moved from near-contemporary stories to concern himself with earlier days in Scotland, and then to earlier times in the lands of *Ivanhoe*, *Kenilworth*, and *Talisman*, Canadian writers followed willingly. The feeling that the past is more rich, more mysterious, and at the same time more satisfying as a subject for reverie than the present was a natural feeling in "this barren wooden country." The "lack of a past" disturbed many early writers; the assumption that the sense of the past is a rich and essential part of human experience animates the early Canadian leap into historical fiction. In 1824, Cushing's *Saratoga, A Tale of the Revolution*, took readers back "sixty years since," as *Waverley* had done, and Cheney's *A Peep at the Pilgrims* followed Sir Walter into remoter eras. The year 1826 added Cushing's *York Town: A Historical Romance*, and Cheney's *Rivals of Acadia*. A much more successful Canadian follower of Scott was Major John Richardson: *Wacousta* (1832) is an excellent example of the transplanting of the Scott tradition. Professor Carl Klinck, in introducing a New Canadian Library edition of *Wacousta* says, "Here is stock material of Scottish romance in the age of Sir Walter Scott, effectively but unexpectedly introduced in the war tent of a savage."

A second Scottish influence came to supplement that of Scott. John Galt had been hailed in Scotland as the man likely to succeed to Scott's romantic mantle (and rewarding sales record). But Galt's more sociological approach, his dour realism, failed to hold the popular Scottish audience. These very qualities constituted his appeal in Canada. The novels of the '20s, set in the Lowlands and in London, were reminders of the common-place aspects of the life left behind by immigrants; the two novels with American settings, *Lawrie Todd* (1830) and *Bogle Corbet* (1831), added vigorous, anti-heroic portraiture of Scottish expatriates, and an ironic, reductive plot of grudging acceptance of the new frontier life. Galt's own life in Canada was very colourful and controversial, but his fictional account of life in the settlements established a strain of wry, low-keyed reporting of undramatic, unaccented "roughing it."

Galt democratized Canadian fiction twenty years before *Uncle Tom's Cabin* did this job for American best sellers. He democratized it in a way distinct from Dickens's way – in a way divested of caricature or exaggeration. No doubt it was a way more appropriate for a country where eccentricity was never encouraged, and where "leveling" (*vide* Mrs. Moodie) was rigorous. This Galt strain of robust ironic realism was paralleled in the writings of another Scottish Canadian, Thomas McCulloch. *The Letters of Mephibosheth Stepsure* (1821-22) predated and may have influenced Haliburton's "Sam Slick" (1836-1860). Here the dour self-mocking tone may owe something to Galt, and the comic portrait of a jaunty opportunist may sound echoes of Scott's Andrew Fairservice and Dugald Dalgetty; or one may say that Haliburton's kind of irony is simply a drawing on the joint-stock of Scottish humour – a humour based on the enjoyment of smartness or "canniness," wry laughter, without rancour.

A third Scottish-born novelist who exercised enormous influence on Canadian fiction in pre-Confederation years was R.M. Ballantyne. In an unceasing flow of books for young readers, Ballantyne capitalized on the image of the Canadian frontier. *Hudson's Bay* began the series in 1843. Canadian novelists for years continued to feed the demand for boys' books established by Ballantyne. The Ballantyne school helped fix the image of the Canadian barrens as barren indeed – barren of social or intellectual interest fit for adult consumption. Ballantyne's work made familiar the great stretches of Canada controlled by the Hudson's Bay Company and administered largely by Hudson's Bay factors who were young Scots, like Ballantyne himself. This image of the adventurous North supplemented the more domestic settlement scenes scrutinized by Galt. Together these two Scots, Galt and Ballantyne, added to the influence of Scott himself, dominated the work of Canadian fiction writers up to the Confederation period.

PERSISTENCE OF LOWLAND INFLUENCE IN MID-CENTURY

Once again it is the story of an influence that lasted too long. Galt's annals of Canadian parishes, like Ballantyne's tales of boyish northern adventures and Scott's swashbuckling historical romances, satisfied audiences that might well have been turning to the new Canadian realities of urbanization, new ethnic tensions *vis-a-vis* French Canada and the States, or to the subtler social and psychological probings of the age of Hawthorne and Melville. *The Scarlet Letter* in 1850 and *Moby Dick* in 1851 were apparently by-passed by the Canadian novelists, who went on grinding out such pseudo-Scottish romances as Richardson's *The Monk of Saint John* (1850); Somerville's *The Life of Robert Mowbray* (1853); McDougall's *Lady of the Beacon of Aheera* (1857); Noel's *The Abbey of Rathmore*; Fleming's *Sybil Campbell, or the Queen of the Isles* (1863); Daniel's *William and Anne, A Tale of Love and War* (1864).

Professor John Matthews, in *Tradition in Exile*, offers a feasible thesis. Literary forms of the Old Country – in this case, forms of Lowland Scotland – would transplant to Canada because the terrain and the social patterns in early days were comparable. These transplants assuaged the need for imaginative expression. In the States, and in Australia, the inappropriateness of songs about moors and crags and of stories of genteel travellers led to early cultural uneasiness on the part of the exiles, and consequently to an earlier development of new folk forms. Canada stayed with Scottish models because of the continuing closeness of physical and social forms.

Another major reason that the taste for Lowland themes and measures dominated Canadian readers was the preponderance of Scots in the printing, publishing, and book selling business. From the very first phase of Canadian history, publishing matured under Scottish direction. Many of the first printers in the Maritimes and Quebec were Scots, such as William Brown and James Robertson. Early journal editors included John Strachan (*Christian Examiner*, 1819); Hugh Thomson (*Upper Canada Herald*, 1872); David Chisholme (*Canadian Magazine and Literary Repository*, 1823, and *Canadian Review and Magazine* 1824); A.J. Christie (*Canadian Magazine and Literary Repository*, taken over in 1824); George Stewart (*Literary Magazine*) and Alex Spark (*Quebec Gazette*, 1792, and *Quebec Magazine*). These editors were complemented by Scottish book publishers such as Andrew Armour and Hew Ramsay of Montreal in the mid-30s, G. Mercer Adam of Montreal and Toronto, Robert Middleton of Quebec, Thomas Maclear and Hunter and G.M. Rose of Toronto, and A. and W. Mackinlay of Halifax. Bookstores were often run as an adjunct to a press or a journal. These added further Scottish bias. Publishers were John Neilson in Quebec, James Lesslie in Toronto and later in Kingston and Dundas, John McMillan of Saint John, Samuel Thomson in Toronto and James Campbell in the same city. All were well-established between 1824 and 1850. And all were naturally well-disposed towards the acceptance of books with a Scottish flavour.

Lowland Scots in Canada moved into other areas where their taste exercised a crucial influence on the continuing development of Canadian culture. They dominated the Mechanics' Institutes and the literary and historical societies; they led the militia; they rallied the temperance movements and presided over the Free Masons. James Rattray in *The Scot in British North America* provides long lists of the Scots in all these positions: the long lists add up to illumination of the way Scottish motifs and tastes continued to dominate Canada even after the percentage of Scots in the total number of immigrants began to dwindle. Above all, Scots dominated Canadian schools and politics in the pre-Confederation period. Sir Daniel Wilson is one good example among many of those who exercised strong educational leadership.

Learned societies based on Scottish models reflected Scottish interests and intellectual ambitions. Law, medicine, science, architecture – in all Scottish taste and values were imprinted, all with influence both direct and indirect on the growth of Canadian literature. The influence of Scots as governors-general must be noted too, from Dalhousie to Lorne, as a pressure on cultural development.

Scottish-flavoured work continued to be published. Following Scottish models, and imbued with Scottish love of historical research, regional histories flourished: from John Ross, 1819, to Alex Ross, 1848, from George Simpson to Thomas Simpson, 1843, from Gourlay, Haliburton and Fisher in 1836 to Atkinson, Murray and McGregor in 1844. Statistical methods culminated with Christie's six volume *History of The Late Province of Lower Canada* in 1855, but regional histories continued with Beamish Murdock, 1865; Duncan Campbell, 1873; Alexander Begg, 1871; James Hannay in 1879. Accounts of the War of 1812 and the search for Franklin engaged two other Scottish Canadians, Auchinleck and McClintock.

Memoirs and light essays of the *Noctes Ambrosianae* ilk appeared from Tiger Dunlop to Alex Rae Garvie's *Thistledown*, 1875. More vigorous, and more topical, was the work in journalism of William Lyon Mackenzie, Neilson, Richardson and others. In all, comparison with Scottish journals will show a source for tone and topic.

Journalism and history were the genres in which the most impressive Canadian work was done between the 1830s, when Haliburton and Richardson reached the peak of work in fiction, and the 1880s, when the poetry of Roberts and Lampman began to appear. The period from 1840 to 1880 represented lean years in the creative arts in Canada.

Meanwhile, back in Scotland, a similar story of a long hiatus marks the middle years of the nineteenth century. In the '40s, '50s, and '60s, when such ex-Scots as Carlyle and Ruskin were helping to animate the great mid-Victorian flowering in London, Scottish writers in Scotland were turning out school-of-Scott novels, school-of-Burns poems. This long dull period in Scottish letters lasted until the dramatic emergence of Robert Louis Stevenson. When Stevenson did appear, he found a Canadian audience very ready to respond.

THE INFLUENCE OF ROBERT LOUIS STEVENSON

In Scotland during the cultural low between the period of Burns and Scott and the emergence in the 1880s and '90s of Stevenson and the Kailyard School, followers of Galt such as Hugh Miller and William Alexander continued to publish parochial idylls. Among Scottish expatriates in England, Thomas Carlyle and George Macdonald did most to keep Lowland themes and values before the general public, but Carlyle's interests were increasingly retrospective, and Macdonald's focus swung from the contemporary worlds of *David Elginbrod* (1863) and *Robert Falconer* (1868) to the fantasy worlds of *At the Back of the North Wind* (1871) and *The Princess and the Goblins* (1872) and their successors. Such writings, taken with the persistence in Scottish poetry of imitations of Burns and Scott, may be interpreted as sad and dangerous, as escapist, and as a negation of

216

the changing economy and the structure and direction of real life in the industrializing, centralizing, and secularizing Lowlands. In this literary interregnum, Scottish genius directed itself largely into technology: the great names of the '50s to '70s are those of engineers and business magnates.

In Canada, the same persistence of parochialism and romantic adventure in literature is less escapist. Canadians still lived out the life that Scott and Carlyle hymned. Canada was reliving a Scottish stage long gone by, in the still-rural, still-atomistic settlements of the pre-railroad era, as well as in the northern barrens and in the barely accessible northwestern plains. So, even though some non-Scottish literary influences began to be strongly felt – Tennyson and Whitman, *David Copperfield* and *Uncle Tom's Cabin* – the Scottish themes remained appropriate as well as powerful. Lowland machinists manning the printing presses, Lowland clerks working in and buying out the bookselling shops, Lowland journalists moving into publishing and editorial positions, all ensured that these appropriate themes would also remain widely available.

It was into a society still clearly attuned to Scottish tastes that the sense of a new renascence in Scottish letters moved swiftly and pervasively. Robert Louis Stevenson began publishing his short stories in 1878, with "Lodging for the Night" and "The Sire de Malétroit's Door." His essays, first appearing in British periodicals from 1877, soon drew wider attention: *Virginibus Puerisque*, for instance, appeared in book form in 1884. His frivolous travel books such as *Travels with a Donkey* and *The Amateur Emigrant*, began to be widely read from 1878-9. Of his novels, *Treasure Island* appeared in book form in 1883, *Dr. Jekyll and Mr. Hyde* in 1886, and *Kidnapped* in 1887. In every one of these areas he found a Canadian audience very ready to respond, and a group of Canadian writers very ready to imitate. Through him, a new pressure of Scottish tensions was felt, first directly from his own books, later through the works of Canadian imitators.

Stevenson caught some of the traditional Scottish relish for romantic adventure, quest and quarrel, and epitomized also the nineteenth century revolt against some of the trammels of Calvinism. His own rebellion against the values of his father and mother in Edinburgh focused the aesthetic, joyful reaction against the soul-searching gloom of orthodoxy. It was not a Burnsian revolt; Stevenson erupted not into passions for women, for native land, or for drinking; instead he flung back into the freedoms of the child-world, of far away places, and into experiments in the macabre. But these too, like Burns's avenues, were native paths for the Scottish soul in its mood of revolt. Stevenson's sea-going romances, his children's poetry, his vagabond lyrics, are all rooted in Scottish traditions. Transplanted to Canada, they flourished with equal charm, equal colour – and equal shock value.

Stevenson himself was a legendary figure: his Bohemian life, his agnosticism, his marriage to a divorcee, his quest for life in the South Seas, all

217

jumbled together in the world's imagination to make him seem the epitome of revolt against convention. His warmth, sincerity and optimism made the revolt appear wholesome rather than effete. He appeared frivolous and charming rather than dangerous, even to orthodox elders. Altogether, Robert Louis Stevenson offered an attractive model of innovation to the rather timid rebels among Canadian artists of the 1880s and 1890s.

His eloquence and devotion to style made him a hero to short story writers like Duncan Campbell Scott and Gilbert Parker. His emphasis on the romance of life, and the value of an art set against the practicality of an industrializing scientific age, stirred such poets as Isabella Crawford, G.F. Cameron, and Wilfred Campbell. Bliss Carman was encouraged by his example to play with the notion of vagabondage, and to experiment with poems of childhood and with short singing verse forms. In the novel, Stevenson's lead was followed by Lily Dougall, A.C. Laut and Charles G.D. Roberts, among others, in their flippant, fanciful play with history, their cast of characters – rogues, charmers, sensible young men caught in perilous quests – and in their emphasis on action and chance in plotting. Essays in late nineteenth century Canadian journals show a stylistic elegance, a radical loosening from Confederation pomposity in manner; they too have been touched by the rather dandified charm of Robert Louis Stevenson. Children's novels, always a major genre for Canadian writers since Ballantyne, swelled in numbers and in strength: Marshall Saunders wrote both in this genre and in the historical romance. Finally, Stevenson pointed the way for experiments in the macabre; Duncan Campbell Scott's work in such a tale as "The Witching of Elspie" owes more to *Dr. Jekyll and Mr. Hyde* than to the earlier models provided by Poe.

Of all these Canadian writers, Bliss Carman shows most clearly, Isabella Valancey Crawford least clearly, the influence of Robert Louis Stevenson. Carman had spent two years at Edinburgh University in 1881 and 1882, years when *Virginibus Puerisque*, *A Gossip on Romance*, and other essays were creating a great stir. In Carman the influence of Stevenson transfigured his earlier dependence on the Pre-Raphaelites and on Tennyson. "A Seamark," a threnody published on Stevenson's death, acknowledges the influence of Stevenson as man and as poet on the young Canadian. *Songs from Vagabondia* and most of the later volumes implicitly contain the same acknowledgment of debt, in their themes, rhythms and tone. In Carman, the legendary, the sensational, the mystic and the marvellous combine with grimmer ironic tones in a mix very much like Stevenson's. Pairs of lines rise in the mind: "Under a wide and starless sky" / "Here by the gray north sea"; "Shovel them in, shovel them in, shovel them in to shore . . . . " / "Yo-ho-ho, and a bottle of rum!"; "When I was sick and lay a-bed." / "When I was just a little boy, Before I went to school . . . . "

Among the novelists, the writer most strongly influenced by Stevenson was Gilbert Parker. Here was a young man from Napanee, in that part of eastern Ontario dominated in politics and in education by the Scottish powers at Queen's University. Parker's early tales deal with Scots and voyageurs in the Northland. The greatest of his mature novels, *The Seats of the Mighty* (1896), parallel to Stevenson in style and tone and in inventiveness, is also parallel in its basic plot: the canny, honorable, Whiggish hero, Major Stobo, has been "kidnapped" into an alien, romantic world. He is both attracted and repelled by the dashing, bragging, witty, and amoral Doltaire – a French-Canadian variant of Alan Breck Stewart. Parker's romance is almost as inhibited and sexless as Stevenson's. Its central adventurous voyage down the St. Lawrence has the dash, the sensationalism, and the essential cruelty of Stevenson's fight-filled stories.

Stevenson was popular in the United States. F.L. Mott, in *Golden Multitudes*, a study of best sellers in America, shows him as rivalling the sales of F. Crawford, W.D. Howells, Mark Twain, and Marie Corelli in the 1880s. But in Canada, the vogue for Stevenson outstripped all contemporary rivals. To me this indicates not only the particular popularity of Stevenson's manner here, but also the persistent openness to Scottish work. For Stevenson, in spite of his rebellion against Scottish orthodoxies of business and theology, re-introduces essentially Scottish materials. Response to a grey huddle of hills and a bright thread of river, tenderness and laughter, respect for the past, pleasure in rhythmic song, love of a voyage or of a good fight – Stevenson's trademarks are stamped on most Scottish characters.

In the plethora of Canadian novels from the late 1880s on, many of the titles bear witness to the Stevenson influence in particular, and to the Scottish bias in general. Marshall Saunders, who had been educated in Scotland and France, began professional writing with *My Spanish Sailor*, 1889, and added other Stevensonian adventure stories over the years, such as *Rose a Charlitte*, 1898. Lily Dougall, educated at Edinburgh University, published *Beggars All* as the first of a long series of novels in 1891. John Campbell, a graduate in theology from Edinburgh after earlier education at Toronto, published *Two Knapsacks* in 1892, reminiscent in subject and tone of Stevenson's *Travels with a Donkey*. Parker, in *The Chief Factor*, also 1892, presented a Scottish company factor, one of the staples of fiction about the adventurous North. Parker's portrait was in part a recognition of the local fact, in part an exploitation of the vogue for Scots dialect which Stevenson had revived. John Mackie, turning to the new West for adventurous setting, also made vivid use of Scottish elements in *Devil's Playground* (1894) and other novels featuring the Mounted Police. Robert Barr's *In the Midst of Alarms*, 1894, a comic version of the time of Fenian raids in the Detroit district, exploited some of Stevenson's pace and the rush of incident familiar from *Treasure Island*. Barr, who later became a prolific novelist, had come to Canada from Glasgow. Agnes Laut in 1900 began her concern with Canadian historical writing with the romantic, adventurous *Lords of the North*, featuring rival groups of Scottish fur traders in the Montreal of McTavish, Fraser, and Mackenzie. Miss Laut, daughter of the Principal of Queen's University, got her Scottishness at second hand, but her early novels in particular show the persistence of

Scott, refreshed by Stevenson. William McLennan published *Spanish John* in 1898 and *The Span of Life* in 1899 in collaboration with Jean McIlwraith. Miss McIlwraith, a graduate of Glasgow, went on to publish her own novel, *The Curious Career of Roderick Campbell* in 1901, the same year as Ralph Connor's *Man From Glengarry*. Roderick Campbell, a turncoat before Culloden, is an engaging Falstaffian figure, an opportunist, who stirs memories in his readers of a long roll of literary prototypes from Scott to Stevenson. A Nova Scotian, W.A. Fraser, exploited the conventional antithesis of the canny Lowlander, dashing Highlander in *Blood Lilies* (1903). In the opening years of the new century, titles reminiscent of this same strain continued to appear: e.g. in Richardson's *The Camerons of Bruce* and W.W. Campbell's *Ian of the Orcades* (both 1906). Imitations of *Kidnapped*, designed for child readers, appear as late as Frank Baird's *Rob MacNab, a Story of old Preston* (1923).

THE IMPACT OF THE KAILYARD SCHOOL

The elegant romanticism of Robert Louis Stevenson thus provided a very powerful model and stimulus from the 1890s on for Canadian novelists, many of them Scottish by inheritance and by education. A different and even stronger Scottish influence began to be felt within Stevenson's last years. This was the influence, also in the '90s, of the "Kailyard School" of Scottish fiction.

The Kailyard writers – J.M. Barrie, S.R. Crockett, Ian MacLaren – are usually considered by Scottish critics as a debased and deleterious group of writers. These novelists, "hankering for a homely rural past," presented faint caricature versions of a picturesque and disappearing way of life. Village humour, village pathos, sentiment and whimsy were all presented in a way that seems to most modern Scottish critics vulgar, bathetic and basically dishonest. The motives for writing such fiction in Scotland were bound up in the displacement from rural, familial, and religiously orthodox life, into the fragmentation of the turn-of-the century period. Barrie's *Auld Licht Idylls* (1888), *Sentimental Tommy* (1889), and *A Window in Thrums* (1891) came out of his own dislocation from home, village, mother and native land. Crockett's *The Lilac Sunbonnet* (1894) and the novels of "Ian MacLaren" (John Watson), *Beside the Bonnie Brier Bush* and *Days of Auld Lang Syne*, satisfied demands for more about "the auld name, the wee hoose, and the whaups crying on the moors" – and added the other elements which became the stock of these homely novels: sentimental treatment of the "Dominie" and the minister, plot manipulation of poignant family losses and the inhibition of passion, graveyard tremors and coy glances at inebriation.

Immensely popular in Great Britain, these books (*Beside the Bonnie Brier Bush* in particular) also outsold such contemporary rivals as *The Prisoner of Zenda* and *Trilby* in the United States. In Canada, the impact of the Kailyard novels was greater still. Canadian cities had perhaps not produced a reading public needing such exotic escapism as *Trilby* and *Zenda*. Canadian readers had not developed a taste complex enough for the niceties and nuances of Henry James, or on the other hand distressed enough to welcome the muckraking wrath of Frank Norris and his school. The Canadian society, predominantly middle class, still predominantly rural and Protestant in mores, had maintained a taste not ranging beyond regional dialect annals. The Scottish parochial sentimental romances found an avid readership in Canada, and a group of writers all too ready to imitate.

Why not? There was hardly a Canadian village throughout the later nineteenth century without its dominating Kirk, its Scottish schoolmaster and its Scottish-trained printer and journalist. The Lowland thread was much more visible and significant in Canadian towns than in those of the United States. And the Kailyard values, seen in a kindly rather than a satiric light, were still really present in many Canadian villages, perhaps long after they had disappeared in the homeland. Humour, gossip, sweetness, sentimentality – these were the values, presented in annals of the parishes from John Galt on, still present and possible in Canadian town life. So when, at the end of the century, the Lowlands produced the new popular idylls, Canadian taste was quickly responsive.

"Ralph Connor," like "Ian MacLaren" a minister writing village fiction under a pseudonym, had a Kailyard fondness for chronicling regional detail; and like Barrie, Crockett and MacLaren, Ralph Connor is most effective when retrospective, when hovering with loving accuracy over the "bees," and wakes, the tavern fights, the Bible classes of Glengarry, rather than when moving into the emerging tensions of city society or political manoeuvres. His hero is a current version of the Robbie Burns type, with fine instincts, powerful passions, natural intelligence, a beautiful singing voice, and magnificent physical strength. Ralph Connor adds the "mother figure" popularized in the *A Window in Thrums* in his hero's patroness, the minister's wife. He modifies the anti-city hysteria of the Scottish Kailyard stories: his hero meets success in Montreal business, although he whimsically realizes the ultimate impossibility of converting real worldlings to his own moral values. (Here he is closer to the hard core of Scottish common sense in Barrie's plays, such as *The Admirable Crichton* and *A Kiss for Cinderella*, with their anti-idyllic recognition of the impenetrability of social and economic barriers, even by a Burns type.) The Lowland strain appears everywhere in Ralph Connor, in spite of his initial choice of Highlanders for his cast – Macdonald Dhu, Macdonald Bain, the MacRaes and the McGregors. He soon turns to the Lowland pleasures of endless debates on predestination, and the application of a Calvinist conscience to the exigencies of Montreal commerce, and of a romance involving a sophisticated charmer and also a simpler, more pious maiden.

Ralph Connor was soon joined in the Canadian Kailyard by R.L. Richardson, with *Colin of the Ninth Concession*, 1903. Here are memories of schoolyard fights, of a sadistic dominie, and of the warmth of a Scottish Canadian farm home – all capped with a romance ending more in the manner of Disraeli than of MacLaren. W.A. Fraser in *The Lone Furrow*, 1907, presents the story of a village minister and his wife set against the narrowness of village morality. He works his dialect with accuracy and charm.

More strongly marked by the mawkish mannerisms of the Kailyard is the work of "Marion Keith" (minister's wife, this time). *Duncan Polite* (1905) presents a Highlander and a Lowlander as two old friends keeping an eye on the life of the village of Glenora. Piety, temper, and affection characterize the Lowlander, "splinterin' Andra" Johnstone. The plot of young romance and of theological changes (broadening, softening, secularizing) lacks tension. But in this too the author follows the desultory sequence of Barrie's *Idylls*, or of *Beside the Bonnie Brier Bush*. Perhaps we see here a continuance of the "statistical" method so dear to the annalists as a rejection of fanciful artistic manipulating. Perhaps there is a link still with the unorganic plotting of Scott. Perhaps a combination of such theological and aesthetic concepts is reinforced in Marion Keith by Canadian and feminine timidity.

The same qualities may appear effeminate in R.E. Knowles's *Saint Cuthbert's* (1905). Here the dour Old Testament rigidity of the village Scot is sentimentalized, and connected with an idyllic rehash of the parable of the Prodigal Son. "Only those who understand the Scottish temperament would have known there had been a struggle," the book announces in its opening sentence, and proceeds to exploit the Kailyard clichés about the stern Scots father, the delicate suffering mother, and the wandering boy. Knowles's *The Dawn at Shanty Bay* (1907) continues the moral and sociological strain; so do many other popular Canadian novels in the ensuing years. The best in the type is Isabel Ecclestone Mackay's *Mist of Morning* (1919).

Didacticism, sentiment and whimsy mark all these novels. Perhaps the high incidence of ministers among the producing novelists is responsible. Religious bias among the publishers, plus the successful examples in Canada and Scotland of clerical authors, fostered these ministerial efforts. The results show the presence of some occupational hazards: vapid moralizing, blindness to ironies, and censorship of moral and psychological blasphemies.

There were some ironic counterblasts among the Canadian novelists, presaging the anti-Kailyard tone of Brown's *The House with the Green Shutter*. There is the anti-idyllic humour of E.E. Sheppard's *Dolly the Young Widder* (1886), the farcical humour of Arch McKishnie's *Gaff Linkum* (1907) and the wider ethnic range of John MacLean's *Warden of the Plains* (1896), in which a Scots missionary hero tackles vices other than those of Ontario villages. Robert Stead's *Bail Jumper* (1914) presents life on the western farms, where only Scottish names remain as reminders of heritage, and where no use of dialect or Lowland manner-isms seems significant enough for record.

But Kailyard strains at their best survive in the work of Sarah Jeanette Duncan, fused there with a Jamesian fineness of technique and an ironic tone which reminds us of the best of John Galt. There are two Scottish ministers in *The Imperialist* (1904), representing perhaps two generations of Lowland theology, or else representing a Scottish newcomer and a Scot tempered and restructured by Canadian experience. The heroine's father, Mr. Murchison, represents another Lowland type, the type that had in fact ensured the dominance of Scottish ways and values in Canada throughout the first years of the life of the Dominion. In Duncan's novel, the Kailyard qualities still appear – gentleness and humour and family tenderness – but leavened by wit and a bit of malice. Henry James may have shown her the basis of her fictional technique, but she added to James, not from Hamlin Garland or Theodore Dreiser, and not from Conrad or Hardy, but from Barrie and Ian MacLaren. The world these Scottish writers pictured, and the tone they chose, was not only pleasanter but also actually closer to Canadian reality than the American or English alternatives.

POETS AFTER CONFEDERATION

To turn from fiction to poetry, before moving on to the consideration of non-literary aspects of Canadian culture, is to enter an area where influences from the Lowlands are more nebulous. Here, as in fiction, there is a striking preponderance of Scottish names among the writers: Campbells and Camerons and Macraes join the Dougalls and Frasers and Gordons and Duncans.

Every year saw volumes of verse by Scots or descendants of Scots, a few in Gaelic, but mostly in dialects of the Lowlands. We could start with McLachlan's volumes in 1855 and 1858, and then skim through the following list:

1858: MacGeorge, *Tales, Sketches and Lyrics*
1861: McLachlan, *The Emigrant*
1863: Ascher (not a Scot but using the popular dialect) *Voices of the Hearth*
1860: William Murdock, *Song of the Emigrant*
1868: Charles Mair, *Dreamland and Other Poems*
1867: Alexander Muir, "The Maple Leaf Forever"
1874: Machar, *For King and Country*
1875: Alex Rae Garvie, *Thistledown*
1878: Hunter-Dewar, *Emigration of the Fairies*
1866: Lachlan MacGoun, "Tramp Tramp Tramp" (anti-Fenian song)
1880: W.W. Smith, *Poems*
1881: K.S. MacLean, *Coming of the Princess, the Lady of Lorne*
(1883: Evan MacColl, *Poems and Songs in Gaelic*)

1884: I.V. Crawford, *Malcolm's Katie*
1887: G.F. Cameron, *Lyrics on Freedom*
1887: Mary Morgan ("Gowan Lee"), *Woodnotes in the Gloaming*
1889: W.W. Campbell, *Lake Lyrics*
(1889: W.D. Lighthall, ed., *Songs of the Great Dominion*)
1890: D. Anderson, *Lays of Canada*
1891: G. Murray, *Verses and Versions*
1891: John Imrie, *Songs*
1893: Elizabeth MacLeod, *Carols of Canada*
1893: D.C. Scott, *The Magic House*
1893: J.D. Edgar, *This Canada of Ours*
1894: Robert Reid, *Poems Songs and Sonnets*
(1895: D. Anderson, *Scottish Folklore*)
(1895: J.A. Lockhart, *Beside the Maraganeywa*
(1896: W.W. Smith, *New Testament in Broad Scots*)
1897: John Macfarlane, *Heather and Harebell* (R.L.S. echoes)
1899: A.M. Machar, *Lays of the True North*
1902: J.W. Bengough, *Echoes of Drumtochty* (includes "To Ian MacLaren")
1900: F.G. Scott, *Poems*

Names of authors, and titles of their publications prepare us for the predominance of echoes from Scott, Burns and Carlyle. *The Literary History of Canada* comments that "a direct connection between the best poems [of this period] and contemporary events hardly exists." The conventions in Burns which had been valid for the poets of the '40s and '50s remained as artifice in the '60s and '70s. The stance of the village poet voicing in a common vernacular the shared joys and sorrows of a tightly-knit community became a pose in the poets – and poetesses – of greater sophistication. These poets chose to write in "braid Scots" for sentimental effect. The range of poetry in this vein appears best in *Selections of Scottish Canadian Poetry*, edited by William Campbell (1913). Much of it is third-rate, bathetic and sentimental. It is not popular art or folk art – much too self-conscious for that. But it has an interest as revelation of mass taste, a taste still dominated by one ethnic strain, even though that strain had became numerically less and less significant.

Major poets of the late nineteenth century – Lampman, Carman, Roberts, Campbell, Crawford and Duncan Campbell Scott – do not work in this blatantly "auld hame" vein. But they too show the remnants of Lowland attitudes, inculcated through family ties, educational system, the press, and politics. Essentially they are bourgeois poets, writing in a vein of moderate commonsense gentility. The Scottish educational ideal might point to these poets as its best products. Knox's dream of a school in every parish, a college in every city had come close to fulfilment in the young Dominion. Such a system guaranteed a freedom from class divisions, reinforcing the kinship or clan feeling of the early days, when bonds were strong enough to counteract economic separations or stratifications. There is consequently a level homogeneous tone in Canadian expression in the decades after Confederation. The Canadian poets manifest neither the sparkle of the aesthetic aristocratic wits, the Wildes and the Beardsleys, nor the hammer of the new proletarian language of Whitman, the early Frost, or E.A. Robinson. The dignity of the Canadian tone also reflects the Scottish strain in school discipline, and the Scottish balance between respect for technology and respect for poetic gifts. The poet trained in such a school – different both from the classicism of the best English education, and the levelling practicality of contemporary American schools – might be expected to manifest a modest self-confidence, self-respect in the face of scientific contemporaries, and no need to withdraw into effete aestheticism, nor to align with assertive mass movements. The stance of self-respecting bourgeois gentility, which differs from the posture of poets of the '90s both in England and in the States, is noticeable in all the turn-of-the-century Canadians (with the possible and rather self-conscious exception of Carman).

Related is the pallor of these poets' works. Their propriety, their gentility, their poetic thinness, may come also from the very decency of their upbringing. The upright, fair-minded Scottish school masters, inculcating a taste for the spare, the sparse, the controlled, left their mark on this generation of poets. Again it is a mark differentiating them from the more opulent tone of English decadence, and from the greater angularity of American conflict-conscious muckrakers (to mention contemporary non-Canadian alternatives in poetic tone). We see the effect in Lampman's "November" poems, in his taste for a decorous pastel beauty, in his choice of tight forms like the sonnet. There is a kind of poetic thrift in this pallor. The same tone – honest, affable, controlled, rather pale – appears in the New Brunswick poems of Charles G.D. Roberts.

Mentioning Roberts and Lampman we remember another quality of their work which seems rooted in the Scottish inheritance. This is localism, a focus on regional detail. In that turn-of-the-century period, so stirred by nationalisms in Europe and America, Canadians achieved (by Yeats's definition) "provincial" rather than "national" poetry. The orientation to small culture pockets in Scotland had been especially strong in old days when water channels and spurs of hill effectively separated each little plain or glen from its neighbours. In Canada this local differentiation survived, even after transportation had erased much of it in Scotland. So Lampman in Ottawa and Roberts in the Maritimes focused on local patches of landscape in a way reminiscent of an earlier day in Scotland. And the landscape, whether in the Gatineau hills or on the Tantramar shores, still resembled Scotland in its dun colouring and its angularities.

Lampman's strongest note is his sense of reaction against an idyllic romantic response to the landscape. Lampman, set against nature, wrapped in thought, "draining the heat," creates his own "nameless and unnatural cheer, a pleasure secret and austere." It is a mood familiar to the

Scot, who husbands his resources and preserves his identity by drawing in to his own fire.

The need to preserve identity is a constant theme in Roberts and Lampman. Canada in the post-Confederation period was feeling the pressures of a border state – a position familiar in Scots tradition. In the new nation, buffetted by counter-ideologies British and American, a kind of dogged resistance emerged, individual as well as national, not flaming or passionate, but close to the mood long sustained in Scotland during centuries of political and economic orphanage. Lampman's focus on his own moods, in the face of the impinging realities of nature, suggest the dour insistence on identity of the eighteenth and nineteenth century Scot. Examination of the conscience, self-help, ironic downrightness and honesty – these are the marks also of many of Lampman's compatriots, and especially of George Frederick Cameron.

One of the qualities honestly recognized and explored by these poets was their pleasure in retrospect. Nostalgia for a passing world was strong in fiction at this time, as has already been suggested in reference to *The Man From Glengarry*. Leacock's "Mariposa" and L.M. Montgomery's "Avonlea" rose to popularity on the same nostalgic thrust. In the poets, the hankering back, the longing for a remembered world of childhood, a countryside of pre-industrial simplicity, is endemic. "Yet will I stay my steps," Roberts says in "Tantramar Revisited," " . . . Muse and recall far off, rather remember than see." This corresponds to the contemporary Kailyard longing for childhood and countryside and continues the emigrants' cry of longing for the old home. The theme of displacement – displacement in time, in place, in sociological and theological values – is dominant in Canada as in Scotland, and to an extent unequalled in the States or in Europe or England.

In the poetry of Roberts, Lampman, Carman, Scott, and Campbell, there are many qualities other than these I have mentioned. But these qualities – thrift, pallor, nostalgia, independence, self-assertion against nature – seem to be important traits, and they seem to be arguably Scottish ones. I do not mean that the qualities emerging at the end of the nineteenth century were merely late marks of the Scottish heritage. I *do* mean that nothing in the Scottish heritage impeded the direction Canadian poetry was taking – and many elements in that heritage implemented the development, and cleared a path for it.

Although there is much that is admirable and interesting in these poets, they did not create a body of outstanding poems, any more than their contemporaries in Scotland did. Nor did they play an appreciable part in voicing or directing national culture, in the way Burns or Scott or even Stevenson had done. The major cultural force in the last quarter of the century may be said to have inhered not in a single writer or in a coterie of writers, but in the strong, serious, popular press.

226

GENERAL INFLUENCES ON POPULAR TASTE

An army of newspapers, grinding out editorials, reviews, essays, short stories, and occasional verse, kept the taste for reading widespread, and kept the readiness for a national literature apparent. It directed the cultural as well as the political and economic growth of the country along lines alien to American democratic forms, even while deviating from British principles. And that popular Canadian press still found its editors, its writers, its printers and its publishers largely among the Hunters and the Roses, the Andersons and the Middletons, the Browns, the Dougalls, the Stewarts and the Christies. All these men from Glasgow and Aberdeen and Paisley were trained to be practical and hard-headed. But they were ready, like their unsung predecessor at Kilmarnock, to take a chance on local talent and popular taste. Particularly were they ready, of course, to recognize a new poetic voice when it spoke with a Scottish burr.

Contributing to the tendency to patronize and push Scottish trends was the incredible roll-call of Scottish Canadian success stories. A tradition that produced so many successes carried its own validation. The success of such men as Strathcona and Macdonald was itself a cultural force. Scottish values had given Canadian railroading its creators, from Strathcona to Sandford Fleming; had produced merchant powers like Renfrew and Simpson, lords of the liquor and tobacco empires like Seagram and Macdonald, educational leaders like George Grant, politics from George Brown and John A. Macdonald to Alexander Mackenzie and Alexander Galt. Who could argue with a set of assumptions and a code of behaviour that produced such performances? The percentage of Scottish immigrants dwindled, but the power of Scottish mores waxed.

Diminution in the numerical proportion of Scottish immigrants was particularly noticeable out West. After the 1880s, when we speak of Canadian culture we must look beyond Lake Superior to include the life of the prairies and the west coast. Throughout the early years of the nineteenth century, hardy travellers who pushed beyond the Sault had recorded a passage from one Hudson's Bay factory to the next. It was a record of a chain of isolated Scottish families, offering warmth and friendship, and creating a myth of Canadian western hospitality that has its base in Scottish conventions. As towns grew up in the West, many focused around the established "first family" of the Scots factor. Such a family at the core of new settlement gave a social tone, decent, law-abiding, and hard-working, to the Canadian West. The tone is recorded in travel accounts from Sladen to Kipling; and most accounts add glimpses of the Scots from whom the tone emanates. After 1886, new settlers flooded in, many of central European, Slavic, or Scandinavian background; but the early tone persisted. Bryce's *The Scot in the North West* summarizes the extent of influence.

East *and* west, the continued Scottish dominance in Canadian schools ensured continuing relish for literature and for the national past. Scottish teachers also inculcated respect for the creative man, a tradition rooted in the idolatry of Burns and Scott, and one that marked a sharp difference from the increasingly irreverent anti-creative bias in the States (the bias which forced Mark Twain into the pose of non-poetic "funny man" for so many years). The respect for learning in Canada had as a negative result – a rather pretenious erudite style, even in the semi-learned.

The combination of bookshop, printing establishment and newspaper office in small towns and in the rising cities continued to be another channel through which Lowland ideas were diffused. The *Canadian Monthly and National Review*, for instance, so powerful an intellectual influence, was the brain child of a Scot, Graeme Mercer Adam. Associated in this enterprise as in so many of national importance was Stevenson; the printers were Hunter and Rose. (George McLean Hunter had moved into this venture from earlier work with the Montreal *Witness*.) The great city journals continued to be dominated by Scottish Canadians like George Brown of the *Globe*, David Chisholme of the Montreal *Gazette*, Dr. A.J. Christie who went from the *Gazette* to the *Canadian Magazine*, and John Ross Robertson of the Toronto *Telegram*. In smaller centres, from a profusion of Scottish names one might select Thomas McQueen of the Goderich *Huron Signal*, James Innis of the Guelph *Mercury*, James Somerville of the Ayr *Observer*, Robert Sellar of the Huntingdon (Que.) *Gleaner*. Histories of Canadian journals sound like a directory of Aberdeen or Glasgow: Hugh Scobie, Hugh Graham, J.A. Macdonald, David Creighton – the Lowland names are legion.

Domination over politics was another means by which Scottish cultural values were made to prevail in Canadian communities as the nineteenth century drew to its close. Traces of this bias appear in the whole spectrum of political life – a curious alternative to the story of Tammany domination in the United States, and without comparable undertones of corruption by an ethnic group.

Finally, the pressure of Scottish values can be seen in the English-Canadian view of history. In the first *Makers of Canada Series*, how many Scottish names appear among the historians, as well as among the men who "made" history! As Canada moved into the twentieth century, two massive studies summarized the effects of the Scot in this country: James Rattray's *The Scot in British North America* (1884) and W.W. Campbell's *The Scotsmen in Canada* (1911). Both authors catalogued Scottish success stories in every conceivable field; both also attempted to generalize on the Scottish qualities that emerged from these stories. Campbell specified elements dominant in Scottish character, and persistently successful in the Canadian scene: "dour, kindly, dignified, stubborn, strenuous." Daniel Clark, in *Selections from Scottish-Canadian Poets*, concocted another list: "reticent, slow, purposeful, philosophic, grim in humour, given to melancholy . . . but preserving an inward chuckle." Both lists sum the Scottish strain in nineteenth century art and life.

In cultural terms, the story of the nineteenth century might now be summarized: an early direct imitation, followed by long continuance of

228

Scottish themes and styles in the mid-century, and culminated by a late return to direct imitation. The Lowland stream had reached its fullest expression in Canadian art early, when Canadian conditions made its use possible, successful and satisfying. The Scottish stream became narrow and thin, but Canadians persisted in following a less-and-less appropriate tradition. By the end of the century Canadian writers, though refreshed by the facile flavour of the new sentimental and escapist Scottish art, wandered into an illusory land, a parched terrain. Yet the solider values of the earlier tradition remained powerful in Canadian folk and popular culture.

INTO THE TWENTIETH CENTURY

As the world moved towards World War I, no single new Scottish voice caught the Canadian ear. Writers and painters of the Celtic Renaissance such as "Fiona MacLeod" stirred little response. Duncan Campbell's "Piper of Arll" is probably the most important of Canadian attempts at the mystic qualities of the "Celtic twilight." *Art nouveau* prettiness and the swing into symbolism and fairy tale magic sat uneasily on Canadian poets. Perhaps Presbyterianism had established too strong a distrust of illogic, too great a defence against the luxury of stained glass, incense and jewelling. In Canadian symbolism when it did emerge, more important poetic influences were to be felt from American, Irish and English contemporaries, and from earlier poets like Donne and Blake.

Glasgow played its part in stirring the experiments of emerging Canadian painters of the '20s. William Cruikshank and William Wood are among many Scots who brought new infusions of talent in the early century, and one may speculate on the deep-grained effect of Scottish attitudes toward art on the life of Tom Thomson at Leith, and of others growing up in still-Scottish communities in rural Canada. But one would see this Scottish strain as very minor compared to Scandinavian, German, and French influences on the Group of Seven and their successors in Canadian art.

In less serious art terms, the same diminution of influence appears. In escapist fiction, although some Scottish novelists have been very popular (notably John Buchan and A.J. Cronin, and more recently Michael Innis, J.I.M. Stewart) the days of dominance seem over. Modern historical novelists such as Neil Munro, James Lorimer and D.T.H. McLellan have made little impact. The genre has remained popular with Canadian writers like Thomas Costain and Thomas Raddall, however, and perhaps the Scottish flavour in these Canadian names suggests that this is one of many examples of a different growth, but from a common root – the old Scott tradition.

Similarly, Scottish dialect humorists such as Eric Linklater have had little sale, now that the Scottish rhythm and localisms are no longer familiar (in the literal sense of family nearness) to Canadian ears. But Canadian writers as diverse as Earle Birney and Sheila Watson still catch the flavour of dialect for ironic effect – a persistence of the old near-scientific pleasure in linguistic oddities.

The literature most controversial in modern Scotland has fostered little following in Canada. We have found our own forms of irony, of irreverence, of radicalism; but we have not followed the lines of George Brown or "Hugh MacDiarmid" or Louis MacNeice. We have had innovative political movements but they have not shown much debt to Dr. Grieve's form of nationalism or communism. We have had our own kind of reaction against the regional idyll, in writers like Ernest Buckler, Margaret Laurence, and Sinclair Ross, but the reaction shows little trace of being aroused by Brown's *The House with the Green Shutters*. Canadian poets have danced mockingly around our own "blasted pine," but the ironists like A.J.M. Smith and Frank Scott show little affinity with MacNeice, though they may be echoing the essence of his cry, "It's no go the gossip column, it's no go the Ceilidh."

Now Buckler grew up in Dalhousie West, Nova Scotia; Margaret Laurence's Neepawa was Scottish-founded and Scottish-dominated; and Sinclair Ross and Frank Scott bear testimony to the Scottish influence in their very names. But the range in ethnic backgrounds of contemporary Canadian writers is actually very great. The Canadians who have achieved "best seller" status include Pierre Berton, Morley Callaghan, Leonard Cohen, Robertson Davies, Margaret Laurence, W.O. Mitchell, Hugh MacLennan, and Mordecai Richler. Even so condensed a list suggests how little the contemporary Canadians can be said to follow a subsidiary stream from a Scottish source. Yet Klein, Layton, Gustafson, Cohen – as well as Ross, MacLennan, and Graeme Gibson – seem most Canadian when they strike notes closest to the Lowland strain. Love of home, tenderness for children, combined with dour recognition of the "cauld blast" in the universe, and a self-mocking reductiveness – these qualities remain strong in most major Canadian artists. For even when the Lowland groups no longer predominate at immigration points, and even when Lowland names no longer sound most persistently in the roll call of poets, novelists, essayists, journalists, painters, musicians, architects and sculptors, values and tastes which we recognize as Scottish still permeate Canadian life and art.

Love of the land is still a major theme. This is not a paradisal land, but it is a land that can be tamed and possessed. It appears still in terms Burns would recognize. Grove, Ostenso, Buckler, and Laurence anatomize the hard work, frugality and independence of Canadian farm life in ironic terms. Realistic animal stories also persist: a direct line seems to run from Burns to C.G.D. Roberts to Farley Mowat, in tenderness, humour and sympathy, presenting honest encounters with our "fellow mortals." Irreverence and impropriety, also taken from Burns's book, mark contemporary love songs, but in Canadian lyrics the other strand of Burns's manner persists also – tenderness, gentleness, sentiment.

Dualistic psychology, which critics of literature see as characteristic of the Scottish outlook, still dominates Canadian novels. Critics have attributed Scott's double focus – on genteel hero and pawky follower – to the divided loyalty of the Scot, the sense of Highland and Lowland alternatives, or to a Calvinist sense of duality. Critics have added Stevenson's dichotomies – Jekyll and Hyde, David and Alan – to the dualistic scheme. If such dualism is indeed peculiarly Scottish, it has been thoroughly adopted in Canada. In MacLennan's *The Watch that Ends the Night* George and Jerome offer such a double focus; the twin theme recurs in Buckler's David and Anna in *The Mountain and The Valley*; and one might add for an obviously non-Scottish Canadian example the double hero-villain of Cohen's *Beautiful Losers*. Such a duality appropriately represents the bicultural strains in Canada, just as it once reflected the double culture of Scotland.

Today, Canadians dream of a flowering of native literature. Our situation is not unlike that in Scotland in the opening years of the nineteenth century, a time of frustration because of economic and cultural encroachments by a rich and powerful neighbour, and of determination to resist "cultural imperialism" by rediscovering national essences. Lockhart in those days exhorted his fellow Scots, in terms that could be modified to fit Canadian needs:

> Scotland should learn to consider her own national character as a mine of intellectual wealth, which remains in a great measure unexplored . . . . . She should by no means regard English literature as an expression of her mind, or as superseding the examination of what intellectual resources remain unemployed within her own domains.

Adapting this exhortation to Canadian terms, we might suggest that Canadian culture may now be ready to free itself from dependence on any imported models as a "mine of intellectual wealth," or "expression-... mind." We may also however further explore the notion that many of our "intellectual resources" remain as a naturalized form of Scottish values. These values are powerful here both as a heritage from a day when Scottish threads were the strongest inweavings of the Canadian fabric, and also as a continuing, inevitable and appropriate response to an environment similar to Scotland in geographic forms, in climate, and in politico-sociological structures.

TWELVE

The Gaelic Tradition in Canadian Culture

George S. Emmerson

The term "Celtic" is more precisely applied to a culture than to a race, a culture which has jostled with its principal rival, the Germanic, for a place in Europe over the centuries. In the eighteenth century, the geographic boundary between the two cultures in Scotland was roughly defined by the merging of the mountains of the northwest with the lowlands of the southeast, and were distinguished by their respective languages – Gaelic and "Lowland Scots." The latter language, now usually referred to simply as "Scots," is a northern branch of English or Anglian with its own infusions from the low countries and France and from Gaelic itself.

In Medieval times, Gaelic was the language of the Scots and was then referred to as Erse (Irish) by the English speakers of the southeast and eastern ports. In 1363-5 Fordoun wrote:

> The manners and customs of the Scots vary with the diversity of their speech. For two languages are spoken among them, the Scottish and the Teuton, the last of which is the language of those who occupy the seaboard and the plains while the race of Scottish speech inhabit the Highlands and outlying islands. The people of the coast of the islands, on the other hand, are a savage and untamed nation, rude and independent, given to rapine, ease-loving, of a docile and warm disposition, comely in persons but unsightly in dress, hostile to the English people and language and, owing to diversity of speech, even to their own nation, and exceedingly cruel. They are, however, faithful and obedient to their king and country and easily made to submit if properly governed.

This seems a remarkably perceptive report.

The Norse marauders and settlers of the Hebridean and West-Highland fringe had some impact on names and no doubt also on social customs, lore and music, but in these higher arts the Celtic strain was overwhelmingly the stronger. The first rulers of the united kingdom of Scotland (844

232

A.D.) spoke Gaelic. It was the Anglo-Normans who established the Anglian dialect in Scotland as the language of state even before it was so established in England, where French remained the dominant language at court practically to the time of Henry VIII. King James IV (c.1500) of Scotland, who married Henry's sister, Margaret, was the last of the Scottish kings to be fluent in Gaelic. It was he, too, who broke the Norwegian king's hold on the Hebridean clansmen and set up the Earl of Argyll, chief of Clan Campbell, to erode the dominion of the Macdonald clan over the Isles. This is the true origin of the well-known Macdonald-Campbell feud. It is ironical that it was to the Macdonalds and their associates, adherents to the Roman Church, that James IV's direct line of descent had ultimately to look for its support in the eighteenth century. It was from these clans that a large proportion of the earliest settlers in the New World were drawn.

By this time (1707) Scotland had entered into an incorporating union with England while retaining her own church, educational structure and law. It is to Scotland's control over these vital institutions that Canada owes so much, a phenomenon which provides the subject for several other articles in this symposium. It is certain that when the British government decided to recruit the Scottish Gaels (or Highlanders) into the British army and form Highland regiments, it could not have imagined the many ramifications of this which would develop within the British Empire and its influences on the spread of Scottish Gaelic culture in the world. Its contribution to the depopulation of the Scottish Highlands was seen as an advantage. Through these regiments hundred of Gaels reached North America and remained there to form Gaelic-speaking communities on lands granted by the Imperial government. The first really major Gaelic settlements in Canada began in this way, that in Glengarry, Ontario, being the most noteworthy. The Highland military tradition in such settlements remained strong over the years and it is therefore surprising that the tradition of the great Highland bagpipe as a military instrument did not share this strength. The Scots, both Highland and Lowland, and the Irish too, were often led into battle by a bagpiper in centuries past; but it is the Highland Gaels who cultivated their Great Bagpipe (*Piob Mohr*), so-called from its size, and its music, for a military role. With the creation of Highland regiments went the development of the combination of piper and drummer which evolved into pipes and drums – the military pipe band – thus founding a new tradition of bagpipe music for marching which is now as strong in Canada, and as indigenous, as it is in Scotland itself. Yet one looks in vain to the Canadian Gaelic settlements for a tradition of piping that reaches back to their origins.

In the tradition of the Gael, the Great Pipe had its own unique art music – Pibroch – a theme and variations form of great variety and subtlety both melodically and acoustically. While Pibrochs have most frequently been composed to commemorate some warlike achievements, or lament the death of a hero or a loved one, they are not restricted to heroic themes.

They require great technical skill and musicianship which is not easily acquired without much study and practice. This has often called for something like full-time devotion to the instrument, restricting it, if you will, to professionals. The great patrons of the professional pipers in Scotland were clan chiefs or lairds and the study required of such a piper often involved a few years at one of the special piping schools or colleges such as that of the MacCrimmons in Skye, or under the tutelage of a master of the art. Conditions in the pioneering settlements were not conducive to this kind of application. As for dance music, the fiddle was, in Canada, a more accessible and less temperamental instrument, requiring less skill to play acceptably.

The principal Gaelic-speaking Scottish settlements in Canada by the middle of the nineteenth century were well-established in Nova Scotia, particularly in Cape Breton, Pictou and Antigonish, parts of Prince Edward Island and New Brunswick, the Ottawa River Valley, the Red River in Manitoba, and in parts of Ontario – particularly Glengarry, Stormont, Zorra, Elgin, Bruce and Baldoon. There were others of less significance and kindred settlements of Lowland and Ulster Scots whose native tongue was modern English and Scots.

Apart from the distinctions associated with their respective languages, the Highland and Lowland Scots were – in general – products of different environments. By the eighteenth century, the Highlander was predominantly a hunter and fisherman or a crofter picking meagre crops from a thin and rocky soil. He lived very close to nature, and was inured to hardship. The cold and wet of the North Atlantic climate held no terrors for him. The Hebridean, living in the eternal presence of the sea, on bare windswept islands, remote and magical, was a different person from the Gaelic-speaking Highlander of the mountains, of the old Pictish regions of Breadalbane and Strathspey, and both differed again in some degree from their brethren in the broad moorlands and glens of Sutherland and Caithness. Their pronunciation of their common language was different, just as the dialects and pronunciation of English differed with fine gradations from the borders with England to John o' Groats, Orkney and Shetland.

Associated with the Gaelic language was an ancient and rich oral tradition of literature, descended from the great bardic culture of former days and largely devoted to the legendary heroes of the race. By the eighteenth century the long bardic epics were preserved in whole or in part in the mouths of the story-tellers with which every clan abounded, mixed with a multitude of those folk tales which John F. Campbell has recorded for us and which Helen Creighton has traced anew in Nova Scotia. In addition to this was the wonderful inheritance of song – the work song, the rowing song, the song of incantation, the love song and the song of live experience. What a treasury was there! [1]

In eighteenth century Scotland, a notable development in Gaelic literature was the emergence of Gaelic poets who turned from the traditional subjects of their predecessors and composed poems on the themes of their daily life, in the manner of poets in the other European languages. Some of these poets could read and write Gaelic, but most did not. Duncan Ban Macintyre, perhaps the most gifted of these, had all his compositions committed to memory. The Rev. Dr. Stuart of Luss wrote down many of Macintyre's poems from the poet's dictation and published them in 1768. Similar collections of other Gaelic poets followed, but much remained only in oral circulation, for the Gaelic tradition was yet essentially oral.

In his *The Literature of the Highlands*, Magnus Maclean wrote:

> At the beginning of the nineteenth century quite an unprecedented number of Highland bards existed; among others Duncan Ban MacIntyre, Ewen Maclachlan, Alan MacDougall, Alexander Mackinnon, John Maclean, Donald Macleod, Kenneth Mackenzie, James Shaw, James Macgregor, John Macdonald, Donald Macdonald, Angus Fletcher and Allan MacIntyre. The splendid renaissance of the '45 had thus culminated in the remarkable result that there was scarcely a parish or a clachan throughout the Highlands and Islands that had not its own poet. And yet the noontide glory had already departed for of the great sons of the Muses, Macdonald, Maccodrum, Macintyre, Roy Stuart, Macpherson, Buchanan, Rob Donn and William Ross, only one was still living [Macintyre], the venerable hunter-bard of Glenorchy, who outlived his peers and died at Edinburgh in 1812.

It was the society which produced this outpouring which was now breaking up and transplanting itself on the opposite Atlantic shore. Although the tension which is the mainspring of great art was present in this experience, the leisure for its expression had to give way to the unfamiliar tasks of clearing forests and coping with the problems of survival in an unfamiliar terrain and climate of extremes of sunshine and ice.

Bard MacLean in Nova Scotia despaired in his desolation:

> Tha mulad diomhair an deigh mo lionadh
> Bho'n 's eiginn striochdadh an seo ri m' bheo
> Air bheag toilinntinn 's a' choille chruim seo
> Gun duine faighneachd an seinn mi ceol.
>
> Cha b' e sin m' abhaist an tus mo laithean;
> 'S ann bhithinn rabhartach aig gach bord,
> Gu cridheil sunndach an comunn cuirteil,
> A' ruith ar n'uine gun churam oirnn.

A hidden grief has overfilled me since I've been doomed to stagnate here for the rest of my life with little amusement in this gnarled forest and without anyone to ask me if I'd sing a song.

That was not my custom in the early days; then I used to be frolicking

235

at every table, happy and contented among cultured companions, passing the time without any care.[2]

This, however, was a passing phase. MacLean soon began to appreciate some of the recompenses of the new land, and Charles Dunn truly observes that if MacLean had written in English he would have been more widely esteemed as a classic poet of pioneer life. He was the most versatile and renowned of the Highland poets to settle in the New World.[3] None of the several Gaelic poets who emigrated to Canada was quite of this calibre. Nevertheless, one must comment on the Rev. Duncan Black Blair who was inspired to write a number of poems on the Canadian scene, of which the following is a good example:

Anns a' gheamhradh neo-chaoin
This a' ghaoth le fead ghoineant',
'S bidh cruaidh ghaoir feadh nan craobh,
'S iad for shraonadh na doininn.
Bidh sneachd trom air gach gleann,
'S cathadh teann mu gach dorus;
Ach bidh lon againn 's blaths,
'S bidh sinn manranach, sona.

In the surly winter the wind comes with its shrill whistle, and there's a loud moaning among the trees under the blast of the storm. There's deep snow in each valley and heavy drifts around every door; but we have food and warmth, and we're companionable and contented.[4]

Other Gaelic poets emerged from the new settlements in some profusion, and the work of the best of them has that same vigour and unsentimental awareness of nature that was characteristic of the compositions of the great eighteenth century Gaelic poets.

In contrast, the emigré Lowland Scots writing poetry in their own tongue were constrained by its associations of "hame and infancy" and pawky humour. They came to its traditions via the works of Burns and his contemporary song writers, and imitated these models, but in a way that often tended to artificiality and the rudest sentimentality. This corruption of taste was somehow a peculiarity of their associations with modern English, and the postures of the period. Modern English was now the dominant dialect for serious literature and discourse in Scotland although, curiously enough, it made remarkably slower progress within the legal profession. With its increasing ascendancy for higher literary purposes since the appearance of the King James translation of the Bible, it caused the decline of the growing Lowland Scots literary tradition of the fifteenth and sixteenth centuries.

Gaelic has had a much longer run as a working language and is consequently a more fully developed language than Scots had a chance to become. But Scots was the language of "feeling" for most non-Gaelic speakers in Scotland and remains so to the present day although to a lesser

extent than formerly, with the exception of those brought up within the
Glasgow industrial region, in which the vernacular is a corrupt patois.
Great poetry on universal themes has been written in Scotland in the
vernacular Scots tongue, or its literary synthesis, in recent times, starting
with Hugh Macdiarmid's *Sangschaw, Penny Wheep,* and *A Drunk Man
Looks at the Thistle* of the 1920s. This development has had no manifestation in Canada corresponding to that which one can trace among the
nineteenth century immigrants and which is the subject of another contribution to this symposium. Gaelic poetry in Scotland has been touched by
this modern movement, its crowning glory being the work of Sorley Mac-
Lean, but this also has had no impact in Canada – as yet.

The poetry of the pioneering Gael in Canada expresses the simple wonder of his new habitat and the struggle of the experience in a more immediate way than the corresponding endeavours in English or Scots. Nevertheless, being in a minority language, this poetry has had no apparent
effect on the mainstream of English or French literature in Canada. This
does not preclude the discovery of Canadian works here and there which
draw their expression from the Gaelic tradition, just as one encounters
Gaelic constructions and expressions in the English speech of people
raised where Gaelic was indigenous in Canada. That "indigenous" is not
too strong a word is well illustrated by the experiences of that great Scottish divine, Norman Macleod, when he toured the eastern provinces in
1841. While proceeding by steamboat from Kingston, Ontario, to Toronto, for instance, he heard a number of voices from a lower deck singing
a Gaelic chorus. After seeking them out, the following dialogue ensued:

> "Pray what language is that?"
> "Gael, sir . . . . "
> . . .
> "Is it a language?"
> "It's the *only* true *langidge.* English is no *langidge*
>   at all, at all."
> "It must be banished; it is savage."
> "It's no you, or any other, will banish it."
> "Pray let me hear you speak a sentence of it.
>   Address a question to me."
> "*Co as a thanaig thu*?" (Where do you come from?)
> "*Thanaig mis as an Eilean Sgianach*!" (I come from
>   the Isle of Skye.)
> "*O, fheûdail! 'Se Gael tha am.*" (Oh goodness!
>   He is a Gael!)[5]

None of these men had ever been in Scotland; all were natives of Glengarry, Ontario. This did not surprise Macleod; he was meeting with this
sort of thing wherever he travelled in Upper Canada and the Maritimes
and, not long before, he had participated in open air religious services in

237

Gaelic at Pictou, to which nearly five thousand people had thronged from near and far. He had never seen the like in Scotland.

When formal education was introduced to the Gaelic-speaking communities in Canada the principal use of the language in the schoolroom was to teach English – just as in Scotland. Thus most Gaels everywhere came to read and write English better than they could read and write their parent tongue, the tongue in which they expressed themselves best, the vehicle of their literature! A considerable incentive towards literacy in Gaelic, however, was provided by the publication, in 1841, of a valuable collection of the best Gaelic poets of the eighteenth century, entitled *Sar Obar nam Bard Gaeloch* (*Masterpieces of the Gaelic Bards*). This was compiled by John Mackenzie and published in Glasgow. The poems were in the original Gaelic and the biographies of the poets and an introductory dissertation were presented in English. Charles Dunn, whose study of the Gaelic literature of Nova Scotia[6] is an indispensable guide to this subject, tells us that *Sar Obar nam Bard Gaeloch* had a remarkable effect on the cultural life of Canadian Gaels, enticing the curious into learning to read their own language.

The attachment of the emigrant Gaels to their native islands and mountains was deep and intense. Unlike their Germanic tormentors, the Vikings of the Middle Ages, the Gaels, as a people, were not maritime adventurers. Perhaps their internecine feuds, to which they were peculiarly addicted, provided sufficient release for their aggressive instincts. In their days of crisis in the eighteenth century, however, these feuds melted into insignificance and the more civilized side of Gaelic life enjoyed the greater prominence it so richly deserved, although observers were usually deceived by the trappings of poverty.

The Protestant Reformation spread into Sutherland and Caithness in the seventeenth century but was much slower in penetrating the remoter Highlands. A Gaelic translation of the Bible was not available until the late eighteenth century. When the missionary zeal of the reforming ministers bore fruit, it was with a startling fervour and earnestness which was quickly reinforced by the anguish of parting from friends and relatives in the time of wholesale clearances, and by the resulting desolation. Thus a peculiarly puritanical branch of the Protestant church made great headway throughout the West Highlands during the nineteenth century. The Gael was ever close to the supernatural and wove some of his superstitious propensities into whatever creed he adopted. Not even the strictest Calvinist in the Hebrides would readily scoff at the phenomenon of "second sight," for instance. This was the most common and best authenticated form of extra-sensory perception within nearly everyone's experience. The Gaels took this with them and their heightened sense of the "other World" to their new home in the forest and by the sea of new shores. The Rev. W.A. Ross of Zorra, for instance, recorded that nearly all the superstitious Halloween rites described by Burns were practised by the Zorra pioneers, a Protestant Gaelic community.[7]

The Catholic part of the Scottish Highlands still embraces the Great Glen, Glengarry, Ardnamurchan, Knoydart, Moidart, and the islands of Rum, Eigg, Canna, Barra, South Uist and Eriskay. It is from these regions that the Catholic Gaels of Canada set forth, settling mainly in Cape Breton, Antigonish, Prince Edward Island and Glengarry, Ontario. It is among these that the traditions of the Gael have been most tenaciously preserved in both Scotland and Canada. The relationship between the Catholic and Protestant Highlanders has been traditionally cordial and tolerant. The binding force of the Gaelic language was proof against sectarian hostility. It was a very different case in Ireland, where Catholics spoke Gaelic and Protestants spoke English. The Rev. Norman Macleod the elder, father of the minister of the same name mentioned above and composer of the favourite Gaelic song, "Farewell to Fiunary" (*Fiunary* was the name of his manse in Morven), frequently entertained "old Mr. Cattanach," the local Roman Catholic priest at Campbeltown, and often provided board for the priest of his parish in Morven.[8] But we can find many examples of this spirit in the ministrations in Glengarry of Bishop MacDonell, whose unbigoted acts of Christian charity earned a generous encomium from the Orange Body of the City of Toronto (c.1835).[9] The divisions which developed among the Protestant brethren, however, were sometimes more deeply felt, and were a vexatious intrusion into immigrant Highland settlements.

The Scottish Kirk, however, was an influential democratic power in Scotland, largely taking the place of a parliament. It was a great force towards literacy – in English – and it produced or fostered a disputatious body of parishioners, particularly in the Lowlands, who made "points of doctrine" and consequently philosophy, theology and science their profound concern. The West Highland Presbyterians were more likely to follow their ministers and fall under the spell of repressive piety. Many regarded their misfortunes as judgements for sinful living, and for these the rejection of all expression of secular joy seemed only too appropriate. Some of this is seen in the Gaelic-speaking pioneer settlements of Nova Scotia, and where it is strong it has had an inhibitory effect, as in Scotland, on the preservation of the traditional customs, dances and songs. The Catholic communities have largely been spared this cloud of guilt, but they have had their puritan devotees too. Nevertheless music and dance have occupied a paramount place in the culture of all Gaels. The folk music of the British Isles is predominantly Celtic in origin and no community in Europe has exceeded Ireland and Gaelic Scotland in the variety, extent and beauty of its instrumental music and songs.

In both music and dance, Gaelic society developed sophisticated art forms: the *port* of the *clarsach*, the *piobairechd* of the *piob mor*, or great bagpipe, and Highland dancing. The Gaelic-speaking pioneer communities of North America were heirs to these, but had little apparent opportunity to cultivate them. In their recreational life they took inspiration from the smaller folk forms – the traditional dance music and martial airs played on both fiddle and bagpipe and the immense resources of song. The latter included the work or occupational songs which lightened every task. Communal tasks – such as waulking the cloth and rowing the long boat – were accompanied by the appropriate songs, usually comprising alternating lines of solo and chorus. Survivals of this great accumulation reaching back into distant time are still being collected in Nova Scotia and the Hebrides. As J.L. Campbell expressed it, "Work in the Gaelic-speaking Highlands and Islands was performed as a joyful social creative activity, integrated into the lives of the people and expressing their personalities- . . . their great store of traditional folksong enriched their lives and lightened their labours."[10]

That great Gaelic social institution, the *ceilidh*, a domestic gathering combining entertainment and conversation, has survived as a vital characteristic of life in the Gaelic communities of Canada right into modern times although, recently, it has more commonly been replaced by public concerts. Public Gaelic concerts, as distinct from those of the Gaelic societies of the cities, are more of an institution in Cape Breton than elsewhere in Canada, for it is there that the Gaelic language has been most tenaciously preserved. Nevertheless, the visitor to many concerts in Glengarry County, Ontario, would be excused for thinking that he had arrived in the Scottish Highlands, for, although English is the language now used, it is the music, songs and dances of Scotland that dominate the programme. There are still a few districts in Scotland in which one could summon up a band of twenty fiddlers at short notice, but it would startle any Scot today to walk into a hall in Maxville, Ontario, or Sydney or Halifax, Nova Scotia, and find a score of fiddlers who had never seen Scotland, crowding onto a platform to play reels, hornpipes, jigs and Strathspeys with all the love and fervour in the world. This, in large measure, is the very stuff of Canada, let alone of Scotland, in the experience of thousands of Canadians.

Traditional Scottish dance music can be categorized under two generic heads – reels and jigs. The sub-categories of reel to which special names have been given are: rant, Scottish Measure and Strathspey.[11] The common-time hornpipe which has been a great favourite in New England and in the Maritimes is a class of tune which was developed from the Scottish Measure in the eighteenth century and was widely used as the vehicle of theatrical character step-dances at that time and subsequently. The Irish hornpipe has a different rhythm and style. Prior to the vogue of the new hornpipes, the name was given to a step-dance measure in 3/2 which was a favourite in England, in the Scottish border country and to some extent in Ireland. The common-time hornpipe, so called, was widely used in Scottish dancing schools for a character dance called Jacky Tar and for Country Dances. It was clearly a relative, a mutation, of the traditional Scottish rant, although many of the stage hornpipes named after dancing masters (Fishar's, Durang's, etc.) are obviously not Scottish in origin at all. The different classes of jigs are not so clearly differentiated and, although they form the bulk of the corpus of Irish dance music, they are hardly less essential to the dance music of England and form a considerable component of that of Scotland.

The jig cannot compete with the rant and hornpipe in the affections of Canadian fiddlers, nor can the Strathspey, still less the slow Strathspey so much enjoyed by Scottish fiddlers. This certainly has something to do with the prevailing dance forms and also the fiddling technique. The self-taught, uncultivated, traditional fiddler uses a very short bowing action, vigorously scraping out the tune with a stroke to each note and producing but very small sound. The more tutored fiddler has acquired the advantages of a more varied bowing technique and larger sound, although in some cases at the sacrifice of what the Scots call "pith and birr." The long bow is most advantageous, if not essential, to the slow Strathspey. As already remarked, the Cape Bretoner's partiality for rants, common-time hornpipes and, to a lesser extent, jigs, is undoubtedly due to the prevailing tradition of step-dancing which has also given rise to the name of "clog" for a particular class of hornpipe tune, the "Scottish Measure."

A considerable proportion of this body of dance music has been composed by fiddlers – and pipers – within the past two hundred years. It remains a living tradition and nowhere more so than in the regions of Gaelic settlement in Canada, particularly in Cape Breton, Glengarry and the Ottawa River Valley. More than that, each region has developed its own characteristic style of fiddling as well as its favourite versions of old tunes and even favourite tunes of its own. Hence certain characteristics distinguish the typical fiddler from Cape Breton from his counterpart in Glengarry or by the Ottawa River. The same could once be said, and to a lesser extent can still be said, of fiddlers in Scotland itself, and of fiddle and pipe tunes. The printed music collections, improved technique, and the disruption of the old communities have conspired towards greater uniformity in Scotland. Nevertheless, there is a clear difference between the Irish and Scottish styles, and mainland and island styles, of performing the same tunes, and no less a difference in the technique of the instrumentalist.

The Cape Breton fiddlers often seem to form a bridge between the Scottish and Irish styles. There is, too, a difference between the Cape Breton and Nova Scotian styles recognized by the cognoscenti. In addition there are the related musical traditions of Acadia and New England in which fiddling plays an equally prominent role. In all of these regions rants and common-time hornpipes reign supreme. It is fascinating to hear the transmutations of Scottish rants and even of Strathspeys, suitably renamed, by French-Canadian fiddlers, among whom Jean Carignan, a Quebecer, takes pride of place. Another offshoot of the Gaelic tradition in fiddling in Canada is what is called "Country Music," the "hoe-down" square dance idiom, very different from the Scottish tradition of fiddling which is its natural progenitor. This subject has not yet been studied and treated with the scholarship it deserves and the different styles of fiddling are not so easily discussed on paper in any case. The "Scotch," Cape Breton, Nova Scotian, Acadian and "Country" styles of fiddling are identifiable and have their respective devotees.

The most distinctive characteristic of the Scotch style is the absence of the drone effect of frequent doubling with the open string common to the other two styles. Double-stopping, staccato, and what some call the "skirl" – a quick figure or arabesque employing the four working fingers – are also distinctive characteristics of the Scotch style. The Acadian style bends all tunes, even if they be Strathspeys or Scottish Measures, into an impetuous filigree of graceful notes. The accents of the tunes – Scottish tunes though they be – are changed, making them no longer Strathspeys, etc. This style is at its best with rants and hornpipes. Indeed, one is tempted to say that it was uniquely devised for these rhythms. In the hands of such an artist as Jean Carignan the effect is incomparably exciting. In other categories of Scottish dance tune it is not nearly so effective and, in any case, to the Scottish ear its accent is "wrong." The same can be said of the "Country" style which now rather predominates in Canada.

The social dances brought to Cape Breton by its Gaelic-speaking settlers were several variants of what are now called the "four-handed reel" and the "eight-handed reel," or, in Gaelic, the *Ruidhleadh Bheag* ("small reel") and the *Ruidhleadh Mor* ("big reel"). These dances comprised eight bars of travel in a circle alternating with eight bars of setting to partners, either in a line or in a square.[12] The setting took the form of hornpipe stepping – trebles and beats, brushing and heel and toe movements – a style of dancing for clad feet, and of which little trace survives in Scotland but which is certainly essential to Irish dancing. Nevertheless there is sufficient evidence in written record and within comparatively recent memory to confirm the Cape Breton round reels as authentic survivors of a favourite dance form of the Hebrides and contiguous parts of the Scottish mainland at the time of the large scale emigrations.[13] Stepping was commonly employed for setting in country dances in the rural communities of the Scottish Lowlands and was certainly taught by itinerant dancing masters in Ayrshire and Galloway in the early nineteenth century.[14] The term "Country Dance," it must be pointed out, refers to a specific longwise dance form characterized by a system of progression by which each couple has an opportunity of leading through the dance as "dancing couple" in regular sequence. There are "Scottish," "English" and "Irish" Country Dances, differing more in technique than in figures and, of course, in music, although there are large scale mutual borrowings.

Country Dances are performed to all classes of reel, hornpipe and jig and were popular in the rural and formal ballrooms of Canadian and New England towns in the nineteenth century. American ballroom manuals called them "Contra-Dances," a name appropriate to their longwise formation of male and female ranged in opposing lines, in contradistinction of the couples facing each other in square formation, which, incidentally, is the original *contra-dance* formation. Other than by providing tunes, there was no Scottish influence on these dances. The technique was mainly stepping; but the ballroom manuals of the period leave no doubt that hornpipe stepping was appropriate only to vulgar assemblies.

The so-called "Square Dance" is a rustic form of the Quadrille, which was a more decorous dance and, originally, one demanding much classical dance skill and a large repertoire of steps. The Square Dance has therefore been referred to as a "country dance," but this is not the same as "Country Dance" with capital "C" and "D." The Scottish Country Dance which emerged from the Lowland dance assemblies of the eighteenth century was unknown to the Gaelic immigrants of Canada. If the latter encountered Country Dances in their new home it would be through the social dancing of their neighbours who had derived them from America or England. Nothing replaced their own reels and music in the esteem of the Gaels in both Scotland and Canada.

The Country Dance, as it evolved in Scotland, took on a character influenced by the technique of the Scotch Reel in its Atholl and Strathspey forms. It was a favourite social dance form of many Lowland regions and has been introduced in strength to Canada since the 1940s through the work of the Royal Scottish Country Dance Society, founded in 1923. There are now numerous groups of devotees of Scottish Country Dancing in Canada, providing and receiving continuous instruction in the art. Many new dances in the idiom have been devised in Canada, even by native-born Canadians, and have found a place in the repertoire, but these can scarcely yet be considered a uniquely Canadian strain of the genre. It is a notable fact that some of the most accomplished exponents of the art, dancers and musicians, are resident in Canada and many are Canadian-born. One of the Canadian bands which provide music for the great Scottish Country Dance occasions is acknowledged to rank with the best in the world.[15]

The style of this dance, while energetic, is controlled and courtly in the ballroom. It is slowly being accepted in the Gaelic regions of Canada where, except for its music, it has no roots. It puts a premium on a limited range of dancing skill in the style of Highland Dance – a Gaelic source – and, above all, it provides an incomparable opportunity to dance socially to all categories of the traditional dance music played in the Scottish style.

The dramatic or mimetic jigs and reels which were once an essential feature of every *ceilidh* in the Scottish West Highlands and even of like occasions in the non-Gaelic southwest[16] were a vague recollection among some old people in Cape Breton and the Hebrides in recent times.[17] The milieu which preserved these very simple performances, with their connotations of ancient ritual, has passed away. This is not to be confused with what is known as Highland dancing.

What we call Highland dancing, today, is really a cultivated art form which has developed from Gaelic culture's traditions of music and dance. It is analogous to the development of ballet – or the associatied cultivated dance forms of the sixteenth century French court – from the raw material of the folk. But unlike its European analogue, it belonged to the folk and developed within the folk. Its centre of development was the central Highlands of Scotland and its social expression was in that dance known in the eighteenth century and later as the Highland Reel – for three or four dancers. A peculiarly elegant and sprightly form of its varied and exacting technique was fostered in the Strathspey and contiguous regions of the northeast Highlands, and from its variety of steps developed the enchainments which were later given such names as "Highland Fling."

It is not our purpose here to enter into the details of the nature and historical development of Highland dance. For this, the reader is referred to the relevant works cited in the notes. Suffice to say that the eighteenth century was a "dancing" century in Scotland – and elsewhere – if ever there was one, and that dance served as much for exercise as diversion among even the Highland soldiery of the period.

It is a curious fact that Highland dancing is not indigenous to Cape Breton or to Nova Scotia generally nor to Prince Edward Island. Although one sees much of it in these provinces today, it has there little history prior to the early years of the present century. By contrast it seems to have had a longer run in the Glengarry settlement where living memory and tradition regard hornpipe stepping as an intrusion. If this is true, it could very neatly be explained by the fact that Glengarry was heir to military traditions which included Highland dancing.

One would look to Glengarry also for a tradition of military piping, but historians have not been interested or knowledgeable in this and there is no visibly greater interest in piping in Glengarry than in many other regions of Ontario. The great vogue of female pipe bands in Nova Scotia underlines the relative weakness of the tradition there. It is appropriate at this point to mention that the great strength of pipe bands in Canada lies in Ontario where there are, at time of writing, three of the best bands in the world. These are civilian bands. Civilian pipe bands now greatly excel military pipe bands, and they are constantly pitting themselves against one another in competition at the many Highland games which have long been characteristic of the Canadian scene.

The modern piping and dancing competitions began with the efforts of the Highland Society of London, England, founded around 1780. The Society comprised a large number of Gaels of the military and other professions who were imbued with a nostalgia for the associations of their language and who wished to take action to preserve it and its literature, and, not least, their great inheritance of bagpipe music and dance. Gaelic clubs and Highland societies which sprang up wherever Gaels congregated sought affiliation to the *the* Highland Society. The first of these, in Canada, was initiated by Bishop Macdonell in Glengarry in 1818. The institutional meeting took place at St. Raphael's on November 10 of that year, on which occasion the charter was presented by Simon McGillivray, one of the vice-presidents of the London parent body, to William

McGillivray, Angus Shaw, John Macdonell (of Gart), Henry Mackenzie and the Rev. Alexander Macdonell, forming the original committee of application. The Society extended its mandate to include the relief of distressed Gaelic immigrants. Grants in aid of the production of scholarly works on the Gaelic language, the collection of Gaelic poetry, and prizes for Gaelic scholars and pipers were established. After some years of usefulness the Society suffered a decline on account of the death or removal of its founders and, after a brief restoration under Macdonell of Gart, the decline continued until the Society came to an end around 1870.[18] Meantime, in 1842, another branch of the Highland Society was founded in Hamilton, Ontario, on the instigation of Sir Allan MacNab and Sir Charles Bagot. There was, too, a Celtic Society of Upper Canada at this period. Gaelic clubs and Caledonian societies are still active in most Canadian cities, but now exist primarily to bring Gaelic speakers together for social diversion.

The original Highland Society of London sponsored the first Highland bagpipe competition in 1782 and extended premiums to dancing a few years later. The modern Highland Gathering dates from this period, but did not extend to Canada until the second half of the nineteenth century. All the Gaelic settlements in Canada now conduct important annual Highland games, and numerous others, if less important, are found wherever Scottish sentiment exists. Competition piping and Highland dancing are now extensively developed from coast to coast, with a multitude of native Canadian dancers and teachers reinforced by the continued influx over the years of skilled devotees from Scotland itself. Like all athletic competitions in general, Highland dance competitions were originally for males and thus a male character was placed on competition dance. The first competition dances were the Highland Reel, the Strathspey Twasome and, a little later, the *Gille Callum*. In more recent times, the *Gille Callum* has been joined by a Highland Fling and the *Seam Triubhas* and, since World War I, girls and women have largely dominated the activity.

Highland games, Highland dancing and pipe bands are now so characteristic of the Canadian scene that they are for many as much Canadian as they are Scottish. They are primarily maintained by the Canadian descendants of Scottish immigrants and their attainments are salutary, the standards achieved being comparable to the best anywhere and often better.

Turning, now, to the less obvious manifestations of Gaelic cultural influence in Canada, we are faced with a dearth of scholarship. Poetry we have touched upon; what of the related art of imaginative prose – the novel? Students of Canadian literature have not been at pains to identify Gaelic influence on Canadian writing, yet one suspects that writers imbued with an inheritance of Gaelic manners, taste and expression would be influenced by it, as was Niel Gunn in Scotland, for instance. The mention of Gunn, a native of the county of Caithness, where Gaelic, Scots and Norse elements meet, turns one's eyes to Canada's Farley Mowat whose family came from the same region of Scotland. Is Farley Mowat in this tradition? He is recognizably closer to it than he is to English models; but this subject deserves closer study than anyone has yet been able to give it.

Much the same has to be said of the visual arts. Scottish painting is not well known in Canada, yet the Gaelic (or Celtic) influence on Scottish painting is considerable – love of colour, light and design. People familiar with the work of the "Scottish Colourists" of the earlier part of the present century find parallels in the aspirations and tastes of the Canadian Group of Seven. Are they both manifestations of Gaelic tradition? The Celts are nothing if not artistic. The great Scottish architectural genius, Charles Rennie Mackintosh, a Gael in the great Celtic tradition of design, has attracted the interest of Canadians but this is as yet a very peripheral aspect of Gaelic influence in Canada.

While it is in the arts that one naturally seeks Celtic influence with greatest expectation, there is more than a probability that Canada has derived at least one of its national games from the Gaels, namely, ice hockey. The most popular Scottish Gaelic game is shinty, played with sticks or clubs and a wooden ball. In some parts of the Highlands the word shinty was corrupted to "shinnie," and it is an interesting fact that "shinnie" was played upon ice in Canada before the word "hockey" was used of the game. Ice hockey has been so widely adopted in Canada, however, that apart from the name of its progenitor, the Gaels have not retained identity with it as, for instance, the Scots as a whole have with that other great Canadian winter game, curling.

Curling has been a much loved game in Scotland, at least since Medieval times, and although it was, and is, particularly popular in the central Highlands of that country, it was really a game of the Lowlands as its original technical terms reveal. The earliest established curling club in Canada was created in Montreal in 1807, largely supported by the Scottish officers of the garrisons. Soon thereafter, similar clubs began to form in other towns, as, for example, Quebec (1821), Kingston (1820), Toronto (1836), Fergus (1834), Galt and Guelph (1838), and Halifax (c.1838).[19] Soon it followed Scots – Gaels and Lowlanders alike – across the continent, until now it is a game which Canadians have made peculiarly their own, while paying salutary honour to the game's origins, with tartans, blue bonnets, bagpipes and conviviality. The game of frozen winter locks and ponds in the open air has become a game of indoor arenas and artifical ice and its language, wonderfully poetic and expressive in Scots, has comparatively recently been replaced by prosaic English in Canada; this is a loss.

If Highland games and dancing, Gaelic mods, bagpiping, fiddling, ice shinty and, to some extent, curling, cannot testify to the strength of Gaelic cultural influence in Canada, one cannot ignore the many war memorials surmounted by kilted soldiers. Surely these are a visible reminder to every immigrant that to be Scottish is also, in a very deep sense, to be Canadian, and especially if the blood is Highland and dreams are of the Hebrides.

NOTES

1. Cf. J.F. Campbell, *Popular Tales of the West Highlands* (Paisley: A. Gardner, 1890-1893), 4 vols.; H. Creighton, *Songs and Ballads from Nova Scotia* (Toronto: Dent, 1932); *Maritime Folk Songs* (Toronto: Ryerson, 1962)

2. Charles W. Dunn, *Highland Settlers: A Portrait of the Scottish Gael in Nova Scotia* (Toronto: University of Toronto Press, 1953), p. 58.

3. *Ibid.*, p. 60.

4. *Ibid.*, p. 63.

5. Donald Macleod, *Memoir of Norman Macleod* (Toronto: Belford, 1876).

6. Dunn, *op. cit.*

7. W.A. Ross, *History of Zorra and Embro* (Embro, 1909).

8. Macleod, p. 26.

9. J.A. Macdonell, *Sketches of Glengarry* (Montreal: Foster, Brown, 1893), p. 327.

10. J.L. Campbell, ed., *Hebridean Folksongs* (Oxford: Oxford University Press, 1969), p. 16.

11. For a fuller discussion of this see George S. Emmerson, *Rantin' Pipe and Tremblin' String: A History of Scottish Dance Music* (Montreal: McGill-Queen's, 1964), pp. 267-285.

12. F. Rhodes, "Dancing in Cape Breton, Nova Scotia," in J.F. and T.M. Flett, *Traditional Dancing in Scotland* (London: Routledge, 1964), pp.267-285.

13. See George S. Emmerson, *A Social History of Scottish Dance* (Montreal: McGill-Queen's, 1972), and Rhodes, *loc. cit.*

14. *Ibid.*, p. 157-60.

15. Stan Hamilton's band, essentially comprising Stan Hamilton (piano), Robert Frew and Robert Brown (accordians), all raised in Scotland, supported by drummer and bass.

16. Emmerson, *Social History* pp. 231-39.

17. Rhodes, *loc. cit.*

18. MacDonell, pp. 326-7.

19. John A. Stevenson, *Curling in Ontario: 1846-1946* (Toronto: Ontario Curling Association, 1950); John Kerr, *Curling in Canada and the United States* (Toronto: Morton, 1904).

THIRTEEN

The Scottish Tradition
in Higher Education

D. C. Masters

The story of the role of the Scots in Canadian higher education is concerned with two types: the Scot directly from Scotland, such as Thomas McCulloch at Dalhousie, Thomas Liddell at Queen's and Daniel Wilson at Toronto, and the Canadian Scot, like G.M. Grant and D.H. MacVicar. The latter were still close to the traditions and cultural influences of Scotland, but they had experienced them at one stage removed. They represent Scottish culture transmitted through Canadian conditions.

To some extent there was tension between the two groups. Thus when MacVicar was being considered as professor in the projected Presbyterian college in Montreal in 1868 a local clergyman, the minister of Erskine Church, argued that the church should attempt to secure a scholar from Scotland. This, wrote MacVicar's biographer, was typical of many discussions in the Scottish Presbyterian community in Canada. "One party felt it an indispensable condition for success that some scholar of established standing should be brought across the ocean: the other party thought it a pity that Canadian-trained ministers, in relation to high and responsible positions, should never be allowed to show what was in them."[1] Nevertheless both groups of Scots reflected the influence of the Scottish university system. The Scottish universities contributed many of the leaders in the founding of Canadian colleges and a number of influential Canadian Scots had also studied in Scotland. Thus Sir William Dawson studied at Edinburgh and George Munro Grant at Glasgow.

Although the Scottish universities (Aberdeen, Edinburgh, Glasgow and St. Andrews) possessed important differences, in the late eighteenth and early nineteenth centuries the four had developed what may be regarded as a "system." One of its distinctive characteristics was a concentration upon lectures as the principal means of academic instruction. There was little emphasis upon the tutorial system as it had been developed in the English universities. The Scottish system was based on the idea that education would best be facilitated if young people listened to addresses of mature and presumably distinguished scholars. A famous critic of higher

248

education in early nineteenth century Scotland, the Reverend Michael Russel, in his *View of the System of Education at present Pursued in the Universities of Scotland*, particularly deplored the teaching of philosophy solely by lectures at Edinburgh. He objected to a system in which there were no examinations, no compulsory attendance at lectures and no tutorials. He admitted that an eminent and specialist professor would "afford a clearer light, and more extensive information to the student, than the discourse of a young tutor employed in teaching several branches of learning," but maintained that "a very extensive and brilliant display of knowledge, so far from being useful to lads who have still to learn the rudiments of mental science, only dazzles and bewilders them."

Like Edinburgh, the other Scottish universities laid great stress on lectures. John Strachan, who was educated at Aberdeen and St. Andrews, liked the Scottish lecture system and argued that it was better suited to Canadian conditions than the English system. He wrote in 1815, when he was considering the establishment of a college in Montreal:

> I prefer the form of the Scotch and German Universities to the English or rather a mixture of both plans because much more may be done at one fourth of the Expence. In the English Universities the public Professors seldom lecture more than once a week – many of them not at all – the whole system of Teaching is conducted by Tutor ... Our Professors must each during the Session give two, three or even four courses of Lectures till the Funds afford the means of increasing their numbers.[3]

The curriculum in the Scottish universities laid considerable emphasis on philosophy in its various guises (mental and moral philosophy, metaphysics, etc.) and on science, some of it concealed under the title Natural Philosophy. Thus the staff at St. Andrews in 1747 included the principal, three professors of philosophy, teaching respectively (1) logic, rhetoric and metaphysics (2) ethics and pneumatics (3) natural and experimental philosophy; one professor each of Greek, humanity, civil history, mathematics and medicine.[4] The Edinburgh curriculum in 1831 provided that candidates who survived a three-day examination in classics, mathematics and philosophy qualified for the degree of MA.[5] The Glasgow course in arts in 1826 included Latin, Greek, logic, natural philosophy and moral philosophy. Lectures were given in natural history although the Chair of Natural History was outside the regular curriculum.[6] The recommendations of the Scottish Royal Commission of 1858 represented the culmination of the curriculum which the Scottish universities had built up. It provided that the M.A. course should be in three parts: (1) classics (2) mathematics and natural philosophy (3) philosophy and English literature.[7]

In the granting of degrees the Scottish universities in the late eighteenth and early nineteenth century showed a preference for the MA and a reluctance to grant BAs. The Commission of Visitation appointed by the British government in 1826 to inspect the Scottish universities recommended a course of three years to be followed by an additional year of work prior to the granting of an MA degree. The fourth year was to include courses in natural history, chemistry and political economy. As a result Edinburgh introduced the BA degree in 1842 and granted from six to twelve BAs each year between 1843 and 1858. St. Andrews granted the BA degree between 1839 and 1861. After the Executive Commission on the Scottish Universities, appointed under the Universities Act of 1858 (Scotland), had recommended the granting of only an MA, both universities abandoned the BA degree.[8]

John Machar, later to be Principal of Queen's University, had provided a picture of the academic milieu which was the background of so many Scottish educators in Canada. Machar, a native of Forfarshire, was educated at King's College, Aberdeen, and studied theology at Edinburgh. In addition to theology, Machar at Edinburgh also continued his classical and mathematical studies. Excerpts from his journal give the picture of an institution in which the Presbyterian and Scottish academic worlds were closely associated:

> March 1st, 1816 – Mathematics. Called on Dr. Buchanan. Walked out by Merchiston Castle, where Napier discovered the Logarithms .... Attended the Theological Society. Essay on the Evidence of Prophecy.

> March 6th – Mathematics. Attended College as usual. Teaching from five to six. Read sixty pages of Horne on the Psalms – a very fine preface. Consulted Poole's synopsis on Psalms, CXXI, and other passages. Read forty lines of Homer.[9]

In May, 1816 Machar attended meetings of the General Assembly of the Church of Scotland. His journal for May 17 read:

> Teaching as usual. Read eighty lines of Third Book of Iliad. Heard Dr. Chalmers, now of Glasgow, preach from Acts XX, 35; "It is more blessed to give than to receive;" an eloquent sermon and in some parts highly wrought up. Read a hundred and twenty pages of Thompson's Lectures. Attended the General Assembly. Read some of Cicero, Horace, etc.[10]

II

The Scottish tradition in Canada was transmitted through two sorts of colleges. The first group was Presbyterian and dominated by Scots. Pictou Academy, in Nova Scotia, Queen's in Kingston, Manitoba College in Winnipeg and Morrin College in Quebec City were examples. Dalhousie, although nominally non-sectarian from 1818, was in reality a Presbyterian college for much of the nineteenth century. Even more Presbyterian and equally Scottish were the theological colleges like Knox in Toronto, the Presbyterian College in Montreal and the Presbyterian theological colleges in the Maritimes.[11] The second group of colleges comprised those which were not dominantly Scottish and Presbyterian but in which Scots had an important influence. Examples were McGill, King's College, Fredericton (later to be the University of New Brunswick), King's College, Toronto, the University of Toronto, Trinity College, Woodstock College and the English-speaking Roman Catholic colleges. In these non-Presbyterian colleges, such men as Daniel Wilson at the University of Toronto and R.A. Fyfe, a Baptist, were of importance.

In the quest for employment in non-Scottish and non-Presbyterian institutions, Scots had certain assets. There is some evidence that Scots were popular with educational administrators because of the idea that they would work harder and for less money than would English professors. John Strachan, in his preliminary ideas about a college in Montreal, explained in 1815 why the English system was unsuited to Canada:

> The great opulence of Cambridge & Oxford is far beyond our reach, and altho I should be sorry ever to see them lose a shilling for I think them wisely adapted to so rich and populous and learned a country as England I think them unfit for this country . . . . Learning they may have in abundance, but the industry the labour (I may say drudgery) and accommodation to circumstances cannot be expected from them.[12]

Bishop Mountain, the real founder of Bishop's College, an Anglican institution in Lennoxville, wrote in 1845 about Henry Miles who had been educated at Edinburgh and Aberdeen and who had been appointed to teach mathematics at Bishop's:

> He is, I believe, about 30 – an intelligent, steady sort of man . . . of exceedingly good attainments & most successful experience in tuition (judging from his testimonials). We could not have expected to get anybody from an English university at the same rate.[13]

III

The study of the Scottish tradition in education may largely be considered in terms of personalities. These may be classified in three broad groups: men who were teachers and also administrators such as Thomas McCulloch at Pictou Academy, Sir Daniel Wilson at Toronto, Sir William Dawson at McGill and George Munro Grant at Queen's; men who were exclusively teachers, such as John Watson at Queen's, Clark Murray at McGill, George Paxton Young, H.A. Nicholson and Ramsay Wright at Toronto,[14] and men who were not professional educators but who took a considerable interest in education.

The third group were of a type described later by Rupert Lodge, the Canadian philosopher as "Knights errant." Some of them exerted some influence upon the development of Canadian education. In this third class were James McGill, the Montreal merchant whose bequest of land and ten thousand pounds made possible the founding of McGill University; Lord Dalhousie, the founder of Dalhousie University; and the Roman Catholic Bishop of Kingston, Alexander Macdonell, the founder of Regiopolis College. William Lyon Mackenzie was a most notable "Knight errant," taking a great interest in the college question. Mackenzie had a characteristic concern for equality of opportunity in higher education in Upper Canada. He was an especial foe of special privileges in this area, vigorously attacking Bishop Strachan and the Anglicans. In the first number of his paper, the *Colonial Advocate*, Mackenzie asserted:

> We coincide with Mr. Strachan, in opinion respecting the very urgent necessity which exists in Canada, for the establishment of a university . . . . If it is to be an arm of our hierarchy; if students are to be tied down by tests and oaths, to support particular dogmas, as in the case in Oxford, the institution will answer here no good purpose . . . . [15]

Two of the Scottish educators listed in this section were of especial importance in the earliest period of higher education in Canada: Thomas McCulloch and John Strachan. McCulloch presided over the first of the Presbyterian colleges, Pictou Academy, and ended his career as Principal of Dalhousie (1838-43). He was largely responsible for Pictou's influence and for the lead which it gave to higher education in the Maritimes. Born in Renfrewshire and educated at Glasgow University, McCulloch emigrated to Nova Scotia in 1803. With a group of associates representing the Secession Presbyterian Church, McCulloch established Pictou Academy which began teaching in 1818. Although chartered as an academy, Pictou was really a college, teaching a considerable range of college courses. It had a notable but comparatively brief career as an instrument of higher education. The connection with the Secession Church involved the Academy in controversy with adherents of the Church of Scotland who were eventually able to reduce Pictou to the status of a grammar school.[16] By 1838 its influence as a significant element in higher education was over.

McCulloch was a fine scholar in Hebrew and the classics and had a considerable interest in science. He gave popular lectures in science and accumulated an ornithological collection which became the property of Dalhousie University.[17] He was also a popular writer of note, the author of *Colonial Gleanings* (1826) and *Letters of Mephibosheth Stepsure*, 1821-2, (Halifax, 1860). McCulloch was a vigorous apologist for his religious faith. He has been described by a modern writer as "a learned, frustrated, waspish little man in whom an enlarged ego was continuously assailed by a strong instinct of self preservation."[18] Yet he is one of the great names in the development of the Scottish tradition in education.

John Strachan has been much maligned because of his undoubted desire to maintain Anglican control over secondary and higher education. His real services to education have often been overlooked. He was an excellent teacher who established an influence over his pupils which lasted throughout his career and theirs.[19] He helped to establish a tradition of disciplined and practical education, adjusted to the capacities of the boys and the needs of education. At Cornwall he developed an interesting method based on the principle that the boys should expound the lesson in turn.[20] His lessons in arithmetic were especially adjusted to the needs of boys, many of whom were slated for mercantile careers. His insistence on religious instruction in secondary education left its mark, even though modified by the influence of Egerton Ryerson.[21]

In the field of higher education, Strachan failed to maintain Anglican control over the provincial university which began as King's and which was secularized as the University of Toronto in 1849; but his preference for the Scottish lecture system[22] made its mark on King's and probably carried over into the University of Toronto. His insistence on denominational control of higher education in the end helped to produce the distinctive Canadian invention, the pluralistic university with affiliated church colleges. In the King's College period Strachan's effort at Anglican control pushed the Methodists and Presbyterians into founding Victoria and Queen's respectively. Trinity, Strachan's answer to the secularization of King's, finally affiliated with the University of Toronto in 1904.[23]

IV

The Scottish influence in Canada made for a broader curriculum than was current in Canadian colleges like King's Nova Scotia, King's Fredericton and Bishop's, which were derived from the Anglican tradition. These institutions concentrated pretty narrowly on classics and mathematics.[24] King's College Fredericton is a case in point. Prior to 1840 its curriculum looked very broad, including not only classical authors and mathematics, but also mental and moral philosophy, the evidences and general principles of the Christian religion, logic, rhetoric and history. However, the principal, Dr. Edwin Jacob, a graduate of Corpus Christi College, Oxford, maintained that, while the aim of the college was to impart intellectual and moral culture, he believed that this was to be achieved almost solely through the study of the ancient classical languages and literature.[25]

The emphasis of the Scottish universities on philosophy and science has been noted and when Scots in Canada had anything to say about university curricula they reflected this influence. When William Brydone Jack, a graduate of St. Andrews and a student of Sir David Brewster, a famous mathematician, arrived at King's College Fredericton, he soon made his influence felt. Having been appointed professor of mathematics and natural philosophy, Jack challenged the dominance of the classics at the college and sought to expand the curriculum to include more "practical subjects."

He persuaded the College Council to acquire a fine equitorial telescope, then the best of its kind in North America, and initiated a course in surveying which led at a later date to the establishment of a department of engineering.[26]

McCulloch's curriculum at Pictou included classics, Hebrew, history, philosophy, mathematics and natural philosophy.[27] When John Strachan was discussing the curriculum for King's College, York, in 1826, his scheme called for

1.   Classical Literature, including English Composition
2.   Mathematics, Practical and Theoretic
3.   Natural History, including Botany
4.   Natural Philosophy and Chemistry
5.   Moral Philosophy and Divinity
6.   Surgery and Anatomy.[28]

At Queen's the early curriculum was largely a replica of that being offered at Edinburgh. This is not surprising since the teaching staff in 1846-7 consisted of three Edinburgh men (the Rev. John Machar, the Rev. James Williamson, the Rev. George Romanes) and two other Scots, the Rev. James George (St. Andrews) and the Rev. Hugh Urquhart. The subjects listed in the Queen's College calendar of 1845-6 were theology, church history and biblical criticism, oriental languages, natural philosophy [physics], moral philosophy, logic, mathematics and classics. The natural philosophy course included "Mechanics, Hydrostatics and Hydrodynamics, Pneumatics, Light, Heat, Fixed and Locomotive Steam Engines, Electricity, Galvanism, Magnetism, Electromagnetism and Electro-Chemistry."

While Scottish colleges in Canada tended to reproduce the Scottish curricula, they did not follow the Scottish abandonment of the BA degree. Queen's showed the effects of the Scottish attempt to revive the BA after 1826. The earliest Queen's curriculum provided for a BA in three years and an MA in four; but after the Scottish universities abandoned the BA, following the Report of the Royal Commission of 1858, it was retained at Queen's and by other Canadian universities such as McGill[29].

V

It was inevitable that the Scottish influence on Canadian education should be largely a Presbyterian influence. William Rattray in his work, *The Scot in British North America*, has described the impact of Presbyterian thinking on the general cast of the Scottish mentality: "Whatever may be thought of the dogmatic value of the Presbyterian standards, it is certain that they deepened the sense of duty, the feeling of manly independence and the impatience of external restraint in matters of faith and practice."[30] The influence of Presbyterianism was apparent in Canadian education, particularly in the dominantly Presbyterian colleges. One gets a picture of the polemical, Calvinist tone of theology at Queen's in its early days, in the description of the courses in theology as described in the calendar for 1845-6. They included

> Lectures on the Person, Character and Offices of Christ, as disclosed in various ways, both in the Old and New Testament . . . . Lectures on the Principal Doctrinal Heresies of the Primitive Christian Church, and the various modifications of these heresies presented in modern times [including, no doubt, Arminianism]. Lectures on the leading Doctrinal tenets of the various Christian Churches.

and also

> Lectures on the connection between Moral Philosophy and Christian Theology and particularly on the principles of moral obligation.[31]

The clearest examples of the undiluted Presbyterian tradition were the theological colleges such as Knox, which was established in Toronto in 1844 by the Presbyterian Church of Canada, the offshoot of the Free Church in Scotland, and Presbyterian College, which was established in Montreal in 1868. Presbyterian College had a charter similar to that of Knox and, at the outset, a staff of three who were all graduates of Knox.

D.H. MacVicar, the first Principal of Presbyterian College, was almost a type figure of the solid Calvinist Presbyterian. His lectures always showed the influence of such divines as Charles Hodge and Jonathan Edwards as well as Calvin himself. J.H. MacVicar's *Life* of his father indicates the character of D.H. MacVicar's lectures and of his theology: "In the earlier days . . . the doctrine of election, perhaps, received larger attention in the classroom than later on, though it was never tabooed. He believed too intensely in the sovereignty of God to pass it over in silence; but he grew accustomed to expect questions at this point. There was sure to be some one ready to voice a personal difficulty about reconciling the mission to preach a free gospel with the inscrutable decrees."[32]

According to MacVicar's son, his father would meet this criticism by drawing a church on the blackboard with the people sitting in the pews. "Now," he would say, "Jones here may be elect, Smith over there may not. The preacher in the pulpit knows nothing about that, however, and the only thing he can do is preach the Gospel to both."[33]

While Presbyterianism was dominant in the theological colleges it also exercised a strong influence upon the general Scottish philosophy of education. Presbyterians brought to the educational world certain attitudes which were not uniquely Presbyterian, but merely Christian; but they were put forward by the Presbyterians with particular vigour and consistency. One was the idea that the whole universe was made and controlled by the Lord: "This is my Father's world." The tremendous emphasis of Calvin and other Reformers on God's sovereignty was basic in Presbyterian educational theory. Related to it was the proposition that all our vocations and schemes of education are for the Lord. Thus a writer in the

Canadian Christian Examiner and Presbyterian Review for August, 1839, asserted, "Education consists, not merely in a knowledge of reading, writing and cyphering . . . but in bringing to maturity the powers of the mind, and in giving them such a direction, and finding them such employment, as will best answer the ends of our creation; namely the glory of God, and the enjoyment of his favor."[34]

William Snodgrass, the Principal of Queen's from 1866 to 1877, presented a very clear exposition of the Christian approach to learning in his inaugural address, entitled *The Sacredness of Learning*. Snodgrass attributed all truth and all knowledge to the great, sovereign God, the author of all things. He asserted that the distinction between sacred and secular learning was a man-made distinction. Really all learning comes from God, "the Author of that volume which is usually, but not consistently, divided into the two great sections, natural and revealed."[35] Snodgrass asserted that God's authority is decisively determined when we appeal to his written word. He adjured the students at Queen's:

> Gentlemen, this authority is supreme. By the holiest and most constraining considerations you are bound to defer to it. Recognize it in every exercise of those intellectual powers and moral sentiments with which your Maker hath endowed you. Recognize it in all the sources and means of instruction, which, by a divinely beneficent arrangement, profusely and invitingly surround you – in your perusal of the records of history, every page of which bears convincing testimony to the invisible but omnipresent hand that holds the direction and shapes the issue of all events in your study of the book of nature where each relation you observe, each law you discover, each symbol you interpret, is an exponent of the marvellous skill with which the Father of lights both, everywhere, on land and skies, on air and seas, photographed the glory of his perfections in your inquiries into the physical structure and spiritual organization of the individual man, and into the universal conditions, diversifying distinctions, and ultimate destiny of humanity, all of which demand the belief, as they are pregnant with the evidence of, a moral government.[36]

Lord Elgin, who was a Presbyterian, provided an example of the conjunction of Christian theology and educational philosophy in his speech at the opening of the Toronto Normal and Model School on July 4, 1851. Asserting that the foundation of the Canadian Common School System was "laid deep in the rock of our common Christianity," Elgin continued:

> While the very semblance of dictation is to be avoided, it is desired and earnestly recommended and confidently expected that every child who attends our Common Schools shall learn that he is a being who has an interest in eternity as well as in time; that he has a Father, towards whom he stands in a closer and more affecting relationship

than to any earthly father, and that that Father is in heaven
.... That that Father's kingdom may come, and that he has a duty
which like that of the sun in our celestial system, stands in the centre
of his moral obligations, shedding upon them a light which they in
their turn reflect and absorb, the duty of striving to prove by his life
and conversation the sincerity of his prayer that the Father's will may
be done upon earth as it is done in heaven.[37]

VI

While some Canadian Scots brought orthodox Christian thought to bear
upon the development of higher education, others, more liberal in theology, helped to carry the universities out of the orbit of Christian orthodoxy. Herein lies much of the importance of G.M. Grant at Queen's and of
the Scottish-Canadian philosophers John Watson, Clark Murray and
George Paxton Young. They helped to carry Queen's, McGill and Toronto away from their Christian origins and into the position of pluralistic, non-sectarian universities.[38]

   Watson, Young and Murray were appointed to chairs of philosophy at
Queen's, Toronto and McGill respectively in 1871-2. Under their influence philosophy achieved an influence over the whole tone of university
life which it has not since recaptured. They succeeded three professors of
philosophy who were clergymen and whose primary interest was theology: James Beaven at Toronto, James George at Queen's and W.T. Leach
at McGill.[39] Watson, Young and Clark were all trained in Scottish universities (Watson at Glasgow, Young at Edinburgh and Murray at Glasgow
and Edinburgh). All three had orthodox, Presbyterian backgrounds (indeed Young was a Presbyterian clergyman). All three could be classified
as ethical idealists.[40] Each repudiated the supernatural aspects of Christianity in the attempt to devise a rational defence for the ethical values of
Christianity. Watson could well have been speaking for the three in comments which he made on the lectures of his great teacher, Edward Caird,
after the latter's death:

> The close shell of traditional Calvinism was burst .... As time went
> on, and the walls, behind which the traditional philosophy and theol-
> ogy had for so long sheltered themselves, fell as by a miracle, as the
> walls of Jericho collapsed at the sound of the trumpet, it was discov-
> ered that the new philosophy, if it indeed disclosed a new heaven and
> a new earth, did not in reality destroy Christianity but fulfilled it. The
> older men, and especially the older clergymen, who found their fa-
> vourite formulas quietly set aside might grumble and prophesy disas-
> ter, but the younger men, more alive to the advance of scientific dis-
> covery and of an aggressive enlightenment, which threatened to de-
> stroy all faith in higher things, felt that the new philosophy enabled
> them to preserve the essence of religion while giving to it a more
> rational form.[41]

G.M. Grant, who arrived at Queen's as principal in 1877, six years after Watson's appointment, exercised the same liberalizing influence. Like Watson and others he helped to effect the transition at Queen's from an orthodox Presbyterian to an essentially non-sectarian institution. Born in Nova Scotia, the son of Scottish parents, Grant was educated at Pictou Academy and the University of Glasgow where he obtained the highest honours in philosophy. Ordained to the ministry of the Church of Scotland in 1860, he was minister of St. Matthew's Church, Halifax, from 1863 to 1877. He is chiefly remembered as the greatest single influence in the development of Queen's during a long tenure of office, 1877-1902.

Grant prided himself on his moderation. He accepted the findings of the scientists and the biblical critics while insisting that people should be critical about them. In his inaugural speech in 1877 he urged his audience to

> cultivate then a cordial spirit towards criticism and science. Accept thankfully the undoubted results of the one, the facts of the other . . . . Collect all the facts and rightly interpret them and you will find that they prove subversive of all anti-Christian theories. You say that they invade the province of theology proper. Well the theologians first taught them the bad lesson by treating the Bible as an inspired scientific text book.[42]

Grant's early reputation at Queen's was indicated by a student's song at his inauguration. It rejoiced that after years of financial privation, Queen's was being sent "a liberal Grant."[43]

Grant, Watson and the other philosophers, despite their liberalism, still reflected their early Presbyterian backgrounds. Grant's relation to the Presbyterian church was always close and indeed he was one of the architects of Presbyterian union in 1875. Watson always opened his lectures with prayer: "Prevent us, O Lord, in all our doings with thy most gracious favour and further us with thy continual help."[44] The group was in the tradition of Scottish moderation rather than that of the Scottish evangelicals. It was not without significance that Grant was identified with the Auld Kirk, rather than with one of the more evangelical off-shoots of the Auld Kirk such as the Free Church. While Young was a Free Church minister, his reaction to the Free Church was very like that of a moderate.

Sir William Dawson, the great Principal of McGill (1855-1893), on the other hand represented the influence of Christian evangelicalism in the field of higher education. His role was to attempt to counteract the liberalizing influence of Grant and the Scottish philosophers, particularly his own McGill philosopher, Clark Murray.

Dawson, a Nova Scotian Scot, educated at Pictou Academy and the University of Edinburgh, early developed an interest in the geology of Nova Scotia. He was associated with the Scottish scientist Sir Charles

Lyell in investigating the geology and mineralogy of the Maritime provinces. After serving as superintendent of education in Nova Scotia (1950-54) he came to McGill where he served as principal with great distinction over a long period (1855-1893). Dawson was of special importance in establishing the study of science at McGill and in Canada. According to a recent authority he always had a Calvinist suspicion of the Arts faculty as being too humanist.[45] Dawson was a leading protagonist in the scientific and religious controversies of the late nineteenth century. He represented a detailed and sustained attempt to maintain a synthesis between the theories and observations of the scientists and the record of Scripture.

The most spectacular feature of Dawson's career was his sustained attack on the position of Darwin, Huxley, Asa Gray and other evolutionists. Dawson maintained that species were specially created by God and were immutable, although all species, including man, could vary widely and rapidly, within certain limits. As a geologist he utilized a good deal of Canadian data in support of his position. His writings on evolution have been described by a recent authority as "futile, valid, respectable and just plain cranky."[46] He represented a not unsuccessful attempt, in his day, to continue the two theological traditions (natural and revealed) as developed by Paley in the eighteenth century and Hugh Miller in the nineteenth. Under his jurisdiction young Canadians were encouraged to pursue scientific investigation while remaining within the evangelical fold. Thus in its calendar for 1876-7, the Presbyterian College in Montreal could assert:

> The Senate of the Presbyterian College, having a full knowledge of the nature of the training given, and the religious influence exerted on students in the McGill University, confidently recommend parents to send their sons to it, whether they are designed for the Christian Ministry or for any of the learned Professions.[47]

VII

The Scots in Canada were divided on one of the principal problems in relation to university education, the appropriate relationship between the church and the university. Adherents of the Auld Kirk maintained that church-related colleges should include arts and other faculties as well as the theological school. Queen's in its early period came out of an Auld Kirk community. When the university was in the process of establishment, a meeting of its sympathizers held in Toronto on December 10, 1839, passed a resolution "that the circumstances of the Presbyterians in these Provinces require that means be adopted to afford them the benefit of a literary and scientific education, based on scriptural principles."[48]

Adherents of the various groups which had seceded from the Auld Kirk, particularly the Presbyterian Church of Canada (the Canadian projection of the Free Church of Scotland) believed that the arts and science faculties should be entirely under secular control, with the church controlling only the professional training of candidates for the ministry. Thus Knox and Presbyterian College in Montreal represented the Free Church tradition. This distinction between the adherents of the Auld Kirk and its opponents was more the rule in Central Canada than in the Maritimes. Pictou College, under the auspices of the Secession Presbyterian Church, was an example of a church college comprising arts as well as theological training.

Among the leading advocates of a church-controlled arts college were Thomas McCulloch and John Strachan. In Strachan's case, of course, the controlling church was to be the Church of England. In the proposed plan for the organization of King's College, York, which he submitted to Sir Peregrime Maitland, the Lieutenant-Governor of Upper Canada in 1826, he stipulated, "The Principal and Professors, except those of medecine and law, should be clergymen of the Established Church; and no tutor, teacher or officer, who is not a member of that Church, should ever be employed in that institution."

The list of Scots favouring a purely secular university was impressive. Perhaps the most famous pronouncement in support of this position was that of Lord Dalhousie at the laying of the cornerstone of Dalhousie University on May 22, 1820:

> Before I proceed in this ceremony, I think it necessary to state to you, gentlemen, the object and intention of this important work . . . . This College of Halifax is founded for the instruction of youth in the higher Classics and in all Philosophic studies, it is formed in imitation of the University of Edinburgh; its doors will be open to all who profess the Christian religion; to the youth of His Majesty's North American Colonies, to strangers residing here, to gentlemen of the military as well as the learned professions, to all, in short, who may be disposed to devote a small part of their time to study . . . . It is founded upon the principles of religious toleration secured to you by the laws, and upon that paternal protection which the King of England extends to all his subjects.[49]

Thirty years later in Toronto, Lord Elgin displayed the same preference for a non-sectarian university. His views were similar to those of Robert Baldwin, the real architect of university secularization in Toronto, but they were in accordance with Elgin's own philosophy. He vigorously supported the policy of secularizing King's as the University of Toronto and envisaged a strong non-sectarian institution with affiliated divinity schools representing the various denominations. He hoped that Queen's and Victoria would come into the university and agreed only with reluctance to grant a charter to Strachan's new institution, Trinity, as a church-related arts college. He pointed out to Earl Grey, the Colonial Secretary, on October 25, 1850, "At the same time it must be remembered that the object of our recent legislation on the University question has been to set up one great Institution in the Province where a high Educational standard might be maintained and which should give degrees which shall be worth having."[50]

Shortly after the establishment of the University of Toronto, a young Scot, Daniel Wilson, was appointed Professor of History and English Literature. He proved to be one of the leading advocates of the non-sectarian university. Wilson (1816-1892) had been born in Edinburgh and educated at the Edinburgh High School and Edinburgh University, before coming to Toronto in 1853. In 1880 he became President of University College and in 1887 President of the University of Toronto. Wilson's churchmanship was rather unusual for a Scot: he was an Anglican evangelical and one of the founders of Wycliffe College.[51]

Wilson's views on the church-related arts college were similar to those of the Baptists and the Free Church Presbyterians. In 1877 when the Bishop of Huron, Isaac Hellmuth, who was about to establish Western University at London, offered Wilson the position of Provost and Vice-Chancellor at a very considerable salary for that time Wilson was not gratified. Reporting the incident in his diary on May 3, 1877, he described Western as a Protestant university with an Anglican theological faculty and added, "I do not believe in denominational colleges other than theological. Orthodox science is generally another name for shallow bigotry."[52] In a letter to Hellmuth on May 4, Wilson explained:

> I need not assure you of my sympathy in reference to all that pertains to the clear setting forth of evangelical truth, for I have battled for that through evil as well as good in a tolerably unmistakable manner. But I must inform you that I no less strongly desire to see the untrammeled freedom of scientific and philosophic research. Truth has nothing to fear in the long run from the researches of such men as Darwin and Huxley. I think it suffers far more from the shackles with which orthodox zeal would hamper inquiry with the most honest intentions .... Truth has everything to gain from the most absolute freedom of inquiry.[53]

While Queen's as an Auld Kirk institution was originally in the tradition of a church-related university, its constituency changed drastically after the completion of Presbyterian church union in 1875. Queen's was subjected to the Free Church influence and became in effect a non-sectarian university with an affiliated theological college.[54] This dispensation was perfectly acceptable to Grant when he became principal in 1877. During his career in Nova Scotia he had not been keen on the idea of denominational colleges and had favoured the idea of one good interdenominational university for the province. Speaking in March, 1876, Grant deplored the fact that "denominational colleges have been fastened upon us for a generation, and are to be continued forever."[55] He preferred the position of Joseph Howe, the great Nova Scotian reformer, who,

Grant asserted, had advocated "an institution where young Nova Scotians without distinction of class or creed could contend in that literary contest where defeat is no dishonour and where victory ensures modesty."[56] When Grant came to Queen's in the following year he was quite happy to accept the changed status of the university.[57] He was willing to concede to the University of Toronto the whole of the endowment from the land set apart by the province for university education.[58] He did not, of course, conclude that Queen's should merge with the University of Toronto. Instead he conceived of two secular universities, one, the University of Toronto, supported by the provincial government and the other, Queen's, supported by a national private constituency.

Manitoba College, which began classes in Winnipeg in 1869, in a sense represented both the early Queen's and the Knox traditions.[59] The College showed some signs of the Queen's Auld Kirk idea of maintaining the union of arts and theology and late in its career it made a brief experiment (1910-1914) in offering an arts course. It was a classical college which combined mathematics with classics. True to its Scottish background the college also stressed mental and moral philosophy. Yet, under the influence of its early teachers, John Black, James Robertson and George Bryce, it was primarily in the Knox tradition and made training in theology its principal concern.

VIII

The Roman Catholic Scots were in a different position from the Presbyterian Scots in regard to higher education. As members of a religious organization which was largely composed in Canada of other ethnic groups, the French and the Irish, the Scots were not able to dominate church colleges, with the possible exception of St. Francis Xavier, in the manner in which Presbyterian Scots dominated such institutions as Pictou, Queen's, Manitoba College and the Presbyterian divinity schools. However, the Scottish strain was paramount in some of the early colleges, Iona and St. Andrews, and the Scots played a leading role in St. Dunstan's in Prince Edward Island. In the Roman Catholic polity the role of the bishop in the founding of colleges was just as important as that played by Anglican bishops like John Strachan and G.J. Mountain. Three early bishops, Alexander Macdonnell (1762-1840), Angus MacEachern (1759-1835) and Colin MacKinnon (1810-1879), should be particularly noted.

Bishop Macdonnell made a beginning in "higher education" with the establishment of a school in his house at St. Raphael's in Upper Canada in 1821. Like other Protestant and Roman Catholic establishments it commenced as a combination of high school and divinity school.[60] In 1826 the institution opened as Iona College with Fr. W.P. MacDonald as its first rector. In 1828 the bishop reported eight divinity students in the second year, one in the first year and two in philosophy. Macdonnell's removal to Kingston in 1836 ended the career of Iona, which was succeeded by a new institution at Kingston, Regiopolis. The Scottish influence in Regiopolis is clear from the fact that it was established by Bishop Macdonnell in 1838 and its first rector was his nephew, Fr. Angus Macdonnell. Regiopolis secured a university charter in 1866 but was closed in 1869, as a result of the decision of the Ontario government not to support denominational colleges.[61]

The Scots were active in the establishment of colleges in Prince Edward Island. Bishop Angus MacEachern, the first Bishop of Charlottetown, was the moving spirit in the establishment of St. Andrews College. MacEachern, who was born at Kinloch Moidart in Scotland, was trained at the Royal Scots college, Valladolid, Spain. After ordination by the Bishop of Valladolid he served in western Scotland before emigrating to Prince Edward Island.[62] MacEachern, with the support of William Fraser, the first Bishop of Antigonish, established St. Andrews near the head of the Hillsborough River in 1831, with the Reverend Edward Walsh, an Irish priest, as rector. Walsh was succeeded in 1835 by another Irish-born priest, Charles Macdonald.[63] St. Andrews was more the forerunner of a college than a college in its own right. MacMillan, the historian of the early Catholic Church in Prince Edward Island, reports that the curriculum consisted of Greek, Latin, French and mathematics, as well as the subjects taught in an ordinary commercial course.[64] The school attempted to secure students from the Protestant community in Prince Edward Island and exacted no religious tests from its students. Under MacEachern the emphasis was no doubt heavily Scottish. He was always anxious that his ordinands should have the Gaelic and wanted his seminarians studying in Quebec to read Gaelic so that they could minister to the Gaelic-speaking Roman Catholics of the Maritimes.[65] Unfortunately his quasi-Scottish college was short-lived. After a series of rapid changes in staff it was closed in 1844.

St. Dunstan's College succeeded St. Andrews in 1855 after an interval of eleven years and provided a new area of activity for Scottish educators. St. Dunstan's in its early period had a curriculum the rough equivalent of a French classical college, and prepared candidates for the priesthood for further study in the seminaries of Quebec and Montreal. Its first rector, Angus MacDonald, was succeeded in 1869 by James MacDonald (1869-1880). The names of appointees to the teaching staff under James MacDonald indicates the variegated character of the faculty: James Charles MacDonald, Michael J. Macmillan, Cornelius O'Brien, Stanislaus Boudreault and Allan J. MacDonald. A subsequent list of the staff in 1889-90 indicates the same ethnic variety: J.C. MacDonald, Greek and mathematics; J.A. MacDonald, physics and mental philosophy; J.A. Blaquière, Latin and French; Ronald MacDonald, history and mathematics; J.M. Sullivan, bookkeeping, business and telegraphy; W.P. McNally, French and English.[66]

In Nova Scotia, as in the other two Maritime colonies, the Scots were associated first with a small, short-lived college and afterwards with a larger one which survived. Bishop Colin MacKinnon, the Bishop of Arichat, was the moving force in the establishment of Arichat Seminary on Cape Breton Island in 1853. Dr. John Cameron, perhaps the most distinguished of the early Scottish Roman Catholic educators, became its principal in 1854. Born in Antigonish and educated at Rome, Cameron has been described as "a thorough scholar and an eloquent preacher."[67] Later, in 1877, he became Bishop of Arichat.

In 1855 the seminary was moved to Antigonish and its character changed. Instead of an advanced seminary, the plan at Arichat, it became a 'college for the public' and was intended to be a training school not only for priests, but also for others. Thus it became St. Francis Xavier College (it was so named in 1859), with a curriculum resembling that of a French-Canadian college. Many of its graduates proceeding towards the priest-hood went to the Laval Seminary. St. Francis Xavier was dominantly but not completely under Scottish control. Cameron was its first rector, holding office until 1863. Its initial staff was largely Scottish, including two Camerons, Father William Chisholm, Mr. Rod MacDonald but also Dr. John Schulte. Unlike Presbyterian institutions like Knox and Presbyterian College, Montreal, which began and remained purely theological schools, St. Francis Xavier did not become a theological school, but instead had a long and distinguished career as the most Scottish of the Roman Catholic universities.[68]

IX

A consideration of some leading educators in the latter part of our period provides further evidence of the ubiquitous Scottish influence. Some were Presbyterians; but others made their contributions in other Protestant academic communities. George Douglas began his life as a Presbyterian but made his great contribution in another denomination. His father was a staunch Presbyterian who reared his family in that faith. After the arrival of the family in Montreal in 1832, George was converted to Methodism and in 1850 ordained to the Wesleyan ministry. After holding charges in Bermuda and in several Canadian cities he became Principal of Wesleyan Theological College, Montreal, in 1874. As principal he laid especial emphasis on the study of metaphysics; but he is chiefly noted for his eloquence as a preacher. Rattray asserts, "It is a remarkable fact that the most eloquent preachers of the Methodist Church in Canada are Scots, and Dr. Douglas is one of the most eloquent."[69] A consideration of Douglas's published *Sermons and Discourses* indicated that he was indeed eloquent in the nineteenth century sense with a highly rhetorical style.[70]

R.A. Fyfe (1816-1878), a Canadian Scot, was ordained to the Baptist ministry and was briefly (1843-44) Principal of the Canadian Baptist College in Montreal.[71] Fyfe played a large role in changing the thinking of Ontario Baptists in regard to education. Prior to 1850 they were opposed to church participation in education at any level, except for the training of the clergy. While opposing King's College in the period 1827-1849, the Baptists made no effort to establish a Baptist college, nor did they favour denominational participation in primary and secondary education. In the 1850s Fyfe undertook to change the thinking of his fellow Baptists. In the Baptist periodical, the *Christian Messenger*, in an article bearing the unobtrusive title, "A Proposal," Fyfe suggested founding an academy in a western locality, where Baptist parents might send their sons and daughters. He proposed that the academy should provide theological training and a good secondary school under Christian supervision. He asserted that education under religious influence was the best training for other spheres of Christian activity as well as for the pulpit. Largely as a result of Fyfe's influence the Canadian Literary Institute (later Woodstock College) was established. Under Fyfe's principalship three departments (preparatory, literary and theological) were developed. So was begun a train of events which culminated in the establishment of McMaster University in 1887.

Malcolm MacVicar, a leading Baptist teacher, was a brother of the equally redoubtable Presbyterian academic, Donald Harvey MacVicar, the Principal of Presbyterian College, Montreal. Malcolm MacVicar, born in Argyleshire, Scotland, held various academic posts in the United States and was appointed to Toronto Baptist College in 1888.[72] He played an active role at Baptist College, representing the institution in negotiations with the University of Toronto in 1884 and was the first Chancellor of McMaster University.

In Winnipeg, St. John's College was derived from a church school, Red River Academy, which was established in 1833. During the regime of the first Bishop of Rupert's Land, David Anderson, the Academy became a theological college as well as a secondary school. Anderson mentioned St. John's Collegiate School and St. John's College in his charge of 1850; but by 1865 little was left of the institution but some dilapidated buildings. The revival and real beginnings of St. John's College was the work of the second Bishop of Rupert's Land, Robert Machray (1832-1904).[73] Born in Aberdeen, Machray had been trained at King's College, Aberdeen, where he took the traditional Scottish combination of courses in mathematics, natural philosophy and moral philosophy. Later he graduated from Sidney Sussex College, Cambridge. A Presbyterian during his early career, Machray joined the Church of England while at Cambridge and in 1856 took holy orders. Shortly after his consecration as bishop in 1865 he displayed great concern for the development of education in his diocese at every level. Under his vigorous support St. John's was reorganized and was incorporated in 1871. The Scottish influence in the college was exercised not only by Machray himself but also by others including the first warden, Reverend John McLean, a classmate of Machray's at Aberdeen and a prizeman in Latin, Greek, natural and moral philosophy;[74] Canon S.P. Matheson, who became Professor of Exegetical Theology in 1873;

and Canon Robert Machray, the Bishop's nephew, who became Professor of Church History and Liturgics in 1883.

Of the early teachers at Manitoba College, George Bryce, a Canadian Scot, was the real founder, a brilliant and versatile figure, prominent in the life of the college, the Presbyterian Church, the Manitoba and Winnipeg school systems and a prolific writer on the history of Manitoba. His publications included *Manitoba: Its Infancy, Progress, and Present Condition* (London, 1882), *A Short History of the Canadian People* (London, 1887), and the *Life of Lord Selkirk* (1912). Dr. Andrew Baird, one of Bryce's colleagues, wrote, "Dr. Bryce was admirably fitted for his work as a pioneer. Quite competent in his own department, he was versatile and capable of giving help and leadership in all sorts of spheres. Always cheerful, always ready, there were few benevolent or religious enterprises in which he had no hand."[75]

Thomas Hart, a Canadian Scot and another early teacher at Manitoba, had been trained at Queen's and Edinburgh. A quieter type than Bryce, he confined his activities to teaching. Baird wrote dryly that Hart, with fewer outside commitments, "was always on hand and kept the wheels going round. One of the gentlest and kindliest of men, . . . was so memorable that men who had no gift for Greek, which was compulsory in those days, plugged faithfully because even their modest degree of success so pleased their beloved teacher."[76]

Dr. John Mark King, born and trained in Scotland, became Principal of Manitoba College in 1883 and carried on in the Scottish tradition. A graduate of the University of Edinburgh, who had distinguished himself in the departments of philosophy and mathematics and who had supplemented this with post-graduate training at the University of Marburg in Germany, King was a great administrator. A man of penetrating critical judgment, he had unusual gifts as a teacher. According to Baird, "His mind was analytical and delighted in making distinctions between things or opinions which are liable to be confused with each other but which ought to be kept separate. Quite beyond his gifts as a teacher was the impression made by the intensity and weight of his moral character."[77] He had many of the qualities obviously derived from a Calvinist background.

X

The history of a "tradition" is twofold: it is concerned with thought and action. This article has been an account not only of Scottish thought but also of the roles of particular Scots in Canadian education. The role of both the native Scot and also of his Canadian descendant has been to project into Canada a Scottish intellectual tradition. Largely it has been a tradition of Christian orthodoxy and of a Scottish university curriculum, transmitted by Presbyterians like McCulloch, MacVicar, Dawson and Bryce; by other Scottish Protestants like Fyfe, Strachan and Wilson and by Roman Catholic educators like MacEachern, Macdonell and John Cameron. Other Scots, like Grant, Watson, Young and Murray were no less a product of Christian orthodoxy, although they were in reaction against much of the orthodox Christian position.

So much for the background of the Scottish tradition in higher education; but to say that their basic ideas were derived from Scotland is only to tell part of the story of the Scots in Canada. Their chief contribution was to identify themselves with the Canadian environment and to make their ideas part of the intellectual tradition of the Canadian community. Of all the ethnic groups who have come to Canada, the Scots were the quickest in acclimatizing themselves. Witness the long list of Scottish politicians, clergymen, bankers, textile manufacturers, lawyers and others who made so considerable a contribution to Canadian development. The Scots in higher education were part of this tradition. Probably the Scots born in Canada, like Grant and Dawson, were more completely adjusted to the local milieu than were those born in Scotland, like Strachan and Daniel Wilson. Yet Strachan was sufficiently Canadian to realize the importance of developing a native clergy, as distinct from one trained in Great Britain,[78] and Wilson was regarded as sufficiently Canadian to be offered the post of Minister of Public Instruction in the Ontario government in 1875.[79]

The long-run influence of the Scots in Canadian higher education has been profound. In the Roman Catholic world Scots helped to organize colleges which preserved the Scottish identity in a religious community in which the Scots were in a minority. In the Protestant world in Canada the quality of academic life has often reflected the influence of Scottish Calvinism. Its rigorous intellectual discipline tended to produce men with a capacity for sheer hard work and with a penetrating, critical spirit. Thomas McCulloch, the great religious controversialist in Nova Scotia; John King, who delighted to make distinctions between things often confused; G.P. Young, vigorously denouncing competing philosophies as "palpable absurdities,"[80] reflected this influence; but there were many more who displayed the same qualities. They exemplified the Puritan spirit, and the Puritan tradition in Canada was largely, although not completely, Scottish in its origins.

NOTES

1. John H. MacVicar, *Life and Work of Donald Harvey MacVicar* (Toronto: 1904), pp. 69-70. Actually MacVicar was born in Scotland (Dunglass, Argyleshire) although he came to Canada at an early age.
2. Quoted in D.B. Horn, *A Short History of the University of Edinburgh 1556-1889* (Edinburgh: the University Press, 1967), pp. 119-120.

3. George W. Spragge, ed., *The John Strachan Letter Book: 1812-1834* (Toronto: 1946), pp. 67-8, Strachan to Samuel Sherwood, Andrew Stewart and James Stewart, February 14, 1815.

4. R.G. Cant, *The University of St. Andrews, A Short History* (Edinburgh: Oliver and Boyd, 1946), p. 89.

5. Horn, pp. 161-162.

6. James Coutts, *A History of the University of Glasgow* (Glasgow: James Maclehose & Sons, 1909), p. 343.

7. Robert Falconer, "The Scottish Influence in the Higher Education of Canada," *Royal Society of Canada, Proceedings and Transactions*, XXI (1927, Third Series), Section 2, p. 14.

8. Horn, p. 160; Cant, p. 107; Falconer, pp. 13-14.

9. *Memorials of the Life and Ministry of the Rev'd John Machar, D.D.* (Toronto: John Campbell & Son, 1873), pp. 14-15.

10. *Ibid.*, p. 16.

11. For an account of the small Presbyterian theological colleges which functioned in the Maritime Provinces between 1839 and 1863 see D.C. Masters, *Protestant Church Colleges in Canada* (Toronto: University of Toronto Press, 1966), pp. 81-82.

12. Strachan to S. Sherwood, Andrew Stewart and James Stewart, February 14, 1815. There is some evidence that Strachan was originally brought over to Canada for much the same reasons as he later advanced for bringing Scots to Canadian colleges. Henry Scadding, who was one of Strachan's clergy, wrote that the Kingston families who brought Strachan to Canada "when casting about for the education of their sons appear to have looked toward Scotland rather than England, partly perhaps from national predilection, and partly from a reasonable impression that the economic and primitive university system of Scotland was better adapted to a community constituted as that of Upper Canada then was, than the more costly and more complicated systems of England." *Scadding: The First Bishop of Toronto*, p. 12, quoted in W.J. Rattray, *The Scot in British North America* (Toronto: Maclear and Company, 1880) II, 430.

13. Bishop's University, Nicolls Papers, G.J. Mountain to Jasper Nicolls, June 12, 1845.

14. H.A. Nicholson, a medical graduate of Edinburgh, held the chair of natural history at Toronto, 1871-73. Robert Ramsay Wright, an Edinburgh graduate, held the chair of natural science, later biology, at Toronto 1874-1901. From 1901 to 1912 he was vice-president of the university.

15. *Colonial Advocate*, Queenston, May 18, 1824.

16. H.L. Scammell, "The Rise and Fall of a College," *Dalhousie Review*, XXXII (1), 1952. The opponents of the college insisted on the letter of its charter which entitled it to be merely an "Academy" and not a "College."

17. H.M. Tory, *A History of Science in Canada* (Toronto: Ryerson Press, 1939), p. 44.

18. H.L. Scammell, "Why did Thomas McCulloch come to Dalhousie," *Nova Scotia Historical Society Collections, 31, (1957), 68.*

19. One gets a very human picture of Strachan in a letter from young George Ridout to his parents in York shortly after George and his brother Tom had arrived at Strachan's Cornwall school; "Mr. Strachan asked us to night, as we went to get some paper from him whether Tom had rather be called Tom than Tam as he generally calls him. Tom told him which he had rather be called and Mr. Strachan laughed and when he does he laughs hearty." Ontario Archives, *Ridout Papers*, George Ridout to his parents, January 27, 1806.

20. Henry Scadding, *Toronto of Old* (Toronto: Adam, Stevenson & Co., 1873), p. 162.

21. John Strachan, *The Christian religion recommended in a letter to his pupils* (Montreal, 1807).

22. See above.

23. Some of the early Scottish educators can merely be mentioned. At Dalhousie: James Ross, born in Forfarshire and trained at Pictou College, Principal of Dalhousie (1864-1885) and Professor of Ethics and Political Economy; James Gordon MacGregor, a Dalhousie graduate who studied at Edinburgh and held the chair of Physics at Dalhousie (1879-1901); Charles Macdonald, a graduate of Aberdeen and Professor of Mathematics at Dalhousie from 1863 to 1901.

    The McGill Medical Institution, the earliest active part of McGill College, was founded by Dr. Stephenson, a native of Montreal, who studied at Edinburgh. Dr. Caldwell, the first holder of the chair of medicine, was born in Ayrshire, studied in Edinburgh and had been a surgeon in the 13th Regiment of Dragoons. Dr. Robertson, first lecturer in midwifery and diseases of women and children was descended from a Perthshire family and a graduate of Edinburgh. Like Caldwell he had been a military surgeon. See J.J. Heagerty, "Medical Practice in Canada under the British Régime," in *Tory*, pp. 73-75.

24. Masters, pp. 12, 66-68, 70-71.

25. Frances A. Firth, "King's College, Fredericton, 1829-1859," *The University of New Brunswick Memorial Volume*, Alfred G. Bailey, ed. (Fredericton, 1950), p. 25.

26. *Ibid.*, p. 26.

27. Scammell, "The Rise and Fall of a College."

28. J. George Hodgins, *Documentary History of Education in Upper Canada*, 1 (Toronto: Warwick Brothers and Rutter, 1894), 1790-1830, 214. Strachan's proposed curriculum for a college in Montreal in 1815 was very similar to the York proposal. Strachan to Sherwood, A. Stewart, J. Stewart, February 14, 1815.

29. Falconer, p. 14.

30. Rattray, I, 191.

31. *Queen's College Calendar*, 1845-1846, p. 5.

32. MacVicar, pp. 121-122.

33. *Ibid.*, p. 122.
34. *Canadian Christian Examiner and Presbyterian Review*, August, 1839, p. 252.
35. William Snodgrass, *The Sacredness of Learning*, Address delivered at the Opening of Session 1864-5, Queen's College, Kingston, 1864, p. 13.
36. *Ibid.*, pp. 9-10.
37. Toronto *Globe*, July 5, 1871. Elgin's immediate concern in this speech was primary and secondary education; but it indicates a general attitude which is relevant to this paper, since Elgin was also concerned with higher education, i.e. the problem of the University of Toronto.
38. John Irving, "The Development of Philosophy in Central Canada from 1850 to 1900," *Canadian Historical Review*, XXXI (1950), 252-287.
39. Two of these three, Leach and George, were Scots, the former educated at Edinburgh and the latter at St. Andrews and Glasgow. Beaven was English and a most rigid Anglican.
40. Murray was more difficult to classify than Watson and Young. Irving describes his final position as "eclectic idealism." Irving, p. 279.
41. John Watson, "Edward Caird as a Teacher and Thinker," *Queen's Quarterly*, XVI (1909), 303-313.
42. *Queen's College Journal*, December 15, 1877, pp. 5-6.
43. W.L. Grant and F. Hamilton, *Principal Grant* (Toronto: Morang & Co. Limited, 1904), p. 206.
44. T.R. Clover and D.D. Calvin, *A Corner of Empire* [Queen's], (Cambridge: At the University Press, 1937), p. 146; Irving, p. 272.
45. Charles F. O'Brien, *Sir William Dawson, A Life in Science and Religion* (Philadelphia: American Philosophical Society, 1971), p. 2. For other material on Dawson's career see also Sir William Dawson, *Fifty Years of Work in Canada Scientific and Educational* (London and Edinburgh: Ballantyne, Hanson & Co., 1901).
46. O'Brien, p. 144.
47. *Annual Calendar Presbyterian College Montreal*, Session 1876-77, p. 16.
48. *Queen's University Domesday Book*, 1831-1924, p. 32.
49. Quoted in D.C. Harvey, *An Introduction to the History of Dalhousie University* (Halifax: McCurdy Printing Company, 1938), pp. 19-20. Dalhousie did not persevere in the plan of making the College an imitation of Edinburgh.
50. *The Elgin-Grey Papers 1846-1852* (Ottawa: J.O. Patenaude, King's Printer, 1937) Public Archives of Canada, II, 726-727, Elgin to Grey, October 25, 1850.
51. Scottish episcopalians were usually high, not evangelical.
52. H.H. Langton, *Sir Daniel Wilson* (Edinburgh: Nelson, 1929), p. 88.
53. *Ibid.*, pp. 88-89.
54. That the members of the Church of Scotland were anxious to maintain Queen's as a Presbyterian institution was indicated by a pamphlet published in 1871, *Presbyterian Union and the College Question* (Kingston,

1971), by an alumnus of Queen's College. The alumnus argued that the Church of Scotland must reject union with the Canada Presbyterian Church if its members insisted upon secularization of Queen's.

55. Grant and Hamilton, p. 184.

56. *Ibid.*, p. 185.

57. Masters, p. 110. The footing of Queen's had been a delicate point in the negotiations leading to the union of 1875. An arrangement was effected which left Queen's nominally Presbyterian, but which virtually transformed it into a private institution. Hitherto, the governing body, the Board of Trustees, had been elected by the Synod from a list of persons nominated by the individual congregations. After union, the Board became a self-perpetuating body. Theoretically the corporation of the University consisted of the communicants of the Presbyterian Church in Canada; but practically the church as a body had no control of the university.

58. Grant and Hamilton, pp. 208-9.

59. Masters, pp. 93-94; A.B. Baird, The Story of Manitoba College, radio script, February 12, 1930.

60. Lawrence K. Shook, *Catholic post-secondary education in English-speaking Canada: A History* (Toronto: University of Toronto Press, 1971), pp. 18-19.

61. *The Universities of Canada Their History and Organization,* Appendix to the Report of the Ontario Minister of Education, 1896 (Toronto: Warwick Bros. & Rutter, 1896), pp. 142-143.

62. Rev. John C. MacMillan, *The Early History of the Catholic Church in Prince Edward Island* (Quebec: Evenment Printing Company, 1905), pp. 51-55.

63. Shook, p. 37.

64. MacMillan, p. 293.

65. Shook, p. 14. When MacEachern was in failing health he stipulated that a possible coadjutor should be able to speak English, French and Gaelic. He preached a sermon in Gaelic shortly before his death. MacMillan, pp. 300-301.

66. Shook, pp. 39-44.

67. Rattray, III, 845-846.

68. Shook, pp. 75-78.

69. Rattray, III, 842.

70. See Douglas's "Educational Address" in his *Discourses and Addresses* (Toronto: William Briggs, 1894), pp. 299-311.

71. A.J. MacLachlan, "Canadian Baptists and Public Questions before 1850," unpublished BD thesis, McMaster University, R. Hamilton, "The Founding of McMaster University," unpublished BD thesis, McMaster University. For a brief biographical note on Fyfe see *The Universities of Canada*, pp. 128-129.

72. In 1881 the Theological Department of the Canadian Literary Institute was moved to Toronto where it became the Toronto Baptist College.

73. Rev. Charles H. Mockridge, *The Bishops of the Church of England in Canada and Newfoundland* (Toronto: F.N.W. Brown, 1896), pp. 209-230; T.C.B. Boon, *The Anglican Church from the Bay to the Rockies* (Toronto: Ryerson Press, 1962), pp. 67-70, 95-96; Masters, pp. 87-88; Rattray, Vol. III, p. 847.

74. After his consecration as Bishop of Saskatoon in 1874 Bishop McLean founded Emmanuel College, Saskatoon.

75. Baird, *op. cit.*, Rattray, III, 848-9.

76. Baird, *op. cit.*

77. *Ibid.*

78. Strachan, "An Appeal to the Friends of Religion and Literature, in behalf of the University of Upper Canada," [1827], Hodgins, *Documentary History of Education in Upper Canada,*" I, 217.

79. Langton, p. 86.

80. John Watson, *op. cit.*

FOURTEEN

The Scot
as Politician

A. Margaret MacLaren Evans

The first task of Scottish emigrants to the New World was to acquire a home and means of livelihood. As soon as it was accomplished, many of them, accustomed to years of struggle for economic and political freedom in their own land, began to turn their attention to public affairs.[1] Politically articulate Scots made their appearance in the British colonies which are today Canada towards the end of the eighteenth century. In 1789, James Glenie, a brilliant St. Andrew's graduate recently turned lumberman in New Brunswick, was elected to the Colonial Assembly. There he rapidly came to the front by his fearless attacks on what he called the "Governor's pitiful Junto" for their system of land granting, their policy in military matters, their favouritism toward the Anglican Church, and their obstruction of measures passed by the Assembly. He lost support, however, when he went so far as to attempt a vote of censure of the governor, and the popular movement which he had begun collapsed for want of a leader when he left New Brunswick. Glenie was far from being the "violent Democrat and Jacobin" that the government had labelled him. He and his supporters had been motivated less by principle than by envy of the power and patronage of office. Yet they had made some claims concerning the constitutional rights of an assembly which were forerunners of the Reformers' claims of the next century.[2]

In the politics of Quebec in the same period, a Scot from Edinburgh, Dr. Adam Mabane, was prominent on the side opposing reform. After arriving in 1760 in the lowly position of surgeon's mate in the army, he had risen steadily in his profession, and in 1764 Governor James Murray had made him a councillor and a judge in the Court of Common Pleas. "Possessing marked ability, a strong character, and a warm Scottish heart," Mabane was one of the individuals with the most weight in the administration from these first civil appointments until his death in 1792.[3] With his natural sympathy for the French Canadians, and his suspicion of the British merchants in Montreal and Quebec whom he regarded as republican innovators, he was the favoured adviser not only of Murray but also

273

eventually of the next governor, Guy Carleton, and of his successor, Frederick Haldimand, who both believed in conciliating the French. Mabane left a dual imprint on Canadian politics. He was a reactionary who opposed immigration into Quebec and supported the old system, including seigneurialism. His warnings of the dangers in American democracy and of the need for resistance to political change were echoed in later Toryism. At the same time, as the chief builder of the "French party," Mabane expressed the vague hopes of French-Canadian nationalism which were given substance by the French-speaking reformers in the Assembly after 1791. Thus "the two parties to the constitutional struggle of the nineteenth century shared the political heritage of this half-forgotten leader."[4]

It was clear even in the late eighteenth century that the Scots' experience with the English at home would affect their thinking on what should be done about practical questions arising in Canada. When Chief Justice William Smith ruled in 1786 that under the Quebec Act no British-born subject had lost his right to English law, he implied that all those born in Quebec since 1763 came under English law. Not only the French Canadians were horrified, but also Scottish officials such as Mabane in Quebec. To him, used to Scottish law, it was completely illogical to assert that British subjects must have English laws.

Similarly the career of Adam Lymburner, a Kilmarnock Scot who had become one of the wealthy Quebec merchants so much disliked by Mabane, exemplified the influence of the Scottish political background. When amendment of the Quebec Act was being considered following the Loyalist influx into the interior west of Montreal, Lymburner went twice to England as the trusted delegate of the British mercantile minority and the few French Canadians who favoured constitutional revision. In 1788 he urged on the British government the granting of an assembly in which representation would be apportioned "parmi les anciens et les nouveaux sujets."[5] In 1791 he pleaded with the British government not to divide Quebec into two separate provinces. As a merchant he foresaw that the division would create problems in the commerce of the St. Lawrence valley and disputes "très dangereuses à la tranquillité et sécurité." As a Scot he maintained that the difference in religion and civil law between the two parts of the province was not a reason for division. Such a difference was not "de grande conséquence," he argued, using the analogy of his native land: the laws of Scotland were not those of England but were "presque les mêmes comme ceux de France."[6]

But these Scots in the early period of Canada's history, political-minded though they had been, were actually just leaders of groups or local factions. The words "politician" and "party" can be applied only loosely until after 1815 when the colonies first had conditions favouring the emergence of political parties in the modern sense: rapidly enlarging populations, maturing societies and economies, and particularly expanding communications which made possible the spread of political ideas and the discussion of political problems. This chapter on the Scot as politican, which must be highly selective because of its length, will concentrate on the nineteenth century, the time when the bases of the important Canadian political traditions were laid and also when persons of Scottish origin were more readily distinguishable than they are in the twentieth century. And the emphasis will be on the Scots who were in the political arena as elected members in the lower houses and on the issues which engaged them. The many Scottish governors and members of upper houses would constitute a chapter in themselves.

I

As men began to align with Tory and Reform parties, or their successors, the Conservatives and Liberals, Scots ranged themselves, with all the vigour and intensity of their nature, on both sides. Glengarry County in eastern Ontario is a predominantly Scottish area which illustrates this political cleavage. From the days of the original settlement by Scots Loyalists and the later immigration of a disbanded Highland regiment under its chaplain, Alexander Macdonell, the county was Conservative. Macdonell, as well as becoming the first Roman Catholic Bishop of Upper Canada, was a Legislative Councillor who stood resolutely against the Reformers to the point of co-operating with the Orangemen. It is not surprising, then, that the Glengarrian community of Maxville reminisces about staunch Conservatives like James Burton who "fought many strenuous battles . . . against those terrible Grits." But Maxville also remembers unswerving Liberals such as Malcolm J. Fisher who believed in "the political infallibility of Gladstone, Blake and Mowat," and James Ferguson who was "too generous to decry the Conservatives the right to enter within the pearly gates" but felt that "any of that ilk who gained such a favour would be located in the north east corner of Heaven – the most forbidding location."[7]

Since the Scots took their politics with such earnestness and such élan, some of the most entertaining, if disorderly, election contests occurred when the opposing political parties nominated Scottish candidates. In 1841 the Canada Company brought the prestigious James McGill Strachan into Huron County to oust the individualistic Dr. William "Tiger" Dunlop, a descendant of Robert the Bruce. The "Tiger," as a Canada Company officer, had promoted the settlement of that western part of the Company's tract in Upper Canada, but had become increasingly critical of the Company's policies. The story of the Huron election is a medley of bonneted Highlanders, marching children, blocked roads, military aid rushed from London to quell the threatening battle, a partisan returning officer, and finally investigation by a select committee which declared Dunlop the victor according to the "legal" votes.[8]

While it is easy to see the political enthusiasm of the Scots, it is more difficult to identify the factors which determined their party allegiance.

Many nineteenth century emigrants left the British Isles with liberal political ideas formed by events there, but they did not necessarily stay of the same mind in the different environment of America. For many Scots, as for English and Irish, migration had a conservatizing effect. Patrick Shirreff reported after his tour of North America that "a feeling of toryism pervaded most people in the Canadas" with whom he had come in contact; he believed that men usually changed from being Whigs "after sharing the pickings of Tory governments."[9] Adam Fergusson also, on his visit to Upper Canada, was assured by the solicitor-general that "however turbulent or discontented individuals may have been prior to their arrival in the province, comfort and plenty soon work wonders."[10] In each colony there were Scots who grew more conservative as they attained prosperity or office. In Nova Scotia, Alexander Stewart, the son of a Scottish Presbyterian minister and himself a proficient lawyer, led a popular attack on the governing clique in the 1820s while he was the member for Cumberland; then, after being appointed an Executive Councillor, he turned to a defence of the Tory system with its checks against too much democracy. And earlier, in the young colonies of the late eighteenth century and the first years of the nineteenth century, Scots had had little reason to be political reformers since they practically controlled the governments: for example, John Fraser, William Grant, Hugh Finlay, James McGill, John Richardson, John Young, James Stuart, in the councils of Lower Canada; and John Munro, Robert Hamilton, Alexander Grant, John McGill, Thomas Scott, William Dickson, James Crooks in those of Upper Canada. In fact, in the latter province around the turn of the century, Scots so predominated in the government that it was called "the Scotch faction" or "the clan."[11]

Nevertheless, as the 1820s and 1830s wore on, numerous Scots manifested varying degrees of reformism and radicalism. They found inspiration in Jacksonian democracy to the south and the liberal movements in Britain and Europe. But most of all their own independent spirit reacted against the privileged oligarchies which were entrenched in British North America, controlling the government, the church and the economy, and overruling the wishes of the people represented in the assemblies. Scots who settled at a distance from the colonial capitals tended to develop a deeper feeling of separateness and of dissatisfaction with government policies. Although geographical and economic groups were never homogeneous politically, the division between the hinterland and the metropolis, between the farmer or fisherman and the urban classes, was reflected in the opposition of the Scots in Cape Breton to the Council of Twelve at Halifax, and of those in the western peninsula of Upper Canada to the Family Compact at Toronto.

Religion was also a strong determinant of party orientations. The Scot in nineteenth century Canada was affected both by the religious disputes of his native country and by the religio-political controversies on this side of the ocean. Here the Church of Scotland and the Church of England were very similar in their conservatism and social respectability, their urban character and their belief in a strong tie between church and state. Generally the Scots who belonged to either of these churches were Tories, whereas the Reform supporters came from the Dissenting churches with their special grievances such as the clergy reserves in Upper Canada or the government's refusal of an endowment to Pictou Academy in Nova Scotia. The Academy was a Presbyterian institution for higher learning founded in 1816 by the scholarly Thomas McCulloch, a Secession Church minister and educationalist from Renfrewshire. The Provincial Assembly's continuing inability to get its bill for a permanent grant passed in the Council pointed up the faults in the system of government and gave rise to a reform movement led by the Pictou Secessionists. Their organ for open criticism of the government was the *Colonial Patriot*, a weekly begun in 1827 and edited by Jotham Blanchard who had been a pupil of McCulloch. For the Scots of the area who adhered to the Church of Scotland, however, McCulloch's views were too radical. The Kirkmen sided with the Council of Twelve and in 1831 launched another weekly, the *Pictou Observer*, as the mouthpiece of Scottish conservatism. So strong was the politico-religious discord in Pictou that at one point the sheriff built a fence ten feet high across the main street to keep the contenders apart.[12]

The two Pictou weeklies demonstrate not only the interconnection between the religious and the political convictions of the Scots, but also the relation between politics and the founding of newspapers, a sizable number of which were managed or edited by Scots. Unlike the modern "independent" press, these papers took sides openly in the political conflicts of the day. G.M. Grant has remarked that at that time "it was almost impossible to be an editor without being a politician."[13] For a populace without telephone, automobile, radio and television, newspapers were about the only means of public information and were very influential. Indeed, Joseph Howe, who began as a mild Tory and became the leading Maritime Reformer, credited his conversion to the "Pictou Scribblers."[14]

Family was another component in the partisanship of a Scot. If he was born of a Liberal or a Conservative father in Canada, he was likely to maintain the same party connection and hand it on to his children. Some of the families became virtually political dynasties. The well-educated John Young of Falkirk, Scotland, settled in Nova Scotia in 1815 with his sons William and George; they were all to be famous in the affairs of that province. John, whose "Letters of Agricola" published in the *Acadian Recorder* stimulated the improvement of agriculture, represented Sydney in the Assembly for twelve years. George, a writer like his father, founded and edited the weekly *Novascotian* in Halifax, and was one of the first reporters of the proceedings of the Provincial Assembly. He and his brother were associates with Howe in the Reform opposition which worked successfully for a system whereby the government would depend for tenure on its command of a majority in the elected House and would thus be responsible to the people. William, a shrewd lawyer who would be the distinguished Chief Justice of Nova Scotia for the last twenty years of his life, was chosen Liberal leader in 1854 and elected premier in 1859. Throughout the 1850s he was active in the discussion of the topics vital to Nova Scotians: reciprocity with the United States, the public school system, and integration of the provinces by a maritime or larger union.

The Laird family had a similarly long relationship with the politics of Prince Edward Island. The father, Alexander, a Scottish farmer of high character who migrated from Renfrewshire in 1819, represented Queen's County for sixteen years. He was a Reform colleague of George Coles, the head of the first "responsible" ministry in the Island. Both of Laird's sons rose to be Liberal ministers too – Alexander in the province and David at Ottawa. The latter, the founder of the Charlottetown *Patriot*, spoke out against the Quebec scheme for federal union in 1864 because it did not provide for settlement of his province's perennial land problem or for communications with the mainland. In 1873 he was a member of the delegation which, having reached agreement on these matters with the Dominion government, brought Prince Edward Island into Confederation. Taking his seat as a new member in the House of Commons just at the time of the Pacific Scandal, "Dour Davie," always "the keeper of an alert Presbyterian conscience,"[15] proceeded to denounce the government of John A. Macdonald for its lack of morality. His maiden speech resulted in instant Cabinet rank as Minister of the Interior under Alexander Mackenzie, and that was followed by appointment in 1876 as the first Lieutenant-Governor of the North West Territories – a big step from his Island home.

But some Scots politicians did not keep to the party affiliation of their families. Oliver Mowat, who by the 1890s was the Grand Old Man of the Canadian Liberal party, was the son of the Caithness immigrant, John Mowat, one of the leading Conservatives in Kingston. Some other Scots changed their political opinions several times during their careers. William McDougall was one of these. A smooth and capable politician, but prone to take up with each new movement, he began as a radical at mid-century, modified to become one of the foremost Liberals in the decade preceding Confederation, endorsed representation according to population as the remedy for the united Province of Canada, and then abandoned it for the principle of the double majority when he accepted office in the government of John Sandfield Macdonald and L.V. Sicotte in 1862. After 1867 he stayed on in the "coalition" ministry at Ottawa, in 1875 was elected to the Ontario Legislature as an Independent, and in 1878 returned to the House of Commons as a Conservative. "Wandering Willie" had been a source of embarrassment to his earlier Reform co-workers; he was an uncertain colleague of John A. Macdonald also. As the dispute over the northwest boundary of Ontario dragged on, he warned Macdonald that if it were "not soon disposed of," he and the other Ontario politicians who had seceded from the Liberals would be compelled to make their "peace with Blake & Co."[16] Still, Mowat and McDougall were exceptions. The pattern among Scottish politicians was usually one of hereditary party identification and fervent party loyalty.

II

In the rapidly changing provinces of the early nineteenth century, the small ruling elites were sure to be challenged by Scots and others who wanted governments more popularly-based and responsive to public opinion. In Upper Canada the Constitution of 1791 and the frontier environment, in which not many people had the time and the aptitude for office, had combined to produce a government by the few – the so-called Family Compact. The most powerful member of the Compact was John Strachan, the indomitable little Aberdeen schoolmaster who had come to Kingston in 1799 without money or influence, considering provincial politics "hardly worth notice,"[17] but who had gone on to dominate for two decades the Legislative and Executive Councils. Imbued with characteristic Scottish concern for religion and education, Strachan became the first Anglican Bishop of Toronto, trained a whole generation of future political leaders in his own schools for the "sons of gentlemen," presided over the first provincial Board of Education, and began two institutions of higher learning – King's College and Trinity College. His political design for the province was essentially conservative: Upper Canada should be a balanced society in the Burkean sense with aristocratic leadership and an established church, and should be strongly identified with the British Empire and loyal to Britain. Yet his anti-democratic concept of government was entirely compatible with material progress. Strachan and his colleague William Allan, another transplant from Aberdeen, were both interested in the promotion of ambitious projects in land settlement, banking and canal-building. Allan exemplified the purposeful Scottish businessman in politics. As merchant, first President of the Bank of Upper Canada, Canada Company commissioner, first Governor of the British America Assurance Company and first President of the Toronto Board of Trade, he was the Compact's principal link with the commercial and financial world.

At the same time in Upper Canada, political radicalism was given an impetus by Robert Fleming Gourlay and reached its peak with William Lyon Mackenzie. The careers of these two Scots had many likenesses. They were the same egotistical, cantankerous and aggressive type, born muckrakers, fearless in exposing political abuses and unrestrained in their harangues against the government. Gourlay began innocently enough after his arrival from Fifeshire in 1817 by seeking statistics on economic conditions so that he might write a guide for emigrants. But his questionnaire to the settlers also invited their opinions on what was retarding provincial progress. Even at this stage Strachan sensed the strain of radicalism in Gourlay: "the man was a dangerous incendiary."[18] The Compact's suspicions were fully aroused when Gourlay organized a series of

279

township meetings at which petitions to Britain would be drawn up and representatives chosen for a provincial convention. In Tory eyes such activities savoured of subversion and republicanism. When prosecutions of Gourlay for criminal libel failed, he was tried under the alien clause of the Sedition Act of 1804 and banished from the province.

Similarly Mackenzie, of humble Dundee background, seemed harmless at the outset. His biting editorials in the *Colonial Advocate* made that weekly the main anti-government organ in the 1820s. Nevertheless, he was the spokesman not of radicalism but of agrarian conservatism in his attacks on the Compact's economic policies. Like the rest of the Reformers, Mackenzie seems parochial and reactionary when his insistence upon economic retrenchment is compared with the forward-looking provincial schemes of the Scots in the government. In his political views in the 1830s, however, he swung decidedly to the left. The Seventh Report of the Select Committee on Grievances which he chaired in 1835 was an omnibus condemnation of Compact rule. While he was increasingly convinced that fundamental constitutional change was necessary and that there was no hope of obtaining it by appeals to London, he was also coming to admire the American elective system. By 1837 he was proclaiming in his new paper, *The Constitution*, that Upper Canada would achieve real self-government only by resort to arms and separation from Great Britain. "The clan Mackenzie was at war again with England," comments Mackenzie's biographer.[19]

As in the Gourlay incident, the oligarchy equated democratic reform with disloyalty, this time with some justification. In his disillusionment with Britain, Mackenzie had said, "I am less loyal than I was." Gourlay, on the other hand, had been no rebel. He thoroughly disapproved of the Mackenzie uprising, and was in fact one of the early proponents of a union of British North America in order to bind it closer to the mother country. The government contained the threat posed by Mackenzie almost as easily as that by Gourlay two decades earlier. Mackenzie's extremism had split the Reform movement and alienated the moderates; in the end he led a mini-rebellion and like Gourlay was exiled. Some years before, Thomas Talbot, dismayed at the Reform sympathies among the Highland settlers in his tract north of Lake Erie, had predicted that they would become "most inveterate Rebels."[20] In 1837, however, Mackenzie's help came not from the Scottish Presbyterians in the western peninsula but from sections of the province settled largely by Americans. The option offered between Strachan, stability and the British connection on the one side, and Mackenzie, violence and "Yankee" republicanism on the other, made very clear the conservative bias of the great majority of Scots as of other Upper Canadians.

Although the province would have had a more tranquil history without the assertive Scots, Strachan, Gourlay and Mackenzie, the three with all their faults had been sincere in pursuing what they thought was best for Upper Canada. Strachan, if too high-handed and too exclusive in his point of view, perhaps "the most imperious and obdurate tory who has left his stamp on Canadian history,"[21] had done much for cultural and economic advancement and had established the Tory political tradition which would carry forward into mid-century Conservatism. Gourlay and Mackenzie, for their part, had established a radical Reform tradition emphasizing anti-privilege and anti-monopoly, American democratic principles, the separation of church and state, and economic policies to serve an agrarian society. Gourlay had prepared the stage for the Reform leaders of the 1820s by making the different communities of Upper Canada aware that they had common grievances which called for common political remedies, and by supplying Reform editors and assembly-men with a martyr, for the conservative forces had over-reacted in their proceedings against him. Mackenzie's rebellion along with that in Lower Canada ultimately cut through the political confusion in the colonies by prompting Lord Durham's investigation, the first step towards the peaceful democratic revolution of the 1840s. In the long view of political development, there is surely a place for the agitators like Gourlay and Mackenzie who rouse attention to political ills, even though they themselves are not of the stuff to devise the remedies. W.L. Mackenzie King, at any rate, found great satisfaction in thinking of his grandfather as a "true patriot" who had struggled for the "rights of free men."[22]

In Lower Canada the "state of things" culminating in rebellion in 1837 was characterized by Lord Durham as a "struggle, not of principles, but of races."[23] Although in large measure Durham was right, a glance at the divergence among the Scots alone tempers the impression left by his *Report* that the English-speaking population of the province was all on one side, and the French-speaking on the other. Scots, it is true, were powerful in the British-controlled councils. The "Scotch party" was another name for the Château Clique which managed affairs as the Compact did in Upper Canada. Also, Scots were active in the English-language Tory press, especially in Montreal where both the *Gazette* and the *Herald* crusaded against the French popular party. The bilingual *Gazette* was bought in 1822 by Thomas Andrew Turner of Aberdeenshire. Publishing it in English only, he made it the organ of the commercial interests in the city. The *Herald* had a series of Scots associated with it: William Gray and Mungo Kay as founders, to whom John Strachan advanced some of the necessary money; Archibald Ferguson and Robert Weir as subsequent owners; Dr. Alexander Christie and Adam Thom as editors. The paper's bias was especially strong under Thom, a lawyer and schoolteacher, who wrote the abusive "Anti-Gallic Letters" and advocated severe punishment for the rebels of 1837-38.

On the other hand, there were Scottish editors and members in the *canadien*-dominated Assembly who worked with the French Canadians for reform. The best-known was John Neilson, a man well informed on the currents of political thought in the western world and respected for his integrity. He had come from Kirkcudbrightshire in 1790 as a protégé of his uncle, William Brown, owner of the bilingual *Quebec Gazette*, and later inherited the journal. Under his direction for over half a century, it was one of the principal papers in the province. Neilson, as a member of the Assembly after 1818, evinced a liberalism "of a sober and sedate cast,"[24] which led to warm friendship and close political collaboration with the French-Canadian leader, Louis-Joseph Papineau. For some years Neilson had prestige in the French party as high as that of Papineau. On two occasions the Assembly sent him to England as their very effective representative: in 1823 with Papineau to oppose the proposed union of the Canadas, and in 1828 with Papineau's cousin, Denis Viger, and Augustin Cuvillier to urge that the Assembly should have a larger voice in the government of the colony. In the early 1830s, however, the moderate Neilson, who still thought that the Constitution of 1791 could be made to work without radical change, drew apart from the extremist Papineau, who like Mackenzie in the sister province had come to believe an elective council and other amendments essential. Neilson's editorials in the *Gazette* after 1834 made "des attaques très dures contre le parti canadien."[25] But the Scot, whom Papineau had termed "tout bon canadien," was deserting *les patriotes* or the Papineau radicals, not the French-Canadian cause as he conceived it. After the rebellion, since Neilson considered that the projected union of Lower Canada with Upper Canada would be dangerous to French rights and society, he headed a movement, which included the French clergy, for the maintenance of the Constitution of 1791.

Outside the cities, too, there were Scots who sided with the French. A "fiery, flaxen Celt,"[26] the merchant William Henry Scott of Saint-Eustache west of Montreal, represented Deux-Montagnes in the Assembly from 1829. Although an adamant Presbyterian, he had the confidence of the Roman Catholic French Canadians. Feeling their grievances against the ruling cliques his own, he gave steadfast support to Papineau until the very eve of the rebellion. Then he vacillated, and finally, in spite of pressure and threats, refused to lead the local *patriotes*. Moreover, he and his younger brother Neil tried to dissuade Dr. Jean-Olivier Chénier who was resolved on using arms. The Scotts, however, had had such close assocations with the *patriotes* that they were compromised in the eyes of the authorities and were imprisoned. Yet William, though less moderate in disposition than Neilson, had had a moderating effect on the events at Saint-Eustache by failing to join in the insurrection. Amury Girod, the adventurer who prodded the local *patriotes* on to military action, wrote in his diary for December 5, 1837: "Depuis que Scott nous a abandonnés, les habitants sont sans courage."[27] The French case in Lower Canada obviously had not been presented by that race alone.

The Atlantic provinces did not have the racial division of Lower Canada or the bitterness engendered in Upper Canada by the alien question and clergy reserves to breed radicalism and rebellions. Each colony, however, had its own inequities and Scottish settlers who worked for reforms.[28] In winning two notable victories of the first half of the century – representative government in Newfoundland and responsible government in Nova Scotia – Scots had conspicuous roles. Soon after coming to St. John's from Kirkcudbrightshire in 1808, the public-spirited Dr. William Carson began criticizing naval rule. He demanded that Newfoundland be governed like a typical British colony by governor, upper house and popular assembly. For a quarter of a century he kept the issue of representative government alive through pamphlets and letters in the Newfoundland *Patriot*, a Reform paper which he set up. A Liberal party, predominantly Roman Catholic, gradually gathered around the Protestant Carson in the Assembly granted by Britain in 1832. The alliance was not unlike that of Neilson and Scott with the French Catholics in Quebec. In Nova Scotia, the Loyalist Joseph Howe was the outstanding Reformer, but several others in the embryonic Liberal Party were Scots: William and George Young, the sons of "Agricola"; Beamish Murdoch, the author of a history of the province, and S.G.W. Archibald, a learned lawyer from an old and respected family, who were moderate Reformers of the 1820s; Hugh Bell and James McNab, both of whom in 1848 entered the first "responsible" government in Nova Scotia; and especially William Annand. Annand, the son of a well-to-do Banffshire merchant, had a lengthy career alongside Howe, from the 1830s when he entered the Assembly, through to the 1860s when with Howe he vehemently opposed Confederation. The *Novascotian*, edited by Annand from 1843 and widely read in the province, was in the van of the Reform movement during the struggle for responsible government; and the *Morning Chronicle*, founded by Annand in 1844, was the vehicle for Howe's "Botheration Scheme" letters and other vigorous anti-Confederation articles in 1865.

Between these Reformers or Liberals and James William Johnstone there was a long political duel in Nova Scotia. Johnstone, Jamaica-born but of a lineage going back to the estate of Annandale in Scotland, was talented and striking in appearance, an excellent constitutional lawyer and the champion of the large Baptist denomination in the province. When the old council was reconstructed in 1838, Governor Sir Colin Campbell acted wisely in choosing a man with such qualifications as chief adviser. By the 1840s, Johnstone was recognized as the leader of a second political party which the Liberals called "Tory." Yet Johnstone, in spite of his aristocratic instincts, was not opposed to reforms. He believed that government should be responsible to the people in that the executive should not continue if it lost the confidence of the Assembly. But he did not agree that the ministers should be members of that Assembly, where they would dominate policy-making and themselves be exposed to undesirable political pressures. In the 1850s Johnstone outdid the Liberals by favouring the democratic electoral practices of simultaneous voting and full manhood suffrage. As first minister until 1848, leader of the opposition from 1848 to 1857 and 1860 to 1863, and premier from 1857 to 1860 and again in 1863, he established the Conservative Party in Nova Scotia on a progressive base. The Scots in the Maritime provinces did not agree politically any more than Scots elsewhere. But they had in common that they were dedicated and extraordinarily durable politicians.

III

With the achievement of responsible government towards the middle of the century, the Tories and Reformers in the Maritimes thus merged almost imperceptibly into Conservatives and Liberals, whereas in the united Province of Canada a variety of political groupings appeared. Out of these, two new parties were fashioned. They did not represent a division between right and left like the Tories and radicals, but were centrist combinations. After Confederation they would evolve into Canada's first national parties – the Conservatives and, a generation later, the Liberals. Since each of these parties owed its beginnings to Scots in Canada in the 1850s, the politicians of that province merit attention.[29]

On the Canadian Assemblies of the 1840s and 1850s, the Scots were bound to leave their mark because of their numbers and their individual strengths. The veterans of the pre-rebellion era who were members would now play out the last acts of their careers in a province adjusting to the union of Upper and Lower Canada and to the idea of responsible government. Among the old-timers were Neilson and William Scott, still enjoying the trust of constituencies in Canada East though they had defected from the *patriotes*. Neilson was not reconciled to the union or willing like Louis LaFontaine to make common cause with the Reformers of Canada West led by Robert Baldwin. On the contrary, Neilson agreed with Viger and Papineau that *la survivance* could best be achieved by separatism. It was to strive for repeal of the union that Neilson participated temporarily in the united Legislature and directed the editorials in the *Quebec Gazette* in the 1840s.[30] Back, too, from Canada East were Robert Christie, the Gaspé merchant who had been expelled from the Assembly five times by the popular party between 1829 and 1834 because he had slighted the Reformers; and James Leslie, a Montreal merchant and old Reformer, who accompanied LaFontaine into the first responsible ministry in Canada in 1848.

From Canada West as well there were two Scots whose paths had crossed many times – Colonel Allan Napier MacNab and the amnestied Mackenzie. Not only had they had fierce encounters in the old Assembly, but also it was under MacNab's leadership that the militia had easily dispersed the Mackenzie rebels in 1837. Although a man of great ambition and of business and political prestige in the Hamilton area, MacNab had never made his way into the inner circle of Strachan's Compact at Toronto. By the 1840s he was at last one of the main Tory leaders. As such he led a frenzied attack on the Rebellion Losses Bill of 1849, charging that it indemnified treason in Lower Canada, and in extravagant statements stigmatizing the whole French-Canadian race as rebels and aliens. Yet in the political flux of the early 1850s, even a vehement Scot like MacNab found himself setting aside some of his prejudices and forming a partnership with the French Canadians. From 1854 to 1856 he headed a ministry with A.N. Morin and in 1856 with E.P. Taché. MacNab is usually depicted as attaining this high office only by seniority and as being a liability to his party in the 1850s because he was a demagogue without real ability and with political views of the old order.[31] His famous remark, however, that "my politics now are railroads" suggests that, as far as economic developments were concerned, he was very much in tune with the political philosophy of the decade. His forte, like that of some other Scottish politicians, had always been in projects for the commercial prosperity of the young province – roads, canals, steamship companies, railways.

Mackenzie was less attuned to the new age. Unruly as ever, he re-entered political life in 1851 as the member for Haldimand, and launched another paper to berate the government – the *Weekly Message*, unsuitably named for it came out only when he could find the funds. He never accepted the union or the principle of responsible government. Perhaps this attitude was natural in one so thoroughly an independent as Mackenzie, one whom it is impossible to imagine at the head of a department in a collectively responsible cabinet. Paradoxically, though, he helped to condition the working of the new type of government when, as Chairman of the Committee on Public Accounts 1854-55, he made certain that the ministers discharged their responsibility to the Assembly in spending the public money.

Other Scots such as the two Macdonalds were just beginning their political careers. John Sandfield Macdonald, a native of Glengarry County who had become a lawyer of repute in Cornwall, entered the Assembly in 1841. Proud and sensitive, he would prove a somewhat difficult member in Reform ranks. But with his Highland blood and the Gaelic tongue, he wore well in eastern Ontario for thirty years. The Kingston lawyer, John Alexander Macdonald, did not leave political life from his election as a Tory in 1844 until his death in 1891. He would be criticized at times for opportunism and procrastination. Nevertheless, "Old Tomorrow" would be acknowledged as a superb party tactician and the most charismatic of all the Scots in Canadian political history. At first he had a strong rival among the young Tories in John Hillyard Cameron, an eminent Toronto lawyer, who had influence in the Church of England and the Orange Order as well as connections with the Toronto *British Colonist* edited by another Scot, Hugh Scobie. Cameron, however, remained with MacNab on the dogmatic right wing of the party whereas Macdonald adapted to the moderating currents of the 1850s. Two others who embarked on politics – Alexander Campbell in the Legislative Council, which was elective after 1856, and Alexander Morris in the Assembly – would hold office under Macdonald after Confederation, which each had a hand in initiating. The moderate Morris, a son of William Morris, the member for

Lanark from 1820 to 1836 who had been the Church of Scotland's champion for a share in the clergy reserves, was the go-between who helped to bring about the Great Coalition in 1864. The urbane Campbell, who accompanied Macdonald to the Charlottetown and Quebec Conferences, was one of the official "Fathers" of Confederation.

Among other new Scottish members in the Canadian Assemblies was John Young, a Liberal Montreal businessman, who was a member of the Hincks-Morin ministry which replaced the faltering Baldwin-LaFontaine ministry in 1851. Concerned as other business politicians were in the 1850s with improving commerce and transportation, Young favoured free trade and an intercolonial railway. On the other hand, the Toronto Liberal, Isaac Buchanan, one of the wealthiest merchants in Canada West, supported a protective tariff and the Great Western Railway which was designed to tap the trade of the American midwest. Buchanan was linked with the early career of the forceful George Brown, who was to be John A. Macdonald's greatest adversary. Strongly sympathetic to the Free Church, Buchanan backed the Toronto *Banner*, begun in 1843 as the Free Kirk journal under Peter Brown and his son George. But the latter, a British Whig in background, found the religious paper less challenging than the political controversies of the province. In 1844 he founded the Toronto *Globe* as the organ of the Baldwin Reformers. Brown's stirring editorials coupled with modern publishing methods steadily advanced the circulation of this paper. In 1851 he started the other side of his political career when, reacting against the "state churchism" of the Hincks government, he was elected as an independent Reform member for Kent in the southwest corner of the peninsula.

During the years between the achievement of responsible government and Confederation, this imposing array of Scots had plenty of scope for their varied talents and political beliefs in the many shifting party alignments in the Province of Canada. After the triumph of moderation and of biracial co-operation in achieving responsible government in 1848, political extremes had quickly reappeared. It looked as if the Tory forces on the right might be reconstructed on a platform of friendly separation from Great Britain. The majority of the signers of the Annexation Manifesto issued in Montreal in 1849 were big business Tories, among whom were a number of Scots – Peter Redpath, David L. Macpherson, D. Lorne Macdougall, James Ferrier, John Rose, and Alexander Tilloch Galt – all connected with the financial, commercial or railway interests of the city. They took this step not because they were inherently disloyal, but because, discouraged by the depression of the late 1840's, they resented Britain's apparent desertion of her colonies in moving toward free trade, and her upholding of the Rebellion Losses Bill. Tory annexationism so motivated died with the return of prosperity and did not become a party policy. At the same time, Scots not satisfied with the Baldwin-LaFontaine brand of liberalism or moderate reform took part in a revival on the radical left in both parts of Canada. In the East, Galt, the clever son of the Scottish novelist John Galt, allied himself with *le parti rouge*, while in the West a small band of advanced Reformers meeting in the Toronto office of William McDougall organized the Clear Grits. Of the eight or nine men who were the leaders of the original Clear Grits, four were Scottish Canadians. Two of these were young radicals – the lawyer McDougall and Edinburgh-born David Christie, an affluent farmer. The other two – the businessman James Lesslie, a native of Dundee, and the Sarnia lumberman and shipbuilder Malcolm "Coon" Cameron – represented continuity with the rebellion years. Lesslie had been labelled by Sir Francis Bond Head a "notorious rebel" and had been imprisoned in 1837. Since 1844 he had kept Mackenzie's ideas before the public in the Toronto *Examiner* of which he was the proprietor and editor. Cameron had been a radical assemblyman since 1836. Blunt and confident, he was very popular in western Ontario, where he represented at different times Kent, Lambton and Huron. He threw himself into the temperance movement and was the introducer of the first prohibition measure in the Canadian Legislature. Like many Scottish politicians he founded political newspapers – the *Bathurst Courier* at Perth in eastern Ontario, and at Goderich the *Huron Signal*, which he put under the able editorship of his friend, Thomas McQueen, a native of Ayrshire.

On February 14, 1851, the *North American*, McDougall's new paper instituted to be the mouthpiece of the Clear Grits, published their platform. It called for secularization of the clergy reserves, retrenchment in government expenditure, biennial parliaments, abolition of property qualifications for parliamentary representatives, application of the elective principle to all government offices, extension of the suffrage, and vote by ballot. The platform was a mixture of the earlier radicalism of Mackenzie, contemporary British Chartism, and North American frontier democracy. To Brown it amounted to American republicanism. He disapproved of the Clear Grits as much as he did of the Hincksites. In the very section of the province from which the Grits derived their strength the independent Reformer soon had his own following. In 1853 the *Globe* became a daily paper and began to be the "Scotchman's Bible" from Toronto westward. It won Brown lifelong political friends in two fellow-Scots Archibald McKellar of Chatham, too jovial to make a discreet politican but efficient in organization, and Alexander Mackenzie, thoroughly upright and reliable, the self-educated Perthshire stonemason who was now a rising contractor in Sarnia. Brown had other firm friends in western Ontario in William Notman, a Free Church Scot and Reformer who sat for Middlesex and later for Wentworth North, and Adam Johnston Fergusson Blair, the member for Waterloo and later for South Wellington whose father had originated the Scottish settlement of Fergus. Brown did not have strength, however, in eastern Ontario, the domain of the moderate Roman Catholic Sandfield Macdonald, who had more rapport with the French Liberals of Canada East than with the Presbyterian voluntaryist Brown.

Thus, with the high Tories MacNab and Hillyard Cameron, the moderate Tory John A. Macdonald, the British Liberals Brown and Alexander Mackenzie, the virtually independent Reformer Sandfield Macdonald and independent radical Lyon Mackenzie, the *rouge* Galt, and the radical Grits Lesslie, Malcolm Cameron, McDougall and Christie, Scots were prominent in all the political fragments resulting from the break-up of the old Tory and Reform parties in the 1850s. But along with the divisive tendencies there were centripetal political forces activated by some of these same Scots. Professor Donald Creighton has unfolded the development of John A. Macdonald's idea of a "great, middle, constitutional party" to achieve which it would be necessary to build friendly relations with the French Canadians and to liberalize the "old Conservative programme" in Canada West. These objectives Macdonald did, in fact, accomplish in the broadly-based coalition of 1854 between the conservative *bleus* of Canada East, the Tories and liberal Conservatives of Canada West, and the conservative Liberals of both sections. MacNab was the nominal leader from the West, but Macdonald was his heir apparent. In 1856 the latter succeeded to the leadership.[32] The great bi-racial Liberal-Conservative party of the future had been born. Macdonald's adroitness in winning men to his party of the centre can be seen in his overtures to Galt:

> You call yourself a Rouge. There may have been at one time a reddish tinge about you, but I could observe it becoming by degrees fainter. In fact you are like Byron's Dying Dolphin, exhibiting a series of colours – "the last still loveliest" – and that last is "true blue," being the colour I affect . . . pray do become true blue at once: it is a good standing colour and bears washing.[33]

Yet the Toryism of Strachan, MacNab and Hillyard Cameron did not die. It remained "a strong constituent element in the party, without which Liberal-Conservatism would have lost its essential character."[34]

Although Macdonald's success in uniting political groups in 1854-56 further weakened the Reformers, the other powerful Scot, George Brown, would begin the task of rebuilding them. The gradual rapprochement between the Brownites and the original Clear Grits is described by Brown's biographer, Professor J.M.S. Careless.[35] The disunity in the Reform press at least was ended by 1855 when the *Globe* absorbed both Lesslie's *Examiner* and McDougall's *North American*. Opposition to separate schools, representation by population, and westward expansion – persistent themes in the *Globe* – were issues on which the Grits and Brown agreed. By the time of the Reform Convention in Toronto in 1859, the original Clear Grits, though still possessing their power base in agrarian western Ontario, had been transformed into a Grit-Reform Party under the leadership of an urban and professional group dominated by Brown and his metropolitan paper. This party was as middle-of-the-road and respectably British as were the Conservatives; it, too, linked with the business community, had a major concern for material development. In the legislature Brown now had the assistance of McDougall, a former political foe, as well as of newer members, notably the canny lawyer Mowat. The latter had entered politics with a victory in 1857 over J.C. Morrison, also of Scottish descent, one of the moderate Liberals enticed by Macdonald into the Conservative ministry.

Still, Brown's Reformers were very decidedly a sectional party. Not until they became associated with the movement for Confederation was it clear that they, like John A. Macdonald, could enter into a harmonious working relationship with Canada East. The two days' Brown-Dorion administration in 1858 had hardly been a test. Confederation was also the issue which led the new Conservative and Reform parties in Canada to join forces with the rising Conservative and Liberal parties in the Maritimes.

The main Fathers of Confederation from Canada, except for George E. Cartier and D'Arcy McGee, were Scots. Their contributions have been fully recognized: Macdonald's efforts to establish a strong central government and his genius in reconciling differences amongst the delegates and in conveying his own vision of a nation *a mari usque ad mare*; Brown's decisive step in joining his political opponents, Macdonald and Cartier, in 1864 which alone made possible the Great Coalition, and his expositions of the constitutional details of a federal union both at the conferences and through the *Globe*; Galt's expertise in effecting the financial terms under which the provinces would enter the Dominion; and Mowat's and McDougall's work on the division of powers between federal and local legislatures. Not nearly so well-known are the Scottish politicians from the Atlantic provinces who were associated with Confederation.[36]

In New Brunswick, which was the key province since it connected the Canadas and Nova Scotia geographically, two men of Scottish extraction gave valuable aid to the Liberal premier, Samuel Leonard Tilley, in obtaining finally a verdict favourable to Confederation. The first was the eloquent and elegant lawyer, John Hamilton Gray, a Conservative, who, after attending the Charlottetown and Quebec Conferences, had a firm belief in union and began a series of public meetings with Tilley to explain the scheme to New Brunswickers. But Gray went down to defeat along with the Tilley government in 1865 when the people of the province renounced Confederation. Gray was right when he assured George Brown that the setback was transitory. The man who had much to do with reversing the results of 1865 was the headstrong and energetic Peter Mitchell, a Reform lawyer and lumber merchant whose parents had come from Scotland. Hand in hand with Lieutenant-Governor A.H. Gordon, who had been instructed by Britain to use every means possible to carry Confederation, and aided by Canadian money and a fortuitous Fenian raid on the border, Mitchell engineered the sweeping defeat of the anti-Confederate government in 1866 – thereafter being dubbed by his enemies Bismarck'' Mitchell.[37] He headed the new government which hastened to carry through the legislature a resolution for union contingent upon the building of an intercolonial railway.

In Nova Scotia the Conservative premier, Dr. Charles Tupper, also faced with strong opposition to Confederation, had urgent need of support from both parties to prevent a hostile vote. The polite but firm Scottish Canadian, Robert B. Dickey, a Conservative delegate at Charlottetown and Quebec, was not won over to the Quebec terms. His place at the London Conference was given to a strong unionist, John W. Ritchie, a member of a Scottish family in the province distinguished throughout the century in politics and law. But most important to Tupper and the Confederate cause was the calm, cool Adams George Archibald, of Scottish descent and irreproachable character, an assemblyman since 1851 and Howe's successor as Liberal leader. At Quebec Archibald was on the special committee which arranged the financial resolutions; and it was his consistent support of Confederation which kept it from taking on the complexion of a Conservative party scheme in Nova Scotia, for other leading Liberals followed Howe in opposition to it. For instance, A.W. McLelan, a level-headed, practical Scot, was afraid of the financial consequences for his native province; and Hugh McDonald, a lawyer of Scottish lineage in Inverness county, went with Annand and Howe to England in 1866 to affirm that the people should be consulted before the Constitution was changed. Archibald's reply to such arguments was to refer to the union of Scotland with England on which there had not been an appeal to the people. The Scots then, like the anti-Confederates in Nova Scotia now, had feared that the smaller state would be swamped by the larger. But, Archibald declared, this had not happened; instead, "Scotchmen could take their place with Englishmen in any part of the world."[38]

In Prince Edward Island the Conservative premier, the other John Hamilton Gray, a retired army officer of Glasgow descent, had been caught by the spirit of a great new nation at the Charlottetown Conference, of which he was chairman. But in December, 1864, realizing that he could not convey his enthusiasm to the Islanders, he resigned office. Professor Waite maintains that, although the loss of Gray, "a strong man politically," was serious, the opposition of the people to Confederation was such that no party could have taken up the cause and survived, and nothing any man could do would have altered their attitudes.[39] Until 1873 the province was controlled by the anti-Confederates. Typical of their belief that the Quebec Resolutions were not fair to the Island's small population either politically or economically was the Liberal, Andrew Archibald Macdonald, who at Quebec had contended unsuccessfully for the appointment of senators by the provincial legislatures and for equal representation for each province in the Senate in accord with the American example.[40]

Thus the Scots in the eastern provinces included opponents to union just as the Reformer Sandfield Macdonald and the Conservative Matthew Crooks Cameron stood aloof in Canada West, while the Scottish Protestant *Witness* run by John Dougall raised its voice in Montreal against Confederation. On the other hand, the Maritime Scots who were unionists had set aside party differences and staked their political futures on Confederation. At the conferences they had mostly upheld the rights of the provinces, especially the smaller provinces. In comparison with the Canadians they had had a small impact on the negotiations. Their major contributions had been in their own bailiwicks as they attempted to overcome the reluctance and suspicions of the people. They failed in Prince Edward Island until 1873; but they had been among the forces which carried New Brunswick and Nova Scotia into the Dominion in 1867. Archibald and Mitchell were rewarded by places in Macdonald's first ministry. An Ottawa post was one of the ways in which provincial politicians would coalesce into the national parties after Confederation.

IV

In the last third of the century, Canadian Confederation "only yet in the gristle" had to harden "into bone."[41] During this critical time newspapers still expressed the opinions of the parties, and again a number of the politically powerful editors had Scottish blood: John Cameron, the founder of the *London Advertiser* and the Toronto *Liberal*, who took over the editorship of the *Globe* after the Browns, and who in turn was followed by John S. Willison; John Ross Robertson of the *Toronto Telegram*; A.H.U. Colquhoun of the Toronto *Empire*; P.D. Ross of the *Ottawa Journal*; Hugh Graham (later Lord Atholstan) of the *Montreal Star*; and J.J. Stewart of the *Halifax Herald*. Though the daily paper published in the large urban centres was now the main forum for political discussion, the weekly still held sway in some smaller communities. Here, too, there were Scots editors with frank political leanings, such as M.Y. McLean of the *Huron Expositor* in Seaforth or Robert Sellar of the *Gleaner* in Huntingdon, Quebec.

In this period, while the political creation of 1867 was being tested, only about 16% of Canada's population gave their ethnic origin as Scottish. Yet for a generation the new national government was headed by Scots – the Conservative John A. Macdonald and the Liberal Alexander Mackenzie. During his first ministry, a coalition which rapidly took on a Conservative complexion, Macdonald realized his goal of a nation extending from ocean to ocean.[42] He rounded out the Dominion territorially by adding the Provinces of Manitoba, British Columbia and Prince Edward Island, and he combated the repeal movement in Nova Scotia by granting "better terms" which won over Howe and McLelan. Only Newfoundland resisted his expansionist programme. But the young nation already had problems which Macdonald would have to face in the future. In Nova Scotia the provincial government was still controlled by the anti-Confederates under the obdurate Scottish premier, Annand. Perhaps Sir John Bourinot was right in suggesting that Annand saw his chance at leadership when the last of his rivals in the party reconciled themselves to the union.[43] At any rate Annand, becoming vituperative towards Howe, his former friend and idol, continued to charge that the province had been wronged by the way in which it had been forced into Confederation. This last-ditch campaign to release Nova Scotia ceased with Annand's premiership in 1875, but the seeds of secessionism would spring up again in the next decade. As for the West, Macdonald's handling of the Red River rebellion in 1870 left a legacy of racial and religious bitterness in Canada, and his promise to British Columbia of a railway involved the government in negotiations with financiers which led to the "Pacific Scandal" of 1873 and resignation.

Mackenzie, who succeeded as prime minister for the next five years, epitomized the good qualities often attributed to Scots – intelligence, industry, conscientiousness, rectitude, and the inner strength which comes from profound faith in God.[44] With Scottish grit he served the country until his death in 1892, seldom absent from his seat in the Commons, faithful to his committee duties even though a throat malady made it increasingly difficult for him to speak. In administration he stood for honesty, economy and efficiency. If these are criteria of good government, Canada has never been so well governed as in the Mackenzie interlude of the 1870s. In his way, too, Mackenzie was a nation-builder. His government's discussions with Great Britain through Edward Blake, the Minister of Justice, on such matters as the Supreme Court Act, the prerogatives of the Governor-General, the treaty-making power, and authority over extradition and merchant shipping, advanced Canada along the path towards national autonomy within the Empire. Mackenzie's railway policy, slower-going than the Conservatives, but realistic in view of the small population and capital in the country, resulted in considerable stretches of completed road. Yet it aroused the anger of British Columbia which thought it a repudiation of the agreement to build a line to the coast within ten years. Mackenzie's greatest disadvantage, however, was the economic depression which just coincided with his term in office. To Canadians, discouraged in the hard times, the strait-laced prime minister with his careful programmes seemed unimaginative and uninspiring, while his aversion to bestowing the accustomed partisan favours heightened his image as a parsimonious Scot. The people rejected him in the elections of 1878 and, forgetting the Pacific Scandal, swept back into power the dynamic Macdonald who promised benefits to all parts of the country through his "National Policy."

Macdonald, prime minister again until 1891, devoted himself to uniting the country economically through protective tariffs to encourage industry, a transcontinental railway, the populating of the prairies, and the promotion of trade on an east-west axis. The completion of the Canadian Pacific Railway in 1885 was his most dramatic achievement. It took great faith in the future of Canada to embark on this vast undertaking, and great resolution to persevere with it in face of the immense problems in construction and financing. Macdonald was fortunate to secure the aid of a sagacious group of men, all Scots by birth, for the syndicate with whom the contract was made to build the railway: George Stephen of the Bank of Montreal, his cousin Donald A. Smith, who had first-hand knowledge of the West, the wealthy businessmen Duncan McIntyre and Robert B. Angus, and John Rose, formerly Macdonald's Finance Minister, who was now a member of a London banking house. The skilful chief engineer, Sandford Fleming, was also a Scot.[45] When Macdonald died, the Liberal leader, Wilfrid Laurier, rightly paid tribute in the Commons to his statesmanship, his patriotism, and his great gifts in the "supreme art of governing men" and in the "intricate management of a party."[46] In Macdonald's hands, the organized and disciplined national political party had been made a unifying agency in the far-flung country with its disparities in resources and development, languages and creeds.

Meanwhile the Liberals could not compete in national organization. Brown before 1867 had not been able to make the unionist cause a bond to tie the Liberals in British America together, as Macdonald had with the Conservatives. Nor had Mackenzie succeeded in welding the loose alliance of provincial Liberal parties over which he presided. Still, in the provinces strong men arose whom Laurier would merge in the 1890s into a compact national Liberal party. One of these was Andrew George Blair, a New Brunswick lawyer of Scottish ancestry and high reputation, who found only six Liberals in the provincial assembly of 41 members when he was elected to it in 1878. Five years later under his leadership the Liberals had the majority. Blair remained as Premier of New Brunswick until Laurier called him to head the busy Department of Railways and Canals in 1896, and was noted as a progressive though cautious administrator. Another Scottish premier, the veteran Mowat of Ontario, was invited by Laurier into his "ministry of all the talents" in 1896 as Minister of Justice.[47] Mowat had the prestige of having given his own province since 1872 sound and just government, including the deft handling of several thorny Protestant-Catholic problems. Moreover, he had already helped to strengthen the federal Liberal party by influencing its convention in 1893 to approve a revenue tariff. This platform healed the divisions on fiscal policy which had plagued the Liberals nationally, gave electors an acceptable alternative to the Conservative National Policy, and was one of the major factors in Laurier's victory in 1896.

George Bryce felt that the large number of Scotsmen occupying "representative positions of trust" in the world could be accounted for by "the interest in national affairs, so general among Scotsmen."[48] Scottish Canadians had, if possible, more zest for politics after Confederation than before, since now there were both federal and provincial elections to be fought. Not just among leading men in the parties, but among the grassroots Scots as well, political interest was a vital part of everyday life.

Letters passing between Scottish friends made frequent mention of public figures and events. If the writers were Liberals, a common theme was righteous indignation at Conservative tactics:

> We had some excitement at our election. We did not expect any opposition in our County but the Tories got a man out of the Lunatic Asylum to oppose Mills and took us all by surprise. Half of our party did not know there was any opposition, and consequently would not go near the polls if not roused to action. I was counting I drove my team about forty miles election day after voters. However, we got our man elected with over 500 majority but the way the Tory party acted in our County this election was just as disgraceful as the selling of the Pacific Railroad Charter to Sir Hugh Allan.[49]

Reinforcement for the Liberals' sureness of their own higher political morality – as if any were needed – came in letters from friends in Scotland:

> In reading the paper you kindly sent me I was very much struck with the extraordinary amount of corruption and jobbery that obtains in the Canadian Government. I hope the leader of the Reform Party will soon gain the victory. I thought that when you had the government in your own hands that you would be perfection. If Ireland when it gets Home Rule will do no better it will be a bad job.[50]

Political interest, however, was not enough to solidify provincial parties either in New Brunswick or in the new western provinces of Manitoba and British Columbia in the nineteenth century. In the other old provinces, coherent modern parties did develop, often under Scottish leaders such as the Conservative Simon Hugh Holmes and the Liberal George H. Murray in Nova Scotia, or the Conservative Neil MacLeod in Prince Edward Island. Even the French-speaking province of Quebec had a premier with a Scottish name in the Conservative John Jones Ross (1884-87). But, above all, it was Ontario under Mowat which effectually dispelled the notion abroad at the time of Confederation that political parties would have no place at provincial level in the new Dominion.[51]

Though performing on a smaller political stage than Macdonald, the wary Mowat was as skilful in the craft. He had the same faculty for sensing the aspirations of the people, and he understood equally well the brokerage function which a strongly-organized and broadly based political party can fulfill in reconciling conflicting interests. The opposition cried "ascendancy" and "exclusiveness" because of the number of Scots in Mowat's cabinets. But it was primarily because they were efficient and hard-working that the premier appointed such men as James Young, a businessman from Galt who had been the publisher of the *Dumfries Reformer*; the scholarly Adam Crooks and buoyant George W. Ross, the first two Ministers of Education; the Roman Catholic Christopher Findlay

Fraser, who directed Public Works for twenty years; the meticulous Alexander McLagan Ross, Provincial Treasurer; and John Morison Gibson, the author of several social welfare bills. Mowat and his colleagues took over the moderate Brownite Reform tradition of Canada West, and gave it new emphases to suit the needs of a province which was moving rapidly into the industrial age and which, with the acquisition of the disputed territory to the northwest, doubled in size. The many social and economic services added by the Ontario government under Mowat, together with its victories in several constitutional disputes with the Dominion, destroyed permanently the concept of the Fathers that the provinces would be no more than large municipalities. And the stability parties achieved in Ontario over the twenty-four years of his premiership was evidence that responsible government by party would obtain in the provinces as at Ottawa.

V

Although the Scots had had their faults and failures as well as their strengths and successes, they had, as parliamentarians, been connected in impressive numbers with every important Canadian political development of the formative nineteenth century. Never so numerous in the population as the English or the Irish, they had nevertheless played significant parts in originating the Tory and radical traditions, in shaping the Reform movements which preceded responsible government in the Maritimes and Canada, in building the provincial Conservative and Liberal parties before 1867, and in moulding the political policies in the new nation both federally and provincially after 1867. In the events leading to Confederation they had been constructive leaders. Also, a remarkable number of Scots had been managers or editors of influential newspapers; they had understood the power of the press in that century in diffusing opinion on political questions. As late as 1908, Goldwin Smith remarked: "The voting is in Parliament, but the national debate is in the press."[52]

In evaluating the qualities which the Scots brought into Canadian politics, it would be correct enough to include courage, stubbornness, diligence, competence, astuteness, resourcefulness, and even colour, wit, humour and eloquence. But these, after all, were not unique to Scottish politicians. More distinctive were their combinations of qualities. They had the capacity at the same time to dream dreams and to be practical, to emphasize stability and to promote economic and social progress, to hold firm views of their own and to co-operate with others of a different political or religious stripe. Possibly there was an instinct inherited, as some writers have surmised,[53] from ancestors in the days of the "Auld Alliance" between Scotland and France which helped them to be effective politically in the cultural dualism of Canada. Noteworthy, too, were their high levels of education – lawyers predominating – and of adaptability. The latter enabled them to move throughout the century with the growing country, the changing concepts of government, and the altering nature of the political party.

Finally, whichever party label the Scots chose to wear, they were, on the whole, men who sought the middle course politically and the British mode of action. Gourlay and Strachan, John A. Macdonald and Alexander Mackenzie, were equally "loyal." Neilson, the Archibalds, Johnstone and Blair were typical of the Scots of the centre. The name of Canada's first national party, which had been fathered by a Scot, was "Liberal" Conservative, and the temperate Reform principles of Brown and Mowat were modelled on those of British Victorian Liberalism. Even though a few Scots had moved farther to the left or the right, the Toryism of MacÑab was only relatively "High," the extremism and republicanism of William Lyon Mackenzie was rejected by his fellow countrymen, and the Clear Grit radicalism and Americanism of McDougall and "Coon" Cameron were soon watered down. This essential moderation and Britishism of the Scots who occupied such a large place in the mainstream of Canadian public life in the nineteenth century passed into the political tradition of Canada.

Richard Van Loon, in analyzing the ethnic origins of Canadian members of Parliament and cabinet ministers, has commented on the continuing "Scottish proclivity for gaining the seats of the mighty" in the first four decades of the twentieth century. Persons of Scots derivation had declined to about 12% of the population by the census of 1941. Yet from 1896 they had been the largest ethnic group in the House of Commons – constituting over one-quarter of its membership – and in the administration. According to Van Loon, 20% of Wilfrid Laurier's cabinet appointees were Scottish Canadians, 13.3 of R.L. Borden's, 26.9 of Arthur Meighen's, 23.9 of W.L.M. King's, and 28.6 of R.B. Bennett's.[54]

As in the nineteenth century, a number of Canadian Scots have gained political prominence at both provincial and national levels. The best known of the Scottish-Canadian politicians is William Lyon MacKenzie King, descendant of the "old rebel" William Lyon Mackenzie and of a Scottish officer of the Royal Horse Artillery, and the man who held the office of prime minister longer than any other politician in the British Commonwealth. Thomas Alexander Crerar, active in western farm politics, was appointed Minister of Agriculture in the Union Government (1917-19), led the National Progressive Party (1921-22), and served in King's Liberal government as Minister of Railways (1929-30) and Minister of Mines (1935-45). Charles Stewart, the Premier of Alberta (1917-21), became King's Minister of the Interior (1921-30). The Scots-born Ian Alastair Mackenzie, Provincial Secretary in British Columbia in 1928, accepted in succession the federal portfolios of immigration (1930), national defence (1935-39), pensions and national health (1939-44), and veterans affairs (1944-48). Simon Fraser Tolmie, the Minister of Agriculture under both Borden and Meighen (1919-21, 1926), returned to British Columbia as the provincial Conservative leader and premier (1928-33). James G. Gardiner, the Saskatchewan premier (1926-29, 1934-35), headed the Canadian Department of Agriculture under King and Louis St. Laurent (1935-57). Similarly, Stuart Sinclair Garson left the premiership of Manitoba (1943-48) for the post of Minister of Justice under St. Laurent (1948-57), and Hugh John Flemming, the premiership of New Brunswick (1952-60) for the post of Forestry under the Conservative government(1960-63). Angus L.Macdonald interrupted his tenure as premier in Nova Scotia (1933-40, 1945-54) to aid King as Minister of National Defence for naval services (1940-45). Thomas C. Douglas, a native of Falkirk, Scotland, went from the CCF premiership of Saskatchewan (1944-61) to the national leadership of the New Democratic Party (1961-71).

Since about 1940 there has been a growing tendency among parliamentarians to call themselves simply "Canadian" or "British." Nevertheless, the Scottish penchant for politics is still clearly identifiable in the House of Commons of 1975, headed as it is by the Prime Minister, the Right Honourable Pierre Trudeau, whose mother was Grace Elliott, and enlivened by former prime minister John George Diefenbaker, who acknowledges his descent from the Highland emigrants to the Red River Valley in 1813. Many other members are of Scottish stock: for example, Allan Joseph MacEachen, Minister of External Affairs; John Carr Munro, Minister of Labour; Mitchell W. Sharp; J. Angus MacLean, former Conservative Minister of Fisheries (1957-63); and Donald MacInnis, Conservative member from Cape Breton.

In the last half-century a new component has entered Canadian political history. After World War I paved the way for the participation of women in politics, the pioneers at Ottawa again were of Scots blood: Agnes Campbell Macphail, the first woman elected to the House of Commons (1921), and Cairine Mackay Wilson, the first appointed to the Senate (1930). Today, Flora Isabel MacDonald, a native of Nova Scotia who represents the Conservative riding of Kingston and the Islands, is the first woman seriously to compete for the leadership of a major national party. The presence of women with such ability and spirit as these promises enrichment of the Scots political tradition in Canada in the coming years.

NOTES

1.   The four volumes of W.J. Rattray, *The Scot in British North America* (Toronto: Maclear, 1880) contain considerable information about Scots in Canadian politics but this, like the material in works on the Scots in

Canada, is mainly useful for biographical background. Political analysis must be drawn from other sources, such as those indicated in subsequent notes.

2. S.D. Clark, *Movements of Political Protest in Canada, 1640-1840* (Toronto: University of Toronto Press, 1959), pp. 158-164, 166-167; W.S. MacNutt, *New Brunswick: A History 1784-1867* (Toronto: Macmillan, 1963), pp. 100-117.

3. A.L. Burt, *The Old Province of Quebec*, Carleton Library Series (Toronto: McClelland and Stewart, 1968), I, 77.

4. Hilda Neatby, "The Political Career of Adam Mabane," *Canadian Historical Review*, XVI (1935), 150.

5. See "Instructions . . . à Adam Lymburner," *Bulletin des Recherches Historiques*, XXXVII (1931), 691.

6. Louis François Georges Baby Collection, Public Archives of Canada, Adam Lymburner (Londres) à J. Perrault l'aîné, 5 janvier 1791. Copy of original in the Archives of the University of Montreal.

7. Maxville Women's Institute, *History of Maxville and the Community* (Maxville, 1967), pp. 50, 51, 53.

8. Robina and Kathleen M. Lizars, *In the Days of the Canada Company 1825-1850* (Toronto: Briggs, 1896), pp. 236-280.

9. Patrick Shirreff, *A Tour through North America* (Edinburgh: Oliver and Boyd, 1835), p. 104.

10. Adam Fergusson, *Practical Notes Made during a Tour in Canada*, 2nd ed. (Edinburgh: Blackwood, 1834), p. 115.

11. W. Stewart Wallace, *The Family Compact*, Chronicles of Canada, XXIV (Toronto: Glasgow, Brook, 1915), p. 4.

12. George Patterson, *History of the County of Pictou* (New Glasgow, N.S., 1877), pp. 321-363.

13. G.M. Grant, *Joseph Howe*, 2d ed. (Halifax: A. and W. MacKinlay, 1906), p. 28.

14. D.C. Harvey, "The Intellectual Awakening of Nova Scotia," *Historical Essays on the Atlantic Provinces*, G.A. Rawlyk, ed., Carleton Library Series (Toronto: McClelland and Stewart, 1967), p. 117.

15. M.O. Hammond, *Confederation and Its Leaders* (Toronto: McClelland, 1917), p. 309.

16. John A. Macdonald Papers, PAC, McDougall to Macdonald, April 11, 1881.

17. *John Strachan: Documents and Opinions*, J.L.H. Henderson, ed., Carleton Library Series (Toronto: McClelland and Stewart, 1969), p. 21, Strachan to Dr. James Brown, March 31, 1801.

18. George W. Spragge, ed., *The John Strachan Letter Book: 1812-1834* (Toronto: Ontario Historical Society, 1946), p. 163, Strachan to Colonel John Harvey, June 22, 1818.

19. William Kilbourn, *The Firebrand* (Toronto: Clarke, Irwin, 1956), p. 160.

20. U.C. Sundries, PAC, Talbot to Secretary George Hillier, March 19, 1824.

21. Aileen Dunham, *Political Unrest in Upper Canada 1815-1836*, Carleton

Library Series (Toronto: McClelland and Stewart, 1963), p. 53. Cf. Gerald M. Craig, *Upper Canada: The Formative Years 1784-1841* (Toronto: McClelland and Stewart, 1966), p. 170.

22. J.W. Pickersgill, *The Mackenzie King Record*, I, (1939-1944) (Toronto: University of Toronto Press, 1960), p. 565. Cf. Wilfred Campbell, *The Scotsman in Canada: Eastern Canada* (Toronto: Musson, n.d.), p. 335 ff.

23. *Lord Durham's Report*, Gerald M. Craig, ed., Carleton Library Series (Toronto: McClelland and Stewart, 1963), p. 23.

24. Helen Taft Manning, *The Revolt of French Canada 1800-1835* (Toronto: Macmillan, 1962), p. 161.

25. André Beaulieu et Jean Hamelin, *Les Journaux du Québec de 1764 à 1964* (Québec: Les Presses de l'Université Laval, 1965), p. 212. See also Mason Wade, *The French Canadians 1760-1967*, rev. ed. (Toronto: Macmillan, 1968), I, 138-144, on the division in the popular party between the followers of Papineau and of Neilson.

26. Joseph Schull, *Rebellion: The Rising in French Canada 1837* (Toronto: Macmillan, 1971), p. 94.

27. Aegidius Fauteux, *Patriotes de 1837-1838* (Montréal: Les Editions des Dix, 1950), p. 373.

28. A general background for the reform movement in the Maritimes is found in W.S. MacNutt, *The Atlantic Provinces* (Toronto: McClelland and Stewart, 1968). Edward Manning Saunders, *Three Premiers of Nova Scotia* (Toronto: Briggs, 1909) is detailed on J.W. Johnstone.

29. For general discussions of the politics of the Province of Canada consult: J.M.S. Careless, *The Union of the Canadas* (Toronto: McClelland and Stewart, 1972); and Paul G. Cornell, *The Alignment of Political Groups in Canada, 1841-1867* (Toronto: University of Toronto Press, 1962).

30. On this stage of Neilson's career see: *Racism or Responsible Government: The French Canadian Dilemma of the 1840's*, Elizabeth Nish, ed., "Issues in Canadian History," ed. Morris Zaslow (Toronto: Copp Clark, 1967), pp. 2-5, 23, 31-34, 94, 102, 118-119, 173-174.

31. E.g., J.C. Dent, *The Last Forty Years: The Union of 1841 to Confederation* (1881), Carleton Library Series (Toronto: McClelland and Stewart, 1972), pp. 40, 248, 256. A more favourable view is taken in: Carl F. Smith, "The Political Career of Allan Napier MacNab (1825-1836): A Study in Detemination," M.A. thesis, University of Guelph, 1971.

32. Donald Creighton, *John A. Macdonald: The Young Politician* (Toronto: Macmillan, 1952), pp. 174-237. Cf. James A. Roy, *The Scot and Canada* (Toronto: McClelland and Stewart, 1947), pp. 104-105.

33. O.D. Skelton, *The Life and Times of Sir Alexander Tilloch Galt* (Toronto: Oxford, 1920), pp. 229-230, Macdonald to Galt, November 2, 1857.

34. Creighton, p. 238.

35. J.M.S. Careless, *Brown of the Globe* (Toronto: Macmillan, 1959-1963), I, 195-237, II, 13-14; and "The Toronto Globe and Agrarian Radicalism, 1850-67," *Canadian Historical Review*, XXIX (1948), 14-39.

299

36. Scattered references are found in such works as: Lorne C. Callbeck, *The Cradle of Confederation* (Fredericton: Brunswick Press, 1964); Donald Creighton, *The Road to Confederation* (Toronto: Macmillan, 1964); W.L. Morton, *The Critical Years* (Toronto: McClelland and Stewart, 1964); W.M. Whitelaw, *The Maritimes and Canada before Confederation* (1934; reprinted Toronto: Oxford University Press, 1966).

37. George Stewart, *Canada under the Administration of the Earl of Dufferin* (Toronto: Rose-Belford, 1878), pp. 240-241.

38. J.C. Dent, *The Canadian Portrait Gallery* (Toronto: Magurn, 1880), I, 88.

39. P.B. Waite, *The Life and Times of Confederation* (2d ed.; Toronto: University of Toronto Press, 1962), pp. 180, 183, 191-192.

40. [A.A. Macdonald], "Notes on the Quebec Conference, 1864," *Canadian Historical Review*, I (1920), 35-37. Macdonald was one of the few who kept notes of the proceedings at Quebec; he reported his own speeches in some detail.

41. *Correspondence of Sir John Macdonald,* Sir Joseph Pope, ed. (Toronto: Oxford University Press, n.d.), p. 165, Macdonald to John Rose, March 5, 1872.

42. On Macdonald as Prime Minister, see Donald Creighton, *John A. Macdonald: The Old Chieftain* (Toronto: Macmillan, 1965).

43. Sir John G. Bourinot, *Builders of Nova Scotia* (Toronto: Copp Clark, 1900), p. 82.

44. On Mackenzie as Prime Minister, see Dale C. Thomson, *Alexander Mackenzie: Clear Grit* (Toronto: Macmillan, 1960), pp. 169-343.

45. John Murray Gibbon, *Scots in Canada* (Toronto: Musson, 1911), pp. 137-138.

46. Canada, House of Commons, *Debates*, 1891, pp. 884-887.

47. On Mowat's career see: A. Margaret Evans, "The Mowat Era, 1872-1896: Stability and Progress," *Profiles of a Province* (Toronto: Ontario Historical Society, 1967), pp. 97-106; and "Oliver Mowat: The Pre-Premier and Post-Premier Years," *Ontario History*, LXII (1970), 137-150.

48. George Bryce, *The Scotsman in Canda: Western Canada* (Toronto: Musson, 1911), p. 328.

49. Private collection, MacLaren Family Papers, Donald McLaren, Kent County, to Robert MacLaren, Huron County, Ontario (author's great-grandfather), January 31, 1874. The reference is to David Mills who was returned as the member for Bothwell in the federal elections of January 22, 1874.

50. MacLaren Family Papers, Robert Fergusson, Stirling, Scotland, to Robert MacLaren, June 6, 1892.

51. Martin Robin, ed., *Canadian Provincial Politics* (Scarborough: Prentice-Hall, 1972), *passim*.

52. Quoted in Alexander Brady, *Democracy in the Dominions* (3d ed.; Toronto: University of Toronto Press, 1968), p. 568.

53. John Murray Gibbon, *Canadian Mosaic* (Toronto: McClelland and Stewart, 1938), p. 109; Roy, *Scot and Canada*, p. 109.
54. Richard Van Loon, *The Structure and Membership of the Canadian Cabinet*, Report no. 8, Royal Commission on Bilingualism and Biculturalism (1966), pp. 44-48.

FIFTEEN

The Scot
and Canadian Identity

W. Stanford Reid

The preceding chapters of this book have indicated that Scots have played an important role in Canada from the very beginning of its history. Scottish names appear repeatedly at crucial turning points in the Canadian story as well as in the more mundane aspects of its development. In this, Scots have contributed certain characteristics to Canadian identity. While some Canadians themselves may feel that there is no truly Canadian identity or that what identity has developed is now being eroded, to many who come to the country for the first time, one thing stands out. It is the Scottish influence, which, although metamorphosed by the Canadian geographical and social environment, still remains strongly Scottish in flavor.

THE SCOT IN TWENTIETH CENTURY CANADA

While most of the chapters tend to end their story of the Scot in Canada around 1900, the reason for this is not far to seek. From the opening decade of the present century the pattern of Canadian immigration has changed radically from what it was in earlier years. Ever-increasing numbers of Europeans, particularly from eastern Europe, Asiatics, West Indians and Americans have moved into Canada to create a widely variegated ethnic mosaic. As a result the proportion of the native English-speaking element in the population has declined steadily, and as Scots were only a relatively small part of that group their share in the population has likewise become smaller.

This development is indicated at least in part by the immigration and population statistics. During the years 1898-1901, Scottish immigration averaged around 1200 immigrants a year out of a population in Scotland of 4,500,000. English and Welsh immigration, on the other hand, was running at about 8,500 out of a home population of 32,000,000 to 33,-000,000. Thus Scotland was sending to Canada an average proportion of its population. By 1967 the number of Scots entering the country had risen

302

to 15,575, although since that time the figure has dropped to about one-third of that figure. While the reasons for the increase in immigration in this century is not always clear, some factors, both old and new, have acted to maintain the flow of Scottish people of all classes and social strata. The fact that friends and relatives have already migrated sometimes acts as an incentive for a move to Canada. Perhaps more important is the fact that ever since the 1820s Canada has been regarded as the land of opportunity. This has been particularly true as a result of the Depression of the 1930s and two world wars. Canada did not seem to have been as hard hit by the Depression as were some areas of Scotland where up to 25% of the labouring population were, at the depth of the slump, out of work. Furthermore, during the bombing raids of World War II Canada seemed to be a very peaceful place to live, as testified by some of the children who were evacuated to relatives in Canada for safety. Another of the more recent causes has been the fear of the growing socialism in Great Britain which has caused middle class families to move. And probably one of the factors which went along with all the others was the fact that it was felt that in Canada there were more of the comforts of life, such as central heating! But even with the increase in Scottish immigration since 1900, the Scottish proportion of the population has declined. In 1901 it was just under 15%, by 1921 it had fallen to 13.3% and since 1941 it has remained stationary at around 10%, although in the latest census the differentiation between English, Welsh and Scottish has been dropped in favour of "British." Yet Canadians of Scottish origin, from what we can determine, still form the third largest ethnic group in the country, with a total of around 2,000,000, as compared with 5,000,000 in Scotland.

In spite of the proportional decline of Scots and Canadians of Scottish descent within the population, they still play an important part in Canadian life and activity. Scots continue to come to Canada from all levels of society: skilled workmen, professionals, financiers, manufacturers. Moreover, even though they may have no relations in Canada, they soon find that they are involved with other Scots or Scottish Canadians who are very conscious of their Scottish background and heritage, and of what Scots have meant to the development of Canada and Canadian self-consciousness.

One manifestation of the strength of the continuing Scottish tradition in Canada is the number of Scottish organizations in the country. Scots and Scottish Canadians seem to have a penchant for organizing St. Andrews societies, Burns associations and the like. Many of the St. Andrews societies commenced as friendly societies to help newly-arrived immigrants, but have now become important social organizations performing a number of other functions. Burns societies also fill somewhat the same function, although their principal interest is to perpetuate "the immortal memory." Alongside these more or less Lowland organizations, whose members, however, often wear the kilt, are the various Scottish clan societies: McLeods, MacDonalds, MacRaes and all the rest, who have their *ceilidhs* (social gatherings) and welcome their travelling chieftains who come to grace their meetings with their presence.

While in a good many cases these societies are held together largely by nostalgia, in academic circles the study of the Scot both at home and in Canada is coming to be recognized as a valid field of investigation and interest. This is natural not only because the Scot has played a considerable part in Canadian development generally, but also because there are still areas in Canada, such as Cape Breton, where Scottish pockets have survived, keeping alive not only "the language" but also many of the customs and arts which their forefathers brought from their native heath. Marius Barbeau, the indefatigable folklorist, recorded many of the Scottish songs and stories which are gradually disappearing even from these Scottish settlements. Of great importance in the preservation of spoken Gaelic, music and dance has been the Gaelic College at St. Ann's, Cape Breton, founded by A.W.R. Mackenzie, with its summer courses attended by many from across Canada and the United States. The CBC has also assisted by making regular Gaelic broadcasts, and although for a time these were suspended, such an outcry has been raised that they have been restored. A further centre of Celtic studies is to be found at St. Francis Xavier University, Antigonish, which has an active Department of Celtic Studies. In Ontario the University of Guelph has pioneered studies in Scottish history and culture, and in Scottish contributions to the Canadian scene. Not only is there an inter-departmental committee which sponsors semi-annual colloquia and publishes the proceedings, but it has also been responsible for organizing on a continent-wide basis The Conference on Scottish Studies which publishes a quarterly journal, *Scottish Tradition*. Partly as a result of these influences, the American Society of Eighteenth Century Studies has now established a Scottish section which will concentrate on Scottish intellectual and literary endeavours in that period. Thus Canadians are able to gain a greater understanding of the part Scots have played in the history of their country.

Many Canadians who are not of Scottish origin also appreciate, perhaps even unconsciously, what the Scot has meant to Canada. Not only do they attend the various Highland games which are held across the country every summer, but a large proportion of the population in summer enjoys a round of golf and in winter spends considerable time participating in or watching curling bonspiels, both games having been brought from Scotland, although the names of many players are anything but Scottish! Scottish dance societies also have a large following, many of whom are Dutch, German, Ukrainian and even English. In this way not only Scottish folk dances but also Scottish music is more than surviving. It is playing a significant role in the development of a Canadian popular culture.

Yet while such organizations and activities are important and influential, their impact on a country cannot but be somewhat limited. Despite the contemporary love of statistics, the use of the computer to deal with large aggregates and the tendency to think in terms of mass effects, the individual is still of paramount importance. In this situation Scots and Scottish Canadians, despite their relatively small numbers within the population, are by no means a negligible quantity. It is impossible in a few pages to list or even mention all those of Scottish origin who have played an important part in Canada during the past seventy-five years. Yet, lest some sceptics think that the Scots have lost all significance and that today the Scottish tradition is largely non-existent, let us examine a few areas in twentieth century Canadian life to see something of the contemporary position of the Scottish tradition.

Before looking at individuals, however, one point which we must keep in mind is that the Scots in Canada, like the rest of the population, have tended to become urbanized. The descendants of the original settlers who located in Cape Breton, New Brunswick, the Eastern Townships of Quebec, the Glengarry, Dundas and Stormont districts of eastern Ontario and the west and southwest of that province, and who subsequently often relocated in groups on the western prairies, have steadily migrated to Montreal, Toronto, Winnipeg, Vancouver and other cities to enter the professions, business or government service. The newly-arrived Scottish immigrants have usually done the same thing with the result that some rural areas which before World War I were almost solidly Scottish have few if any Scots still resident. Therefore, we must look for Scots primarily in urban settings and occupations.

As in the earlier days of the country, the professions have in the twentieth century exercised a great attraction for the Scot and the Scottish Canadian. Many Scottish doctors have migrated to Canada to take a large part in the development of medical education. At the same time Scottish names appear very frequently in the lists of doctors born and trained in Canada. Many of these men have been known for their accomplishments in other fields. For example, Dr. Tait MacKenzie also gained a reputation as a sculptor, Dr. W.H. Drummond as a writer of "habitant" poems, Sir Andrew MacPhail as an educator, Dr. Thomas Gibson as a pianist, and Dr. H. Rock Robertson as the organizer of the medical faculty at the University of British Columbia and subsequently Principal of McGill University. Probably one of the most widely-known Canadian medical practitioners was Dr. Norman Bethune, a descendant of the Rev. John Bethune of Montreal and Williamstown, Ont., who died while serving with Mao Tse Tung's forces in China.

Law, too, has been a field which has attracted individuals of Scottish origin, probably because of the argumentative Calvinistic tradition from which they have come. Like Sir John A. MacDonald earlier, many of these men have entered politics to become important in both law-making and law enforcement at provincial and federal levels. A glance at the directory of the legal profession reveals so many Scottish names that it is virtually impossible to single out individuals for comment.

When we come to the Protestant ministry and the Roman Catholic priesthood, again we are faced with a plethora of Scottish names. MacDonals or Macdonells, MacLeans, Reids, Sutherlands, Mackinnons, MacQueens and others are almost innumerable. They are particularly numberous in the Presbyterian, United and Roman Catholic churches, although some also appear in the rolls of the Anglican, Baptist and other denominations. One example of the Scottish influence is that of the seventy-three moderators of the General Assembly of the Presbyterian Church in Canada since 1900, sixty-seven have had distinctly Scottish names, although one or two of these may have had ancestors who came to this country via Northern Ireland. While the same is not equally true of the United Church in Canada, yet out of moderators since 1925 eleven have had Scottish names.

In the arts also, Canadians of Scottish descent have played an important role, although a number have migrated to the United States. Dr. Tait MacKenzie, mentioned above, has been one of Canada's outstanding sculptors, William Cruickshank, a Scot who taught art in Toronto for twenty-five years, had among his students some of the Group of Seven, of which J.E. MacDonald was a member. Among the more recent Scottish-Canadian artists are the late Evan MacDonald of Guelph and Arthur McKay of Regina. In music one of the best known Scottish Canadians was the late Sir Ernest MacMillan, from 1926 to 1952 Principal of the Toronto Conservatory of Music and from 1931 to 1956 the conductor of the Toronto Symphony Orchestra. In the field of classical vocal music Maureen Forrester, whose father was a Scot, is outstanding, while in the "popular" field are such artists as Gisèle (La Fleche) MacKenzie, Catherine MacKinnon and Anne Murray. In the literary field there are novelists such as Charles Gordon (Ralph Connor), Lucy Maud Montgomery, Hugh MacLennan, Grace Campbell and David Walker; poets William Wilfrid Campbell, Duncan Campbell Scott, John MacRae and Frank Scott; folklorists and historians such as Cyrus MacMillan and W.L. Morton; and journalists-travellers-conservationists such as Blair Fraser and Farley Mowat. On the stage Brian Macdonald, who began his career with the Winnipeg Ballet, has gained an international reputation for his directing and choreography. Many actors from Scotland have contributed to Canadian theatre, two of the best known being Douglas Campbell and Hugh Webster, who have participated in the Stratford Festival and have played important parts in other productions. Norman McLaren, another Scot, has made a considerable reputation in the production of films for the National Film Board. On the radio and television names such as Gordon Sinclair and Ross MacLean indicate that Scots are also involved in the newer communication media.

In the field of education Scots still carry on the old tradition which goes back to and beyond the Reformation. Dr. Norman MacKenzie, a Nova Scotian, for instance, who has been Principal of both the University of New Brunswick and the University of British Columbia, is one of the leading moulders of Canadian university education. One of his successors at UNB was Dr. Colin MacKay and at UBC was Dr. J.B. MacDonald, both of Scottish origin. On the other hand, Dr. J.S. Thomson came from Scotland to be Principal of the University of Saskatchewan and later Dean of Divinity at McGill University. Another educationalist of great influence was Prof. Harold A. Innis of Toronto who has been described as the leading social scientist in Canada. Needless to say St. Francis Xavier University is well-staffed with faculty and administration of Highland origin. In professional education, medicine, law and similar fields the same is true, for many of the deans and university professors bear Scottish names.

Business and finance also continue to be one of the preoccupations of many who bear Scottish names. One may think of the Robert Simpson Co. which was founded in Markham, Ontario, in 1872, by a Scot who had recently arrived from Scotland and who later moved to Toronto. One of the early business men of Newfoundland was Sir R.G. Reid who came from Cupar Angus via Australia to Canada where he became one of the major railway builders of the East, eventually owning large tracts of land in Newfoundland as well as controlling most of the island's railway system, for which he was none too popular. In finance Scots have also maintained their reputations. Many have risen to influential positions in this field, one of the most important being James Muir who came from Scotland in 1912 to join the Royal Bank of Canada, of which he became the president in 1954.

Probably the most outstanding of the Scots involved in Canadian business life during the first sixty years of the present century was the late Donald Gordon. Born in Old Meldrum, Aberdeenshire, in 1901, he came with his parents to Canada at the age of twelve. Commencing his career with the Bank of Nova Scotia, he studied at night and by correspondence in order to gain a better education. In 1935 he was appointed secretary of the newly-established Bank of Canada and later deputy-governor. During World War II he served Canada in many capacities, the most important being that of Chairman of the War Time Prices and Trade Board and Executive Director of the International Bank for Reconstruction and Development. Following the cessation of hostilities he was made Chairman and President of the Canadian National Railways and on retiring from the CNR became President of the British Newfoundland Company, with all its financial problems. The night the problems seemed to be finally solved, he died in his sleep. A quotation from an address delivered at McGill University in 1965 reveals not only his outlook, but that of many other Scots:

> For my part, I see nothing old-fashioned about such virtues as honesty and truthfulness, a keen sense of public duty, and an obligation to do the right thing simply because it is the right thing to do. Moreover, I believe that the importance of integrity and good faith in the business world cannot be overstated; and it would confound many a

cynic to know how often our hard-headed bankers look upon the integrity of management as the best and surest of all collateral.

The combination of business acumen and success with philanthropy of different kinds has been continued in the present century by many Scottish Canadians. Lord Beaverbrook's donations to the University of New Brunswick are well-known examples. Probably one of the most outstanding demonstrations of the Scottish approach, however, has been that of Sir William Macdonald and his successors Walter and David Stewart. Sir William, who was born in Glenaladale, PEI, in 1831 acquired his wealth in the tobacco industry and disbursed it liberally for educational projects, being particularly interested in the training of young people in practical matters. He gave large sums for the creation of "consolidated" schools in Eastern Canada, established the Macdonald Institute and Macdonald Hall, one of the first university residences for women in Canada, at Guelph, in affiliation with the Ontario Agricultural and Veterinary Colleges, now part of the University of Guelph, and made very large donations to McGill University, Montreal. To the latter institution he not only gave Macdonald College, St. Anne de Bellevue, which housed both the agricultural and home economics faculties, but also paid for the erection on the Montreal campus of the Engineering Building, the Chemistry and Mining Building and the Physics Building. When the Engineering Building was destroyed by fire he paid for its reconstruction and provided so well for the equipment of the Physics Building that it was one of the foremost research centers in the world. It was there that Ernest Rutherford made his fundamental nuclear discoveries that ushered in the Atomic Age. Sir William also endowed a number of professorships which still bear his name.

Sir William died in 1917 and in his will left his tobacco business to Howard and Walter Stewart, the two sons of his long-time confidential aide and advisor, David Stewart. Before long Howard withdrew from the business and Walter became the sole owner. He also continued Sir William's policy of assisting in the development of education, particularly at McGill University. Under his son, David, the Macdonald Tobacco Company has been sold, but much of the money received has been used to establish the Macdonald Stewart Foundation whose interest is primarily in the field of education, providing funds for conferences on Canada's British heritage, assisting institutions such as the University of Guelph to obtain collections of materials which enable scholars to investigate the impact which Scots have had on Canadian development and promoting other educational projects. In this way, the Scottish tradition of the successful businessman employing his wealth to assist worthy social causes is being continued to the present.

Turning from business to politics, despite their relatively small proportion of the population we find that Scottish names appear in considerable profusion in the various political parties both at the provincial and the federal levels. The present Trudeau Cabinet, for instance, has ten members out of thirty bearing Scottish names, and practically every Provincial Cabinet, with the exception of Quebec, has three or four ministers whose lines go back to Scotland. It is not necessary, however, to recapitulate the information on this aspect of Scottish activity given in the preceding chapter.

It would be possible to keep on listing other names in many different fields. For instance Margaret (Polson) Murray, wife of Professor J. Clark Murray, Professor of Philosophy at Queen's and McGill Universities, founded the Imperial Order of the Daughters of the Empire in 1900. In a completely different field, J.A.D. McCurdy made the first airplane flight in the British Empire on February 23, 1903, when he flew his *Silver Dart* on a test flight at Baddeck, N.S. Turning to more warlike activities, the most prominent Canadian military leader in World War II was A.G.L. McNaughton who commanded the First Canadian Division in World War I, became chief of Canadian General Staff in 1929, President of the National Research Council in 1935, and commanded the Canadian Forces overseas in World War II until he returned to Canada to become Minister of National Defence in 1944. Later he became Chairman of the Canadian-United States Permanent Joint Board of Defence and Canada's permanent representative to the United Nations. Enough has been said, however, to indicate that even in the twentieth century when Canada is becoming increasingly cosmopolitan, the Scots and the Scottish tradition still continue to be influential.

THE SCOT AND CANADIAN IDENTITY

From its earliest beginnings Canada has tended to develop an identity which has differentiated it from France, Great Britain and the United States. Some, however, may feel that its identity is not strong or unique enough to make Canadians truly "different." While this may be partially true, and while Canadians do tend to squabble among themselves, French with English, easterners with westerners, Canada has, particularly since 1867, developed something of a personality. And in this development Scots have played a not inconsiderable part.

We may go back to the days of John Neilson and Adam Lymburner shortly after the cession of New France, when they sought for some form of Canadian identity. Or we can think of men such as William Lyon Mackenzie, George Brown and Lord Elgin in the mid-nineteenth century insisting upon the rights of Canadians to direct their own affairs. Sir John A. MacDonald, Sir. A.T. Galt, Sir William MacKenzie, Sir Oliver Mowat, and John Sandfield MacDonald followed in their footsteps, seeking to establish Canadian identity by means of the unification of the various British North American colonies. The twentieth century has seen many non-Scottish advocates of this point of view, but probably the most outstanding leader, whether one agrees with his methods or not, was W.L.

Mackenzie King. Another more recent example is Walter Gordon, the protagonist of Canadian economic nationalism. Even at the grass roots level, the Scots and Scottish Canadians have always seemed to show a desire to insist upon Canada's independence and individuality, which has been one of the reasons perhaps why they have usually been able to understand the French-Canadian aspirations more easily than members of other non-French-speaking ethnic groups. Thus throughout Canada, Canadians of Scottish origin have generally supported the idea of Canadian national identity.

One of the principal reasons for this desire for national identity is the historical heritage of the Scottish peoples. As pointed out in the first chapter, the Scot almost since the day of the Roman invasions has had to fight to maintain his independence whether against Anglo-Saxons, Danes, Anglo-Normans, English or even French. It seems almost to be an inbred condition, a conditioned reflex that he should have to battle to maintain the fact that he is a Scot. Although some of the Scots such as Bishop Strachan or Sir Alan MacNab do not seem to have been willing to take a stand for Canadian self-assertion, most seem to have felt that they had to defend their Canadianism against the influences of both the mighty neighbour to the south and the mother country across the Atlantic. While cherishing their Scottish heritage they have transferred their primary loyalty to Canada, echoing the words of George Brown of *The Globe* after he had paid a visit to Scotland: "It is Canada for me."

It is not surprising, therefore, that the Scots who have come to Canada and their descendants have been an influential factor in Canadian history. It has not been because of their large numbers, but primarily because of their historical inheritance, the Scottish Tradition. And, in this day and age when Canadian governments at every level, big business and big labour often appear to have little real interest in maintaining a distinctive Canadian identity, it is perhaps time that Canadians of Scottish origin should refurbish their sense of independence to insist that Canadian identity must be not only maintained but also strengthened and reinvigorated, in order that all Canadians, of whatever ethnic origin, may take pride in being Canadians.

APPENDIX

Scottish Place-Names in Canada

Watson Kirkconnell

INTRODUCTION

This monograph* began as an address to the Celtic Society of Wolfville, Nova Scotia. So many challenging questions were raised that a systematic study was undertaken by its author, in order to prepare a toponymical roster and to analyse its significance.

THE PEOPLES AND SURNAMES OF SCOTLAND

At the outset, one should remember that Scotland, from which the Scottish Canadians have come, is not homogeneous in either race or language. In other words, there is no "Scotch race" and no "Scotch language." The ethnologist, whose definition of race is based on physical characterisitcs and measurements, distinguishes carefully between the flaxenhaired ex-Scandinavians in the extreme north, the "Black Breed" in the Western Highlands, the red-heads in the Eastern Highlands, the tall, dark-haired, blue-eyed Galwegian blend, the short, dark Strathclyde type, and the Anglo-Danish mixture of the Lowlands generally. So far as language is concerned, the English of the Lowlands is still waxing and the Gaelic of the Highlands is waning. The Welsh language of the Kingdom of Strathclyde, which persisted from the fifth century until the eleventh, has disappeared, and the Norse that was spoken in the Shetlands as late as the eighteenth century survives only in a host of place-names and dialect terms. Still older linguistic traces, found on Roman maps and no doubt borrowed by them from primordial people, are the Clyde *(Clota)*, the Nith *(Novius)*, the Hebrides *(Hebudes)* and the Orkneys *(Orcades)*. Clan-names, while not identical in pattern with the racial and linguistic background,

* From Watson Kirkconnell, "Scottish Place Names in Canada," A Paper Delivered at the Third Annual Meeting of the Canadian institute of Onomastica Sciences, York University, Toronto, June 13, 1969, in J.B. Rudnyckyj, ed., *Onomastica*, No. 39 (Winnipeg, 1970).

are nevertheless clear evidences as to diversity of national origins. Gaelic in origin are the clan-names Angus, Campbell and MacGregor. Norman-French are Bruce, Cummings, Fraser, Grant and Sinclair. Ultimately Norse are Gunn, Lamont, Macdonald, MacLeod, MacNeill (of Colonsay) and Sutherland. English are Johnson, Leslie and Stewart (although this final family was originally Breton and came over with the Normans).

Since the majority of Scottish place-names in Canada are actually based on surnames, some analysis of the latter is in order. The main types are occupational, descriptive, patronymic and territorial. Examples hereunder will be limited to actual place-names in Canada.

Examples of occupational names are Avenir (OF. *avener*, oat merchant), Faulkner (falconer), Gardiner (gardener), Lymburner (limeburner), Milner (miller), Pender (impounder of strayed cattle), Sclater (slater), Sellars (M.E. *seler*, a saddler), Shearer (cutter of cloth), Spence (dispenser of food from the larder) and Stewart (originally the "steward" or chief manager of the royal household). Patronymic derivatives of occupational names are Macoun or Macgowan (son of the *Gow* or blacksmith) and MacIntyre (son of the carpenter).

Descriptive names are Auld (old), Young or Yonge, Baine (G. *ban*, white or flaxen-haired), Reid (red-headed), Duff (F. *dubh*, dark), Campbell (G. *Caimbeaul*, crooked mouth), Cameron (G. *cam-shron*, hooked nose), Strang, strong, or else OF. *estrange*, a foreigner), and Tod (nickname, "the fox").

Patronymic names may be Scandinavian (with a suffixed-*son*), Gaelic (with a prefixed *Mac* "son of"), and English (with a suffixed genitival -*s*).

Formed on the Scandinavian model are Allison (son of Ellis), Anderson (son of Andrew), Dawson (son of Dawe or David), Ferguson (son of Olr. *Fergus*, the grandfather of Saint Columba), Jameson (son of James), Matheson (son of Matthew), Paterson or Patterson (son of Patrick), Nicolson (son of Nicol), Robertson (son of Robert), Robinson (son of Robin), Simpson (son of Sim or Simeon).

Gaelic patronymics have a wide range of application. Based on straight personal names are MacAdam (son of Adam), MacAlister (son of Alexander), MacAlpine (son of Ailpean), MacArthur (son of Arthur), MacAulay (son of Amhalghaidh), MacCormack (son of Cormack), MacCreary and Macrorie (son of Ruadhri), MacEwen (son of Ewen), MacFarlane (son of Bartholomew), MacGregor (son of Gregory), MacKay or MacKee (son of Aodh), MacKendrick (son of Henry), MacKenzie (son of Coinneach), McKim (son of Simon), MacKinnon (son of Fhionnghain), MacLaren (son of Laurence), MacLaughlin (son of Lachlann), MacMahon (son of Matthew), MacMurdo (son of Murdoch), MacNaughton and MacCracken (son of Neachdain), MacNeill (son of Neill), MacTavish (son of Tammas, i.e. Thomas), MacVeigh (son of Bheatha), MacWatters (son of Walter). Of special note are Macdougall or Macdowall (son of Dougal, eldest son of Somerled, Norse Lord of the Isles), Macdonald (son of Donald, eldest son of Reginald, second son of Somerled), MacIver (son of Ivarr, a famous Norse chief), and MacKellar (son of Hilarius, bishop of Poitiers). A common ingredient in many old names was the Gaelic *Gille*, "servant," applied especially to those who were consecrated to the service of a saint or of the church in general. This was an element in the older forms of the following surnames: MacBride (son of the servant of Bride, the virgin abbess of Kildare, d. 525), MacCallum (son of the servant of Calum), McClintock (son of the servant of St. Findan), MacLean (son of the servant of St. John), MacLesse (son of the servant of Jesus), MacLennan (son of the servant of St. Finnan), McLure (son of the servant of Odhar), McMunn (son of the servant of St. Munn). Also associated with the church are MacMillan (son of the tonsured man), Macnab (son of the abbot), MacPherson (son of the parson), and MacTaggart (son of the priest). More general are MacEachern (son of the horse-lord), MacIntosh (son of the chieftain), McKague (son of Olr. *Tadhg*, or the poet), McNeily (son of the poet), MacGillivrary (son of the servant of judgment), and MacLeod (probably, son of an old Norse warrior, *Ljot-ulf*, "ugly wolf").

Many a Highland name can shift gears into a Lowland equivalent, depending on the habitat of its owner, e.g. MacIan (MacKean)-Johnson, Macdonald-Donaldson, MacAdam-Adamsonn, MacNeill-Neilson, MacNichol-Nicholson, MacTavish-Thomson, and MacMahon-Matheson.

Examples of the English genitival suffixes are Sellars and Watts.

Hundreds of Scottish surnames are of territorial origin, i.e. they represent the family's original estate or feudal lands. Since these are also place-names, there is often a doubt as to which came first in the Canadian toponymy, the hen or the egg. Wherever the place-name has had wide currency in Scotland as a surname, it has seemed reasonable to count it as a surname in Canada. Thus *Gordon* is the name of a little place in Berwickshire with which some genealogists first associate the family, but it is undoubtedly the family and not the obscure village that is recorded on the Canadian map. Similarly, although the name *Douglas* is derived from the "black water" (G. *dubh glas*) of a stream in Douglasdale, it is the family and not the river that is set down in Canadian gazetteers. In like manner, Blair, Buchan, Caldwell (i.e. "cauld well"), Cochrane, Dundas, Drummond, Glenelg, Harris, Kippen, Lewis, Lumsden, Ross, Selkirk and Sutherland would all seem to have been chosen as Canadian place-names on a surname basis.

SCOTLAND'S MAP AND THE MIGRATIONS

My preliminary survey of place-names by shires on Scotland's map was undertaken hand in hand with the reading of J.M. Gibbon's *Scots in Canada* (Toronto, 1911), Wilfred Campbell's *The Scotsman in Canada: Eastern Canada* (Toronto and London, 1911), George Bryce's *The Scotsman in Canada: Western Canada* (Toronto and London, 1911), and Hazel

C. Mathews's *The Mark of Honour* (Toronto, 1965). It became evident that the bulk of Eastern Canada's Scottish place-names were to be associated with mass migrations in 1770-1840 from Inverness, Argyle, Ross, Sutherland, Caithness, Perthshire, Moray, Skye and the Hebrides. In this period, thousands of crofters were being evicted from the glens, partly by their old chieftain-landlords and partly through the destruction of cottage weaving by the Industrial Revolution. A considerable element in the settlement consisted of Highland regiments which, after Culloden and the defeat of the Jacobite uprising of 1745, had been recruited into the British army, especially after 1757. Marion Gilroy's record, *Loyalists and Land Settlement in Nova Scotia* (Public Archives of Nova Scotia, 1937), shows heavy land grants to Loyalist immigrants, mostly Highland veterans, after 1783, in what are now the counties of Shelburne, Digby, Annapolis, Antigonish and Guysborough. Not a single Loyalist grant was made in Horton and Cornwallis townships, Kings County which had been solidly settled by New England "Planters" in 1761, nor in the Lunenburg South Shore area, settled in 1749-53 by Germans, Swiss and French Huguenots. In Hants County, in a proposed township of "Douglass," a whole battalion of the 84th Highland Regiment simply evaporated, leaving 115,000 acres to escheat to the crown. Most of those in Shelburne left the country before 1800, but an island of Highland population persists in the "Argyle" area, between the Acadians of Pubnico and the Acadians of Clare. After the close of the Napoleonic Wars, and especially after 1820, a severe economic depression swept the industries of the Scottish Lowlands and these also poured their harassed citizens into Canadian settlements.

Mostly unrepresented in Nova Scotia are place-names from the shires of Ayr, Banff, Berwick, Bute, Dunbarton, Kincardine, the Lothians, Nairn, Peebles, Roxburgh, Selkirk, Wigtown and Kirkcudbright. Immigrants from these areas either came too late to affect the naming of communities or did not set up the block settlements that so often perpetuate their own choice of names.

All parts of Scotland are represented in the place-names of Prince Edward Island; their gross number would have been much greater had it not been for a plague of absentee landlords and for the ambitions of surveyors and political persons to have *their* names perpetuated. Settlement goes back to the enterprises of Judge Stewart, of Cantyre, Argyllshire, in 1771; of Captain John MacDonald, of Glenaladale, in 1772; and of Wellwood Waugh, of Lockerbie, Dumfriesshire, in 1774. In 1803, Lord Selkirk brought in a contingent of 800 from Ross, Inverness, Argyle, and especially Skye.

The pattern of Scotch place-names in New Brunswick is not unlike that in Nova Scotia, although there is nothing like the continuing Highland concentration in Cape Breton and Antigonish. In the 1780s, the Loyalists established several regiments (largely Scotch) on the St. Croix and St. John rivers; and there were settlements, direct from Scotland, on the Lower Miramichi and in the county of Restigouche. This latter plantation, largely of fisher-folk, on the Restigouche River and its estuary, has been buried under a community of Acadian French who swarmed in here from exile when the interdict on their presence was removed in 1764.

In Lower Canada, the ultimate province of Quebec, the most important Scottish settlements were those of the Fraser Highlanders, whose mountaineer regiment had scaled the Heights in 1759 and won the battle of the Plains of Abraham.

In Ontario, where no fewer than eleven counties (Bruce, Carleton, Cochrane, Dundas, Elgin, Glengarry, Lanark, Lennox, Perth, Renfrew and Stormont) bear Scottish names, the roster of Scottish place-names is by far the largest in all Canada, yet early mass settlements left a special mark. Such were the Roman Catholic regiments of Glengarry, the Talbot settlements of Argyle Highlanders in Elgin county, the Sutherland crofters in Zorra, and the thousands from Lanark, Renfrew and the west of Scotland who flocked to Lanark county in 1820-21. Veteran resettlement (as in the days of the Caesars) and economic hardship in Scotland were major factors in the situation.

The opening up of the Western provinces came at least two generations later. Not only did immigration agencies (including those of railways and steamship lines) then recruit from all parts of Scotland; but, thanks to the C.P.R., the younger sons of Scotch-Canadian farmers in Ontario swarmed to the Prairies in their thousands. Still earlier had been the striking participation of Scots in the fur trade activities of the Hudson's Bay Company and the Northwest Company. They also played the leading role in the drama of exploration that put the names of Fraser, Simpson and Mackenzie on the maps of the Canadian West and North.

It is sometimes interesting to look for traces of a single known migration. Thus in 1774 a considerable settlement of Lowlanders from Dumfriesshire came to Prince Edward Island. Three years later some of the group, overwhelmed by a plague of grasshoppers, joined the Protestant Highlanders at Pictou. Today, in Prince Edward Island, there is still a "New Annan," and on the mainland, thirty miles northwest of Pictou, there is another "New Annan." Other Dumfriesshire place-names, ascribable to other, later migrations, are Annan, Kirkland (Lake), Moffat and Thornhill in Ontario, Gretna and Thornhill in Manitoba, Bankend in Saskatchewan, and Kirkpatrick in Alberta.

On the other hand, a very considerable contingent of Highlanders from Glenlyon, Perthshire, who settled on the north shore of the Ottawa River near Lachute in 1819, have left no toponymic trace except for Thurso (Caithness) and Lochaber Bay (Inverness), neither one relevant to the area of their origin. After 150 years, a substantial remnant of lineal descendants is still in the area of settlement.

315

THE SCOTS IN THE CENSUS

When in a search for the place of the Scots in Canadian life one turns to the Federal Census of 1961, one arrives at the following Scottish totals by provinces, as compared with Canadians of English, Irish, French, German and Ukrainian origin. The provinces are printed in the descending order of Scottish representation.

Table I: Some Statistics on Ethnic Origins

AREA	SCOTTISH	ENGLISH	IRISH	FRENCH	GERMAN	UKRAINIAN
Ontario	835,590	1,939,867	873,617	647,911	400,717	127,911
Br. Columbia	255,627	518,010	165,631	66,970	118,926	35,640
Nova Scotia	182,823	211,020	93,998	87,883	45,441	1,763
Alberta	165,942	282,961	134,102	83,319	183,314	105,293
Manitoba	119,299	181,607	84,726	83,936	91,846	105,372
Quebec	109,937	322,410	129,326	4,241,851	39,457	16,588
Saskatchewan	102,685	170,296	92,133	59,821	158,200	78,851
New Brunswick	81,082	158,590	82,483	232,127	7,386	379
P. E. I.	32,910	30,191	19,786	17,418	664	66
Newfoundland	9,902	342,070	74,791	17,171	1,829	141
Yukon-N.W.T.	3,475	5,150	2,726	2,403	1,810	703
Totals	1,962,302	4,195,175	1,753,351	5,550,346	1,049,599	473,337

These statistics do not reveal their full significance at a first glance. Thus the 835,590 Scots of Ontario, while they are almost as numerous as all the other Scots in Canada put together, are nevertheless inferior in Ontario to either the English or the Irish and only 29 per cent more numerous than the French. The only province where the Scots are clearly in first place is little Prince Edward Island. The Scots are in second place, behind the English, in Nova Scotia, New Brunswick, Manitoba and British Columbia. Both the English and the Irish outnumber them in Newfoundland; while in Alberta and Saskatchewan they rank numerically behind the English and the Germans. Even in the frontier areas of the Yukon and the Northwest Territories, they run second to the English. Another sort of yardstick is the survival of Gaelic in Nova Scotia, where 3,702 (mostly in Cape Breton) in the 1961 Census still reported it as their mother tongue. Although the English in Canada outnumber the Scots by slightly more than two to one, their ratios to the present total populations of their respective mother countries form a striking contrast; for while the English-Canadians are equivalent to 9 ½ per cent of England's 1961 population, the Scotch-Canadians are equivalent to 38 per cent of Scotland's population. The Canadian Irish are similarly equivalent to 41 per cent of the total population of Ireland (North *plus* South). At the time of Confederation, in 1867, the Scots and the Irish together outnumbered those of English extraction and played a very prominent role in the politics of the new nation. Some 20 of the 34 "Fathers of Confederation" were Scots. The ingredients of these three peoples (English, Irish, Scotch) in Canada's national amalgam is thus very different from that in the "British Isles." The presence of a French sub-nation is another very difficult factor, and now we have nearly five million European-Canadians who are neither British nor French. The Canadians are to be a national blend *sui generis.*

UNFULFILLED BLUEPRINTS FOR "NOVA SCOTIA"

In 1613, (Sir) Samuel Argall, a Kentish-man in the employ of the Virginia colony, led a naval expedition to the Bay of Fundy and destroyed the Acadian settlements as an alleged infringement of the Virginia charter. The region remained under British control until 1631, when Charles I, in order to persuade Louis XIII to hand over the dowry long overdue on his Bourbon wife, Henrietta-Maria, gave the Acadian lands (along with "Canada") back to France. In the meantime, in 1621, Sir William Alexander, a Scottish gentleman at the English court, had been given by James I a royal warrant for the development of a great "New Scotland" here, by a company of Scottish Adventurers. In the Latin text of the warrant, the territory's name was rendered as "Nova Scotia," and this is about all of the original enterprise that remains three and a half centuries later. For a brief time, however, there was great promotional activity. Alexander's notable book, *Encouragement to Colonies*, was published in 1624; and in the same year an Order of Baronets of Nova Scotia was instituted. Bands of colonists were sent out in 1628 and 1629-30.

In maps prepared by Sir William, many toponymical details were worked out (on paper). "New Scotland" was subdivided into two provinces: "New Caledonia" (the modern Nova Scotia, Prince Edward Island

317

and Southern Newfoundland) and "Alexandria" (after his own name), consisting of our New Brunswick, Gaspésie and Anticosti. Cape Breton Island became "New Galloway." Our modern St. John River was named the "Clyde" and the St. Croix River the "Tweed." appropriately separating "New Scotland" from "New England." Our Bay of Fundy was named "Argall Bay." after the man who had destroyed the Acadian Port Royal in 1613. The Bay of Chaleurs was to be the "Firth of Forth." All this paper empire collapsed in 1631, when Charles I snatched Sir William Alexander out of his new domain and handed it over to France. It was reconquered in 1654 by a fleet from Cromwell's England but was restored to France again in 1667 by an ever-obliging Charles II. It came permanently to England in 1713 by the Treaty of Utrecht. Sentimental modern Scots may day-dream over Sir William's geographical terms that remained unimplemented by the course of history.

TYPES OF SCOTTISH PLACE-NAMES IN CANADA

Scottish place-names in Canada are of five main types:
(a) Actual place-names from Scotland, such as Aberdeen, Argyle, Perth, Melrose.
(b) Such place-names with an added element, such as *New* Aberdeen, Argyle *Head*, Perth *Road*, Melrose *Hill*.
(c) Scottish surnames, such as MacDonald, Currie, Duncan, Ferguson.
(d) Scottish surnames with an added element, such as MacDonald's *Corners*, Currie *Road*, Duncan *Cove*, Ferguson's *Falls*.
(e) New coinages, such as Skir Dhu ("Black Rock"), Loch Ban ("White Lake"), and Beinn Breagh ("Beautiful Mountain").

Table II. Analysis of Name-types

PROVINCE	BASED ON SURNAMES	PERCENT OF TOTAL	BASED ON PLACE-NAMES	COINAGES
P.E.I.	7	22.5	24	0
Nova Scotia	75	36	116	16
New Brunswick	51	54	42	1
Ontario	169	54	146	0
Quebec	44	59.5	30	0
Saskatchewan	102	70.5	42	1
Alberta	71	70.5	31	1
Manitoba	65	71	26	0
British Columbia	79	72	30	0
Newfoundland	18	78	7	1
Yukon-N.W.T.	9	82	2	0

FACTORS INFLUENCING CANADIAN TOPONYMY

For an immigrant toponymically this land, the size of Europe, was not a a *tabula rasa*, ready for the imprint of new names. For upwards of 30,000 years it had been occupied by a vast network of aboriginal tribes, so diverse that 176 different Amerindian languages are still recognized in Canada today. Every stream, lake, bay headland and village already had its native name, and thousands of these still survive, from Merigomish, Antigonish and Tatamagouche in the east, through Quebec, Ottawa and Toronto, to Okanagan, Chilliwack, and Nanaimo in the far west. While some of the largest lakes (such as Ontario, Erie, Huron, Nipigon, Winnipeg, Manitoba and Winnipegosis) retain native names, thousands of other lakes and rivers had their Indian names calqued into English in the pioneer days. Virtually all of the famous explorations of the land by the white man were actually guided by Indians who already knew the terrain intimately and had access to its languages.

Earlier than the Scots in much of Canada were the French, and these as they settled staked out their own claims to the naming of places and natural features. They total over six millions today, and their towns provide a striking pageant of municipalized saints – Sainte Anne de Beaupré, Sainte Anne de la Pocatière, Sainte Anne des Chênes, Sainte Anne des Monts, Sainte Anne des Plaines, Sainte Anne du Lac, and all their sisters and brothers. Also competing with the Scots in toponymic aggressiveness were the English and the Irish. In Ontario, for example, the English-Canadians have their London (on the Thames), Stratford (on the Avon), Bath, Brighton, Durham, Portsmouth, Southampton, York and hundreds of others. In the same province, the Irish-Canadians have townships named Cavan, Galway and Monaghan and villages named Dublin, Enniskillen and Killarney. Nova Scotia has its Londonderry and Alberta its Cork.

Also competing during recent decades for a place in the toponymic sun are five million Canadians of European nationalities other than British and French. Thus the Icelanders have given us Arnes, Gimli and Hecla; the Hungarians Esterhazy and Békevar; and the Ukrainians (among scores of other place-names) Halicz, Sich, Julish and Yasna Olana. The Scottish place-names in Canada have had to run the gauntlet of a host of competitors.

In that struggle for survival, some of the more rugged Scottish names have failed to acclimate themselves for Canadian usage. We look in vain for Ecclefechan, Ardnamurchan, Sligachan and Ballachulish. John Milton, in his Sonnet XI, derided cacophonous Scottish surnames – "Gordon, Colkitto [i.e., G. *Coll ciotach*, "Coll the left-handed or crafty"], or Macdonnel, or Galasp [i.e. Gillespie] . . . that would have made Quintilian stare and gasp" – but three of the four have "grown sleek" to our mouths. Pronounceability, however, has no doubt a bearing on viability.

Still another difficulty has sometimes lain in the opposition of officialdom and its friends. The assigning of names to territorial areas and post offices has been commonly in the hands of the Establishment, which has been prompt to donate toponymic immortality to politicians and their cronies. Scots from Prince Edward Island are ready to tell of this sort of chicanery, especially along the east coast. Back in the 1830s, in opening up what became Victoria County, Ontario, a block settlement of Highlanders from Argyllshire and Islay wanted its wholly Scotch township called "Caledonia," but the Family Compact government in Toronto insisted on calling it "Eldon," after the lord chancellor. One cannot get too indignant at this today, however, when one discovers that the name "Caledonia" occurs six times in Canada, three times in Nova Scotia, twice in Ontario, and once in Prince Edward Island, all to the great confusion of postal clerks.

Since 1897, attempts have been made by the Federal Government to achieve a tactful avoidance of so much duplication. A "Canadian Permanent Committee on Geographical Names," with headquarters in Ottawa, has been able, by discretionary consultation with the provinces, to spread hundreds of totally new names across the Canadian West in areas that were being opened up for the first time. There is no "Caledonia" west of Ontario.

Notice may be taken of the wartime drive of public emotion to change place-names. Thus, in 1824, "Berlin" was the cheerfully accepted name for a city in Waterloo County, Ontario, an area first settled in the early 1800's by Swiss-German immigrants from Pennsylvania, later reinforced by settlers direct from Germany. In 1916, however, under excited mass pressure from Ontario Anglo-Canadians, the name was changed to "Kitchener", after Field Marshall Lord Kitchener, who was drowned at sea in that year. Similar ultra-patriotic clamour during World War II, demanding the suppression of "Swastika" as the name of a community in the Timiskaming district of Northern Ontario, was successfully blocked by the town's citizens, who insisted that they had chosen the old folk-symbol as their municipal name long before Hitler and his Nazis had adopted it as a political trade-mark.

TOPONYMY AND DEMOGRAPHIC CHANGE

Even where a place-name may once have been happily appropriate for a community, population changes may come to render it meaningless. The tides of immigration ebb and flow, bringing totally new racial stocks to the surface. A differential birth rate may serve to replace one nationality by another. Canadians are a nomadic people, streaming from the Prairies and the Maritimes to the affluent employment centres of Ontario and Quebec, as well as from rural parts to the cities in every province. We have suffered a hemorrhage of population to the U.S.A. that runs to many millions. The total population of Canada is almost equalled by the number of present-day Americans whose ancestors (or themselves) once lived in Canada.

A number of instances will illustrate the story:

(a) "New Edinburgh," in Digby County, Nova Scotia, was founded and its streets were carefully laid out in 1783 by a Scottish U.E. Loyalist, Anthony Stewart, but demographic changes in the area have made it an Acadian French fishing-village. Of its 40 telephones in 1968, some 39 were French (15 Doucets, 13 Amiraults, etc.) and only one Scottish (a MacCormack).

(b) Shelburne, Nova Scotia, was founded in 1783 by U.E. Loyalists, and by 1786, with a population of over 10,000, it was the largest town in British North America. But the site was ill chosen, storms swept away wharves and warehouses, free rations were cut off at the end of 1786, the settlers fled to England, to Upper Canada, or even back to the U.S.A., and by 1816, according to the Surveyor-General of the province, only 374 persons were left in the town.

(c) In 1784, Preston, Nova Scotia, named by its Scottish Loyalist founders after towns in the Lothians and Berwickshire (unlike Preston, Ontario, which was named after Preston in Lancashire), began its career as a toponymic transplantation from Scotland. In 1814, however, it was used as a depot for Negroes rescued from slavery after the burning of Washington, D.C.; and today the community is solidly Negro.

(d) About 1773, a contingent of Scottish fisher-folk settled along the south shore of the Restigouche River and its estuary, and established such centres as Campbellton and Dawnsonville. Still earlier, however, a flood of Acadians, returning in 1764 from the deportations of 1755, settled on both shores of the Bay of Chaleurs. The Acadians' greater numbers and greater prolificity have submerged the Scottish communities and made them a small minority in a largely French population.

(e) The same process of French replacement is well advanced in the Eastern Townships of Quebec and in the famous old Highland Scottish county of Glengarry.

(f) Colonsay and Saltcoats, shown as apparently Scottish in my place-name list for Saskatchewan, have actually, since 1900-13, become Hungarian communities.

(g) In like manner, the seemingly Scottish towns of Gretna (Manitoba) and Balgonie (Saskatchewan) are now almost completely German.

Expansion rather than shrinkage of the Scots may be noted in the case of Halifax, Nova Scotia. Founded by the English in 1749, and given a famous old Yorkshire name, it has so attracted enterprising Scots from all parts of the Maritimes that its 1968 telephone directory listed 2400 "Macs," some 475 of whom were "Macdonalds." Monuments to Burns and Scott dominate its public gardens and its "North British Society" is perhaps the most powerful organization in the town.

INDEX

Artisans (In Canada): 163, 164, 171-76, 208; skills: 171-74; areas of settlement: 171-76

"Auld Alliance": 15-25, 295

Culture: 5, 9, 12, 13, 88, 100-01, 106, 107, 109, 110, 203-31, 232-46, 247n, 248-67, 286, 304, 306-07, 312; Celtic: 232; curling: 246, 247n; dancing: 13, 88, 110, 239-44, 247n, 304; education: 5, 9, 12, 100-01, 106, 107, 109, 227-28, 248-67, 306, 307, 312; games: 88, 110-11, 239, 244, 245, 246, 304; literature: 203-31, 234-39, 245-46, 306; painting: 229, 246; piping: 233-34, 240, 241, 244-45; publishing: 204, 206, 215, 216, 217, 222, 227, 228, 286; and religion: 238-39; in Scotland: 5, 9, 12, 232-44; and social institutions: 240-46, 247n

Education: 5, 9, 12, 100-01, 106, 107, 109, 227-28, 248-67, 306-07, 312; and Baptist influences: 260, 264-65; church-university relations: 253, 259-62; and the Commission of Visitation (1826): 250; curriculum: 253-54; and orthodoxy: 257-59; personalities: 251-53, 264-66; and Presbyterian influence: 248, 250-51, 254-57, 258; and Roman Catholic influence: 262-64; in Scotland: 248-50, 306-07; and the Scottish Royal Commission (1858): 249; types of colleges: 250-51; and the Universities Act of 1858 (Scotland): 250, 254

Fur Trade (See *Hudson's Bay Company, North West Company*): 27-47, 76-77, 80-81, 94, 122, 180, 184, 185, 200n, 203; background: 27-28; and Canadians: 33-34, 35; conglomerates: 34, 36, 37; *courier de bois*: 28; and exploration: 42-44; pedlars: 33-34, 36; prices: 37; and the Red River Settlement: 76-77; on the Saskatchewan: 33-34, 35

Hudson's Bay Company: 28, 29, 30, 33-46, 60-61, 76, 77, 79, 80-81, 98, 112n, 125, 133, 193, 205, 214, 227; administration: 44-45; *The Beaver*: 46; and Canadians: 33-34, 35, 38, 40; coalition with North West Company (1821): 31, 38, 39, 43, 44, 61, 77; and exploration: 42-44; and Indians: 35, 42; and Massacre of Seven Oaks: 35, 61, 77; officers: 28, 30, 35, 40, 41, 42, 45; organization: 35-36; and Orkneymen: 29-30, 31, 32, 35, 77; and the Puget Sound Agricultural Company: 79; recruiting: 27-31, 41, 81; retrenchment: 38; rivalry with North West Company: 31-38, 39, 60-61, 77; and Sir George Simpson: 39-41; and writers: 45-46

Literature: 10, 12, 13, 46, 118, 120, 132, 203-31, 234-39, 245-46, 306; background: 203-04; before Burns: 204-06; Burns: 10, 13, 88, 132, 203, 204-11, 216, 217, 224, 227, 228, 230, 236, 238; in Gaelic: 233-38; Kailyard School: 216, 220-23, 227; Lowland influence: 203-31; at mid-century: 214-16; poetry after Confederation: 223-29; Scott: 10, 11, 13, 46, 203, 204, 211-14, 216, 217, 222, 224, 227, 228, 229, 231; Stevenson: 12, 13, 14n, 118, 120, 132, 134n, 203, 204, 216-20, 227, 231; in the twentieth century: 229-31

Mercantilism: 8, 179-200, 212; and the

American Revolution: 188; and banking: 197; and fisheries: 182, 184, 188, 189, 190, 192, 200n; and the fur trade: 180, 184, 185, 190, 200n; and the grain trade: 191; and Halifax: 182, 185, 186-89, 190, 192; and Montreal: 185, 186, 189, 190, 194, 195, 196-97; and Newfoundland: 181, 182, 185, 186, 187, 194, 200n; in New Brunswick: 187, 188, 193, 195, 196, 197; and the North West Company: 185, 190; personalities: 183, 186, 187, 188-200; and Pictou: 190; and Quebec: 182, 183, 185, 186, 191, 194, 195, 196, 198; and Scotland: 179-86; and the Seven Years' War: 186, 188, 189, 190, 192, 194, 195; ship-building: 188, 189, 191, 193, 194, 195, 197; smuggling: 182, 184-85; speculating: 189, 190-92, 194, 200n; and the St. Lawrence: 187, 191; timber trade: 188, 189, 190, 191, 193, 194-96, 197; tobacco trade: 181, 182; and War of 1812: 191-92, 193, 194; and West Indies: 180, 182, 186, 187, 188, 190, 191, 192

North West Company: 27, 31, 33-40, 42, 44, 46, 60-61, 77, 95, 97, 112n, 125, 133, 185, 190, 196, 200n; formation: 33-35; and coalition with Hudson's Bay Company (1821): 31, 38, 39, 43, 44, 61, 78; and Massacre of Seven Oaks: 35, 61, 77; and the New North West Company: 37; organization: 36; rivalry with Hudson's Bay Company: 31-38, 39, 60-61, 77; and the xy Company: 37

Politics (See *Political Parties*): 3, 184, 273-97, 298n, 308-09; in Atlantic provinces: 282-84, 289, 290-92; background: 273-75; in British Columbia: 292, 294; Chateau Clique: 281; Clear Grits: 287, 288, 296; after Confederation: 291-97; Council of Twelve (Halifax): 276, 277; Family Compact: 276, 279-81, 284, 298n; in Lower Canada: 281-82, 284-89; Rebellion Losses Bill: 284, 287; and religion: 276-79; in Scotland: 3, 184, 273; in Upper Canada: 279-81, 284-89

Political parties (See *Politics*): CCF: 87, 128, 229; Conservative: 87, 275, 279, 283-84, 288, 289, 290, 291-93, 294, 295; Labour: 87; Liberal: 87, 275, 278, 279, 283, 284, 289, 291, 293-95; NDP: 87, 128, 134, 297; Progressive: 87-88, 91n; Reform: 286, 287, 288-89, 294, 295, 296

Protestant Reformation: 4-6, 10, 12, 111n, 118, 127, 133, 134n, 223, 238; and Theodore Beza: 5; *Book of Discipline*: 5; and Robert Bruce: 5; and Henry Bullinger: 5; and Darwinism: 12; doctrine of: 5; and education: 12; history of: 5-6, 118-19; and John Knox: 4-5, 13, 111n, 118, 127, 131, 132, 133n, 224; and Martin Luther: 4, and Andrew Melville: 5; and James Melville: 5; and Robert Pont: 5; *Scots Confession* (1516): 5; and toleration: 5

Protestant Tradition in Canada (See *Protestant Reformation, Religion*): 118-34; in Alberta: 125; Anglicans (See *Church of England*): 121, 122, 123, 128-29, 130; areas of settlement: 121-22, 123, 124-25, 126; background: 118-21; Baptists: 128, 130-31, 133; Calvanism: 118-19, 120, 128, 132; churches and churchmen: 121-34; Church of England (See *Anglicans*): 121, 122, 123, 125, 128, 129; Church of Scotland (See *Presbyterians*): 119, 121, 122, 123, 124, 125, 126, 127, 128, 129, 130, 133; civil status: 121-22; Congregationalists: 127, 130; Disruption of 1844: 132, 133; division: 123-26; education: 132; Episcopal Church of

Scotland: 119, 121, 128-29; Free Church: 124, 125, 132; influence of Protestant Reformation: 118-20; in Manitoba: 125; occupations: 131; Plymouth Bretheren: 128, 130, 131; Presbyterians (See *Church of Scotland*): 121-27, 128, 129, 130, 131; Presbyterian Church of Canada: 125-26, 127; religious characteristics: 132-34; and Roman Catholicism: 131; in Saskatchewan: 125; Scottish background: 118-21; union: 126-28; United Church: 128

Religion (See particular denominations indexed): in Alberta: 125; and culture: 238-39; and education: 5, 12, 100-01, 106, 107, 109, 132; in Nova Scotia: 121-22, 125; in Manitoba: 125; in Prince Edward Island: 121, 125; at Red River: 79, 127, 128, 130, 133; in Saskatchewan: 125; and toleration: 5, 13, 15, 97, 103, 105-06

Roman Catholic Tradition in Canada (See *Religion*): 93-111, 131; in Acadia: 99-100, 102, 116n; background: 93-94, 95, 105, and culture: 103, 105, 106-07, 110-11; and economics: 100, 109; and education: 100-01, 106, 107, 109; and farming: 99, 100, 104-05, 106, 107; in Glengarry: 93, 94-98, 99, 100, 101, 107, 109, 111, 111n; in Nova Scotia: 99-100, 101-06, 107, 108, 109, 110, 113n, 116n; and Presbyterians: 93-94, 95, 96, 102, 103, 104, 105-06, 108, 109, 110, 111n, 116n; and politics: 99, 109-10; in Prince Edward Island: 99-101, 103, 107, 109, 111, 113n, 116n; reasons for emigration: 101-02; religious characteristics: 106-09; and toleration: 97, 103, 105-06, 113n

Settlement Patterns in the East (See *Free, Military, Proprietary Settlement*): in Acadia: 21-24, 25, 99-100, 102, 142, 166n, 241, 242; Canada Company: 66-67, 74n, 165, 173, 174, 275, 298n; in the Eastern Townships: 67, 68, 167; European attitudes towards: 49; free settlement: 49, 50, 65-72; on the Huron Tract: 66-67, 74n; and land companies: 50; in Lower Canada: 67-68, 165, 167, 170; military settlement: 49, 50-57, 65, 68-69; in New Brunswick: 55, 68; in Nova Scotia: 49, 55, 66, 73n, 99-100, 101-06, 162, 164, 165, 187; in Prince Edward Island: 58-59, 99-101, 162; proprietary settlement: 49, 50, 58-65, 68-69; in Red River: 38, 60-61; in Upper Canada: 58, 59-64, 66-67, 70-72, 77, 93, 94-98, 99, 100, 101

Settlement, free: 65-72; areas of: 66-69, 71; organization of: 69-71; pattern of: 71-72; rationale: 65-66

Settlement, military: 49, 50-57, 65, 68-69; areas of: 51-52, 54, 55; final phase: 56; organization: 52, 56-57; rationale: 50-52; results of: 52-53, 54, 56; second phase: 52-54; third phase: 55

Settlement, proprietary: 58-65; areas of: 58-62; characteristics: 64-65; organization of: 62-64; rationale: 58